They never told me *this* in church!

A call to read the Bible with new eyes

Greg S. Deuble

2nd edition © 2010 • 1st edition © 2006
Restoration Fellowship
www.restorationfellowship.org

Atlanta Bible College
800-347-4261 • 404-362-0052

Cover design by Andrew Deuble of box ten • boxten.com.au

Revised edition ISBN 978-0-9673249-8-2 (formerly 0-9673249-5-5)

Contents

Introduction to Revised and Updated Edition

Thinking he had finished browsing through the large Christian bookstore, the elderly gentleman was about to walk out the door. This man has been a pastor for over 50 years in the evangelical and Protestant tradition and has conducted evangelistic missions around the world and at home in Australia all these decades. He has himself authored a number of best-selling Christian books. Little did he know this day was going to be one of those life-defining days that now and again "happen" in everybody's lives. As he was leaving the store his eyes suddenly glanced upon what he later discovered was the very last copy of *They Never Told Me This in Church!* (This large Christian book chain was about to ban my book, but more on this soon.) Anyway, the Spirit of God spoke directly to his heart that he must buy the book. He obeyed the leading of the Spirit. The rest is history as they say. This pastor's whole Biblical paradigm radically shifted as he read the truths contained in these pages. He has been liberated to see the simple, unifying truth that the God of the Bible is one and not an unexplainable mysterious three-in-one, and that Jesus is His uniquely begotten Son. He now shakes his head, like all of us who once were the victims of unexamined tradition, and wonders how for so long he had it so wrong. He now rejoices in the "new eyes" God our Father has been pleased to grant all who will come to His Scripture with a teachable spirit, an honest mind, the real prayer that He lead us to Himself and away from deception, and the commitment to obey Him no matter what the cost.

It was the Lord Jesus himself who said, "But if your eye is bad, your whole body will be full of darkness" (Matt. 6:23) — which is to say, If your paradigm is wrong, your understanding will be dark. Your head will be befuddled, and your heart heavy. World-view determines our personal joy and fulfilment. And what is true of the individual is equally true of the body which we know as Christianity.

When *They Never Told Me This in Church!* was first published in 2006 I had the conviction that the truths in its pages contained the seed-power to make a difference for the Kingdom of God in these last days. Nevertheless I was very nervous. It's all very well holding certain views but once in print they are there for the world to see and they are there in black and white for a long time! Indeed, I remember handing a copy to a very dear uncle and aunty whom I knew were deeply concerned about reports they had been hearing. Had I lost the faith once delivered to the saints? You cannot imagine how I rejoiced before the LORD when my uncle would ring me after every day's reading excitedly saying over the phone, "Greg, this book is amazing!" So thrilled was he that I got the impression he was actually going to slide right on out through the phone and do a jig for joy in front of me. Bear in mind he had been brought up in the Roman Catholic Church and also attended many evangelical churches in later adult life. His testimony was and still is, "This book has blown nearly 70 years of theological fog out of my head!" And like the pastor I mentioned earlier, my dear uncle is still shaking his head wondering how the simple and liberating truths in this book have for so long been buried under church tradition.

You can also imagine my elation when the book was offered for sale through Amazon books and the very first review came in. You may still read it on their website:

> Greg Deuble's book, *They Never Told Me This in Church!* is a blockbuster. In 50 years of Bible study and having read hundreds of books I would rate this one among the top 5! What a thrill to read a book that pulls no punches and lets the truth fall where it may. Straight to the point and direct it lets one know in no uncertain terms what it takes to become a future participant in the coming Kingdom of God under the Lord Messiah Jesus. This book should be on every believer's bookshelf and taken down and read and re-read often. Hopefully thousands and thousands will order this book; if they do they will have a real treasure on their hands.

It would be possible for me to include in this introduction to this second revised edition a great number of testimonies from pastors, priests, biblical scholars and academics, and a good number of your "average" believers, whose world-view and walk with God have been revolutionized, renewed, and even resurrected. Most touching to my heart is one from a searching lady who was about to convert to Islam. She states how dark her soul was at this time of desperation. But somehow she got hold of *They Never Told Me This in Church!* and again, the rest is history. She testifies that this book brought her to a deep and joyful knowledge of the one true God of heaven and earth through His Messiah, Jesus our Lord.

Now it would be remiss of me not to mention that there has been opposition from the powers that be. This certainly was not unexpected. I indicated earlier that one of the top two Christian bookstores in Australia did place my book on their shelves for a period of two years. This was an amazing window of opportunity that God in His Sovereignty opened up. However, the academic buyer (I call him the gate-keeper!) of that bookstore wrote me a brief note stating that his stores "won't be re-ordering copies of your book, *They Never Told Me This in Church!* The book has caused us considerable problems and we've decided not to continue carrying stock on our shelves." I replied that I hoped and prayed they would review this disappointing decision. It would be so gratifying to see them stand in the true spirit of the evangelical reformers they so loyally promote. Yes, gratifying to see them stand for reasonable dialogue. Surely Truth has nothing to fear from an honest examination under God's light? So far this gate-keeper has not reversed their decision. I can relate to the sadness and the anger of my Master at those hypocrites who deliberately kept the needy and thirsty from his liberating message.

This book comes to you through the dedication and hard work (again!) of Sarah Buzzard (now married as Sarah Jimenez) and her father, Anthony. I am convinced it comes to you as the result of the leading of the Holy Spirit of God. I am convinced you hold it in your hand as a miracle-gift from God Himself. As you read it is my fervent prayer before the God and Father of my Lord and Saviour Jesus Christ that His life-giving word may bless and change your life, bringing you with great joy into His glorious Kingdom.

To the One Whom His own blessed Son called "the only true God" (John 17:3) be the glory ever more!

Greg Deuble

Foreword

Greg Deuble has written a shocking book. My hope is that it will spark a much-needed revolution. The author means to bring nothing but Christian comfort, though the nature of his task in the pages which follow involves him in a ministry of "disturbing the comfortable."

It is my hope that churchgoers of all denominations will take up the challenge Greg issues to his fellow churchmen and women. When they do, reactions may well include a combination of both groans of horror and cries of delight: pain at the discovery that much of what most of us learned in church really has almost nothing in common with the Jesus we have professed to be following, but joy at the discovery of biblical truth formerly unimagined.

It was the late distinguished professor of the Bible, F.F. Bruce, who wisely observed in correspondence with me that "people who adhere to belief in the Bible (as they believe) often adhere in fact to a traditional school of interpretation of 'sola scriptura.' Evangelical Protestants can be as much servants of tradition as Roman Catholics or Greek Orthodox Christians, only they don't realize it is tradition." Over the years I have found this trenchant observation to be exactly on target.

Greg Deuble has spotted in his voluminous reading a number of equally telling quotations which incisively support his conviction that the Church has departed far from the intentions of its founder Jesus. The one from a prominent biblical scholar, Norman Snaith, alerts us to the serious damage which was done to the original Christian faith:

> Our position is that the reinterpretation of Biblical theology in terms of the ideas of the Greek philosophers has been both widespread throughout the centuries and everywhere destructive to the essence of the Christian faith…Neither Catholic nor Protestant theology is based on Biblical theology. In each case we have a domination of Christian theology by Greek thought...We hold that there can be no right (theology) until we have come to a clear view of the distinctive ideas of both Old and New Testaments and their

difference from the pagan ideas which have so largely dominated "Christian" thought.

There are certain types of people who should probably not read this book! I am referring to those who cannot entertain the idea that large bodies of churchgoers could have been misled on fundamental issues of theology. Or those who support their views with a few "proof texts" rather than on the broad evidence of the Bible. But the more adventurous reader is in for a wonderful journey of discovery, with Greg Deuble as guide along the path which has evidently given him so much joy.

Our author has undertaken a complete revision of much of what he learned as a child and as a graduate of Bible college. This does not mean at all that he has given up faith in holy Scripture. Far from it. There is nothing trendy or gimmicky in his approach. Rather, he has learned to read the Bible from its own Hebrew perspective and shedding a large quantity of traditional baggage has made the Bible all the more brilliant and telling. Because he is an honest student of truth, Greg has been rewarded, I believe, with unusual insight. He has a knack for getting to the heart of the issues. He has brought in a wealth of modern scholarly support for his argument, and the quotations gleaned from his wide reading are impressive. He adds a pleasing dose of Aussie humour to his writing while he invites us to re-examine all the major issues of biblical theology. The personal warmth of the author and his pastoral touch are evident in all he writes.

This is no dusty theological tome. It is an impassioned appeal that we take seriously the severely disturbing sayings of Jesus about the dangers of preaching "in his name," and even doing charismatic exploits "in his name" — only to be rejected at the return of Jesus (Matt. 7:21ff). There is everything to be gained by undertaking the "Berean" exercise to which Greg Deuble invites us. There is, as he contends, "another" and compelling way of viewing all the major Bible themes. The author has provided us with a compendium of biblical theology enabling us to become avid readers of the Bible in appreciation of truth newly learned. We will be reading the text of Scripture through Hebrew lenses, which is only reasonable, since our Saviour was a Jew reciting a Jewish creed and claiming to be the Hebrew Messiah.

In my own country of origin some 2% of seven million Londoners attend church with any regularity. The remainder show up in church to be "hatched, matched and dispatched." This is a tragedy of enormous proportions. I believe that Greg Deuble's book if widely distributed could cause a return to the God of the Bible and to Jesus the intrepid and tireless proclaimer of the Gospel of the Kingdom and of immortality. That I am sure would be the author's wish. I sincerely hope that many will gladly take up the challenge to re-examination which Greg so pleasingly and expertly offers us all.

Anthony Buzzard, MA (Oxon.) MA Th.
Atlanta Bible College and Restoration Fellowship

With Thanks

I dedicate this book to a number of folk whose encouragement has been invaluable along the journey. First and foremost I acknowledge **Sir Anthony Buzzard** whose initial gracious and learned contact with me opened my eyes to what I was never told in church. Although I have been careful to duly acknowledge Anthony's work, it has been impossible to cite completely his scholarship, for a lot of the material has come via his personal contact with me. If there is another whose passion is greater for the Kingdom of Christ, I have yet to meet him or her. For the many hours Anthony has spent in editorial suggestions I am deeply grateful.

To **Sarah Buzzard,** Anthony's daughter, I am also deeply indebted. Sarah has spent hours and hours formatting and proofreading the text.

I would like to acknowledge my own brother **Jeff Deuble's** encouragement. To have such a godly brother's support has been a tonic to my own soul.

My son **Andrew Deuble** has given his personal and professional assistance in the design of the cover. A father could not wish for better.

Other great supporters have been **Charles Hunting** and **Jack Townsend** who have given unflinchingly of their time and resources to make this project possible.

Last, but by no means least, I want to thank two very special ladies in my life. First, my dear **wife Chris** has allowed me the many hours necessary to achieve this task. She has sacrificed enormously over our thirty-plus years of marriage, never thinking of herself.

Finally, I want to pay tribute to my own mother **Fay Deuble** who first showed me and taught me to love and honour the God of the Bible.

Introduction

It was the novel of the year, a ripper of a yarn.[1] A thriller based on the heresy that Jesus married Mary Magdalene and that their descendants survive to this day. Dan Brown's bestselling *The Da Vinci Code* has sold a staggering 25 million copies in 44 languages worldwide, enough when piled on top of each other to make a mountain 100 times higher than Everest, or to stretch end to end from London to the Vatican and back again, and then still have plenty to make another daring pilgrimage to the doors of the Vatican! (This fact will impress the Vatican in light of their belated directive to their faithful not to buy or read it!) And we are still counting. The author's thesis is that Jesus was just a man, great and gifted, but totally human. His divinity is a fiction fostered by the Church to bolster its authority. What is more, this man Jesus supposedly married the "fallen" Mary Magdalene and also sired a daughter by her, thus establishing a royal bloodline that lasts to this day, with the couple's descendants still among us. The clues, insists the author, lie in the famous paintings by Leonardo Da Vinci, most notably in his *The Last Supper.* The central message of Brown's *The Da Vinci Code* is that "almost everything our fathers taught us about Christ is false."

There are at least three timeless ingredients that have made *The Da Vinci Code* the most popular novel of all time: a conspiracy theory, the question as to the historical Jesus, and lots of action loaded with imagination. I do not expect my book *They Never Told Me* This *in Church!* to sell 25 million copies (LOL!), even though it contains two of the three ingredients that Dan Brown has so well utilized. Although I am not writing fiction, my book does involve a conspiracy that revolves around Jesus the Christ. Jesus of Nazareth has been the most influential figure in the history of the world. This is suggested by the vigour of the debate about the significance of his life two thousand years after his birth. It is really quite amazing that after all this time the person of Jesus (the) Christ still captures the popular imagination and that of the academics. I write with the

---

[1] *Ripper of a yarn* — a truly gripping story.

conviction that the central issue facing our world today is still the ancient one put by Jesus to his followers: "Who do you say that I am?" There have been any number of popular bestselling books in recent decades, and a mass of academic studies, that have re-examined this critical question in the light of newly discovered materials from antiquity.

The average Christian is not aware that a basic shift in the field of New Testament (NT) studies began to take place in about 1975 in response to these newly discovered materials. A NT scholar named Robert W. Funk founded the Jesus Seminar in the United States. This group of NT scholars, linguists, and historians meets annually and has been at the vanguard of a revolutionary re-examination of Christology. Funk writes that it is not yet clear what the new picture of Jesus will be, "nevertheless it is clear that a revolution is under way." So far, this revolutionary assessment is pretty much contained within the halls of scholarship. However, a swoop on the pews was inevitable. Although most Christians are unaware that such a ground-breaking revolution amongst NT scholars and historians is under way, on a more pragmatic level we should be able to read the "signs of the times." "The Christianized age has come to an end, and with it the colonisation and imperialism of the Christian West. We now inhabit a global village. In that village those of us with Christian or Jewish heritages must compete in a world marketplace of ideas and claims."[2] We have to match Jesus with the Buddha, Lao-tzu, Confucius, Gandhi, Mohammed, New Age "spirituality" and many others. This is a challenge every Bible lover must embrace. Failure to face these challenges will consign the Church to a backwater as stagnant as the proverbial Australian billabong[3] in a big dry. We are at a crossroads. We face a struggle between the forces of light and darkness. I find it exhilarating. It is no less a challenge than Jesus and his apostles faced as they preached the Good News of the Kingdom of God, for their first-century world revered a pantheon with a plethora of gods and goddesses.

Douglas Lockhart in *Jesus the Heretic* observes that the impact of secularism and these new materials means that Christianity has

---

[2] Robert W. Funk, *Honest to Jesus: Jesus for a New Millennium,* Sydney, Australia: Hodder & Stoughton, 1996, pp. 66-67.

[3] *Billabong* — an Australian aboriginal word that means a stagnant backwater. It is formed when a river branch gets cut off from its main source.

lost its grip on the human imagination; it is simply no longer respected. People are waking up to the fact that traditional Christianity has abandoned them, and they are not prepared to be duped by doctrines "which have neither basis in reality nor the psychic energy left in them to keep the religious charade on the move." Lockhart maintains that the assault of this new intellectualism has left our society with the feeling that the Gospel story fails to inspire the Western mind because it has become no more than a series of "culturally hallowed fairytales."[4] Over the last 50 years this loss of respect has left a spiritual vacuum, and as far as Christianity is concerned, there is no longer a healthy scepticism but a sour cynicism born of inner defeat. If these observations are correct, and I think they are spot on, our answer to the question of the identity of Jesus of Nazareth and his message will determine the direction our 21st-century society travels. It's that big. It is no longer acceptable for Christians to live in:

> ill-founded complacency, or…smug self-certainty. Living in a kind of metaphysical dream, the custodians of "old-fashioned" Christianity stumble from one futile explanation of New Testament events to another...Jesus was sexless; Jesus was all-knowing...Jesus *is* God (etc.). Such sentiments slip easily from the lips when the mind has been overtaken by spiritual vertigo due to intellectual under-nourishment.[5]

I want to examine whether "almost everything our fathers taught us about Christ is false," as Dan Brown insists. It is my solid conviction that much is, that fiction has been mixed with truth. The real flesh and blood Jesus has been treated like a piece of plasticine that is pushed and prodded out of historical context by centuries of accrued myth.

There is a generally held view that the apostolic "faith once delivered to the saints" built a strong Church that beat paganism back into the dark recesses of the then-known world. C.S. Lewis imaginatively captured this retreat in one of his novels by having the great magician Merlin imprisoned in a block of ice. Christ is on the throne; the Devil and all his works are more or less under control. At least that's the theory. But what if instead of being so banished, a

---

4 Douglas Lockhart, *Jesus the Heretic: Freedom and Bondage in a Religious World*, Melbourne, Victoria: Element, 1997, p. 1.

5 *Ibid.*, pp. 5-6.

large dose of paganism was actually absorbed into the Christian faith? What if the pure apostolic faith firmly rooted in Jesus of Nazareth was very early on being divorced from its historical context? Many fine Biblical scholars have put forward a seemingly unassailable case that the Jesus of Jewish history has been buried under generations of accumulated myth; the Jesus of history has been supplanted by the Christ of mythology. The well-known dictum of Canon Goudge who considered that the infiltration of Roman and Greek ideas into the Christian church represents "a disaster from which we have never recovered, either in doctrine or practice" is well worth pondering. Could it really be true that "the historical Jesus, the rabbi who had once walked the earth, then died and returned (to life), and who would soon come again to inaugurate his Kingdom, was fading into the background like a figure in an antique mosaic," as Richard Rubenstein argues?[6] Or, as another has it:

> The story of how Greek philosophy, with its synthesis of rationalism and mysticism, rhetorically [i.e. persuasively] penetrated and permeated the Christian tradition, forever altering Christian faith, is virtually an open secret insofar as it oozes out the pores of the literature of Church history and theology. The open secret continues to be kept, no doubt, due to its staggering implications.[7]

That the average Christian today is so unaware of this staggering fact that "Christianity as we have it today is a form of Greco-Roman mythology" is proof that new voices which demand integrity must be heard.[8] Or, as another has said, "In the name of the true Lord of history the false gods in church and society must constantly be demythologized anew."[9] Perhaps the words of Dan Brown's fictitious character Sir Leigh Teabing carry a great deal of

---

[6] Richard E. Rubenstein, *When Jesus Became God: The Epic Fight over Christ's Divinity in the Last Days of Rome,* New York: Harcourt Brace & Co., 1999, p. 146.

[7] Robert Hach, *Possession and Persuasion: The Rhetoric of Christian Faith,* 2000, p. 120. See his website at www.ereflector.blogspot.com

[8] J. Harrold Ellens, *The Ancient Library of Alexandria and Early Christian Theological Development,* quoted in Hach, *Possession and Persuasion*, p. 120.

[9] Karl-Josef Kuschel, *Born Before All Time? The Dispute over Christ's Origin*, New York: Crossroad, 1992, p. 488.

truth after all. Teabing alleges, "Many scholars claim that the early Church literally *stole* Jesus from his original followers, hijacking his human message, shrouding it in an impenetrable cloak of divinity, and using it to expand their own power."[10] Serious and well-respected "conservative" historians and theologians such as N.T. Wright also acknowledge that "it is not only possible, but actually highly likely, that the church has distorted the real Jesus, and needs to repent of this and rediscover who its Lord actually is."[11] This spectrum of voices from the "liberal" to the "conservative" is unanimous.

Much of the New Testament was written to warn of the very possibility of take-over. "Beloved, do not believe every spirit, but test the spirits to see whether they are from God, because many false prophets have gone out into the world" (1 John 4:1). "There are some who are disturbing you, and want to distort the gospel of Christ" (Gal. 1:7). "But I am afraid, lest as the serpent deceived Eve by his craftiness, your minds should be led astray from the simplicity and purity of devotion to Christ" (2 Cor. 11:4). Our Lord himself warned of wolves who would come in sheep's clothing. Evidently, even while the Son of man was sowing his seed of the glorious Gospel of the Kingdom the Enemy was already hot on his heels broadcasting weeds (Matt. 13:25).

I grew up within the Churches of Christ. I was taught early that ours was the New Testament position. This was reinforced to me at Bible College where I learned that we were endeavouring to restore the New Testament Church. Ours is a heritage of reform. We used to be a vibrant people, who challenged the status quo with the great catch-cry: No book but the Bible. Whenever our people moved into a new district, the "establishment" felt threatened. We were convinced we had the truth — not that we believed we were the only Christians, but we were Christians only. We represented the very best of traditional and popular evangelical Christianity: the Bible is the Word of God, our only rule of faith; God is a Trinity in unity, Father, Son and Holy Spirit; Jesus Christ is the second member of this Holy Trinity, God in the flesh who had to become incarnate so that He could die for our sins; Jesus was resurrected and is now in heaven awaiting His Second Coming when He will

---

[10] Dan Brown, *The Da Vinci Code,* Australia: Random House, p. 316.
[11] N.T. Wright, *Who Was Jesus?* London: SPCK, 1992, p. 18.

bring all the saints who have already died and gone to heaven with Him back to rule on earth; all unbelievers will be consigned to everlasting torment in hellfire. Believers' baptism was a key part of Jesus' teaching on conversion. It is with such a heritage in mind that I write this book. *They Never Told Me* This *in Church!* represents a re-evaluation of these issues for the ordinary person. It is not a deeply academic book, though it draws from the best of available scholarship. It tells a story that most of today's Christians are blissfully unaware of: How significantly pagan ideas have infected "the faith once delivered to the saints."

To illustrate how this book came about, allow me to use a familiar example from everyday sporting life in Australia: I am a great rugby league fan. It is a tough, fast, bone-crunching game for the working class man. As a player I learned that one of the worst things you can do to the support-man running next to you is to "sell him the hospital pass." Here is your team-mate running next to you. He holds the ball. You are his support player. The danger is that an opposition player is running full belt right at you. You are covered. You are a second away from collision. You will be tackled. But your mate passes you the ball anyway. What do you do? Take your eyes off the ball, drop it and lose priceless possession for the team? Or do you catch the ball with both hands knowing that in that split-second you cannot defend yourself and will be smashed senseless? It is a horrible feeling being sold the hospital pass.

All my life I have been playing for the "orthodox Christian" team. ("Orthodox" means "straight-thinking.") In fact, I championed the "orthodox" evangelical cause with every ounce of my being. I subscribed to the traditional creeds of the Church: the Nicene Creed, the Apostles' Creed, the Athanasian Creed, the Chalcedonian Creed, the Churches of Christ "No creed but Christ" creed. I was running right alongside all my other "orthodox" team-mates and was in good company, so I thought, stretching all the way back to Jesus and the apostles. But this all changed dramatically for me one fateful night. I met a man who asked me, "Do you believe in the Trinity?" Without blinking an eye I stated with absolute conviction, "Of course I am a firm believer in the Trinity." This man, Sir Anthony Buzzard (who has graciously written the "Foreword" to this book) then asked me a few well-aimed questions that completely threw me. They were questions I had not considered in all my previous Christian life, even at Bible college. They were like well-aimed bolts that hit their mark. To use the football analogy, I was on the ground, severely winded. It had never hit me with such force that my belief structure might be just as biased and error-ridden as others. I had just caught the hospital pass. I needed it — for it jolted me right out of my unquestioned orthodoxy. And now when I stand up to play the ball, I am going to play it for the "heterodox Christian" team! ("Heterodox" means "thinking otherwise.")

It is not easy re-examining our cherished beliefs. We become fiercely and emotionally attached to our "God." Not only that, but surrounding us are the many who subscribe to our dogma. We are family. God is our God. We all belong together. I have often tried to imagine what it must be like being born into a Muslim community, or a Hindu community, or a Buddhist community. Probably no different, really, from being born into a Jehovah's Witness community, or a Baptist community, or a Roman Catholic community or a Churches of Christ community. For those who take their faith seriously it is hard to believe that their perspective may have glaring errors in it. To get a person from any faith to question his position is almost impossible. To raise questions about long-held beliefs usually means the messenger gets shot before the question gets any kind of fair hearing. However, our Lord himself said that it is possible to nullify God's Word in our lives because we refuse to give up human tradition which has been handed down (Mark 7:13). I can relate to the author who said, "In my own case, the hardest — and the most exciting — thing about research into Christian beginnings has been to unlearn what I thought I knew, and to shed presuppositions I had taken for granted."[12]

This book is the result of years of prayerful agonizing before God the Father. It is the result of years of intense study and searching the Scriptures. It has been both a threatening and a liberating journey. Many of my old theological strongholds have been stormed. But every thought must be taken "captive to the obedience of Christ" (2 Cor. 10:5). I am perfectly aware that many who read this will do so with the same spirit I once had. I became a theological policeman, and any doctrine or practice that did not follow this faith that had come to us from the apostles themselves was suspect. I was like a trigger-happy cop who shoots himself in

---

[12] Elaine Pagels, *Beyond Belief: The Secret Gospel of Thomas,* New York: Random House, 2003, p. 181.

the foot without even clearing the holster first. For those self-assured readers like me, may I encourage a moment or two's honest self-reflection? Ask yourself whether you know anybody who has never been wrong about anything. No? Then we may safely say that illusion and deception and error are a part of our human condition. We must therefore walk humbly, for God only promises grace and wisdom to those who know they need help. It is my prayer that *They Never Told Me* This *in Church!* will find its way to the many who are seeking for an authentic spiritual journey and who above all things else are crying out from the depths of their hearts, "Oh God, open my eyes. If I have been deceived, un-deceive me, for no matter what it costs, I want to see You!"

I write this, then, for any who will read it with the same "noble-minded" spirit that the Bereans had, "for they received the word with great eagerness, examining the Scriptures daily, to see whether these things were so" (Acts 17:11). I do not write it with the idea that I have a monopoly on understanding. I am a fellow pilgrim. As a disciple of Christ I am still learning. If at the end of the day, when you have read this book, you consider my ideas too unconventional then I suggest that my book will have served a good purpose. Perhaps my heresy will have served to strengthen your orthodoxy! And while I do write in order to challenge re-examination of our cherished and "traditional" faith, when all is said and done, I am convinced that Christianity will emerge from honest historical and theological enquiry more solid and genuine. This has certainly been my experience since my encounter that eventful night.

Douglas Lockhart notes that when documentaries questioning the efficacy of the Christian faith are aired on television around Easter:

> the reaction of the Church is sometimes quite hysterical. Metaphorically, doors are bolted and windows barred to save the "faithful" from contamination. At the end of one particular BBC programme many years ago, there was a telephone number given which Christians could ring for guidance, a "helpline" to deal with their *expected* doubts and fears. That intrigued me. What had happened to the spirit that had once animated Christians and made them invite the jaws of beasts to devour them? Where was the unshakable certainty, the jutting jaw of immovable faith? What had happened to so reduce Christian certainty that it

> could be so easily threatened? The only conclusion I could come to was that many Christians had realized deep down that the good news was fatally flawed.[13]

I do not agree with this conclusion (nor others) that Lockhart comes to. Mine is the conviction that the holy Scriptures are written by men whose hearts God had spoken through by His Spirit. They are like "a lamp shining in a dark place, until the day dawns" when God brings to pass all that He has promised through His holy prophets and apostles, and has guaranteed through His Son, Jesus our Lord. But I do believe it's time for Christians to honestly face these challenges. It is no longer acceptable for Christians to get upset if somebody is rocking the old boat of belief with fair-minded questions. The attitude that the boat must not be allowed to sink, even if in the end it means taking the boat out of the water, will no longer work. If as Lockhart warns, Christians do not take a stand on behalf of sensible scholarship and spiritual discrimination, they are going to find themselves left intellectually high and dry and caught up in a Church willing to sacrifice growth and discovery in the mistaken and arrogant belief that nothing can or should be added to (or subtracted from) the Christian corpus.

The controversial Bishop John Shelby Spong (controversial because he advocates the ordination of practising homosexuals, the denial of the literal, bodily resurrection of Jesus, and states that his mission is to radically redefine what morality is by "rescuing the Bible from fundamentalism") in the introduction to one of his books wrote:

> Long ago I decided that I could no longer sacrifice scholarship and truth to protect the weak and religiously insecure. I see another audience that the church seems to ignore. That audience is made up of brilliantly educated men and women who find in the church a god too small to be the God of life for them, a knowledge too restricted to be compelling or a superstition too obvious to be entertained with seriousness.[14]

I do not endorse Spong's interpretations and conclusions, but along with the Bishop I realize that my now grown-up children are

---

[13] Lockhart, p. 6.

[14] John Shelby Spong, *Born of a Woman: A Bishop Rethinks the Birth of Jesus,* Harper San Francisco, 1992.

part of that audience. And I want them to find in the Christian church a Gospel that takes seriously the contemporary challenges of modern science and biblical scholarship. I want for them a Gospel free from the binding and blinding strictures of man-made traditions, a Gospel that has contemporary power to worship the God of truth and life, the God of Jesus Christ who does not need to be protected by hiding behind some anti-intellectual pose for fear of the light. Jesus challenged the stereotypes of his day. He would do so again if he was physically here. I want to say that along with every other thinking person with an interest in Christian truth, I have a spiritual investment in discovering the truth, and also in knowing the nature and the seriousness of the lies, if lies they be. Lockhart writes with pathos:

> and neither do I consider my taking a stand against Christianity's claims for Jesus a spiritual impertinence. In fact, I feel the opposite. I feel, deeply, that Jesus the Nazarene has been done a great disservice by many of those claiming to hold him in high esteem. All I see is a sad-eyed prisoner of the Christian imagination locked inside a paradigm he did not, and would not now, condone.[15]

Perhaps, as they say, something in our traditional approach has been lost in translation. So let's see if we can discover what that something is!

What have you got to lose? Maybe you are not sure what to believe any more. Or maybe you sincerely believe you hold the Truth. If it is God's Truth it has nothing to fear from the light. For truth is light. And the wisdom which is from above, from God "is first pure, then peaceable, gentle, reasonable, full of mercy and good fruits, unwavering, without hypocrisy" (James 3:17). God's truth is pure, not mixed (with human philosophy); it is gentle, not roughhouse (rude or domineering); and it is reasonable, not closed-minded (pig-headed). One who holds the truth in all good conscience has nothing to fear from an honest investigation. I will let you decide whether this book passes James' test. And my prayer is that you too may find the joy from the jolt of a well-timed hospital pass. The best part is what they never tell you in church!

---

[15] Lockhart, p. 9.

One
ANOTHER COVER-UP

A nod is as good as a wink to a blind horse.

Winners are grinners and they get to write their own story. Losers just lose and their story is rarely told. Subsequent generations usually learn only a distorted history. Sheer weight of numbers can drown out the story of the minority. The passage of the centuries can dull the collective conscience. Again, if I may quote Dan Brown's Sir Leigh Teabing, "By its very nature, history is always a one-sided account."[1] Or to use the words of Napoleon, "What is history, but a fable agreed upon?" To illustrate how history can be created, not just related, one has only to remember how Hollywood created tales of "cowboys and Indians" to relate "how the West was won," not "how the West was lost." History written by victors conceals as much as it reveals. My aim in this chapter is to show that there is a mass of church history that the average Christian is in the dark about. Time and the majority have conspired to paint a fake picture. The fact that the majority of Christians today believe they hold the pure apostolic faith originally delivered to the Church is proof of the success of the con job "official" church history has bequeathed us.

In 1945 in Egypt a cache of early "Christian" writings called the Nag Hammadi documents was discovered that completely revolutionized our understanding of the Christian church in the first few centuries. The story of Nag Hammadi begins way back in 367 AD when an over-zealous bishop of Alexandria named Athanasius issued an Easter letter. Athanasius demanded that priests in Egypt destroy all "secret writings" that did not conform to his list of acceptable "canon." ("Canon" is a carpenter's term meaning "guideline" and was a string with a weight attached, used to check that a wall was straight.) Athanasius' list of acceptable Christian writings contained most of the 27 books that make up our New Testament. But somebody did not follow Athanasius' directive and

---

[1] Dan Brown, p. 343.

gathered up dozens of these banned books — more than fifty in fact — sealed them in a heavy six-foot jar, and buried them in a hillside near Nag Hammadi, about 600 kilometres south of Cairo. Sixteen hundred years later, a certain Muhammad Ali (not the boxer — this bloke was an Egyptian!) stumbled upon them. Ali's find was, however, in boxing terms the equivalent of a powerful upper-cut into the solar plexus of contemporary belief.

The Nag Hammadi writings have opened up the proverbial can of worms. They confirm that Christianity in the first few centuries was not a monolithic organization. There was massive diversity within churches all over the Roman empire. It seems that today's bewildering number of Christian churches and breakaways is but a pale reflection of the kaleidoscopic scene during the second and third centuries after Christ. Christianity in post-apostolic days was in a liquid state. With the death of the apostles, and the destruction of Jerusalem as the spiritual home of their faith, Christians were scattered far and wide. There were pockets of believers throughout the empire, and larger churches in the big cities like Rome, Antioch, Corinth, Ephesus, and Alexandria. More and more Gentiles were converted and the whole character of the churches changed. The apron strings of the Jewish mother church that had cradled them were well and truly cut. "There was a certain amount of communication between the centres, but nothing approaching an integrated universal Church."[2] Christianity quickly came to terms with the predominantly Hellenistic (Greek) culture surrounding it. Diversity became the order of the day. The confusing of Greek ideas with the Hebrew heritage of the apostolic church:

> began very early, as early as Clement of Alexandria [ca. AD 150-215] and Origen [ca. AD 185-254] and it arose from the fact that these scholars were Hellenists first and Christians second. It was furthered by the fact that all men until Jerome [ca. AD 347-420] tended to read the Greek Bible as a Greek book, and with Hellenistic eyes...The result of this has been that from a very early stage, Christianity itself has tended to suffer from a translation out of the Prophets and into Plato.[3]

---

[2] Hugh Schonfield, *The Passover Plot,* p. 275.

[3] N.H. Snaith, *The Distinctive Ideas of the Old Testament,* Great Britain: The Epworth Press, 1944, p. 161.

Thus, diffusion and confusion became rampant: There were Christians who believed in only one God. Others believed there were two Gods, one inferior to the other. Some accepted the Hebrew Scriptures as the only revelation of the one true God. Others placed the writings of the apostles and their delegates as equal to the old Scriptures. Some Christians held that somehow Christ was both man and God; others said he was a man, but not God; and still others insisted he was a man who had been temporarily indwelt by God. Some Christians believed Christ's death had brought salvation to the world and others claimed his death was incidental, while still others believed Christ had never actually died. Some groups celebrated the eucharist as a "simple meal" of fellowship while others celebrated it in a more macabre way, believing they were eating and drinking actual flesh and blood. Some churches claimed that with the death of the apostles visions and new revelations had ceased; others claimed the Holy Spirit was still speaking to the church in fresh prophecy. Elaine Pagels points out that there were various regions and churches that claimed patron saints as their inspiration: There were the Thomas Christians, the Johannine Christians, the Peter Christians, and even the Mary Magdalene Christians: "Various Christian groups validated their teaching by declaring allegiance to a specific apostle or disciple and claiming him (and sometimes her) as their spiritual founder."[4] This is not surprising, for even as early as 50 to 60 AD the apostle Paul remonstrated with the Corinthians because one group said, "We are of Paul," and another group said, "We are of Apollos," while still others said, "We are of Peter" (1 Cor. 1:12). In other words, Christianity was not a monolithic structure in the second and third centuries. During these second and third centuries — and especially since the Jerusalem church had been razed by the Romans in AD 70 — there was no such thing as "the holy mother church of Rome." Every region, indeed even local congregations, could hold a variety of theologies and doctrines. "There was as yet no established 'orthodoxy,' that is, no basic theological system acknowledged by the majority of church leaders and laity."[5] There were many competing voices:

---

[4] Pagels, p. 65.

[5] Bart D. Ehrman, *The Orthodox Corruption of Scripture: The Effect of Early Christological Controversies on the Text of the New Testament,* Oxford University Press, 1993, p. 4.

> Early Christianity embodied a number of divergent forms, no one of which represented the clear and powerful majority of believers against all others. In some regions, what was later to be termed "heresy" was in fact the original and only form of Christianity...To this extent, "orthodoxy," in the sense of a unified group advocating an apostolic doctrine accepted by the majority of Christians everywhere, did not exist in the second and third centuries.[6]

A pagan philosopher, Celsus, who wrote in the second century, observed that at first when the Christians were few in number they maintained common convictions. However, after the apostles had all died and Christian numbers multiplied across the Roman empire, he observed that they were soon split into many and varied sects which only had the name Christian in common. The history of how one of these competing groups became the dominant party and forced its authority on the rest of Christendom is the story most today are unaware of. It is a shocking historical fact that the Christians who advocated what we call orthodox and the mainstream today, in the second and third centuries "in most cases...represented a minority position."[7] To be sure, later proponents of what became the majority and "orthodox" party (the winners!) were able to write their story, erase other stories to preserve their position, and then insist they represented the opinion of the majority of Christians from the apostles onwards. But in those critical first two centuries "what later came to be known as orthodoxy was simply *one* among a number of competing interpretations of Christianity in the early period."[8] It just so happens that this one was the form adopted by Rome, the church and region that was able to use its superior administrative and economic resources to strategic advantage. Thus, the generally held idea that the early church was one catholic (literally, universal) and unified body, and that heresy was always on the run, needs revision, for "groups later labelled heretical saw themselves as orthodox and sometimes attacked groups that held views they themselves

---

[6] Walter Bauer, *Rechtglaubigkeit und Ketzerei im altesten Christentum,* quoted by Ehrman, p. 7.

[7] Ehrman, p. 8.

[8] *Ibid.,* p. 8.

considered aberrant."[9] We simply have to recognize "that early Christianity is far more diverse than nearly anyone expected."[10]

The "Church Fathers" — the respected bishops and teachers who witnessed to and explained Christianity in the early post-apostolic centuries — on closer examination are often found to espouse views that look decidedly dodgy by later standards. For instance, even though at its inception Christianity had been very positive and liberating for women, it was not very long before the church fathers, influenced by pagan attitudes around them, began to denigrate women and even alienate them from the life of the church. The letters of Jerome "teem with loathing of the female which occasionally sounds deranged."[11] Tertullian (who left the church later) also castigates women as evil temptresses, an eternal danger to mankind:

> Do you not know that you are each an Eve: The sentence of God on this sex of yours lives in this age: the guilt must of necessity live too. *You* are the devil's gateway; *you* are the unsealer of that forbidden tree; *you* are the first deserter of the divine law; *you* are she who persuaded him whom the devil was not valiant enough to attack...*You* so carelessly destroyed man, God's image. On account of *your* desert, even the Son of God had to die.[12]

Augustine agreed: "What is the difference," he wrote to a friend, "whether it is in a wife or a mother, it is still Eve the temptress that we must beware of in any woman."[13] If the church fathers had so soon strayed from the example and teachings of Jesus and his apostles on this issue, we ought not be surprised that these "champions of orthodoxy" could rewrite essential apostolic doctrines — doctrines later condemned as "heresy." Clement of Alexandria, for instance, claimed that Jesus ate food not because he needed the nourishment but simply because he wanted to convince the disciples that he actually had a body. Origen believed that Jesus' body could readily change appearance at will, that is, that he just appeared to have a human body when it suited him (a theory called

---

[9] *Ibid.*, p. 10.

[10] Pagels, p. xxxi.

[11] Karen Armstrong, *A History of God: The 4000-year Quest for God.* London: Mandarin, 1993, p. 145.

[12] *Ibid.*, p. 145.

[13] *Ibid.*, p. 145.

"docetism" from a Greek word meaning "to appear"). Origen was indeed later accused of heresy himself. He had some notion that the holy spirit inserted contradictions into John's Gospel in order to startle the reader into delving into the deeper and hidden meaning of things — although John tells the truth, it is not literal truth but spiritual truth! These were clearly troubled times for the Christian church as the leaders could not get it "right." Many of their views were later branded "heresy," yet we are not openly told this side of the story. These are just a cross-section of those who were the architects of today's mainstream orthodoxy.

It is now a recognized fact by specialists within this field that the many different forms and denominations within the Christian umbrella today "reflect in a pale way the amazing diversity of the first two centuries."[14] Today most Christians of all persuasions confess the Apostolic Creed and accept the New Testament as a fixed canon of Scripture. There is a general consensus among most Christian groups in spite of surface tensions. But there was nothing of a similar nature during the first one and a half centuries of the Church's early dynamic life. During those years of turmoil there were lots of gospels, and they were *all* taken seriously by the disparate congregations. The Gospel of Thomas and the Gospel of Philip and the Gospel of Truth circulated alongside Matthew, Mark, Luke and John, and were held in just as high esteem by many devout believers in Jesus. Some groups like the Ebionite Christians only used Matthew. The Marcionites preferred only Luke. Others followed Irenaeus who "resolved to hack down the forest of 'apocryphal and illegitimate' writings — writings like the Secret Book of James and the Gospel of Mary — and leave only four 'pillars' standing (i.e. Matthew, Mark, Luke and John)."[15] It was only with the turn of the second century that these gospels began to be standardized into today's canon and many disparate Christian groups were brought under the full control of bishops, priests and deacons. This trinity of authority figures came to believe themselves divinely appointed to look after their communities, and eventually took it upon themselves to decide the exact nature of what should and should not be believed about Jesus and his mission. The Roman church then emerged in a leading role, and decided that it had the

[14] Lockhart, p. 266.
[15] Pagels, p. 111.

power to veto community beliefs through the bishops. The Christian canon was considered completed and closed in 367 AD. In the spring of that year, when he was in his sixties, Athanasius, secure as bishop of Alexandria, wrote his most famous letter. He wrote that heretics:

> have tried to set in order for themselves the so-called apocryphal books and to mix these with the divinely inspired Scripture...which those who were eyewitnesses and helpers of the Word handed down to our ancestors. (Therefore) it seemed good to me...to set forth in order the canonized and transmitted writings...believed to be divine books.[16]

This was the point at which somebody took his shovel out to the hills of Nag Hammadi, as mentioned at the beginning of this chapter. As Lockhart says, everything in God's garden which appeared neat and tidy was not really so. When the number of Christian gospels was cut back to four and other sacred writings also axed from the Church's recommended reading list, whole sections of the community of faith were amazed and revolted. Prior to the announcement of the fixed canon there had been a large and sprawling conglomerate of Christian communities all in broad agreement:

> After the announcement, many of these communities not only found themselves disadvantaged by Rome's textual curtailments, but discovered — when the news finally got through — that their particular textual proclivities had pushed them into the category of "heretics." What a shock that must have been. Going to bed one night and being in the fold, but waking up the next day to find you had been classified as "traitorous." Christians one day, heretics the next![17]

The largest group of non-conformists this action affected were the Gnostics. These "knowers" (the Greek word *gnosis* means knowledge) taught that there was an inner, hidden knowledge available only to its members but not open to the rest of the Christian community. Only their Gnostic initiates were privy to the deeper meaning of Christ's teachings. Even so, up until this time

---

[16] *Ibid.,* p. 176, emphasis original.
[17] *Ibid.,* p. 267.

when Rome made her pronouncements about "heresy," Christian writers had tended to regard the Gnostics not as heathens but as "faction-makers," who imported false teachings into the community of Christians. Up until then, Gnostic doctrines warranted rebuke as well as refutation.[18] But from then on, all such different thinking was officially regarded as "heresy" to be punished.

So we see the generally held notion that the great creeds of the Church which evolved from the Council of Nicea in 325 AD onwards are proof that majority "orthodox" Christianity triumphed over the "heretics" of the day, does not stand up to historical scrutiny. The common idea that Arius, one of the main players in the Nicene dispute, was the leader of a little "heretic" splinter group because he did not believe that Jesus was the uncreated God, proves how successful the snow job[19] has been. For it is a fact of church history that along with Arius, believers in God as a single Person, that is, unitarian Christians, were "at the beginning of the third century still forming the large majority."[20]

In his book *When Jesus Became God* Richard Rubenstein points out that the Council of Nicea was not a universal or truly "catholic" council. There were only about 250 bishops present, and almost all of them were from the eastern half of the Roman Empire. In fact, there was only a handful of western bishops at this council of Nicea. Well over half of the church bishops were missing! Arius' sworn opponent was also from Alexandria in Egypt. He was a very short, red-haired man soon to become the most powerful bishop in Christendom. We have already been introduced to him — Athanasius. Years after Nicea voted that Jesus was *wholly* God and *fully* man, the Athanasian Creed declared the true catholic faith was:

> That we worship One God as Trinity, and Trinity in Unity — neither confounding the Persons nor dividing the substance — for there is one Person of the Father, another of the Son, and another of the Holy Ghost, but the Godhead of the Father, and of the Son, and of the Holy Ghost is all one, the glory equal, the majesty co-eternal.

---

[18] Benjamin Walker, *Gnosticism: Its History and Influence,* Northhamptonshire: Crucible, 1989, p. 22.

[19] *Snow job* — a good cover-up that suggests being blinded by a blizzard, equivalent to a con job.

[20] *Encyclopedia Britannica,* 11th ed., vol. 23, p. 963.

Yet, even Athanasius it seems had trouble with his own definitions, for he later wrote that concerning the divinity of the Logos, "the more I thought the less I comprehended; and the more I wrote the less capable was I of expressing my thoughts." To shanghai through this piece of incomprehensible verbalism (that God is a Trinity in unity with the Persons not to be confounded and their substance not to be divided), the Council of Nicea attached an anathema to it, making it binding on the whole church: "The Holy Catholic and Apostolic Church anathematizes those who say that there was a time when the Son of God was not, and that before he was begotten, he was not, and that he was made out of nothing, or out of another substance or essence, and is created, or changeable, or alterable."

Lockhart comments:

> All in all, a tight little package which set the inevitable ball of heresy rolling, the flames rising, the cries and screams of innocent human beings into the fetid air of dank prisons. Because a Church Council composed of people like Athanasius had said so, Jesus was no longer the Jewish Messiah, the Suffering Servant of Isaiah, the Archetypal man...he was the alien Jewish God shoe-horned into a physical body and let loose as a refurbished pagan deity of monstrous proportions.[21]

Now for the real shock. Just a few short years after Nicea where Athanasius and Emperor Constantine rammed their creed through (many of the bishops at Nicea disagreed but signed under duress), another joint council was held that completely *reversed* the Nicene Creed in favour of Arius! Rubenstein notes:

> The joint council of Rimini-Seleucia (359) was attended by more than five hundred bishops from both the East and West. If any meeting deserves the title "ecumenical," that one seems to qualify, but its result — the adoption of an Arian creed — was later repudiated by the Church. Councils whose products were later deemed unorthodox not only lost the "ecumenical" label but virtually disappeared from official church history.[22]

---

[21] Lockhart, p. 131.
[22] Rubenstein, p. 75.

Rubenstein goes on to observe that for more than half a century the document which is today recited in an amended version around the globe as representative of orthodoxy — the Nicene Creed — actually split the Christian community violently. It seems that the bishops present at Nicea were compelled to sign under some duress — the imperial Roman army was, after all, camped outside! All but two or three bishops and a few priests buckled. Arius and these others were excommunicated. But the debate did not go away. In the decades following there was much intrigue and to-ing and fro-ing as one side and then the other side temporarily gained the ascendancy. In a few short years' time when "Arianism" had become even more popular, Constantine found it politically convenient to change sides! This time he exiled all those who did not agree with Arius! In fact, Constantine, as he approached the end of his life, was baptized by the Arian Bishop of Nicomedia.

Constantine presided over the Nicene assembly of bishops himself and according to the *Encyclopedia Britannica* "personally proposed the crucial formula expressing the relationship of Christ to God in the creed issued by the council, 'of one substance with the Father.'" It is a fact that many of the bishops present were opposed to the doctrine of the Trinity and had sided with Arius who was quite skilful at arguing from Scripture that the Son was separate and subordinate to God. However, Constantine sided with Athanasius whose theory that the Son was "made of the same stuff" as the Father was imposed on the assembly. The *American Academic Encyclopedia* notes that "Although this was not Constantine's first attempt to reconcile factions in Christianity, it was the first time he had used the imperial office to *impose* a settlement." One bishop was to write after Nicea the lamentation, "We committed an impious act, O Prince, by subscribing to a blasphemy from fear of you." It is true that some historians disagree that Constantine was heavy handed. They point out that when Constantine saw the scars and wounds of the bishops and priests who had been tortured for their faith in Christ, he actually went around kissing those scars. These historians therefore argue that such warriors of the faith would not have yielded to any coercion, since they had lost eyes and limbs for their beliefs. Most historians, however, understand Constantine to have been the consummate politician, whose record of intrigue and vacillation over the years depended on which party — the Arians or the Athanasians — seemed to have their noses in front at any given time. This record speaks for itself. After the Council of Nicea concluded, Constantine sided with Athanasius against Arius and Arius was exiled to Illyria. It is also a fact that after the Council of Nicea this "Christian" emperor returned home and had his wife suffocated, his mother-in-law Fausta and his son Crispus murdered. He deliberately remained unbaptized until his deathbed so he could continue his political intrigue and still receive the Church's forgiveness by being baptized at the last moment.

The following timeline gives a little of the history in outline form to illustrate how hotly the doctrine of the Trinity and the person and nature of Jesus Christ were contested throughout the Roman Empire. It was not just a simple matter of once and for all time deciding Jesus' divinity by vote in a contrived council meeting. Now observe the machinations.[23]

325 AD — Emperor Constantine convenes the Council of Nicea because the Empire was being torn apart by internal church wrangling over the person and nature of Christ. Christianity had been so successful that the whole Empire was being affected by this dispute. Constantine wanted to unify his domain. He considered himself the high priest of the pagan religion of the Unconquered Sun and thought of himself as a god-incarnate. It is well known that Constantine was a sun worshipper and "converted" to Christianity only on his deathbed. So a council of the church's bishops was convened to resolve the dispute that threatened political schism across the empire.

328 AD — Athanasius becomes bishop of Alexandria.

328 AD — Constantine recalls Arius from Illyria.

335 AD — Constantine sides with Arius and exiles Athanasius to Trier.

336 AD — The eastern bishops meet at Constantinople with the emperor in attendance. "This was the fourth council since Arius' return from exile to pronounce his theology orthodox."

337 AD — The new Emperor Constantius orders the return of Athanasius to Alexandria.

339 AD — Athanasius flees Alexandria having learned he is about to be expelled as a heretic.

---

[23] Juan Baixeras, "So What is This Truth of the Nicene Creed?" www.geocities.com/Athens/Olympus/5257. Used with permission.

341 AD — Two councils are held in Antioch this year. During this time the First, Second and Third Arian Confessions are written in an attempt to produce a formal doctrine of faith to *oppose* the Nicene Creed.

343 AD — At the Council of Sardica, eastern bishops demand the removal of Athanasius.

346 AD — Athanasius is restored to Alexandria.

351 AD — A second anti-Nicene council is held in Sirmium.

353 AD — A council is held at Aries during autumn that is directed against Athanasius.

355 AD — A council is held in Milan which again condemns Athanasius.

356 AD — Athanasius is deposed on February 8th and begins his third exile.

357 AD — The Third Council of Sirmium is convened where it is agreed that the Father is greater than His subordinate Son. (For those interested, the technical terms expressing these ideas, *homo-ousios* and *homoi-ousios,* which denote "made of the same stuff" and "made of like stuff," were avoided as being unbiblical terms.)

359 AD — The council of Seleucia affirms that Christ is "like the Father," but does not specify how the Son is like the Father.

361 AD — A council is held in Antioch to affirm Arius' position.

380 AD — Emperor Theodosius the Great declares Christianity the official state religion of the Empire.

381 AD — The First Council of Constantinople reviews the controversy since Nicea. Emperor Theodosius the Great establishes the creed of Nicea as the standard for his realm. The Nicene Creed is re-evaluated and accepted with the addition of clauses on the Holy Spirit and other matters.

At a glance then — and contrary to popular misconceptions — it can be seen that the Nicene Creed did not just formalize what the Church was already teaching. Conflict raged back and forth. That which was one day deemed "orthodox" was later anathema. Towards the end of the fourth century Hilary, Bishop of Poitiers, wrote despondently:

> Every year, nay, every moon we make new creeds to describe invisible mysteries. We repent of what we have done, we defend those who repent, we anathematise those whom we defended. We condemn either the doctrine of

> others in ourselves, or our own in that of others; and reciprocally tearing one another to pieces, we have been the cause of each other's ruin.[24]

Conflict divided bishops and congregations throughout the empire. When one faction of the Church tried to make its views official, major unrest resulted. Conflict also engulfed Constantine's sons and grandsons when they succeeded him as emperor. As Elaine Pagels states:

> Although Constantine's revolution lent support to the claims of catholic bishops that their church, triumphant through God's grace, alone offered salvation, we would be naive to suppose that Christianity now became, in fact, uniform and homogeneous. Even a glance at the controversies and challenges of the fourth and fifth centuries shows that it did not. What this revolution did accomplish was to enhance the authority of the bishops identified as catholic and to establish their consensus, expressed through the statements of the creed, as defining the boundaries of the newly legitimate faith.[25]

Or, as another commentator puts it, with the passage of time:

> the Jewish-Christianity which had been dominant for decades...was increasingly swept aside and was finally branded heretical, [but] the confessions of a marginal Christianity [i.e. Hellenized Christianity which believed that Jesus was the preexistent God] were very soon to become a kind of normative theology...It would take two hundred years, a great schism in the church, and the rending of Christianity by accusations of heresy and heresy-hunts, before at the Council of Nicea in 325 the "intellectual problem" raised here was translated into a regulation which was binding on the church.[26]

So that which was once the heart of true Jewish-Christianity became increasingly marginalized. The dominant theology of a Church faithful to her Lord and his apostles became increasingly demeaned. The first church historian, Eusebius, born a Gentile Christian towards the end of the third century, "could already

---

[24] E. Gibbon, *The Decline and Fall of the Roman Empire,* Penguin Classics, 1976.

[25] Rubenstein, p. 134.

[26] Pagels, p. 180.

comment disparagingly on Jewish-Christian circles."[27] In short, it is apparent that already in the third century those Christians who did not believe that Jesus Christ was fully God and did not have a personal preexistence before his birth, were being labelled godless![28]

I was always taught that when we come to the fourth century Arius was an annoying heretic, and thank God that the Church so branded him and banished him. Typical of this misconception are the comments of Josh McDowell and Bart Larson who even go so far as to say that until the appearance of Arius (AD 318-320) the debate over Christ's Deity hardly raised an eyebrow. Only with Arius' arrival did "the question *become* a major theological issue within the church."[29] This simply is not true. In fact, the truth is that Arius was considered by *the majority* as the "orthodox conservative"! Richard Rubenstein writes: "From the perspective of our own time, it may seem strange to think of Arian 'heretics' as conservatives, but emphasizing Jesus' humanity and God's transcendent otherness had never seemed heretical in the East."[30]

The truth remains that after countless years of intrigue and debate and political interference today's historic or "mainstream" religion emerged from these days of Constantine.

> As a result of Nicea, Christianity was decriminalised; but only Rome's brand! Free souls who conscientiously objected were increasingly marginalized. Rome became the official centre of Christian orthodoxy, and any deviation from that orthodoxy became a heresy, rather than merely a difference of opinion or interpretation. At Nicea, Jesus' Divinity, and the precise nature of his divinity, were established by means of a "vote." *It is fair to state that Christianity as we know it today derives ultimately not from Jesus' time, but from the Council of Nicea.* And to the extent that Nicea was largely Constantine's handiwork, Christianity is necessarily indebted to him. But this is very

---

[27] Kuschel, pp. 392-393.
[28] *Ibid.*, p. 395.
[29] McDowell and Larson, *Jesus: A Biblical Defense of His Deity,* San Bernadino, CA: Here's Life Publishers, Inc., 1983, p. 80, emphasis added.
[30] *Ibid.*, p. 395.

> different from saying that Constantine was a Christian, or that he "Christianized the Empire."[31]

It is true that Constantine showed great tolerance towards the Christian churches. By the Edict of Milan in 313 he forbade persecution of all forms of monotheism in the Empire. To the extent that this included Christianity, Constantine became somewhat of a saviour for the beleaguered congregations that had suffered centuries of imperial torment. It is also true that Constantine accorded new privileges to the church hierarchy. He let high church dignitaries become part of the civil administration. This paved the way for the Church to consolidate its secular power. Constantine even donated the Lateran Palace to the bishop of Rome, thus helping Rome consolidate its supremacy over other major Christian centres such as Alexandria and Antioch. But for all that, Constantine remained a devotee, not of the Christian God, but of the sun god — Sol Invictus — which had been introduced to the empire from Syrian sources and contained elements of Baal and Astarte worship. "In effect, it posited the sun god as the sum of all attributes of all other gods, and thus peacefully subsumed its potential rivals with no need to eradicate them. They could, in short, be accommodated, without any undue friction."[32] This explains why Constantine could build a Christian church in one part of a city, and in another, erect statues of the mother goddess Cybele and of Sol Invictus, the sun god — the latter in Constantine's own likeness, with his very features! All of which is to say that Constantine was the master politician. He aimed for syncretism in his domain and the cult of Sol Invictus was expedient for the empire's cohesion. Such a state religion included all under its umbrella, achieving this objective beautifully.

And so we see that the Church's dalliance with Constantine came at a heavy price. It is a historical fact that after this flirtation with Constantine, later emperors exercised a significant control over the Church(es) by having a say in the selection of candidates for the position of bishop. For instance, at Constantinople through an ecclesiastical procedure by which the diocesan clergy presented three names for imperial consideration for the position of bishop, it

---

[31] Rubenstein, p. 74.

[32] Michael Baigent, Richard Leigh, and Henry Lincoln, *The Messianic Legacy,* N.S.W., Australia: Transworld Publishers, 1987, pp. 57-58.

was the emperor who gave the final imprimatur to his approved candidate. And even this residual element of communal choice was frequently overruled by the imposition of an outsider favoured by the emperor. "So the foremost episcopal sees in the late antique world, those of Jerusalem, Antioch, Alexandria, Rome and Constantinople, were generally filled by candidates acceptable to the secular authorities."[33] The Church had sold its soul.

But why did the Church swallow this? Why did the Church modify its own tenets of faith and practice in order to capitalize on this opportunity for peace and prosperity? Having withstood sword, flame and wild beasts for centuries why was the Church so willing to get into bed with Constantine, so to speak? The obvious answer is that the Church was composed of human beings who had suffered shockingly for their beliefs for generations. Now they had the opportunity for respectability, for acceptance within the society structures of the day. Of course, this was in exchange for compromise and relaxation of dogma. It was obviously difficult to refuse such alluring concessions, especially when offered with the sweeteners of power, acceptance, social status and prosperity. These accoutrements are appealing to the Church as well as to the world. But is this explanation sufficient?

The Imperial Cult

In order to gauge these "sacred" developments, we need to set them into their "secular" background. The evolving Christian Church did not develop in a cultural and political vacuum. As always, "the world" seeped into the Church. During the first few centuries, the whole Roman Empire was increasingly knit around the worship of Caesar. That which started hesitantly soon gathered momentum. The cult of emperor worship developed in the reign of Augustus, who for reasons of State policy accepted deification. He authorized the construction of temples in which he was worshipped. Augustus was formally decreed Son of God (*Divi Filius*) by the Senate. Upon his death in 14 AD he was deified personally and directly by a senatorial decree. At first, emperor worship was viewed with suspicion. But soon glowing inscriptions like this one from 7 BC started popping up regularly: "Caesar, who reigns over

---

[33] Judith Herrin, *The Formation of Chrisianity,* London: Fontana Press, 1987, p. 63.

the seas and continents, Jupiter, who holds from Jupiter his father the title of Liberator, Master of Europe and Asia, Star of all Greece, who lifts himself up with the glory of great Jupiter, Saviour."

Coins of Julius Caesar show his spirit ascending comet-like to take its place among the eternal deities. A coin of Tiberius Caesar hails him as *pontifex maximus,* supreme bridge builder between earth and heaven, and as high priest of his imperial people.

Gaius Caligula (AD 37-41) became obsessed with the notion of his deity, and his crawling officials played up to him. Suetonius reports that Lucius Vitellius, legate of Syria, returning to Rome at the end of his term of office, adored the Emperor by prostrating himself on the ground and would only appear before him with head veiled. Suetonius also reports that Gaius:

> began to arrogate to himself a divine majesty. He ordered all the images of the gods, which were famous either for their beauty, or the veneration paid to them, among which was that of Zeus Olympius, to be brought to Greece, that he might take their heads off and substitute his own...He also instituted a temple and priests, with choice victims in honour of his divinity. In his temple stood a statue of gold, the exact image of himself...The most opulent persons in the city offered themselves as candidates for the honour of being his priests, and purchased it successively at an immense price.[34]

A later Emperor, Domitian (AD 81-96), insisted that his governors commence their letters to him, "Our Lord and our God commands." Suetonius tells us that it became a rule "that no one should style him otherwise in writing and speaking."[35] It is easy to see how an increasingly Gentile Christian Church (especially so after the destruction of Jerusalem and the land of Palestine by the Romans in AD 66-70) had "no deep-seated objection to paying divine honours to Jesus, [but rather] there was the strongest natural disposition to do so. In due course in some Christian circles under Gnostic influences the result was a movement towards dualism, and monotheism was only saved by the complex doctrine of the Trinity."[36]

---

[34] Suetonius, *Gaius,* xxii.

[35] Suetonius, *Domit,* xiii.

[36] *The Messianic Legacy,* p. 59.

This is to say that in view of the imperial cult it was bound to happen that for many non-Jewish Christians, Jesus the Jewish King Messiah would become the Lord Christ in a Gentile sense, meaning Deity. Schonfield observes that:

> Strange as it may appear to those who think of the deity of Jesus in a religious sense, it was the messianic character of Christianity which contributed directly to his deification among believers from the Gentiles. Messianism represented the conviction that the existing world order would presently be overthrown. The empire ruled by Caesar and his legions would pass away, and in its place there would be the Kingdom of God governed by the Messiah and his people. Christianity identified the Messiah with Jesus. There was "another king," another emperor, to whom allegiance was transferred.[37]

The widespread tendency for the citizens of the Empire to believe the gods came down for intercourse (both in its sexual and commercial meanings) made for a milieu where the deification of cultic figures was customary. After healing a cripple at Lystra Paul and Barnabas were confronted by a frenzied mob who shouted, "The gods are come down to us in the likeness of men." They hailed Barnabas as Zeus and Paul as Hermes (Acts 14:11-12). And after a mighty oration the Greeks of Caesarea hailed King Agrippa I with the words, "The voice of a god and not of a man!" (Acts 12:22). The later deification of Jesus as God or as the Lord God is understandable within this cultural context. And as we shall soon see in the next chapters:

> Christians continue to be troubled today by the Church's contradictory doctrines, which arose from the unhappy endeavour to blend incompatible pagan and Jewish ideas...Christianity became transformed by the assimilation of alien ideas and modes of thought. In the process it ceased to be a reliable guide to its own beginnings.[38]

The authors of *The Messianic Legacy* also agree that there is a cultural explanation for "the final destruction of the historical Jesus" that is not so readily understood. They relate that in 1982 an important book appeared on this subject, *Constantine versus Christ*

---

[37] Schonfield, p. 228.
[38] *Ibid.*, p. 226.

by Alistair Kee, senior lecturer in Religious Studies, University of Glasgow. Kee establishes quite convincingly that Jesus in effect played no part whatever in the religion of Constantine. But if he ignored Jesus, Constantine certainly acknowledged the principle of Messiahship. In fact, he did more than acknowledge it; he took the role of the Anointed One upon himself. For Constantine, the Messiah was precisely what the Messiah had been for Jews in Palestine at the dawn of the Christian era — a warrior-king like David and Solomon, a sovereign and ruler who would reign wisely over a temporal realm, consolidating national unity with divine sanction to legitimize him. To Constantine, Jesus had attempted to be precisely such a Messiah. And Constantine saw himself as following — rather more successfully — in Jesus' footsteps, achieving what Jesus had apparently failed to achieve. As Kee says, "The religion of Constantine takes us back to the context of the Old Testament. It is as if the religion of Abraham...is at last fulfilled not in Jesus but in Constantine." And "Constantine in his day was the fulfilment of the promise of God to send a king like David to save his people. It is this model, so powerful and so pre-Christian, that best describes Constantine's role."

Constantine's belief that he was such a messiah is not so surprising, in view of the fact that he was a pagan king. But according to Kee, what is so astounding is that the Roman church assented to the role Constantine arrogated to himself. The Roman church of the time was quite prepared to concur with Constantine's conception of himself as a genuine Messiah, and a more successful Messiah than Jesus. It was also quite prepared to acknowledge that the Messiah was not a pacific, ethereal, lamb-like saviour, but a rightful and wrathful king, a political and military leader presiding not over any nebulous kingdom of heaven, but over very real terrestrial domains. In short, the Church recognized in Constantine precisely what Messiahship would have entailed for Jesus and his contemporaries. Thus, for example, Eusebius, Bishop of Caesarea, one of the leading theological figures of his day and a close personal associate of the emperor, says of Constantine, "He grows strong in his model of monarchic rule, which the ruler of All has given to the race of man alone of those on earth." Eusebius is very emphatic about the importance of the monarchy: "Monarchy excels all other kinds of constitution and government. For rather do anarchy and civil war result from the alternative, a polyarchy based on equality.

For which reason there is One God, not two or three or even more." Indeed, Eusebius goes much further than this. In a personal address to the Emperor Constantine, he declares the Logos to be incarnate in the Emperor. In fact, Eusebius actually ascribes to Constantine a status and a virtue which should be reserved for Jesus alone: "most God-fearing sovereign, to whom alone of those who have yet been here since the start of time has the Universal All-ruling God Himself given power to purify human life." As Kee insightfully comments on this address by Eusebius: "Since the beginning of the world it is to Constantine *alone* that the power of salvation has been given. Christ is set aside, Christ is excluded and now Christ is formally denied." And "Constantine now stands alone as the saviour of the world. The scene is the fourth century, not the first. The world, spiritual and material, was not saved until Constantine." For Kee, the implications are unavoidable. There is no mention of Jesus. "It is clear that the life and death of Christ have no efficacy in this scheme of things...The salvation of the world is now wrought by the events of the life of Constantine."[39]

The conclusion reached by the authors of *The Messianic Legacy* is that when the Church compromised with Constantine the historical Jesus was officially destroyed, denied, lost. Whilst these authors, I think, then proceed to go much too far in suggesting that the Church and Constantine were erecting an effective bulwark against any possibility of a lineal descendant of Jesus ever stepping up to claim the Davidic throne (Jesus did not marry, and has no flesh descendants, for according to the prophets he died without physical children as Acts 8:33 says), they do have a valid point based on historical reality. Namely, that it is extraordinary to find the Roman Church (1) acquiescing in Constantine's total indifference to Jesus; (2) deferring to Constantine's presentation of himself as the Messiah; and (3) acknowledging the definition of Messiahship — that is, a military and political figure — embodied by Constantine. On the other hand, perhaps in the fourth century, it was not so extraordinary after all, for such attitudes were not as incongruous with Christian belief as they would appear today. Perhaps in the fourth century Christians recognised, far more clearly than their modern counterparts, how closely such attitudes conformed to the historical facts. The historical Jesus had not yet

---

[39] *Ibid.*, p. 233.

disappeared completely under the weight of later accretions. For the Church of the fourth century, there would almost certainly have been some rueful and grudging admission that Constantine was a Messiah who had succeeded where Jesus had failed, and that the Messiah as represented by both Constantine and Jesus was indeed a military and political figure, a king with a mandate to govern.[40]

Douglas Lockhart would draw the same conclusion. He quotes Don Cupitt's analysis that the fourth century's framing of the classical doctrine of Christ reveals an extensive paganization of faith, worship and social organization within the Church. A pagan iconography of Christ was developing under the pressure of political needs, and the Hellenistic philosophy of kingship was at the bottom of it all:

> As God was to the cosmos, and the king was to the state, so the divine Logos indwelt the king and in turn became a king by association. The king, acting in a Godlike manner, and as a shepherd to his people, was seen as a kind of incarnate God, a link between heaven and earth, and the divine Logos as incarnate God was promoted to universal cosmic Emperor who, understandably enough, validated his almost divine deputy's every action. A neat little package which quickly bestowed dignity and privilege, dress and insignia upon the Church's chief ministers, and in turn allowed the king to parade himself as God's earthly representative. Borrowing extensively from court ritual, these chief ministers of the New Christian Order successfully buried Jesus the Jew for a second time.[41]

The inescapable finding, then, is that the cult of emperor worship became a significant part of the developing recipe of the Church's understanding of Jesus the Messiah. Far from being an impenetrable bastion of the faith once delivered to the saints, the Church became a porous sponge that inevitably soaked up the surrounding culture. Don Cupitt catches the pathos of these developments when he says, "Almost the only remaining trace of Jesus is his dark Semitic face, peering out with understandable sadness from his incongruous new setting."[42]

---

[40] Baigent et al, *The Messianic Legacy,* pp. 65-66.

[41] *Ibid.*, p. 27.

[42] Don Cupitt, *The Myth of God Incarnate*, quoted in *Jesus the Heretic,* p. 27.

The battle for "orthodoxy" raged back and forth well after Constantine's death. The Roman Empire was divided between his two sons. And it is a sad fact of this period that "by appealing to the Roman state for support, bishops and theologians had tied their fortunes to the outcome of the struggle between Constans, emperor of the Nicene West, and Constantius, Arian ruler of the East."[43] It is also a fact that the Nicene Creed in these days "became a source of violent contention in the community."[44] So the doctrine of the Trinity was formulated during the power struggles of the fourth century of the Christian era. Later, through the influence of the emperor Theodosius (379-395), this became the "orthodox" doctrine of Roman Christianity enforced on pain of death. In the sixth century the emperor Justinian added the denial of infant baptism to the criminal category, also punishable by death. Tragically then, "the triumph of Nicene Christianity was followed by a violent campaign to impose the new order on outsiders."[45] And "the advocacy of Arian views...and the possession of Arian writings would become crimes punishable by death."[46] So Christianity was gradually metamorphosed. Sadly:

> the Christianity that coalesced and took shape in Constantine's time was in fact a hybrid, containing significant skeins of thought derived from Mithraism and the sun cult. Christianity, as we know it, is in many respects actually closer to those pagan systems of belief than it is to its own Judaic origins.[47]

These conclusions are confirmed by the spade of the archaeologist. In their fascinating book *Excavating Jesus* the authors Crossan and Reed indicate that the further the strata are removed from the first-century world of Jesus (i.e. the more recent the archaeological time) the "tendency is to decrease his Jewish identity; the other [tendency] is to increase his social status." Whether looking at the literature of those centuries, or digging in the dirt, "the farther removed the layers are from the time of Jesus, the more *Christian* they tend to become." In short, "later archaeological layers commemorating Jesus' life tend to efface

---

[43] Rubenstein, p. 169.
[44] *Ibid.,* p. 181.
[45] *Ibid.*, p. 226.
[46] *Ibid.*, p. 223.
[47] *The Messianic Legacy,* p. 60.

signs of his Jewishness...and replace them with features from Rome or Byzantium. On the other hand, the farther removed Jesus is from his first-century Galilean context, the more elite and regal he becomes."[48]

The same metamorphosis can be seen in the evolution of the apostles. A set of ornate capitals was discovered that was carved by French workmen and hidden since 1187, when Sultan Saladin expelled Christians from the Holy Land. They depict scenes from the lives of the apostles, "but the apostles look European not Semitic, their accessories appear medieval not ancient, and their clothes are regal not peasant."[49] These are telling observations.

Saint Augustine?

As the crow flies, it is about 1,600 kilometres from Nazareth to Nicea. However, as Funk writes:

> It is a world away if we are thinking not of geographical space but of the relation of Jesus as Jewish teacher and sage to the theological debates and political intrigue that took place at Nicea. The three hundred years that separate the death of Jesus from the council of Nicea were filled with intrigue, controversy, struggle, martyrdom, conflict, success, triumph.

In other words, notes Funk, by the time the Christian movement arrived at Nicea 300 years after his death, Jesus of Nazareth has receded into the background. The original iconoclast (an iconoclast is a breaker of images, one who attacks cherished beliefs) who subverted the primary world has been replaced by an icon who belongs to the popular expectations and hopes of that world. The enchanting immediacy of his secondary world — the Kingdom of God — has been replaced by the political realism of Constantine's empire.[50] The established Church, instead of living in the energy and freedom of spirit that had characterized its apostolic beginnings, now deteriorated into fear-driven pronouncements from its bureaucracy. The shell was there, perhaps. But the power and inner life of Jesus was buried. In the graphic words of Lockhart, "the psychopathology of a future Church which would repeatedly tear its

---

[48] John Dominic Crossan and Jonathan L Reed, *Excavating Jesus: Beneath the Stones, Behind the Texts,* San Francisco: Harper, 2001, p. 14.
[49] *Ibid.*, p. 24.
[50] Funk, pp. 45, 256.

own living heart and eat it alive was firmly in place."[51] One of the most revered of all "saints" who gave this new direction substance was Augustine of Hippo. Augustine's influence on modern Christianity is almost without parallel. How this man is still revered today in the light of what we know about him, is beyond me. With the rise to political power of the Roman Church, it was Augustine who supplied the theological justification for compulsory measures taken by the state against Christian minorities.[52] Anyone who disagreed with the Church party line was dubbed a heretic and labelled mad or insane. Churches that housed these free spirits were closed with the vengeance of God by "the exquisitely directed anger of men."[53]

The paganization of the Christian Church was complete:

> From being a criminal crucified by Rome, Jesus by proxy ended up on the throne of the Caesars! But what a Jesus. Not the Jesus we know from the New Testament. Not the Jesus who...loved little children. Not the Jesus who wept over Jerusalem's rejection of his messianic message...No, another Jesus displaced the Caesars: the Jesus of orthodoxy's hungry imagination...The demiurge had incarnated and was on the loose, and God help you if you didn't bend the knee. From being the persecuted, Christians became the persecutors, their ego-inflated Jesus lording it over the hearts of men and women *from within!* No escape from this Jesus — *this* Jesus fully backed orthodoxy's claim to power.[54]

As Lockhart wittily remarks, the way Christianity was able to switch Rome from pagan beliefs (!) to a state that held up the failed Jewish Messiah as its central focus was "an amazing cheek, when one thinks about it!"[55]

Of course, every regime needs intellectual backing for justification. One of the giants of this new "catholic" Church, as already observed, was Augustine of Hippo. He was responsible for entrenching the belief that man by nature is intrinsically

---

[51] Lockhart, p. 268.
[52] Joachim Kahl, *The Misery of Christianity: A Plea for Humanity Without God,* Middlesex, England: Pelican Books, 1971, p. 63.
[53] Lockhart, p. 261.
[54] *Ibid.,* pp. 292-293.
[55] *Ibid.,* p. 292.

contaminated with Adam's original sin. Funk observes, "Augustine's notion that the consequences of Adam's sin are transmitted through male sperm is one of the great tragedies of theological history."[56] Almost single-handedly he did away with three centuries of insistence that man in God's image has free will and the power to do good. Now, human beings no longer had the capacity to freely choose to repent and believe the Gospel. Augustine's reversal of the concept of human freedom was offensive to many Christians at the time. This controversy was so great "that riots took place in the streets of Rome in 417 CE between supporters and opponents of the doctrine of Original Sin."[57] Those who upheld the earlier belief that God had gifted men with the ability to make moral choices were soon condemned as heretics. The view that "the soul was self-governed would soon be defunct, and the Rabbinic tradition which saw humanity as made in the living image of the Universal King would fade away with many another shadow of Jewish influence."[58]

Another of the "orthodox" doctrines championed by Augustine was the doctrine of the Trinity. Yet he "confesses" that he was driven to seek God's truth after reading "those books of the [Neo]Platonists."[59] It was these books (probably Plotinus' *Enneads*) which convinced him of the literal Deity of Jesus![60] Prior to this time, his view of Christ had been similar to that of Photinus of Sirmium.[61] That is to say, Augustine believed in Jesus' complete and uncompromised humanity before being persuaded by Neoplatonic philosophy that Jesus had preexisted as God Himself. Augustine, then, did not get his belief in the Trinity from Scripture, but as he honestly admits, from the Greeks! "The Neo-Platonist philosophers whose thought and writings played the most influential part in Augustine's story were Plotinus (c. 204-270 AD) and his disciple Porphyry."[62] In this connection, it is instructive to note that Origen's teacher was Ammonius Saccas, who was Plotinus' master.

---

[56] Funk, p. 313.
[57] Lockhart, p. 190.
[58] *Ibid.*, p. 191.
[59] *Confess.* VII.20.
[60] *Confess.* VII.9; VIII.2.
[61] *Confess.* VII.19.
[62] *The Confessions of St Augustine,* trans. by Maria Boulding, London: Hodder & Stoughton, 1997, p. 16.

It is not difficult to observe the early influence of the Greek philosophers on the church fathers. Justin Martyr for instance calls Heraclitus, Socrates and other Greek philosophers Christians before Christ. And yet another church father, Clement of Alexandria, was so steeped in pagan philosophy that he regarded it as a divine gift to lead men to Christ![63] He explained, "Greek philosophy purges the soul, and prepares it beforehand for the reception of faith, on which the Truth builds up the edifice of Gnosis."[64] And Clement, who is honoured as a saint by the Roman Church, wrote volumes on the "Gnostic" whom he called the "true Christian." He stated, "The Gnostic alone is truly pious...The true Christian is the Gnostic"![65]

That this new triumphant Church was a departure from the Church which the Lord Jesus founded is proved by the centuries of violent persecution that followed. This doctrine produced not the "fruit of the Spirit" but the "works of the flesh" (Gal. 5:19-23). At the end of the fourth century the great library of Alexandria was burned by fanatical "Christians." Orthodoxy had become narrow-minded, even violent. To own a book classified as heretical was to be a criminal. Christian bishops, previously persecuted by Rome, now commanded the civil authorities. In the fifth century, the abbot of the White Monastery at Panopolis in Egypt typically threatened dissenters with, "I shall make you acknowledge...the Archbishop Cyril, or else the sword will wipe out most of you."[66] Not long after, Europe sank into the Dark Ages. Metaphorically speaking, the Church bolted its doors tight so the faithful could be preserved from outside contamination. Instead of the churches of Christ scattered throughout the empire, we had the Church of Intolerance. For more than a thousand years many Christians on the "outside" perished because they remained loyal to the scriptural truth that God is one and Jesus is His Son. With such a sad history we cannot doubt that Jesus the Christ has suffered a huge disservice from those claiming to be his representatives. In the telling words of Lockhart again, "All I see is a sad-eyed prisoner of the Christian imagination locked inside a paradigm he did not, and would not now, condone."[67]

---

[63] *Clement of Alexandria*, xia iii.
[64] *Stromata* 6:26; see also 7:55 and 6.109.
[65] *Stromata* 7:1.
[66] *The Nag Hammadi Library,* ed. James M. Robinson, San Francisco: Harper & Row, 1988, p. 20.
[67] Lockhart, p. 9.

The Church Is Led into Temptation

To gauge how far these historical developments had dragged the Christian Church from the spirit of Jesus of Nazareth its founder and his apostles let us briefly pause to put them into a theological perspective. The baptism of Jesus by John in the Jordan was a defining moment. All four gospel writers mention it. Up till now Jesus has been waiting as the Messiah designate. Now at his water baptism he is publicly marked out as the Christ, the Messiah. God anoints him with the Spirit. Immediately, "the Spirit drives him into the desert" where he fasts and prays for 40 days. At the end of these days, when he is in a seriously weakened condition, Satan approaches him and begins a series of temptations: "**If** you are the Son of God, then..." Many commentators understand that the tempter said to him: "Are you sure that the whole thing is not a delusion? Are you sure that you are not just imagining you are God's Son?" The idea is that a sure way to paralyse a man's actions is to make him doubt his destiny. If at that moment Jesus had allowed a doubt to creep like a canker into his mind, he could not have gone on. But I am not so sure this is the way to best understand what is happening here. It would seem that Jesus understood his own identity and destiny from a very early age. As a lad of 12 he knew of his unique relationship with God as Father (Luke 2:49). There is an alternative interpretation.

The conjunction "if" is many times translated in the NT as "since," and taken this way the devil says to Jesus: "**Since** you are the Son of God, tell this stone to become bread." The Devil is not questioning whether Jesus is the Son of God. His temptation is much more suited to Jesus' mind than that. He is suggesting that because Jesus is in fact the Son of God, the kingly Messiah, why not express that sonship in action to gratify his own needs? Jesus is being confronted with the choice between expressing his conviction of sonship in materialistic and self-aggrandizing terms, or expressing it in terms of an obedience to his Father which could only end on the cross. In other words, Satan's attack was to get Jesus to express his sonship in the wrong way. This peculiar temptation must have had great appeal to Jesus. All through his ministry he was sorely tempted to bypass the way of suffering and humiliation and snatch the throne that was his by God's decree (e.g. Ps. 2:7-12). It is significant that when Peter protested later that Jesus as Messiah should not choose this way of suffering and death, Jesus responded with a savage rebuke: "Get behind me, Satan! You are a stumbling block to me; for you are not setting your mind on God's interests, but man's" (Matt. 16:23). The whole plan of God's redemption for mankind hinged on whether Jesus would take Satan's selfish way or the Father's sacrificial way. Thankfully, the Champion of our Faith chose the way of the cross. He would not use personal power and privilege to achieve God's ends. His Father would take care of him and in the end justify him before the world. But what is the significance of this to our story so far?

In his book *Possession and Persuasion: The Rhetoric of Christian Faith,* Robert Hach develops this idea in relation to the parallel temptations the Church has faced. Jesus' refusal to turn stones into bread can be seen as his unwillingness to allow his miracles, such as feeding the multitudes with a few loaves and fishes, to incite his contemporaries into religious and political fervour. Jesus' refusal to leap from the pinnacle of the Temple may represent his rejection of a Messiahship sanctioning the temple ritual and hierarchy. Jesus' refusal to worship the Devil in exchange for the kingdoms of this world suggests his rejection of the role of Messiah as a kingly figure who would lead the Jewish nation to political supremacy over all the earth by the wrong means of military conquest. In other words Jesus' mission, in rejecting these popular notions of the Kingdom of God, was to radically reorientate his disciples to the nature of his yet future Kingdom. His was to be a Kingdom based on the persuasion of understanding, love, service, equality. In a nutshell, the Devil was trying to tempt Jesus into "embracing a Messianic agenda that would launch his followers on a course of worldwide religious/political/military conquest."[68] Now here's the rub, according to Hach:

> While Jesus successfully resisted the three-fold temptation to build a worldwide empire in fulfilment of his Messianic mission, the same cannot be said for Christendom. The history of Christianity is (with some notable departures from the script) the story of its fall to the very temptations over which Jesus prevailed: in its lust for worldwide power and authority, the Church has, first, appealed to physical and material needs, sometimes through alleged miracle-

[68] Hach, p. 127.

> working, to establish and enforce its kingly rule; second, established its own systems of temple worship (now called "masses" or "worship services" and occurring in temples called "cathedrals" and "churches"), complete with "moneychangers" of various kinds, to appeal to the emotional and psychological desires of its subjects for both sensation and absolution; and third, allied itself with the State to impose its lordship on the masses, appealing (as Dostoevsky's Grand Inquisitor testifies, in *The Brothers Karamazov*) to their neurotic and infantile fears of freedom and responsibility. In short, by succumbing to the very temptations that Jesus resisted Christianity revived and perpetuated the false Messianic hope of world conquest that had characterized first-century Judaism...As early as the mid-second century C.E., the Christian community began to adopt the Gentile authority structures that eventually led to its marriage to the State in the form of the Roman Empire of the fourth century.[69]

Nor is it hard to document how "Christians" have violently disputed and even slaughtered each other throughout the last two thousand years over the way certain passages of Scripture should be interpreted:

> In the coalescence of Christian tradition, this is one principle that has remained constant. In the past, when Church Fathers or other individuals were confronted with one of the various biblical ambiguities and contradictions, they *speculated* about its meaning. They attempted to *interpret* it. Once accepted, the conclusion of their speculation — that is, their interpretation — would become enshrined as dogma. Over the centuries, it then came to be regarded as established fact. Such conclusions are not fact at all. On the contrary, they are speculation and interpretation congealed into a tradition, and it is this tradition which is constantly mistaken for fact.[70]

The Church's long and brutal history is testimony to these truths. As late as 1697 Thomas Aikenhead, a young man of 18 or 20 and a medical student at the University of Edinburgh, was put to

---

[69] *Ibid.*, pp. 39-40.
[70] *The Messianic Legacy,* p. 30.

death by hanging for some unguarded remarks regarding the Trinity. He was allowed no counsel in defending himself and his plea for mercy was disregarded. A graphic story to illustrate how far removed from the spirit of Jesus the "Church" became concerns one of the "super-heroes" of the Protestant Reformation — John Calvin — and what church historians have dubbed "the Servetus affair." During discussions with interested folk I have often asked whether the story of Michael Servetus is known to them. All so far, including some ministers and pastors, have indicated ignorance. I was not taught about this extraordinarily tragic part of Calvin's history in church or even theological college for that matter. Calvin's merciless treatment of Servetus was the single event which led to the consolidation of Calvin's power within Geneva on the one hand, and his vilification as a bloodthirsty tyrant on the other. Yet it is an historical fact that "the trial and execution of Michael Servetus as a heretic have, more than any other event, coloured Calvin's posthumous reputation."[71] Before commenting on it, I set out in full the sad story of Michael Servetus' last moments of life. This comes from the introduction to a book written by the husband and wife team Lawrence and Nancy Goldstone titled *Out of the Flames*:

> Shortly after noon on a cold and rainy late October day in 1553, a procession began at the town hall of Geneva, in western Switzerland, on the border with France. At its head were the local dignitaries — magistrates in their robes and hats, members of the town council, clergymen in their gowns, and the *lieutenant-criminel,* the chief of police. Immediately behind them rode a wave of officers on horseback and a guard of mounted archers. Next came the citizens of the city, first the well-to-do burghers, then the tradespeople and artisans, and, finally, a mob of the city's lower classes. Their destination was a hillside at Champel, about a mile outside the city's walls.
>
> In the midst of these fair-skinned Swiss, one man stood out, a prisoner. He was in his forties, dark, almost Moorish, dirty and weak, with a long, unkempt beard and ragged clothing. He was surrounded by a crowd of pastors exhorting him to confess his sins. An aging churchman

[71] Alister E. McGrath, *A Life of John Calvin: A Study in the Shaping of Western Culture,* Oxford: Blackwell, 1993, p. 115.

walked next to him, whispering in his ear. The prisoner prayed silently in reply. The prisoner's shabby appearance belied his status as one of Europe's leading physicians and preeminent thinkers. His name was Michael Servetus, and his crime was publishing a book that redefined Christianity in a more tolerant and inclusive way. Although this book contained, almost as an afterthought, a great scientific discovery — one which a century later would propel medicine into the modern age — on that October afternoon in 1553, no one in Geneva knew or cared.

Michael Servetus had risked life and position to publish this book...Shortly after its publication, he had been arrested by the inquisitors of France and sentenced to death. On the eve of his execution, he had managed a daring escape and had eluded capture for months. He was on his way to Italy, where he would be safe, but chose instead to stop in Geneva. There his dark skin betrayed him. He was recognized while praying in church and arrested.

Before his supporters could rally to his defence, Michael Servetus was thrown into a dark, airless, vermin-infested cell, where he was kept for seventy-five days, denied a change of clothes, bedding, and often food and water. His access to the outside world was limited to forced participation in a gaudy show trial, where he was to go head to head with his accuser, perhaps the greatest mind of the Reformation. He defended himself brilliantly, but the quality of his arguments never mattered. Servetus' fate had been sealed from the moment he was recognized. He was found guilty of the charges brought by a council and prosecutor hand picked by his archrival and sworn enemy, Jean Chauvin, an obscure failed humanist who had reinvented himself as the reformer John Calvin and risen to be virtual dictator of the great city. On October 26, 1553, Michael Servetus was condemned "to be led to Champel and burned there alive on the next day together with his books."

Torture and cruelty were no strangers to sixteenth-century justice. There was a strict hierarchy of punishment, from relatively painless to gruesomely agonizing, depending on the severity of the crime. Slanderers had their tongues cut out, thieves were impaled. The penalty for murder — beheading — was considered relatively charitable. But of all the punishments, the very worst was to be burned alive, and so this horror was reserved for the most terrible crime there was — heresy. Heretics were especially loathed because they put not only their own souls in mortal jeopardy, but also those of the otherwise innocent people infected by their teachings.

Hollywood has often used burnings as a special effect. The victim is led to a stake atop an immense pile of wood and trussed with ropes. Torches are brought; the pile of wood is set ablaze and huge flames immediately leap up, surrounding the body. The victim screams as the bonfire erupts and the flames leap higher and higher, burning furiously. The camera pans upward as the smoke rises into the sky, and it is understood that all is over, that the victim is past suffering.

Only Hollywood has gotten it wrong. It was never over quickly. The whole point of burning at the stake was to subject the condemned to prolonged, horrible, unendurable pain. That was the type of pain that awaited Michael Servetus — and he knew it.

When Servetus was led to the hill at Champel, the stake and pyre were made of fresh wood, green wood, newly cut branches with the leaves still attached. They sat him on a log and chained him to a post. His neck was bound with thick rope. On his head they put a crown made of straw, doused in sulphur. Chained to his side was what was thought to be the last available copy of his book, the rest having all been zealously hunted down and destroyed. The ideas were to be burnt along with the man. There was no escape.

The fire was lit. Green wood does not burn easily, does not roar up. It smokes and sputters, burning unevenly and slowly. And so Michael Servetus' life was not extinguished quickly in a blazing wall of fire. Rather, he was slowly roasted, agonizingly conscious the entire time, the fire creeping upward inch by inch. The flames licked at him, the sulphur dripped into his eyes, not for minutes but for a full half hour. "Poor me, who cannot finish my life in this fire,"

> the spectators heard him moan. At last, he screamed a final prayer to God, and then his ashes commingled with those of his book.[72]

Having read the story of Servetus' judicial murder it is shocking to see how some historians to this day endeavour to sweep this awful event under the carpet. Calvin's involvement is rationalized: He was "a child of his age" which thought nothing of exterminating "heretics" (free thinkers); Servetus was the only heretic John Calvin ever burned alive; Calvin was historically conditioned and so must be contextualized; Calvin's motives were pure, in that he wanted to save the wider community from infection of heresy; John Calvin was only the chief witness and "technical advisor" of the Genevan authorities; Calvin attempted to alter the mode of execution to the more humane beheading but was ignored; and other crimes of the day are ignored by historians. This only proves that the historians themselves have axes to grind![73] In 1903, a granite monument was erected at the site of Servetus' execution. Its inscription condemns "an error which belonged to his century." It is to us incredible to realize that Calvin was subsequently regarded as the defender of the true faith within Protestant circles!

Such "rationalization" was used by the Nazis on trial at Nuremburg. They were only following orders; they were conditioned by the politics of Germany and Hitler, etc. The prosecutors at Nuremburg, however, quite rightly rejected all such "rationalizations" and the guilty were justly condemned as being fully responsible for their actions. Same for Calvin. I offer you this tragic "Servetus affair" to illustrate the all-too-common spirit the Church and her doctrine has demonstrated throughout the centuries. Jesus said "You will know them by their fruits...Every good tree bears good fruit; but the rotten tree bears bad fruit" (Matt. 7:16-17). It is not my province to pass judgment on individuals who profess the name of Christ. But I have to be honest and ask myself the question about John Calvin, so revered and so respected amongst millions of Christians even to this day: Will a man like this be in the Kingdom of God? Must not a follower of Jesus be like Jesus who was certainly not a child of his evil day? Jesus did not belong to the

---

[72] Lawrence and Nancy Goldstone, *Out of the Flames: The Remarkable Story of a Fearless Scholar, A Fatal Heresy, and One of the Rarest Books in the World,* New York: Broadway Books, 2002, pp. 1-4.

[73] McGrath, p. 115.

authority structures, whether civil or religious. Much less did he commit violence against any fellow human, whether friend or enemy. And the Scripture is clear that "no murderer has eternal life abiding in him" (1 John 3:15). Whilst God is the One who will finally deal with Calvin I am prepared to say that the Church and the doctrine which is guilty of such "fruit" is bad to the core. Sadly, "every major Christian body which traces its history back to the 16th century has blood liberally scattered over its credentials. Roman Catholic, Lutheran, Reformed and Anglican: all have condemned and executed their Servetuses."[74]

With the preceding outline, here is a little questionnaire to test whether you are keeping up with the general trend so far:

True or False?

• Athanasius, the priest (and later the bishop of Alexandria) who was a key power-player in the formulation of the Nicene Creed, enforced his ideas by inciting mob violence, political intrigue and murder of his opponents.

• Augustine (354-430) advocated the massacre of the Donatists, justifying it in the name of promoting Church unity.

• Martin Luther, in later life, advocated the burning of the houses and synagogues, prayer books and Talmuds of what he called "this insufferable devilish burden — the Jews" who refused to convert to Christianity.

• John Calvin personally hunted and finally authorized the torturing to death by slow burning a man by the name of Michael Servetus who refused to bow to Calvin's interpretations of the Trinity.

• Calvin's successor, Beza, dismissed any plea for religious tolerance, calling religious liberty "a most diabolical dogma because it means that every one should be left to go to hell in his own way."

• Melancthon, assistant to Martin Luther in the Reformation days, drafted a memorandum demanding death for Anabaptists (those who believed the official infant baptism under the establishment inadequate).

• The Swiss reformer Zwingli in 1525 launched a campaign to drown Anabaptists.

---

[74] *Ibid.*, pp. 116-120.

If you answered false to any of these questions you have been caught in the traditional snow job. For it is a tragic fact of Church history that some of our greatest saints, theologians and reformers were guilty of such heinous crimes and attitudes. These facts of history are not told us in church, but they can be verified by further investigation in several books.[75] For those not wishing or able to do this, Karen Armstrong's succinct statement is that in order to recreate their religious world the religious reformers sometimes resorted to extreme measures and even to violence. In particular she mentions that Luther, Zwingli and Calvin could be intransigent to the point where anybody who opposed *their* teaching would find their "heretical" books burned, and that in the cases of both Calvin and Zwingli, they were prepared to kill dissidents.[76]

Nor should we be surprised at these things, because they are magnified many times over when we consider other disturbing results of the 'Church's' program throughout the generations. Christians have not only put to sword and flame one another but have crusaded against the very ones their Lord and Master told them to love and bring into God's fold. The sad history of the "Christian Crusaders" who marched off to war against the Muslims in the so-called Dark Ages still rankles Islam to this very day. The story of the Inquisition is another case in point. And how often have I heard my workmates in general conversation say they have no interest in religion because more wars and killings have resulted from religion than any other cause? Mahatma Gandhi was once asked by Howard Thurman, "Mr. Gandhi, what is the greatest enemy of Christ in India today?" Mahatma's one-word reply was "Christianity"! The average Aussie and indeed the average Westerner, it is plain to see, agrees. People are no longer concerned to know and love Jesus. The German theologian Rudolf Bultmann said that Jesus' bones lie rotting somewhere in Palestine; he was not sure whether we can find

---

[75] Richard E. Gade, *A Historical Survey of Anti-Semitism,* Grand Rapids: Baker Book House, 1981. Also, Roland H. Bainton, *The Travail of Religious Liberty: Nine Biographical Studies*, Philadelphia: Westminster Press, 1951 and *The Reformation of the Sixteenth Century*, Boston: Beacon Press, 1952. Another good read along these lines is Will Duran, *The Story of Civilization from Wycliff to Calvin: 1300-1564*, New York, Simon & Schuster, 1957.

[76] Karen Armstrong, *The Battle For God: Fundamentalism in Judaism, Christianity and Islam* London: Harper Collins, 2000, p. 65.

the historical Jesus. He said he was not even concerned with what went on in the heart and mind of Jesus. Modern society, it seems, has adopted this creed, for traditional Christianity is on the nose[77] where I live.

As in the medical field when we vaccinate our children against various diseases by injecting them with a manmade dose of the real disease — so that they can build antibodies — so in the spiritual realm. Once injected by make-believe and falsehood our hearts become immune to the real thing. Yes, I hate "religion" too. It was the religious ones who crucified Jesus. The Devil loves religion. But I have a sneaking suspicion he is afraid the real Jesus of the gospel stories will break out again from under the heavy load of theological baggage that he has been staggering under for generations. As Lockhart again so powerfully states, "There is a sense in which it is necessary for the Jesus who died all those centuries ago to die a second time, not for the sins of the people but for the sins of the Church who made of him more than he ever wished to be."[78]

Over the centuries millions have died because their loyalty to the Bible precluded their acceptance of the unscriptural formulas of Nicea and Chalcedon. They could not accept the triune Being of "God the Father, God the Son, God the Holy Spirit." As impressive as it might sound, it is not found in the Scriptures. If this Trinitarian formula created in the fourth century was of the Holy Spirit, why did it produce centuries of hatred and bloodshed? Why the "works of the flesh" and not the "fruit of the Spirit"? In a later chapter we will discuss who Jesus is, whether he is "God the Son" or "Son of God." For the moment in our brief overview of church history it is important to note that the Bible warned that a false view of who Jesus is would foster an antichristian spirit. The apostle John wrote: "By this you know the Spirit of God: every spirit that confesses that Jesus Christ has come in the flesh is from God; and every spirit that does not confess Jesus is not from God; and this is the spirit of the antichrist" (1 John 4:2-3).

When John tells us that the message of the false teachers is "the spirit of the antichrist" he solves a problem for us: Why have those who believe in the "orthodox" teachings of the mainstream church

---

[77] *On the nose* — out of favour, even to the point of being quite distasteful. Smelly.
[78] Lockhart, p. 180.

always persecuted those who, on good scriptural grounds and out of a pure conscience before God, begged to differ from the accepted line? The reason, according to John, is that the former teaching possesses the spirit of antichrist. Can you imagine those early apostles and disciples of Jesus, those first Christians persecuting and threatening violence to any who refused their message? To ask the question is to give the answer. True, today those like Michael Servetus may not be tortured and killed by the church, (at least in the democratic West) but any who dare to ask questions and who do not toe the party line are nevertheless ostracized and are the victims of more subtle vilification. This ought to be enough in itself to make us re-examine the whole foundation. At last our society is feeling free from the ancient bondage our church fathers led us to. But instead of producing a purer faith, society is growing more secular. Some are atheistic. Some agnostic. Many are experimenting with alternate 'spiritual' ideals. But in any case, "The Church must be held to be a major cause of promoting (the intolerance) it wholeheartedly condemns."[79] As Jesus said, "If the salt loses its flavour, it is good for nothing but to be cast out and to be trampled under foot by men" (Matt. 5:13).

It is time that we in the Church heard this other side of the story. The commonly held mainstream church view that opposition to the doctrine of the Trinity is confined to the "cults" like the Jehovah's Witnesses is just not true. This is a public myth. Some of the greatest thinkers of all time have objected to the doctrine of the Trinity. Sir Isaac Newton, John Locke, Isaac Watts and John Milton all opposed the idea that God is three in one. Thomas Jefferson was a vigorous anti-Trinitarian, too. Most within my own Churches of Christ movement are totally unaware that in our early days in the United States our membership consisted of significant numbers of unitarian believers, which is to say, believers who believed God is one, not three. Churches of Christ folk are largely ignorant that one of our greatest leaders, Barton W. Stone, was an avowed anti-Trinitarian. The amazing thing is that when he and Alexander Campbell made that famous handshake at Cane Ridge joining their respective churches into one fellowship, they all did so as "brothers in the Lord." Barton Stone's own testimony is that "I stumbled at the doctrine of the Trinity...I labored to believe it, but could not

---

[79] Schonfield, p. 13.

conscientiously subscribe to it."[80] Alexander Campbell himself denied the doctrine of the eternal Sonship of Christ, and so had reservations about the Trinity. Very few are also aware that at that time in American history the unitarian movement was so popular within the mainstream Protestant churches that it threatened to change the face of the whole Christian church within that continent. So confident of success was he that Thomas Jefferson predicted that "in the future there will not be a young man in the United States who will not die an Unitarian." The famous American Harvard University became a bulwark for these unitarian views. It is a tragedy that the unitarian movement itself succumbed to an intellectualism that divorced it from its Scriptural moorings and became bogged in the quicksands of rationalism and human philosophy and unbelief.

Yes, winners are grinners and they get to write their own story. Losers just lose. But need they? There is another big untold story out there. Perhaps after all the real Jesus of Jewish history can speak with the same authority that once amazed the crowds who heard him. Even his enemies were impressed. "No man ever spoke like this man" they admitted (John 7:46). Before it is too late, the traditional church must allow Jesus the Messiah, the Jesus who lived in history, the Jesus of the Bible, back into our human existence. Our hearts cry for authenticity. Beyond the stormy winds of "orthodox" persuasion; beyond the earthquakes of "official" church councils; beyond the fires (often literal) of "mainstream" persecutions, is it possible that we can yet hear that authentic word, "You have heard that it was said of old...but **I** say unto you" (Matt. 5:21-22). Perhaps, if we listen to God the Father's command, "This is My beloved Son; **hear him**!" we will in fact "hear the voice of our God" (1 Kings 19:9-14).

---

[80] James Mathes, *Address to the Christian Churches, Works of Elder B.W. Stone*, 2nd edition, vol. 1.

Two
ANOTHER WORLD

Look to the rock from which you were hewn,
And to the quarry from which you were dug.
Look to Abraham your father (Is. 51:1-2).

I first travelled overseas when I was a lad of seventeen. It was a trip to the United States. The first time I had ever seen snow. It was magical. The first time I had ever seen black Americans in real life. Man, were they tall. The first time I had ever been in centrally heated houses, and I found them over-hot. One night I fainted through the curtain of a shower screen right into the bath. When I came to, I thought I had died and was in the waiting room about to see God. It was the first time I began to realize my "lingo" sounded weird to others. In fact, I found it could be downright embarrassing. I remember asking for "a rubber" once. It was an innocent request for what I later found out was in the States called "an eraser." But the looks I got! Another night, we were eating at a restaurant. All sorts of dignified church people were around the table. A certain lady asked us to give her a phone call the next day to make certain arrangements. "I'll give you a tingle[1] in the morning," was the promise, at which point the table of Americans erupted into uncontrollable laughter. What was so funny? On another occasion the airport customs officer noticed my suitcase had one lone shoe. "Where is your other shoe?" he mused with a smile. "It's in another port," I innocently answered. He said, "But there ain't no ships for miles round here!" (Even some Aussies don't know that in Queensland a "port" is a suitcase, short for portmanteau!) These days worldwide travel is commonplace and these kinds of gaffs and stories are familiar to us all. Nevertheless, misunderstandings within the same language and time still frequently occur. Ask an Englishman which football team he barracks for and he will name a soccer team. Ask an American which footy team he supports and he will think you are referring to what Aussies erroneously call "grid

---

[1] *Tingle* — a call on the telephone.

iron." Ask an Aussie from the south of the continent which footy team he supports and he will think you are talking about "Aussie rules football," what we northerners sometimes derogatorily call "aerial ping-pong," but ask another Aussie from up north which football team he barracks for and he may give one of two answers: he will think you are talking about either Rugby Union or Rugby League. Here we see that the word "football," depending on nationality or locality, can mean at least one of five different codes.[2] Although we are much more *au fait* with cultural and language differences these days, understanding each other is still a challenge.

Longstanding Bible myths have been promoted in our popular thinking because of failure to understand such cultural and linguistic differences. A few examples of this will suffice. If we were to ask how many men came to arrest Jesus in the Garden of Gethsemane, the general consensus would probably be around fifty at the most. There were a few Jewish officials, representatives of the High Priest, a contingent of Temple guards and a small "band" of Roman soldiers, as the King James translation gives it (John 18:3). But why do we tend to think in such small numbers? It is because the word traditionally translated as "band of men" or, as some modern translations have it, "a number of men" or even a "Roman cohort," does indeed suggest not many more than forty or fifty men. The Greek word for "band" is *speira,* but to our modern ears, its translation as "cohort" is still rather vague and non-specific. But when we check the organization of the Roman army we learn that a legion consisted of 6000 soldiers, and a "cohort" or *speira* was one tenth of a legion, that is, 600 soldiers. Jesus' arrest in the garden was clearly not a small, quiet affair with just a little "band" of men. This simple example shows how one word can — when not properly understood in its historical context — foster generations of false impression.

Or, take one other brief example. We have the notion that the two criminals who were crucified on either side of Jesus' cross were thieves. However, the word translated "thieves" is the Greek word *lestai* and whilst it may mean "thief," in the context of Roman crucifixion that is not what is meant. Roman justice did not execute thieves. Crucifixion was for the capital offences of sedition, treason, insurrection, rebellion and anarchy. The two crucified next to Jesus

[2] *Football codes* — the various types of football.

were dying for political revolution. They were "freedom fighters." In fact, one of Jesus' own disciples was called Simon the Zealot, and before Jesus called him, Simon was one of these political revolutionaries, the *sicarii*, who carried concealed daggers. Judas *Iscariot* was one of these bandits also. These daggers were used for up-close political stabbing-assassinations. Such *lestai* or "daggermen" were our equivalent of armed terrorists. Yet because this one word has been for generations translated "thief" we have an erroneous idea of Jesus' companions on the cross. These simple examples illustrate how all through the centuries, theologians and biblical scholars have been challenged by problems of translation — or, to be more accurate, mistranslation. By the time a name, a word, a phrase, a sentence, a statement has passed from spoken Hebrew or Aramaic to written Greek, to written Latin, and then to a modern language, it has become utterly divorced from its original meaning.[3] This is not to say that the vast number of English translations are not accurate or largely reliable. The point is that we still need to understand that cultural differences can give nuances not necessarily intended by the original authors of the Bible.

The foundation of our Bible is the Old Testament. The first three-quarters in fact. It stands to reason that if we misunderstand this Hebrew foundation then we construct a system of error. The art of successful reading is generally to let the last quarter of a book agree with the first three-quarters. As the grand finale of the Bible, the NT agrees with and is consistent with its OT heritage. It might sound like an over-simplification to say that the Bible is a Hebrew book and must be approached through "Hebrew eyes." It was written within the culture and thought-forms of the Middle East. In order to understand its message we must become familiar with the thought-forms, the idioms, the culture and customs of those who lived in Bible times. Every sincere reader of the Bible understands this. Doing it is the challenge. We have already had occasion to note Snaith's comment that from as early as the immediate post-apostolic days of the second century, "Christianity itself has tended to suffer from a translation out of the Prophets and into Plato."[4] Snaith's landmark book came to this conclusion: "Our position is that the reinterpretation of Biblical theology in terms of the ideas of the

---

[3] *The Messianic Legacy,* p. 70.

[4] Snaith, p. 161.

Greek philosophers has been both widespread throughout the centuries and everywhere destructive to the essence of the Christian faith."[5] Snaith rings the alarm bells even more vigorously when he makes the astounding remark that if his thesis is correct:

> then neither Catholic nor Protestant theology is based on Biblical theology. In each case we have a domination of Christian theology by Greek thought...We hold that there can be no right (theology) until we have come to a clear view of the distinctive ideas of both Old and New Testaments and their difference from the pagan ideas which have so largely dominated "Christian" thought.[6]

It is a fact that not one of the early church fathers was Jewish. Yet in their polemics against the Jews, notes John Shelby Spong, they wrenched Jewish Scripture badly out of context to justify their position. The bishop writes, "It was a strange and ironic twist of a fateful history to observe gentile Christians beating on Jews with the cudgel of the Jewish person's own holy book." One Jewish scholar arose to protest this misuse of his sacred text. His name was Trypho, and no copies of his work remain intact. We know him only from the response of one of these Gentile church fathers named Justin who wrote a piece called *Dialogue with Trypho.*[7] All of this is to say that with the passing of many centuries since the Scriptures were written much of the original intent has been buried under the accretions of generations of human tradition. This is not to question that we have a most reliable record of what the authors of both Testaments wrote. We do. But each of my chapters in this book will show that there is not one major doctrine held by mainstream Christianity today that has not suffered from a severe poke in the Hebrew eye.

So to begin our journey let's test how clear our "Hebrew eyes" are. I want to spend a little time on this because it is critical to our understanding of who Jesus is. When I was starting to understand these principles, I wrote to a pastor within my own Churches of Christ denomination and showed him what I am about to discuss. He immediately recognized how much hung on this and did not like it, rejecting it out of hand, not because it was not biblical, but

---

[5] *Ibid.,* p. 187.
[6] *Ibid.*, p. 188.
[7] Spong, p. 75.

because it greatly affected his cherished view of our Lord Jesus Christ. This minister's view that because Jesus is God he therefore appears in the Old Testament is very common. It is not new. Irenaeus, so influential as an architect of today's orthodoxy, started teaching it in the second century. Irenaeus believed that wherever the Jewish Scriptures mention God's *word,* or even where they mention the *Lord God* Himself, we find *Jesus Christ.* Irenaeus argued that when God *spoke* to Abraham, it was "our Lord, the *word* of God, who spoke" — not only to Abraham but to all the patriarchs and prophets: "No doubt...the Son of God is implanted everywhere throughout his Scriptures; at one time speaking with Abraham; at another time, with Noah, giving him the dimensions of the ark...At another time, he directs Jacob on his journey, and speaks with Moses from the burning bush."[8]

Irenaeus declared that the One the prophet Ezekiel saw on the throne surrounded by angels was Jesus Christ. In Genesis when "the Lord took clay from the earth, and formed *adam*" (Gen. 2:7), Irenaeus declared that "the Lord God" who created humankind in Paradise was "our Lord Jesus Christ, who 'was made flesh' (John 1:14) and was hung upon the cross." Irenaeus even had the temerity to say that the Jews who did not identify "the word of the Lord" in the Hebrew Bible as Jesus Christ were not true worshippers of God! He averred: "The Jews have departed from God, *since they have not received his word,* but they imagined that they could know the Father...without the word, *being ignorant of the God who spoke in human form* to Abraham and then to Moses."[9]

Because the Jews fail to recognize Jesus as "the God who spoke in human form" to their ancestors, Irenaeus believed God therefore disinherited them. Let us test this popular notion that Jesus appears in the OT in the light of these very Scriptures used by Irenaeus. We will need Hebrew eyes to rightly grasp the message.

The Principle of Agency

In the story of Moses and the burning bush in Exodus 3 just *who* is it who appears to Moses and talks to him? My answer once was typical of the vast majority in the Church. Of course it was God Himself, Yahweh, who spoke to Moses. After all, the text states that

---

[8] Pagels, p. 152.
[9] *Ibid.*, p. 153.

"**God** called to him from the midst of the bush and **said**, 'Moses, Moses!'" (v. 4).

Even more convincing is verse 6, where the same speaker says, "'**I am** the **God** of your father, **the God** of Abraham, **the God** of Isaac, and **the God** of Jacob.' Then Moses hid his face, for he was afraid to look at **God**." Surely it was Jehovah God Himself who appeared to Moses and who personally spoke?

But what do we make of verse 2 that prefaces this narrative by stating that "**the angel of the LORD** appeared" to Moses from the midst of the bush? Many scholars have declared this angel to be God Himself, even the preexistent Christ. They make much of the definite article and point out that this was a particular angel not just any angel. Typical of this school of thought would be these words from R.A. Torrey:

> *The Angel of the LORD in the Old Testament, Who frequently appeared and was seen by Abraham, Manoah, and others, was a Divine Person, God in human form.* A clear distinction is drawn in the Bible between "*an* angel of the LORD," and "*The* Angel of the LORD (or, Jehovah)." The Authorized Version does not always preserve the distinction; the Revised Version, following the Hebrew text of the Old Testament and the Greek text of the New Testament, always does: and "The Angel of the LORD (or, Jehovah)" is a Divine Person.[10]

This is a fancy bit of footwork that disregards the Hebrew text as we shall see. For if we turn to the New Testament's commentary on this incident we see how the Hebrews understood their own Scriptures. But before we turn to the inspired exposition of this incident we need to understand something important about the Jewish mind.

A common feature of the Hebrew Bible is the concept (some even call it the "law") of Jewish agency. All Old Testament (OT) scholars and commentators recognize that in Jewish custom whenever a superior commissioned an agent to act on his behalf, the agent was regarded as the person himself. This is well expressed in *The Encyclopedia of the Jewish Religion*:

---

[10] R.A. Torrey, *The God of the Bible,* New York: George Doran Co., 1923, p. 45.

> Agent (Heb. *Shaliah*): The main point of the Jewish law of agency is expressed in the dictum, "a person's agent is regarded as the person himself" (*Ned.* 72B; *Kidd,* 41b). Therefore any act committed by a duly appointed agent is regarded as having been committed by the principal, who therefore bears full responsibility for it with consequent complete absence of liability on the part of the agent.[11]

Thus in Hebrew custom whenever an agent was sent to act for his master it was as though that lord himself was acting and speaking:

> In Hebrew thought a patriarch's personality extended through his entire household to his wives, his sons and their wives, his daughters, servants in his household and even in some sense his property...In a specialized sense when the patriarch as lord of his household deputized his trusted servant as his *malak* (his messenger or angel) the man was endowed with the authority and resources of his lord to represent him fully and transact business in his name. In Semitic thought this messenger-representative was conceived of as being personally — and in his very words — the presence of the sender.[12]

An equivalent in our culture to the Jewish custom of agency would be one who is authorized to act as Power of Attorney, or more strongly, one who is given Enduring Power of Attorney. Such an agent has virtually unlimited powers to act on behalf of the one who appointed him. This appointed attorney is delegated to carry on all matters of business in the absence of, or inability of, the one who assigned him this office. With this Hebrew "law of agency" in mind — an agent is regarded as the principal himself — let us now turn to answer our question: *Who* is it who appears to Moses and talks to him? The martyr Stephen was a man "filled with the Holy Spirit." Let's listen to his commentary on the burning bush incident. He clearly states that it was "**an angel** [who] appeared to him in the wilderness of Mount Sinai, in the flame of a burning bush" (Acts 7:30). As Moses approached this phenomenon, "there came **the voice of the Lord**: '**I am the God** of your fathers'...**The Lord said**

---

[11] R.J.Z. Werblowsky, G. Wigoder, New York: Adama Books, 1986, p. 15.
[12] R.A. Johnson, *The One and the Many in the Israelite Conception of God,* quoted by Juan Baixeras, "The Blasphemy of Jesus of Nazareth."

to him, 'Take off the sandals from your feet, for the place on which you are standing is holy ground'" (Acts 7:31-33).

Quite clearly this is an example of agency. It is an angel who appears to Moses and it is the angel who speaks. But note that this angel even speaks for God in the *first person.* The angel of the Lord says, "I am God." The angel is distinguished from God yet identified with Him. In Hebrew eyes it is perfectly natural to consider the agent as the person himself. In Hebrew thought, homage given to God's agent or representative is homage ultimately given to God Himself.

There is another instance of agency in Exodus 7. God tells Moses He will make him "God to Pharaoh, and your brother Aaron shall be your prophet" (Ex. 7:1). Moses is to stand before the king of Egypt with the full authority and backing of heaven itself. Then God says, "By this you shall know that I am the LORD: behold, **I will strike** the water that is in the Nile with the staff that is in **My hand**, and it shall be turned to blood" (v. 17). But observe carefully that just two verses later the LORD says to Moses, "Say to **Aaron**, Take **your staff** and stretch out **your hand** over the waters of Egypt...that they may become blood" (v. 19). God says He Himself will strike the waters with the staff in His own hand. Yet, it was Aaron's hand that actually held the rod. It was Aaron who struck the Nile. Clearly, Aaron is not God the LORD. Aaron is standing as God's agent, in the very place of God Himself. There is identification of the agent with his Principal. In Bible terms, Moses and Aaron are "God" (Heb. *elohim*) to Pharaoh!

There are many such OT examples. An agent of God is actually referred to as God, or the Lord Himself. In Genesis 31:11-13 Jacob said to his wives, "**The angel** of God **said** to me in a dream...**I am the God** of Bethel." Here is an angel speaking as though he was God Himself. He speaks in the first person: "I am the God of Bethel." Jacob was comfortable with this concept of agency.

In the next chapter, Jacob wrestled with "**a man**" until dawn, but he says he had "seen **God** face to face" (Gen. 32:24-30). So was this a time when God appeared to Jacob as a man, an event called a theophany? Perhaps as some have suggested it was actually the Lord Jesus himself, as the second member of the triune God, who wrestled with Jacob?

Not at all according to Hosea 12:3-4 which says, "As a man he [Jacob] struggled with **God**; he struggled with **the angel** and overcame him." So the one who is called both "a man" and "God" in Genesis is identified as an angel in Hosea. This is a perfect example of Jewish agency where the agent is considered as the principal.

Here is another example. Exodus 23:20-23 deals with Israel's journey through the wilderness:

> Behold, I [God] am going to **send an angel** before you to guard you along the way, and to bring you into the place which I have prepared. Be on your guard before him and obey his voice; do not be rebellious toward him, for he will not pardon your transgressions, since My name is in him. But if you will truly obey **his voice** and do all that **I say,** then I will be an enemy to your enemies and an adversary to your adversaries. For **My angel** will go before you and bring you in to the land...and **I will** completely destroy them.

Here the angel of the LORD bears Yahweh's name: "My name is in him." This shows that in Hebrew thought an agent may bear the name or title of his principal. When God says that His name was in the angel, it meant that God's authority was invested in the angel. Whatever the angel said and did was in reality what God Himself said and did. In obeying the angel, the Israelites were really obeying God.

Concerning this story of the wilderness wanderings compare these two verses from Exodus:

"And **the LORD was going before** them in a pillar of cloud by day to lead them on the way, and in a pillar of fire by night to give them light, that they might travel by day and by night" (Ex. 13:21).

"And **the angel of God, who had been going before** the camp of Israel, moved and went behind them; and the pillar of cloud moved from before them and stood behind them" (Ex. 14:19).

One verse says it was the LORD Himself there in the pillar of cloud and in the pillar of fire. The parallel verse says it was the angel who was there. So whenever the angel moved it was to the Israelites as if God Himself in person was there. To follow this angelic representative of Jehovah was to follow God Himself.

Sometimes this concept of agency has caused the translators of our Bible difficulties. The Hebrew word for "God" (*elohim*) has a wide range of possible meanings. Depending on context, it can mean the Supreme Deity, or "a god" or "gods" or even "angels" or human "judges." This difficulty is reflected in verses like Exodus 21:6:

The KJV reads, "Then his master shall bring him unto **the judges**."

The NIV says, "Then his master must take him before **the judges**."

But the NASB has it, "Then his master shall bring him **to God**."

So too the RSV: "Then his master shall bring him **to God**."

Clearly, because the judges of Israel represented God as His agents, they are called "God," *elohim*. As the slave gave his vow before these human representatives of God, he was in fact making a binding vow before Jehovah. The agents were as God.

Another OT example. In Judges 6:11-13 "**the angel of the LORD** came and sat under the oak" tree while Gideon was threshing wheat. As "**the angel of the LORD appeared** to him" he greeted Gideon with the words, "**The LORD is with you**, O valiant warrior." We can hear Gideon's disbelief when he says to the angel, "Oh my lord, if the LORD is with us, why then has all this happened to us?" Now notice the change in the text at verse 14: "And **the LORD looked at him** and said, 'Go in this your strength and deliver Israel from the hand of Midian. Have not **I** sent you?'" At this point Gideon demurs and throws up excuses as to why he could not rescue Israel from their enemies. "But **the LORD said** to him, 'Surely **I** will be with you, and you shall defeat Midian as one man.'" Notice how the angel who is speaking on God's behalf actually uses the first person personal pronoun. And the text clearly says that when the angel looked at Gideon it was God Himself who looked at him: "And **the LORD looked at him**." Gideon is not confused as to who he is looking at or who is speaking to him. For as "the angel of the LORD vanished from his sight," he exclaimed, "I have seen **the angel** of the LORD face to face" (v. 22). We know that the angel of the LORD is the agent, and not literally God, because the Scriptures are absolutely clear that no one has ever seen God Himself (John 1:18; 1 Tim. 6:16; 1 John 4:12).

Many scholars have failed to take this very Hebrew way of looking at things into account. They have literally identified the angel of the LORD with God Himself. All confusion is dissipated when we understand the Jewish law of agency: "a person's agent is regarded as the person himself."

One last very clear OT example of the Hebrew principle of agency. It comes from Deuteronomy 29. Moses summons all Israel and says to them, "You have seen all that **the LORD did** before your eyes in the land of Egypt to Pharaoh and all his servants and all his land; the great trials which your eyes have seen, those great signs and wonders" (v. 2-3).

Moses continues to recite for the people all that God has done for them. But notice that in verse 6, while still reciting all God's wonders, Moses suddenly changes to the first person and says, "You have not eaten bread, nor have you drunk wine or strong drink, in order that you might know that **I am the LORD your God**."

It is obvious that God Himself is not personally speaking to the people. Moses is preaching. But Moses as the agent of God can speak *as though he is* the Lord Himself. What is happening here? God is speaking through His man, His appointed representative. Therefore, he can move from speaking in the third person, "the LORD did this and that for you" to the first person: "I am the LORD your God doing this and that."

Let us see how knowing this principle helps us with other apparent difficulties, even seeming contradictions through the Scriptures. Let's take one or two New Testament examples. A story that has created a problem to many minds is the one concerning the healing of the centurion's servant. In Matthew's account (Matt. 8:5-13) it is the centurion himself who comes to Jesus and begs him to heal his servant. The centurion himself says, "Sir, **my** servant is lying paralysed at home, suffering great pain" (v. 6).

However, the parallel account in Luke (Luke 7:1-10) has it that the centurion did not personally go and speak to Jesus. He actually sent or commissioned as his agents "some Jewish elders." These Jewish elders pleaded with Jesus on behalf of the centurion saying, "**He** is worthy for you to grant this to him; for **he** loves our nation, and it was **he** who built us our synagogue" (v. 4-5).

So who actually went to Jesus here? Did these gospel writers get confused? Perhaps the detractors are right to say that the Bible is full of errors and contradictions? Not at all! The difficulty is cleared up when we understand the Hebrew mind behind these Scriptures. The answer to who actually stood before Jesus is the elders. They had been sent by the centurion. But Matthew in typical Hebrew idiom has the centurion *himself* there and *speaking* in the *first person* before Jesus. The agent is as the principal himself.

Take another example. One day the mother of two of Jesus' disciples, James and John, approaches Jesus with a rather bold request: "Command that in your kingdom **these two sons of mine** may sit, one on your right and one on your left" (Matt. 20:21). However, the parallel record in Mark (10:35-37) tells us that James and John were the ones who personally spoke this request: "Teacher, **we** want you to do for **us** whatever **we** ask of you...Grant that **we** may sit in your glory, one on your right, and one on your left."

Again we must ask, Who is actually here before Jesus making this bold request? If we understand the Hebrew concept of agency, the answer is that James and John actually asked their mother to go and speak to Jesus on their behalf. But in the typical Hebrew way Mark says without any thought of contradiction that it was the disciples who personally spoke to Jesus. The agent is as the principal himself.

Let's look at just one more example. In Acts 12 the apostle Peter is in jail about to be executed. But while he was asleep, "behold, an angel of the Lord suddenly appeared, and a light shone in the cell; and he struck Peter's side and roused him, saying, 'Get up quickly.' And his chains fell off his hands. And the angel said to him, 'Gird yourself and put on your sandals...and follow me'" (Acts 12:7-8). Peter thought he was dreaming. As he followed the angel past the guards, out through the iron gate which "opened for them by itself," Peter "did not know that what was being **done by the angel** was real, but thought he was seeing a vision" (v. 9).

Now the church was meeting in a house and praying for Peter's release. Peter started banging on the house door and Rhoda the servant girl went to open the door. She was so shocked to find Peter himself standing there that she raced back inside to tell everybody without first opening the door to let the escapee in. The pray-ers thought Rhoda was mad and had seen a ghost. But as Peter kept banging on the door reality at last prevailed. Once Peter was inside, you can imagine the stir in that place. Peter motioned with his hand for everybody to be quiet. He told them his incredible story. And what did he say? "He described to them how **the Lord** had led him out of the prison" (v. 17).

So who really did get Peter out of jail? The angel or the Lord? The text says both did. But we know that the Lord sent the angel to do the actual work. To the Hebrew mind, it was really the Lord who rescued Peter.

It is a pity that scholars like Irenaeus and R.A. Torrey (quoted above) fail to recognize this simple Hebrew concept. They could have avoided the unbiblical belief that "the angel of the Lord" is actually God Himself, or Jesus himself in a pre-human state.[13] The angel as God's representative is clearly distinct from God, but stands with the full power and backing of God in all he says and does. This commissioned angel can even speak in the first person as though he is God Himself speaking. The same applies to the Jewish judges. To stand before these human magistrates was to stand before "God" and hear His judgments. But no Hebrew ever considered the judge to *be* God. Clearly, we must endeavour to understand the Bible according to its own culture, times and thought-forms.

The significance of all this (and there are other Old and New Testament examples we could cite) is that the principle of agency has huge ramifications for our understanding of who Jesus is and what his purpose and claims were. Jesus claimed to represent God like no other before or after him. He claimed to be the unique spokesman for God his Father and to speak the ultimate words of God. He claimed to act in total accord and harmony with God like no other. He claimed to be the Son of God, the Christ or Messiah, the agent of the Father. The NT claims that he who sees Jesus sees the Father. He who hears Jesus the Son hears the words of God Himself.

The NT puts this theory about the angel of the Lord being Jesus in his preexistence to rest in Hebrews 1: "God, after He spoke long ago to the fathers in the prophets in many portions and in many ways, in these last days has spoken to us in His Son" (v. 1-2). So, the Son of God did *not speak* in the Old Testament days! Back in those days God spoke in various ways and only in "portions," whether by vision or by prophet or by angel. It is only since Jesus Christ was brought into existence at birth and appeared "in these last days" that we have heard God speak "in His Son." This is

---

[13] The identification of the angel of the Lord with a preexistent second member of the Godhead is completely ruled out by Judges 13:16. Here the angel expressly distinguishes himself from God, insisting that a sacrifice not be offered to him, the angel, but to God: "If you prepare a burnt offering then offer it to the LORD."

axiomatic: Jesus Christ was not God's messenger before his appearance as a man, born of Mary in history.

Three
ANOTHER GOD

Little children, guard yourselves from idols (1 John 5:21).

To many Christians the doctrine of the Trinity is confusing but accepted "on faith" because the Church "has always taught it." The Father, the Son and the Holy Spirit are worshipped as three distinct Persons within the Godhead, each being assigned a different function: The Father planned our salvation, the Son executed the plan, and the Holy Spirit applies the plan to us personally today. This doctrine is able to stop short of a fully fledged tritheism by making the proviso that the three deities are all of the same substance, and so are ultimately one. What I did not grow up knowing was that this is only one interpretation of the doctrine of the Trinity. There are in fact differing traditions of the Trinity. For the sake of simplicity we may observe that there are two main groups of Trinitarians: Those who stress the oneness of God and those who stress God's threeness. Those who stress the oneness of God tend to shy away from describing the Being of God as "persons." "Person" suggests an individual centre of consciousness with mind, will and emotions. Clearly, in order to remain loyal to the Bible's central thesis of monotheism, this group says we cannot speak about three centres of consciousness, three divine "I's." They suggest it might be more accurate to talk about a "way of being" or "mode of being." We may indeed talk about the one God subsisting in three distinct manners or modes. The one God may reveal Himself in different ways. God may be present with His people through the unity of Word and Spirit and Son. This view is not so popular today. Pushed to its extreme, this version is called Modalism, and means that the Father *is* the Son *is* the Spirit. This extreme position has been branded as "heretical" by the mainstream Trinitarians!

The second group may be called "social Trinitarians." In contrast to stressing the oneness of God subsisting in three ways, this group holds that God is a divine society of three. Here the Trinity is seen as a community of fully personal and fully divine entities. The divine essence becomes concrete in three Persons. The Father, Son and Holy Spirit are unified by their common divinity or "divine essence." This is the version of the doctrine of the Trinity I grew up believing. Along with most other Christians, I was able to worship the Father, the Son and the Holy Spirit as three distinct Persons within the Godhead. As I said earlier, each "member" of the Trinity was assigned a different function: The Father planned our salvation, the Son executed the plan, and the Holy Spirit applies the plan to us personally today. It is hard for me now to see how social Trinitarianism can avoid the charge of being tritheistic.

If you are not already feeling confused, hang on, because there is more. An essential sub-theme of the doctrine of the Trinity is that Jesus Christ has two natures: his heavenly "God nature" and his earthly "human nature." This is the "orthodox" doctrine that one must believe in order to be saved. I confess that it never occurred to me that these propositions are impossible contradictions. On the one hand we have three "who's" in one "what" (the Godhead as Trinity) and on the other hand we have one "who" in two "whats" (Jesus in his two natures).

In relation to the proposition that God is one Being in three Persons, Martyn Lloyd-Jones, who was one of the greatest 20th-century preachers after the Reformed tradition, states that "no human being would have thought of the doctrine of the Trinity. It comes directly from the Bible." But then astoundingly he adds, "we are simply meant to look at it with wonder, with awe and with worship, and be amazed at it" even though "no single explicit statement of this doctrine is made [in the Bible!]."[1] There are two points of concern raised by Lloyd-Jones' assertion. Firstly, he appears to be ignorant of history. It is quite inaccurate to state that "no human being would have thought of the doctrine of the Trinity." As a matter of historical record, the Babylonians already had a trinity in their Ea-Damkina-Marduk, the Egyptians had already thought of a trinity in Osiris-Isis-Horus, and the Greeks had Zeus-Persephone-Zagreus.[2] No doubt in his defence, Lloyd-Jones would make the point that he was referring to the Christian Trinity with its belief in one God existing in one "essence" in the three Persons.

---

[1] Martyn Lloyd-Jones, *God the Father, God the Son: Great Doctrines Series,* London: Hodder & Stoughton, 1996, pp. 84-85.

[2] Walker, *Gnosticism: Its History and Influence,* p. 73.

However, even on this score his statement that no human would have ever invented this Christian God remains inaccurate. The Gnostics had actually adopted the Babylonian, Egyptian, and Greek trinities, and reworked them into a oneness of essence that Christianity later incorporated into its official doctrine. The Gnostics speculated that within the unitary essence of God there are three manifestations (or Persons). Benjamin Walker says, "This is gnostically stated somewhat as follows. The Godhead reflected, calling forth himself from within himself, and thus it was. And what was, was threefold: *Nous*, 'mind,' *Ennoia,* 'thought' or 'idea,' and *Logos,* 'word' or 'reason.'"[3] The authors of *The Jesus Mysteries,* Timothy Freke and Peter Gandy agree: "Gnostic mythology included a more natural and balanced Holy Trinity of God the Father, God the Son and the mother goddess Sophia." They also write that:

> The notion of a divine trinity is not found in Judaism, but it is prefigured by paganism. Aristotle writes of the Pythagorean doctrine that "the whole and everything in it is comprehended by the number three, for end, middle and beginning have the number of the whole, that is the trinity." Hundreds of years earlier, an ancient Egyptian text has God proclaim: "Being One I became Three." Another reads, "Three are all the gods, Amon, Ra, Ptah; there are none like them. Hidden in his name Amon, he is Ra, his body is Ptah. He is manifested in Amon, with Ra and Ptah, the three united."[4]

Thus, it is established that the later Christian doctrine of the One God in Trinity is paralleled in a number of pre-Christian belief systems.

The second part of Lloyd-Jones' statement that the doctrine of the Trinity "comes directly from the Bible" and that "we are simply meant to look at it with wonder, with awe and with worship, and be amazed at it" even though "no single explicit statement of this doctrine is made [in the Bible!]," I find extraordinary. So are we to worship at the shrine of a doctrine that comes directly from the Bible even though *there is no single explicit statement of it to be*

---

[3] *Ibid.,* p. 30.

[4] Timothy Freke and Peter Gandy, *The Jesus Mysteries: Was the Original Jesus a Pagan God?* London: Harper Collins, 1999, pp. 100-101.

found anywhere in the Bible?! Sound confusing? Contradictory? I would have thought that the dead give-away that a doctrine is man-invented is that it is confusing. Martyn Lloyd-Jones anticipates some trouble with this so he hastens to add that believing in the Trinity does not mean that there are three Gods, for that would be tritheism. He quotes a couple of Bible verses to prove that the Bible teaches there is only one God (Deut. 6:4; John 10:30; James 2:19) and says confusingly again, "So, then, as we consider this great and blessed doctrine of the Holy Trinity, whether we finally understand what we are saying or not, we must keep on saying that we do not believe in three Gods. There is only one God."[5]

What is Lloyd-Jones' explanation, and how does he wiggle out of the corner he has painted himself into? He has to resort to a criticism of the Bible language itself, undermining his own belief in the sufficiency of God's revelation:

> What is the trouble, therefore? Well, the trouble, once more, is due to *the inadequacy of language.* We have to talk about "persons" because we cannot think of a higher category than persons, and as we think of persons we think of individuals, and we are separating them. *But as the Bible uses these expressions, they obviously mean something different.* Now I do not pretend to understand. Nobody understands. The greatest minds in the Church throughout the centuries have been grappling with this and trying to explain it...They say that God is one, but nevertheless that God, who is one, in His ultimate innermost nature exists as three Persons.[6]

Now I have to say that I have many of Martyn Lloyd-Jones' books in my library. He is one of my favourite Bible expositors. I often quote him with approval. You will not find a man of God more thoroughly committed to the authority of the Scriptures. He believes in the accuracy of the Bible as it has come to us directly from the inspiration of God Himself. He is not being deliberately disrespectful to God's revelation, I believe. But this is a classic example of a man whose mind on this point is being man-handled by the heavy hand of tradition. And his last statement just leaves me scratching my head. Did you notice the subtle technique he uses to

---

[5] Lloyd-Jones, *God the Father, God the Son,* p. 86.

[6] *Ibid.,* p. 86.

explain away our trouble with the doctrine of the Trinity? Our problem is that the Bible means "something different" when it talks about "persons" than what we humans mean. We think of individuals when we think of persons, but when the Scriptures talk about Persons within the Godhead it has another meaning altogether! In short, Lloyd-Jones tries to convince us that God is unable to address us in language that is clear, straightforward, unequivocating. Wait a minute. Can't the Almighty speak clearly? If we are rational creatures expected to "hear the word of the Lord" surely the Greatest Mind of all can speak intelligently to us using the ordinary meanings of words? The alternative is to believe that God is free to break all the rules of grammar and vocabulary in order to reveal Himself. In that case the Bible is a slippery revelation!

Anthony Buzzard makes our point trenchantly:

> Language has certain ways of saying things which allow for no ambiguity or uncertainty. This is not true of all the words we use, of course, but some things are unambiguously clear. When we say white, we do not mean black and when we say hello, we do not mean goodbye. If we speak of hot ice cubes or square circles we make no sense — we are talking nonsense, and everyone knows we are. If we did not enjoy a common currency of meaning in the language we use the whole world would come to a grinding halt, and a massive confusion — far greater than we already witness! — would ensue. [Then Buzzard reminds his readers of the humorous words of Humpty Dumpty who said in a rather scornful tone:] "When I use a word it means just what I choose it to mean — neither more nor less."[7]

It is certain that when God speaks to us He does not intend us to use the Humpty Dumpty principle and make up our own private meanings to suit our man-made theories and traditions. It is axiomatic that from the beginning the Christian faith proclaims itself to be the revelation of God's "Word." That means the Christian faith is a message addressed to human understanding using language and logic universally recognized. In the words of Romans 10:17, "faith comes by hearing, and hearing by the word of [or message announced by] Christ." It is by intelligently receiving

---

[7] Lewis Carroll, *Through the Looking-Glass*, *Focus on the Kingdom,* 6:12.

his words that we receive the life of Jesus (John 6:63). In that key parable of the sower and the seed Jesus makes the intelligent reception of his Kingdom message the key condition for salvation (Matt. 13:19; Mark 4:11-12). To believe the revealed message of God through His apostles is to receive His Spirit (Gal. 3:2). Therefore, to believe in the God of the Bible is to believe His spoken word through His prophets and primarily through His Son Jesus (Zech. 7:12; Heb. 1:1-2). The rest of this chapter is based on the straightforward principle that God has told us unambiguously, clearly, simply and many, many times in the Bible just who He is; God has told us that He is one Being, one Person.

Following are a few of the verses in the Hebrew Bible that teach this unambiguously: "Hear, O Israel! The LORD is our God, the LORD is one!" (Deut. 6:4). This was and still is the very first Bible verse that each Jewish boy and girl learns. It is called the *Shema Yisrael* ("Hear, O Israel"). It is the verse that binds Jewish life and community together. Every devout Jew recites it daily. They utter the *Shema* when dying. It is their confession and their identifying mark through the centuries. It was this belief that their God was the only Supreme Deity which distinguished the Israelites from all the surrounding nations who had embraced polytheism. It was to this belief that God called the idolater Abram out of Ur of the Chaldees so that he might become the father of the Hebrew nation. It was this faith to which Joshua challenged the newly founded nation of Israel to adhere; they were to choose either to go back and serve the old gods on the other side of the river, or serve the one true God. "We will serve the LORD," they averred, "for He is our God" (Josh. 24:18). "The LORD is one LORD" is thus Israel's classic statement of monotheism, Judaism's highest confession of faith. It speaks of Yahweh's uniqueness and exclusiveness, that He is one single integral person, not divisible. *The Interpreter's Dictionary of the Bible* tells us that there are two valid ways of interpreting the *Shema* of Deuteronomy 6:4:

> It is possible to translate: "Yahweh, our God, is one Yahweh" — in which case the Shema affirms that Yahweh cannot be divided into several Yahweh manifestations (poly-Yahwism), like the Baals of different sanctuaries [or we might add the Trinity of later Nicene Christianity]. Or we may translate: "Yahweh is our God, Yahweh alone" — in which case the Shema affirms that Yahweh is the only

> and the unique God [we will soon see that Jesus affirmed this creed in John 17:3].[8]

Both nuances are given in other OT passages. The Person of God is indivisible and He has no other in His class for He is alone and unique. He is a single divine Individual: "To you it was shown that you might know that the LORD, He is God; there is no other besides Him...Know therefore today, and take it to your heart, that the LORD, He is God in heaven above and on the earth below; there is no other" (Deut. 4:35, 39).

"See now that I, I am He, and there is no God besides Me" (Deut. 32:39).

"There is no God besides Me...I, the LORD, am the maker of all things, stretching out the heavens by Myself, and spreading out the earth all alone" (Is. 44:6, 24).

These verses could be multiplied many times over. From beginning to end, the Hebrew Bible teaches a strict unitary monotheism. There is one God. And this true God is one Yahweh. He is alone supreme, with no rivals. And in anybody's language one means one, or does it?

Words Taught by God or by Men?

The crucial question about God's identity and how many persons make up His Godhead should be answered by an appeal using biblical language. The Bible more than adequately tells us who God is and it is very confusing to import completely unbiblical language into the discussion. As church history has demonstrated, when such unbiblical language is introduced, the Bible's own clear statements about the unity of God are lost in a cloud of confusion. It is our contention that the multiplied statements of the Scriptures that God Almighty is "one LORD" can all be made using the language of the Bible itself. No appeal to extra-biblical words or explanations is necessary. However, in direct contrast to such unitary monotheistic language, Trinitarian statements on the Being of God require extra-biblical words and definitions — co-eternal, co-equal, co-essential, hypostatic union of the two natures, three in one, one in three, *homoousios* or "of the same substance," unbegotten — to mention just a few! This alerts us to an immediate conflict with the

---

[8] *The Interpreter's Dictionary of the Bible: An Illustrated Encyclopedia,* New York: Abingdon Press, 1962, vol. 2, p. 427.

stated goal of the apostle Paul who states unequivocally that "we speak not in words taught by human wisdom, but in those taught by the Spirit, combining [interpreting/comparing] spiritual thoughts with spiritual words" (1 Cor. 2:13).

We can observe this progression (!?) from the intelligible and simple Bible statements about the God of the Bible and His Son our Lord Jesus the Messiah, by a brief survey of the creedal statements of the Church as they evolved in the post-apostolic centuries. With the passing of the centuries these statements of faith become increasingly complex and contrived:

THE OLD ROMAN CREED, AD + or – 100
I believe in God the Father Almighty;
And in Christ Jesus His only Son our Lord;
Who was born of the Holy Spirit and the virgin Mary;
Crucified under Pontius Pilate and buried;
The third day he rose from the dead;
He ascended into heaven;
He sits at the right hand of the Father;
Thence he shall come to judge the living and the dead;
And in the Holy Spirit, the holy Church,
The remission of sins, the resurrection of the flesh.

APOSTLES' CREED, 2nd century AD
I believe in God, the Father Almighty, Creator of heaven and earth.
I believe in Jesus Christ, his only Son our Lord.
He was conceived by the power of the Holy Spirit and born of the virgin Mary.
He suffered under Pontius Pilate, was crucified, died, and was buried.
He descended to the dead. On the third day he rose again.
He ascended into heaven, and is seated at the right hand of the Father.
He will come again to judge the living and the dead.
I believe in the Holy Spirit, the holy catholic Church, the communion of saints,
the forgiveness of sins, the resurrection of the body, and the life everlasting. Amen.

CONSTANTINOPLE, 381 AD
We believe in one God, the Father, the Almighty,
Maker of heaven and earth, of all that is seen and unseen.

We believe in one Lord, Jesus Christ, the only Son of God,
Eternally begotten of the Father, God from God, Light from Light,
True God from true God, begotten, not made, one Being with the Father,
Through him all things were made.
For us men and for our salvation he came down from heaven;
By the power of the Holy Spirit he was born of the virgin Mary, and became man.
For our sake he was crucified under Pontius Pilate;
He suffered, died and was buried.
On the third day he rose again in fulfilment of the Scriptures;
He ascended into heaven and is seated on the right hand of the Father.
He will come again in glory to judge the living and the dead,
And his kingdom will have no end.

We believe in the Holy Spirit, the Lord, the giver of life,
Who proceeds from the Father and Son.
With the Father and the Son He is worshipped and glorified.
He has spoken through the prophets.

We believe in one holy catholic Church,
We acknowledge one baptism for the forgiveness of sins.
We look for the resurrection of the dead,
And the life of the world to come. Amen.

This Nicene-Constantinople creed is the only ecumenical creed that is accepted as authoritative by the Roman Catholic, Eastern Orthodox, Anglican and the major Protestant churches. This creed made official the terminology of the supporters of Nicene "orthodoxy," namely, that there is "one divine essence, three Persons" (*mia ousia, treis hupostaseis*). This creed affirms that the three Persons, Father, Son and Holy Spirit, are distinct from one another but are equal in their eternity and power. This confirmed the Nicene proclamation that Christ Jesus was "of the same essence as the Father" without arousing suspicion of modalism. The

Encyclopedia Britannica insightfully observes, "Although this doctrine seemed to make problematical the unity of God, it did provide an answer to...the issue of Christ's relation to the Father. *It now became necessary to clarify the second issue — the relation of the divine and the human within Christ.*"[9] The debate now raged over the alleged "two natures" of Jesus Christ. The creation of three Persons in one divine "essence" had now to sort out the "two natures" (one divine and one human) in the person of Jesus. This controversy raged during the 5th century. The resolution was that before his incarnation Christ only had one nature, but after the incarnation there were two natures indissolubly joined in one person. The actual statement came in 451 AD:

CHALCEDON, 451 AD

Our Lord is truly God and truly man, of a reasonable soul and body, consubstantial with the Father according to the Godhead, and consubstantial with us according to the manhood; in all things like unto us without sin; begotten before all ages of the Father according to the Godhead, and in these latter days for us and for our salvation born of the virgin Mary, the mother of God according to the manhood; one and the same Christ, Son, Lord, only begotten, to be acknowledged in two natures, inconfusedly, unchangeably, indivisibly, inseparably, the distinction of natures being by no means taken away by the union, but rather the property of each nature being preserved and concurring in one person and one subsistence; not parted or divided into two persons but one and the same Son, and only begotten, God, the Word, the Lord Jesus Christ.

See how with the passing of time human formulations were invented, new language and phraseology coined in order to explain the Trinity (some of these words are so novel that even my spell-check on the computer keeps reminding me)! This so-called essential and primary article of faith is not found in any divine oracle in Scripture, but depends on the explanations of men. An informative exercise the reader might like to try is to go through the above creeds underlining each and every word and phrase that has been introduced in addition to the simple and beautifully clear creed

---

[9] 22:372, emphasis added.

of Jesus himself as found in Mark 12:29-31. The contrast is stark indeed.

What God has told us of Himself is freely revealed and taught in the words of the Bible, *words taught by the Holy Spirit* (1 Cor. 2:12-13). No appeal to outside "human wisdom" is necessary! Trinitarian scholars acknowledge this conflict. Millard Erickson, a well-known "orthodox" systematic theologian who has written extensively on the Trinity, admits that although the doctrine is held with great vehemence and vigour:

> It is not clearly or explicitly taught anywhere in Scripture, yet it is widely regarded as a central doctrine, indispensable to the Christian faith. In this regard, it goes contrary to what is virtually an axiom [that is, a given, a self-evident truth] of biblical doctrine, namely, that there is a direct correlation between the scriptural clarity of a doctrine and its cruciality to the faith and life of the church.[10]

If this statement does not jolt us enough Erickson goes on to make this staggering admission:

> The question, however is this. It is claimed that the doctrine of the Trinity is a very important, crucial, and even basic doctrine. If that is indeed the case, should it not be somewhere more clearly, directly, and explicitly stated in the Bible? If this is the doctrine that especially constitutes Christianity's uniqueness, as over against unitarian monotheism on the one hand, and polytheism on the other hand, how can it be only implied in the biblical revelation? In response to the complaint that a number of portions of the Bible are ambiguous or unclear, we often hear a statement something like, "It is the peripheral matters that are hazy or on which there seem to be conflicting biblical materials. The core beliefs are clearly and unequivocally revealed." This argument would appear to fail us with respect to the doctrine of the Trinity, however. For here is a seemingly crucial matter where the Scriptures do not speak loudly and clearly...Little direct response can be made to this charge. It is unlikely that any text of Scripture can be

---

[10] Millard J. Erickson, *God in Three Persons: A Contemporary Interpretation of the Trinity,* Grand Rapids: Baker Books, 1995, p. 11.

> shown to teach the doctrine of the Trinity in a clear, direct, and unmistakable fashion.[11]

Let the reader pause and consider the above again! To admit that the so-called essential and primary article of faith is not found in any divine oracle but needs and depends on the explanations of men should ring loud warning bells in any honest student of the Bible's ears. *The Trinitarian has to depart from the revealed language of the Bible in order to justify a teaching not clearly stated anywhere in Scripture!*

Douglas McCready, another Reformed scholar, acknowledges these difficulties of language facing believers in the Trinity:

> From the conservative side, the problem of interpreting the evidence often seems to be one of reading back into the biblical texts the creedal conclusions of early church councils. Because those creeds are considered to have been built on a foundation of biblical evidence, this is illegitimate circular reasoning. The creeds have their proper place in proclaiming Christ's pre-existence, but it is not to justify particular interpretations of biblical text; it is always the biblical texts that must justify the content and wording of the creeds. Moreover, these creeds are not worded in the language of the New Testament but that of Hellenism, although this Hellenistic terminology had been transformed for the purpose of defending New Testament teachings against Hellenistic philosophical concepts. In any case, it is illegitimate to read later theological conclusions back into New Testament texts, tempting as that may be.[12]

McCready offers excellent advice when he cautions us not to read later theological conclusions back into NT texts. However, with the weight of long tradition pushing from this side of the Church creeds, this is now practically impossible advice for most Christians today. Protestants have always said biblical texts must be paramount and primary. But even Protestants have their own set traditions of interpretation. At least McCready is honest enough to admit that the language of Hellenism has been employed to bolster

---

[11] Ibid., p.108-109.

[12] Douglas McCready, *He Came Down From Heaven: The Preexistence of Christ and the Christian Faith,* Intervarsity Press, 2005, p. 48.

and defend the New Testament! McCready notes it was Hans Kung who said "the first paradigmatic change in Christianity occurred when speculative questions about the nature of God and of Jesus replaced the cross and resurrection as the center of Christian thought. The language of Hellenistic metaphysics replaced that of the Bible and Christology 'from above' replaced Christology 'from below.'" McCready justifies his acceptance of Hellenistic language by alleging that "Kung ignores that one reason early Christian theologians used Hellenistic language was that it was the language of the culture in which the early church existed and which it was trying to evangelize."[13] Furthermore, "The orthodox party was forced to use Hellenistic language to refute the Hellenistic thought of the Arian party and preserve the biblical worldview."[14] So, the biblical writings, given to us in "words not taught by human wisdom, but in those taught by the Spirit" now need speculative language in order to effectively communicate the truth of God! On this occasion Hans Kung is certainly more insightful by observing this methodology represents "the first paradigmatic change in Christianity," which in any Bible lover's mind ought to sound a shrill alarm.

Let me put this in a rather graphic way. If I as a believer in the unitary monotheism of the Bible could not find the word "one" applied to God anywhere I would be deeply troubled. If every verse I read said "God is three" and I decided to ignore that and said, "No, God is one. Even though it says He is three all over the place, I know He is one" surely nobody would pay any attention to me. Yet, the staggering truth is that "one" is found in a multitude of passages in the Old and New Testaments that speak of God's identity. However, the word "three" is found nowhere in the Bible in connection with God or any name/title of God. Surely this is a dead giveaway that the doctrine of the Trinity is a doctrine of inference, randomly sewed together. It is not plainly taught in the pages of Scripture. It is built on "human wisdom" and not on clearly revealed Bible language.

Nor can we appeal to the old adage that "it is a mystery to be accepted on faith." A study of the way the NT uses the word "mystery" shows that the opposite is the case. A "mystery" is a

---

[13] Ibid., p. 49.

[14] Ibid., p. 69.

previously unknown, previously unrevealed secret that God has now openly revealed to His people. Here are a few examples:

"Now to Him who is able to establish you according to my gospel and the preaching of Jesus Christ, according to the **revelation of the mystery** which has been kept secret for long ages past, but is **now manifested**, and by the Scriptures of the prophets, according to the commandment of the eternal God, **has been made known to all the nations**" (Rom. 16:25).

"And he was saying to them, '**To you has been given the mystery** of the kingdom of God; but those who are outside get everything in parables'" (Mk. 4:11).

"For **I do not want you, brethren, to be uninformed of this mystery**, lest you be wise in your own estimation" (Rom. 11:25).

"Behold, **I tell you a mystery**" (1 Cor. 15:51).

"He **made known to us the mystery** of His will" (Eph. 1:9).

"And pray on my behalf, that utterance may be given to me in the opening of my mouth, **to make known** with boldness **the mystery** of the gospel" (Eph. 6:19).

"The mystery which has been hidden from the past ages and generations; but **has now been manifested to His saints**" (Col. 1:26).

Each of these examples (and many others might be given) shows that *in Bible understanding a mystery is that which God has revealed and openly spoken about*. A mystery is an open secret for all to understand. There is no such thing as an undeclared mystery to be taken on faith. God's mysteries are given for us to understand! They are addressed to the mind, to the understanding.

On a personal note, I had occasion to enter a well-known large chapel in Auckland, New Zealand. The following statement of faith was posted in the foyer of their large building complex:

> THE TRINITY
> Would you like to understand the doctrine of the Trinity? You can't! That's the conclusion of hundreds of theologians for the last 1600 years. The Trinity is a mystery...Our ordinary, logical skills break down when we try to understand it...It is doubtful the human mind would invent something so opposed to its own capabilities. On the other hand, we still don't understand the Trinity...We are face to face with a mystery...The concept of the Trinity is ideal for meditation. Because you can't understand it we are forced

> to go beyond the realm of our comprehension into the realm of God Himself.

Compare that statement of faith with the Bible's understanding of what a mystery is. At least that church is honest enough to say we can't understand the doctrine of the Trinity, that our human logic breaks down when we try to. Notice also the "mystical" nature of the Trinity because "we are forced to go beyond the realm of our comprehension into the realm of God Himself." What is this but pure Greek philosophical speculation, the very tendency the NT warns against? Metaphysics had no solid rules to the Greeks.

> Reality was not real, so almost anything could exist in the supposedly "real" world and be explained simply as beyond the understanding of humans who occupy the "unreal" (phenomenal) world. A kind of general logic was employed in metaphysical interpretation, but the result of this "logical" analysis did not, itself, have to be logical.[15]

We may put it this way: If the doctrine of the mysterious Trinity were true it would be the only crucial doctrine in the Church *not* plainly taught in the Bible and the only doctrine necessary for salvation relying on the invented words of clever men! The Trinitarian Emil Brunner expresses this finding nicely:

> It was never the intention of the original witnesses to Christ in the New Testament to set before us an intellectual problem — that of Three Divine Persons — then to tell us silently to worship this mystery of the "Three-in-One." There is no trace of such an idea in the New Testament. This "mysterium logicum," the fact that God is Three and yet One, lies wholly outside the message of the Bible. [This mystery has] no connection with the message of Jesus and His Apostles. No Apostle would have dreamt of thinking that there are Three Divine Persons, whose mutual relations and paradoxical unity are beyond our understanding. No "mysterium logicum," no intellectual paradox, no antinomy of Trinity in Unity, has any place in their testimony.[16]

---

[15] Richard R. Hopkins, *How Greek Philosophy Corrupted the Christian Concept of God,* Horizon Publishers, 2005, p. 115.

[16] Emil Brunner, *The Christian Doctrine of God, Dogmatics,* Philadelphia: Westminster Press, 1949, Vol. 1, p. 226.

Compound Unity

When I was a teenager the first book I ever read which systematically set forth who God is was *The God of the Bible* by R.A. Torrey. His book was very influential in convincing my young mind that although there is only one God in both Old and New Testaments, this one God nevertheless exists in three Persons. The first argument Torrey marshals in support of this proposition is that the Hebrew word translated "one" denotes a compound unity, and not a simple unity. Torrey then quotes a number of verses that allegedly back up this notion. Torrey illustrates this widely held belief that "one" can mean "more than one." "For this cause a man shall leave his father and his mother, and shall cleave to his wife; and they shall become **one** flesh" (Gen. 2:24).

Torrey states, "Now the Hebrew word translated 'one' in this passage is the same word translated 'one' in all the passages that declare that there is only '*one* God,' and it can be plainly seen in this passage that not a simple unity but a compound unity is intended: *two,* man and wife, being '*one.*'"

Torrey then turns to another verse: "And the LORD said, 'Behold, they are **one** people'" (Gen. 11:6):

> The same Hebrew word for "one" is used here. Here we are told that *a large number* of people are *one* people; they are at the same time *many* and *one.* We find a similar usage for the Greek word for "one" in the New Testament. Read e.g. 1 Cor. 3:6-8, "I planted, Apollos watered; but God gave the increase. Now **he who plants** and **he who waters are one**." Here we are distinctly told that *two different persons* are *"one."* Turn to 1 Cor. 12:13, "For in one Spirit we were **all** baptized into **one** body, whether Jews or Greeks, whether slaves or free; and we were all made to drink of one Spirit." Here we are distinctly told that all who have become members of the living church by the baptism in the Holy Spirit are *all* together "*one.*"[17]

With "logical" application, Torrey then argues that when the Bible calls God one a compound unity is meant. That is, there can exist a number of Persons within the one Godhead, for "one" can really mean "many"! As a youngster I found this argument that "one" did not necessarily mean a simple unity, but could mean a

[17] R.A. Torrey, *The God of the Bible,* p. 63.

compound unity, rather telling. It was not until I read Professor Buzzard's book *The Doctrine of the Trinity* almost thirty years later that I was shaken out of this misrepresentation of the clear pronouncement of Scripture. Buzzard and Hunting write:

> This argument involves an easily detectable fallacy. *Echad* [the Hebrew word for "one"] appears some 970 times in the Hebrew Bible and in no case does the word itself carry a hint of plurality. It means strictly "one and not two or more." *Echad* is a numerical adjective and naturally enough is sometimes found modifying a collective noun — one family, one herd, one bunch. But we should observe carefully that the sense of plurality resides in the compound noun and not in the word *echad* (one).
>
> Early in Genesis we learn that "the two will become one flesh" (Gen. 2:24). The word "one" here means precisely one and no more (one flesh and not two "fleshes"!). One bunch of grapes is just that — one and not two bunches. Thus when God is said to be "one Lord" (Deut. 6:4) He is a single Lord and no more.
>
> Imagine that someone claimed that the word "one" meant "compound one" in the words "one tripod." Suppose someone thought that "the one United States of America" implied that "one" was really plural in meaning. The specious reasoning is obvious: the idea of plurality belongs to the words "tripod" and "States," *not to the word "one."* It is a subterfuge to transfer to "one" the plurality which belongs only to the following noun. It would be similar to saying that "one" really means "one hundred" when it appears in the combination "one centipede"![18]

So it simply is not true to say that "one" does not mean "one" but can be compound. The Hebrew lexicons of the Bible do not define "one" as meaning "more than one." This compound unity argument is not used by scholars of the Hebrew language. In fact, *echad* is used over 900 times in the Hebrew Bible (it is the most used adjective in the Hebrew Bible) and there is never any question that it can mean anything other than "one," or "a single."

---

[18] Anthony Buzzard and Charles Hunting, *The Doctrine of the Trinity: Christianity's Self-Inflicted Wound,* Lanham, NY: International Scholars Publications, 1998, pp. 25-26.

The expression that a man and his wife will be as "one flesh" simply tells of their physical union and ideal unity of purpose. The couple is as though they are one. They are still one couple, not two couples! (I remember a mother in Tasmania commenting on this verse, "the two shall be one flesh." She pointed to one of her children and said, "That is how two become one flesh!" She had a valid point.) The same idea of unity of purpose is found in Ezekiel 37 where "one stick" is joined to "another stick" and they "become one in your hand" (v. 17). In this acted parable, the prophet is taught that the two kingdoms will be as though they were one stick, ideally united in purpose.

Elohim — The Hebrew Name for God

Well, so much for the first piece of "solid ground" that my doctrine of the Trinity had rested on for all those decades. The next piece of solid ground (?) which R.A. Torrey let me plant my feet on was that the Old Testament Hebrew word most frequently used as the name or title of God is plural in its form. This is the word *elohim*, and literally translated it would read "Gods."

Torrey says:

> For example Deut. 6:4 literally translated would read, "Hear, O Israel, Jehovah our *Gods* is one Jehovah." *Why is it that the Jews with their intense monotheism had a plural name for God?...A plural name was used for the one God, in spite of the intense monotheism of the Jews, because there is a plurality of persons in the one Godhead.* This is a rational explanation of this indubitable fact, and no other explanation is as rational.[19]

Now before specifically refuting this one, it is instructive to note that the Christian fathers (those post-apostolic writers of the first few centuries), who were keen to find Old Testament proofs for the Trinity, never once appealed to this argument from the word *elohim*. This fact in itself is rather suspicious for those seeking to find a plurality of persons within the God of the Bible. The argument from the plural ending on *elohim* dates from around 1,000 AD. It is a relatively recent invention.

What R.A. Torrey and the many who use this argument fail to tell us is that *elohim* is used in various ways in Scripture. It is not

---

[19] R.A. Torrey, *The God of the Bible,* p. 64.

only used to describe the Almighty, but also individual pagan gods and even mighty human beings. As we pointed out in the previous chapter *elohim* may be translated as God, god, angels, judges, or even a human being who stands as God's representative or agent. For example, the sons of Heth address Abraham as "a mighty prince," the word for "mighty" being *elohim* (Gen. 23:6). Some translations have Abraham here being called "prince of God." Take another instance. In Exodus 4 the LORD tells Moses that he "shall be as God" (*elohim*) to his brother Aaron. Moses will have God's words in his mouth, and will stand as God's representative before Aaron. Here is a case where an individual human is called *elohim.* Again in Exodus 7:1 the Lord says to Moses, "See, I make you God [*elohim*] to Pharaoh." No one dares to suggest that there is a plurality of persons within Moses because he is called *elohim,* that is, God's representative. The pagan god Dagon is also called *elohim* in the Hebrew Bible. The Philistines lamented that the God of Israel was harshly treating "Dagon our god [*elohim*]" (1 Sam. 5:7). Dagon was a single pagan deity. The same holds true for the single pagan god called Chemosh: "Do you not possess what Chemosh your god [*elohim*] gives you to possess?" (Jud. 11:24). The same for the single deity called Baal.

The Hebrew language has many examples of words which are plural but whose meaning is singular. In Genesis 23 Abraham's wife Sarah dies. The Hebrew text says, "The lives [plural] of Sarah were 127 years" (v. 1). Even the plural verb that accompanies the plural noun does not mean Sarah lived multiple lives. The Hebrews never taught reincarnation or plurality of personhood. Another example of this kind of anomaly in the Hebrew language is found in Genesis 43. After Joseph wept to see his brothers, we read that Joseph "washed his faces" (plural). This is another instance where in the Hebrew language the plural noun functions as a singular noun with a singular meaning, unless, of course, Joseph was a multi-faced human being! The same in Genesis 16:8 where Hagar flees from "the faces" (plural) of her mistress Sarah. These are "anomalies" of the Hebrew language that are clearly understood by Hebrew scholars who rightly translate to a singular form in English. Take the word for "master" (*adonim*). The *-im* ending is plural. So what do translators make of verses like the following from Genesis 39? "And he [Joseph] was in the house of his master [plural word *adonim*] the Egyptian. Now his master [plural word *adonim*] saw that the LORD was with him" (v. 2-3). Then in verses 7-8 of the same chapter we read that "his master's wife" (plural word *adonim*, with singular meaning) looked lustfully at Joseph but he "refused and said to his master's wife..." (plural *adonim* with singular meaning). Verse 16: "his master [plural *adonim*] came home." In all these cases the plural word for master (*adonim*) is paired with singular verbs and pronouns. Nobody suggests for a minute that Potiphar was a multi-personal being or that his wife was a plurality of persons just because the Hebrew word describing them is in the plural! The better explanation is that the Hebrews used a form of speech called "the plural of majesty." Put simply this means that someone whose position was one of dignity was spoken of in this way as a sign of honour. The plural acted as a means of intensification:

"The fanciful idea that *elohim* referred to the Trinity of persons in the Godhead hardly finds now a supporter among scholars. It is either what the grammarians call the plural of majesty, or it denotes the fullness of divine strength, the sum of powers displayed by God."[20]

"*Elohim* must rather be explained as an intensive plural, denoting greatness and majesty."[21]

"Early dogmaticians were of the opinion that so essential a doctrine as that of the Trinity could not have been unknown to the men of the Old Testament...No modern theologian...can longer maintain such a view. Only an inaccurate exegesis which overlooks the more immediate grounds of interpretation can see references to the Trinity in the plural form of the divine name *elohim*."[22]

Elohim occurs about 2,500 times in the Hebrew Bible and depending on context is variously translated as God, god, goddess, gods or human judges. We have English words that can also carry a plural or a singular meaning, depending on context. Take the word "sheep" for instance. I know you mean a plurality when you say to me, "These sheep are lost" because of the plural pronoun "these" and the plural verb "are." But if you say to me, "This sheep is lost" I

---

[20] William Smith, *A Dictionary of the Bible,* ed. Peloubet, MacDonald Pub. Co., 1948, p. 220.
[21] *The American Journal of Semitic Language and Literature,* 1905, vol. XXI, p. 208.
[22] *The New Schaff-Herzog Encyclopedia of Religious Knowledge,* vol. 12, p. 18.

know you mean one particular individual because the pronoun "this" is singular as is the verb "is." The same applies to the Hebrew word *elohim.* The Hebrew ending *-im* is plural in form but can be singular in meaning. How can we tell? Just as we can in English from the context. The simple truth is that whenever the one God of the Hebrew Bible is referred to, the word *elohim* is accompanied by singular personal pronouns and singular verbs.

Besides the plural form *elohim* the Hebrew Bible also has two singular words for God, *El* and *Eloah.* Both refer to the one true God of Israel. (See e.g. Gen. 17:1; Ex. 34:6; Josh. 3:10; Is. 5:16 for *El* and Deut. 32:15; Neh. 9:17; Ps. 50:22; 114:7; Is. 44:8 for *Eloah* in Hebrew lexicons.)

The oldest Greek translation of the Hebrew Bible is called the *Septuagint* (LXX). It was translated by 72 Hebrew scholars in about 250 BC in Alexandria, Egypt. The king of Egypt, Ptolemy Philadelphus, sponsored this massive project. According to Josephus the Jewish historian, the Jewish translators did their work by the sea in idyllic conditions, with their food laid on in abundance. Now here is the telling fact. Whenever the word *elohim* refers to the God of Israel the Septuagint uses the singular and not the plural. From Genesis 1:1 consistently right through, this holds good. These Hebrews who translated their own Scriptures into Greek simply had no idea that their God could be more than one individual, or a multipersonal Being!

The problem for those who want to believe that the God of the OT is a multi-personal Being is that there is no mention of any diversity in Yahweh. Deuteronomy 6:4, the *Shema Israel,* cannot be tampered with to argue for God's "diversity in unity" for the simple reason that:

> *in the Shema the word "one" qualifies the word "Yahweh" (LORD) not the word "God"* [as rendered in the Greek of Mk. 12:29]. Does Trinitarianism want to argue that Yahweh is a tri-person Being? If so, then Yahweh is not just the Father, but all three persons of the Trinity! Thus all three persons would be manifestations of the one Yahweh (which in theology is called "Modalism" or "Sabellianism"). Or do Trinitarians really want to maintain that Yahweh in the Hebrew Bible is a multi-personal being, contrary to the Bible itself? If not, then what is the point of all the lengthy

> discussion on "unity" and "diversity" in regard to the "one" in Deut. 6:4?[23]

So too when we come to the New Testament. The New Testament nowhere hints at a plurality in the meaning of *elohim* when it reproduces references to the One God as *ho theos*, the One God. Never is *elohim*, referring to the God of Israel, reproduced in the LXX or the Greek NT as *theoi* (Gods). More of this matter shortly. As for Mr. Torrey's assertion that the Jews used the plural word *elohim* for God "because there is a plurality of persons within the Godhead," and "no other explanation is as rational," I will let you decide in light of the facts.

Plural Pronouns for God

So much then for the second bit of "solid ground" that my belief in the Trinity rested on for all those decades. Let's look at Torrey's third argument. It is another bit of shifting sand that so many have traditionally planted their feet on. It is the argument that:

> In the Old Testament God uses plural pronouns in speaking of Himself. He does this in the very first chapter of the Bible in Gen. 1:26 where it is written, "And God said, Let **us** make man in **our** image, after **our** likeness." It is often said that the doctrine of there being three persons in the Godhead is found in the New Testament, but not in the Old Testament, but here it is in the first chapter of the Old Testament...In the 26th verse of the first chapter of the Old Testament the plurality of persons in the Godhead is distinctly taught. We see this same thing again in the vision of God that Jehovah gave to Isaiah in the sixth chapter of Isaiah, where we read in verse 8, "I heard the voice of the Lord, saying, Whom shall I send, and who will go **for us**?" These are not the only instances in which Jehovah is represented in the Old Testament as using plural pronouns in speaking of Himself, but these are sufficient to prove the point.[24]

It is amazing how many sincere believers bring this one up. So let us ask if this really is the case? When God says "Let us make

---

[23] Eric H.H. Chang, *The Only True God: A Study of Biblical Monotheism,* Xlibris, 2009, p. 46, emphasis original.
[24] R.A. Torrey, *The God of the Bible,* pp. 65-66.

man in our image" are we being taught that the Trinity of Father, Son and Holy Spirit are together creating human beings?

Here is a classic case of reading into the text a pre-conceived notion. (This is called *eisegesis,* whereas the correct method is to read out of the text, called *exegesis.*) How is it that when we read that God said, "Let us make man in our image," our minds immediately think it says "Let us three"? (It is surely the result of conditioning over a long period of time.) The verse says nothing about God speaking to the Son or to the Holy Spirit. It simply says that God addressed someone else or some others other than Himself. The "us" could refer to just one other, or to many others. But just for the sake of argument, even if this is a case of a "plural" God speaking, that God is referring to somebody else *in addition* to Himself as the speaker! But who is this someone or who are these others to whom God speaks here?

The Hebrews understood that God addressed His heavenly court, the angelic host and that He allowed them to watch his master-work in creating mankind unfold. This is quite reasonable, for there are other times when God involves the angels in His work. It is certainly the case in Isaiah 6 where God is seen in his Heavenly temple with the cherubs and all the heavenly court. There God asks, "Whom shall I send, and who will go for us?" (v. 8). It is certainly the case in 1 Kings 22:19-20 where the LORD is seen "sitting on His throne, and all the host of heaven standing by Him on His right and on His left" and He asks the heavenly court "'Who will entice Ahab to go up and fall at Ramoth-Gilead?' And one said this while another said that."

So back to Genesis 1:26. Is it reasonable to suggest then that God in some way took the angels into confidence with Himself when He created Adam? After all, there is no doubt that the angels do bear a resemblance to God Himself, for whenever they appear to men on earth they look like men who are also made in the image of God (see e.g. Gen. 18:2; Luke 24:4; Acts 1:10). Angels are also made in the image of their Creator. Therefore, it is not unreasonable to suggest that God could say to the angels, "Let us make man in our image." Now, before you object and say it is preposterous to suggest that angels helped God make Adam, let me hasten to add this. I do not for a moment believe the angels helped God create man, just that God told them to watch! The text is very clear that this is what happened. For the explanatory verse 27 states, "And

God created man in **His** own image, in the image of God **He** created him; male and female **He** created them." The Hebrew text uses the singular pronouns and the singular verb for create, which suggest God Himself acted alone in the creation of Adam and Eve whilst the angelic hosts looked on in awe! This is corroborated in Job 38:4, 7 where God says that when He laid the foundation of the earth "all the sons of God shouted for joy." The sons of God are of course the angels as Job 1:6 and 2:1 confirm. There is an axiomatic statement in Isaiah 44 that the LORD God created "all things" by Himself: "I, the LORD, am the maker of all things, stretching out the heavens by Myself, and spreading out the earth all alone" (Isa. 44:24).

God's own testimony is that the work of creation, "the heavens," "the earth" and "all things" were His work alone. This fact is established right at the very outset in Genesis 1 where we are first introduced to God (*elohim*) the Creator. The Hebrew verb form is in the third person masculine singular whenever we read "God created" or "God said" or "God made." In Hebrew prose, the verb often precedes the noun. Here in Genesis 1:1 before getting to the word God (*elohim*) we read the third person masculine singular form "created" (*bara*) which immediately indicates that the subject (God) is a *single* entity. Nobody but God created. He did it by Himself.

But it is also clear that when He came to create Adam and Eve He told the angels to watch in awe. In this way *the heavenly host participated as spectators* of the miracle of man's creation. Now if you are still not convinced that the God of creation is one God and not three in one, here is our Lord Jesus' own commentary on Genesis 1:26. He will settle this for us, surely. In Matthew 19:4 Jesus answers the Pharisees and says, "Have you not read that **He who** created them from the beginning made them male and female?" According to Jesus himself the creator God was *not* "*We* who made them from the beginning" but a single Person *He*! Jesus does not include himself in the Genesis 1 creation of Adam. The only issue left to settle then is whether we accept Jesus' testimony or cling to our own traditional interpretation?

One clear, simple fact goes unnoticed here. Only four times in the Old Testament does God speak in the plural as here in Genesis 1:26. (The other times are Gen. 3:22; 11:7 and Is. 6:8.) However, the overwhelming fact is that whenever the Old Testament speaks of God it does so by using *singular pronouns*. Over 11,000 times in fact, singular pronouns tell us that God is a single Person. Thousands upon thousands of times God calls Himself "I" or "Me." Thousands and thousands of times when the Bible speaks of God in the third person it reads "He" or "Him" or "His." Never does God hint that He is three.

Hebrew lexicographers are also unanimous in stating this fact: The verbs which follow *elohim*, the one God, are *singular verbs*. And whenever God's personal name, *Yahweh*, occurs all of its 6,800 times it is always accompanied by singular verbs and singular pronouns.

As Professor Anthony Buzzard says, "The Hebrew Bible and the New Testament contain well over ten thousand singular pronouns and verbs describing the One God. Language has no clearer or more obvious way of providing a testimony to Israel's and Jesus' unitary monotheism."[25]

As Anthony Buzzard again notes, "It seems that one would have to suspend all critical faculties to bring oneself to the belief that God is *not* a single Person. The laws of grammar and logic would have to be set aside. Singular pronouns would no longer signify what in normal communication they always denote."[26] In the Hebrew language as in our language singular personal pronouns and singular verbs denote one person — not a plurality and certainly not three!

The only alternative to this plain revelation given us in Scripture to the Being of God is to dismiss the grammatical-historical method of sound exegesis and to propose that God does not use words like we do! We may believe Martyn Lloyd-Jones' claim that language is simply inadequate to tell us who God is. But the consequence of this approach is that we might as well turf out the rest of the Bible as being a reliable source of divine revelation. It is, in short, to propose a God who is unable to communicate up to our human standards. Or else He is very tricky and slippery, to say the least.

Those who still cling to this handful of texts to prove God is a Trinity because He says "Let us" will do so on an undisputed principle of grammar: They insist that "us" and "our" are plural pronouns and must be taken seriously. But in the same breath they dismiss the thousands and thousands of verses that speak of God with singular personal pronouns and singular verbs! For the very

---

[25] Buzzard and Hunting, *The Doctrine of the Trinity,* pp. 17-18.

[26] Anthony Buzzard, *Focus on the Kingdom,* vol. 6, no. 4, p. 5.

rare time God says "Let us" there are *thousands* of times He calls Himself "I" or "Me." Such ignoring of the evidence is a dead give-away that all critical faculties are suspended. Why not stand on the undisputed principle of grammar that "I" and "Me" and "His" and "He" and "Him" in their thousands of references to the One God must be taken seriously? Are we not in danger of ignoring overwhelming evidence, including the Scriptural testimony we have considered concerning the heavenly angelic court?

The first-person plural pronouns "us" and "we" do not tell us anything about the precise number of persons being referred to. Any number from a minimum of two right up to a numberless multitude may be included in these plural pronouns. Furthermore, this argument for the Trinity from the plural pronouns not only tells us nothing about the exact number being referred to but also:

> proves nothing about the *equality* of any persons comprehended within the first person plural. For example, a commander-in-chief of a nation's armed forces could say, "Together we shall win this war"; the first person plural "we" in this statement does not give any indication as to how many officers and men will fight under his command, and even less does it suggest that any of them are his equal. So, what more can be accomplished by using the "us" in Genesis 1:26 than to try to make a case for polytheism, where neither the number nor the rank of the gods matter?[27]

This kind of damning logic does not suit the Trinitarian cause, so of course is never noticed. Also conveniently overlooked (as previously noted) is the thrice repeated *singular* verb in Genesis 1:27 for "created" which emphasizes that only God Himself did the creating of man. "Also, in all subsequent references to this act of God creating human beings, the Scriptures always speak of it in the *singular* whether within Genesis (5:1; 9:6) or in the rest of Scripture (Job 35:10; Ps. 100:3; 149:2; Is. 64:8; Acts 17:24, etc.)."[28]

We must reject R.A. Torrey's contention that God uses plural pronouns when speaking *of* Himself. In Genesis 1:26 God is not speaking "of Himself." He is speaking *to* His audience. Whenever He speaks "of Himself" He constantly uses the first person personal pronoun and a singular verb. This is a stark Biblical fact.

---

[27] Chang, *The Only True God,* p. 211-212.
[28] Ibid.

To close this section, let's take a look at two classic examples of the point we are making. The first is from 1 Kings 18: "The LORD, He [singular pronoun] is God [*elohim*], the LORD, He [singular] is God [*elohim*]" (v. 39). And 2 Samuel 7, quite literally from the Hebrew text: "LORD, Thou [singular] art He [singular], the God [*elohim*] and Thy [singular] words are truth" (v. 28).

There is not one verse in all Scripture that uses the word "God" to indicate a three-in-one Being. Not one. This is an astounding fact. Surely it is unbelievable that in the very book that claims to come from divine inspiration, if this doctrine of the Trinity is supposed to be so foundational, there is not one single instance out of some 12,000 occurrences of the word God and His personal name *Yahweh* where "God" means "three Persons in one" whenever God speaks as "I" or "Me." This is important. Or perhaps after all, the writers of the Bible had not imagined Him to be three Persons?

A Mathematical (or Metaphysical) Explanation

It is evident that God cannot be three and one *in the same sense.* Besides the ruse of playing with the meaning of words, some Trinitarians have turned to another explanation of how God can at the same time be one God yet three. They turn to a philosophico-mathematical explanation. Again, we turn to R.A. Torrey as being typical of this view.

> We do not think that God is three and one in the same sense. In what sense then can He be three and one at the same time? A *perfectly* satisfactory answer to this question is from the very nature of the case manifestly possible. First, because..."God is Spirit," and numbers apply primarily to the physical or material world, and difficulty must always arise when we attempt to conceive Spiritual being in the forms of material thought. Second, because God is Infinite and we are finite. He dwelleth in the light that no man can approach unto (1 Tim. 6:16), and therefore our attempt at a philosophical explanation of the triunity of God is an attempt to put the facts of Infinite Being into the forms of finite thought, an attempt to put the ocean of truth into the pint cup of the human understanding, an attempt which of necessity could at the very best be only partially successful.
>
> Furthermore, number has significance only in the realm of the finite. It is a well-known mathematical fact that when

> you get into the realm of the Infinite finite numbers lose their significance and value. Anyone who has any considerable knowledge of mathematics knows that one divided by Infinity equals nothing, and also that three divided by Infinity equals nothing. Well then, as things equal to the same thing are equal to one another, one as the numerator with Infinity as the denominator equals three as the numerator with Infinity as the denominator, cancel the common denominator, Infinity, and you have, one equals three. Now one does not equal three, but it shows that, when you get into the realm of the Infinite, finite numbers lose their significance and value.[29]

This might possibly sound convincing to our Western minds, but is it as Torrey suggests "a *perfectly* satisfactory answer" to the dilemma of how God can be three and one at the same time? It is ironic that he rejects any "philosophical explanation of the Trinity" but immediately turns to a philosophical, albeit mathematical explanation to prove his point. Before turning specifically to Torrey's "satisfactory answer" concerning the Being of God, let's observe how typical his response to our question is. Trinitarians will always say that God's Being is a *mystery* and that we must accept the Trinity *by faith. In other words, they want us to believe in the ineffable, that is, in the indescribable and unutterable.* At this point, I cannot improve on Robert Hach's excellent response to this argument when he says that appealing to a mystery that must be accepted by faith is:

> To misunderstand the biblical concepts of both revelation and faith. Revelation is, by definition, *the unveiling of a mystery*: once revealed, it is a mystery no longer (see Eph. 1:9-10; 3:1-6; Col. 2:2-3); if it remains a mystery, then it has not been revealed. In other words, revelation on God's side corresponds to understanding on the human side. The fact that Trinitarianism remains a mystery to human understanding, *despite its supposedly having been revealed by God, is the strongest argument against regarding it as a revelation of God: if God had revealed it, it would be understandable.* Trinitarian theology notwithstanding, when it comes to God's being, the fact that words cannot make it

---

[29] R.A. Torrey, *The God of the Bible,* pp. 74-75.

> understandable means that there are no words for it; therefore, it has not been revealed; "The secret things belong to the Lord our God, but the revealed things belong to us and to our children forever" (Deut. 29:29). From a biblical standpoint, there are both "secret things" and "revealed things," the latter being things that are subject to human understanding, the former being things...that are not.
>
> Moreover, to say that the Trinity is an incomprehensible mystery that must be *accepted by faith* is to replace the apostolic faith, which is a matter of persuasion, through understanding, with a mystical faith that must find some means other than understanding to gain entrance into the heart, the alternatives being a variety of more or less coercive forms, both authoritarian and mystical, of possession. (The history of Trinitarian Christianity bears brutal witness to the truth of this observation.)[30]

This is precisely the apostle Paul's position: "For we write nothing else to you than what you read and understand" (2 Cor. 1:13). For Paul there is no such thing as incomprehensible revealed Christian doctrine. There is no esoteric "mystery of the Holy Trinity." Paul's stated aim is to write "nothing else to you than what you read" and "nothing else than what you...understand." He is not promoting an inscrutable enigma. He writes in no riddles. It's all on the table, so to speak. So, if apostolic faith can only rest on what has been revealed, we are now in a position to address Torrey's "*perfectly* satisfactory answer" as to how God can be three in one. (Just by the way, there have been similar "Western" attempts to "illustrate" what the "triune God" is like, by comparing Him to water that can "exist" in three forms, whether liquid, ice or steam, depending on temperature. This is a "scientific" adaptation of Augustine's model of the Trinity as seen parallel to the human soul, with its memory, understanding and will. For Augustine, the Triune God is a unity in threefoldness. Memory, understanding and will are all functions of the mind in its totality. This is the same kind of metaphysical approach as Torrey's mathematical one and is just as unworthy of God's revelation of Himself as given in the Scriptures, as we shall see.)

---

[30] Robert Hach, *Possession and Persuasion,* p. 116.

Firstly, let us remember that to the Hebrew mind thoroughly grounded in his Bible, there would be no way to reduce the LORD to a "what" or an "essence," much less to a mathematical formula. This is a Gentile (Greek), foreign category that is unworthy of the personal God revealed in the Old Testament. To the Hebrew mind, as already noted, there are many things about Himself that God has not chosen to reveal to us. These are "the secret things" and it is foolish speculation to venture there (Deut. 29:29). God is "holy," which is to say, "other" and cannot be limited to either our human language or our human understanding. Jewish belief and Jewish literature of the first century "was never...an analysis of the inner being of God, a kind of numerical statement about, so to speak, what God was like on the inside."[31] It is extremely hard for us "Westerners" to get it into our pattern of thinking that the biblical revelation of God is not metaphysical.

Perhaps a significant part of our trouble is the very word "spirit." To our Western minds the word "spirit" conjures up images of that which is immaterial and invisible. We talk about spirits and ghosts. This is our way of describing that which belongs "over there." That which is "spiritual" is intangible but still very "real." On the other hand "matter" is thought of as whatever is visible, touchable, changeable, temporal. In private correspondence to me, Robert Hach makes the point that:

> the chief fallacy in virtually all the analyses I've read regarding God's "nature" is the Westernization of the term "Spirit." Whenever the text "God is Spirit [or spirit]," or the concept of God as a "Spirit-being," or the overall subject of "spirituality" is addressed, the unquestioned (and therefore, unspoken) assumption is that "Spirit" (or "spirit") is a kind of invisible, eternal *substance*.[32]

Therefore any discussion of God's essence includes metaphysical or Platonic terms. This approach is foreign to the Hebrew and biblical frame.

Hach maintains that to our Western ears the word "spirit" conveys an unfortunate nuance of meaning that is quite foreign to its Hebrew origins. He continues:

---

[31] N.T. Wright, *Who Was Jesus?* p. 49.

[32] 18th Dec., 2004.

> The second-century Christian theologians (who were Gentiles, typically educated in Greek philosophical concepts) rhetorically reinvented the concept of "spirit": the Hebrew "spirit" as God-breathed truth regarding *God's promised future* was exchanged for the Greek "spirit" as the metaphysical/mystical reality of *God's eternal presence*, a concept which had been inherited from Plato.[33]

In contrast to such metaphysical categories the Hebrew Bible says God can only be known by His actions, His work, His deeds. We know God because He has acted and is acting in space-time history. We know what God is like because He has spoken through the prophets. We "see" God in His mighty works in the nation of Israel in the Hebrew Bible. God was known to Israel by what He did in their history, uniquely by His entering into covenant relationship with them: "I am the LORD your **God, who brought you out** of the land of Egypt, out of the house of slavery" (Ex. 20:2). Thus, for the Hebrew mind to explore the subject of theology is to enter a dynamic realm, where life is lived and defined by God's involvement in day-to-day affairs. The Person of God can only be known in the context of relationship with His people. He is the God of Abraham, the God of Isaac and the God of Jacob, that is, the God who has revealed Himself in the personal stories of these men. He is not the God of speculative thought, or systematic theology: "He made known **His ways** to Moses, **His acts** to the people of Israel" (Ps. 103:7). OT theology is fundamentally historical theology. In the New Testament we observe God supremely in His words and miracles in His Son: "God was in Christ reconciling the world to Himself" (2 Cor. 5:18). The faith of Israel stands in contrast, then, to modern categories of speculative thought. As N.H. Snaith in his landmark book of the 20th century, *The Distinctive Ideas of the Old Testament,* puts it:

> The God of the Hebrews was essentially active in the world which He had made. We regard it to be of the utmost importance that this fact should be recognized throughout the whole of Old Testament theology. He was no static God in the sense of the philosophers. He was never thought of by the Hebrews as apart from the world, away in splendid isolation. Any such idea among the Hebrews was a

---

[33] Robert Hach, *Possession and Persuasion*, p. 17.

> development of very much later times, and belongs to the period when the Jews had been influenced by the speculations of the Greeks.[34]

Although God was holy and transcendent to the Hebrew, this did not mean He was remote or passive: "I am God, and not man: the Holy One **in your midst**" (Hosea 11:9). Indeed, He was "other" and unlike anybody else, whether "god" or "flesh," but Jehovah was also always the Living God who was involved in His world sovereignly, dynamically, here and now. Israel was called upon to respond to God's care and deliverance with faithfulness and gratitude, and to always remember and recite and confess His mighty words and deeds. The Bible's revelation of God, then, is simply how we may know what God has done in history and what He is doing in history, as revealed through His prophets, His apostles, and primarily through His Son.

This is perhaps a good reason, as Hach suggests, for rejecting the Western (in this case Latin) translation "spirit" for the more Hebrew understanding of "breath" (The Latin word *spiritus* does mean "breath" or even "wind.") When God spoke to His prophets and apostles it was *as if* He was breathing His message into them, possessing them by His word. To hear the message of the prophets and apostles, then, is to receive God's breath and presence into our lives. To say "God is breath" (rather than "God is spirit") is to put the emphasis back on the biblical notion that God is breathing His presence/spirit into our lives as we hear His word and believe in His work (particularly His word and work in Christ).

To appreciate the fundamental difference between the Hebrew and Hellenistic understanding of God is to recognize that the Bible does not discuss God's Being in metaphysical terms. The Hebrew way of revealing God is to employ *metaphors and not metaphysics.* God uses concrete everyday objects and ideas familiar to ordinary people to illustrate what is abstract and intangible about Himself. The One God must not be reduced to formulas and essences. Whilst it is true that "God is Spirit" we must not think this means He can be reduced to some kind of ethereal, impersonal metaphysical or mathematical formula/substance. God is not a "what." Therefore, we cannot divide three (Persons) by an Infinity (of "Spirit") and come up with one, as R.A. Torrey would like us to. This may be "a

---

[34] N.H. Snaith, *The Distinctive Ideas of the Old Testament,* p. 47.

perfectly satisfactory answer" as to how God can be three in one if we start with the assumption that God exists as such in His very Being, but this will not do when we are talking about the God of the Hebrew Bible. If I may let Robert Hach — whose insights on this subject I freely and thankfully acknowledge — have the last say:

> What God *is in-and-of-Godself* is beyond human comprehension and, therefore, not subject to revelation: no words exist to reveal God's literal *Being* beyond the fundamental Israelite confession of faith: "**Yahweh** our God, **Yahweh** is one" (Deut. 6:4; Mark 12:29). Beyond this, any attempt to describe God's *Being* in literal terms can only amount to theological nonsense, such as the incomprehensible inclusion of three Persons within one *Being,* the second Person of which *being* 100% God and 100% man. God only knows how many intelligent people have been led to reject Christian faith due to the ecclesiastical misrepresentation of God as a theological absurdity.[35]

Does It Really Matter?

So is it really that important whether we believe that God is one Person, or that He is three in one? At the end of the day is this just an academic question for theologians? Does what we believe about the Person of the God of the Bible make any practical difference? Consider the following.

• **Jesus Christ the founder of Christianity said it matters.** One day a certain scribe recognized in Jesus the wisdom of God. So he asked Jesus, "What commandment is the foremost of all?" (Mark 12:28). Jesus answered by giving the unitarian-monotheistic creed which had been recited and believed by Israel for over 1500 years. As already noted, it is called the *Shema Yisrael* and speaks of the unity of God. For Jesus, this is the unassailable revelation of Israel's God and of his God. This non-negotiable starting point for the recognition of the identity of the God of Israel was considered so fundamental that it must be taught to all children (Deut. 6:7). So according to Jesus, the founder of Christianity, the first and most important of all God's commandments: "Hear, O Israel; the LORD

---

[35] Robert Hach, in his paper "The Biblical Concept of Mediation," presented at Atlanta Bible College Theological Conference, 2005.

our God is one LORD; and you shall love the Lord your God with all your heart, and with all your soul, and with all your mind, and with all your strength" (Mark 12:29-30). According to Jesus himself the greatest truth in all the Bible, indeed in all the world, is the fact that "God is one." (Theologically speaking, this doctrine describes the unity of God.) We are to *hear* this, which is to say, pay attention, consider intelligently, and obey. What Jesus said was that Jehovah our God is one Jehovah. And "one" is that Hebrew word *echad* which means single, only, solitary. Jesus says nothing here about plurality in the One God. Surely if God is a tri-unity of Persons Jesus would have set the record straight. Here was Jesus' moment to launch the new doctrine of the tri-unity of God. Here was his chance to include himself in the Godhead: "Hear, O Church, the Lord your God is Three in One! You shall love God the Father, God the Son, God the Holy Spirit with all your heart!" But no, his creed is the faith of the prophets. His faith stands in the unitary monotheistic tradition of Israel. He confesses that Jehovah is one Lord. And you shall love *Him* with all your heart, and with all your understanding, and with all your strength. This truth is for Jesus the foundation of all divine revelation, "the foremost of all." This is Jesus Christ's central statement about the Being of God. God is one Jehovah, one Lord.

The careful reader will observe that when the scribe repeated Jesus' statement, he did so in a slightly different way. The scribe said (depending on which Greek text is used) "Right, teacher, you have truly stated that **God** is one" or "You have truly stated that **He** is one." In other words, when both Jesus and the scribe refer to Israel's God "Lord" and "God" are synonyms. This is important, because some have the erroneous idea that Deuteronomy 6:4 says there is one Lord (YHWH, Jehovah) but not that there is one God (*elohim*), thus asserting that there can be more than one individual God within one "family name" of Jehovah. However, this dialogue between Jesus and the scribe proves both believed Israel's God was just one Individual, the Lord God, and He is the one true Jehovah (YHWH). We may well ask, if this is the central and first commandment for the founder of Christianity, is it our confession too? Jesus' creed was Israel's unitarian creed. At stake here is the question of obedience to Christ. If our God is not the God of the Hebrew Bible, the God of our Lord Jesus Christ, we are floundering in the chaos of belief in another God. Jesus repeats and endorses the same cardinal truth that Moses had laid down as the heart of all religion. Thus, by making this the most important and first of all commandments, Jesus has made faith in the one true God, the Father of Jesus, essential to the Gospel. We cannot afford to be wrong about this greatest of all commandments.

Whenever man refuses to accept God's plain language and revelation of Himself and resorts to philosophy to describe Him, he weaves a complicated web. Compare the simplicity of Jesus' creed with the complexity of those who endeavour to "explain" the Trinity. A certain William Beveridge was an orthodox Anglican bishop of the 17th century and spoke for many when he complained about the impossible complexities of the Trinitarian view of God. The bishop says:

> We are to consider the order of those persons in the Trinity described in the words before us in Matthew 28:19. First, the Father and then the Son and then the Holy Ghost; every one of which is truly God. This is a mystery which we are all bound to believe, but yet must exercise great care in how we speak of it, it being both easy and dangerous to err in expressing so great a truth as this is. If we think of it, how hard it is to imagine one numerically divine *nature* in more than one and the same divine *person.* Or three divine persons in no more than one and the same divine nature. If we speak of it, how hard it is to find out words to express it. If I say, the Father, Son and Holy Ghost be three, and every one a distinct God, it is false. I may say, God the Father is one God, and the Son is one God, and the Holy Ghost is one God, but I cannot say that the Father is one God and the Son is another God and the Holy Ghost is a third God. I may say that the Father begat another who is God; yet I cannot say that He begat another God. I may say that from the Father and Son there proceeds another who is God; yet I cannot say that from the Father and Son there proceeds another God. For though their nature be the same their persons are distinct; and though their persons be distinct, yet still their nature is the same. So that, though the Father be the first person in the Godhead, the Son the second and the Holy Ghost the third, yet the Father is not the first, the Son the second and the Holy Ghost a third God. So hard a thing is it to word so great a mystery aright; or to fit so high a truth

> with expressions suitable and proper to it, without going one way or another from it.[36]

How complicated we have made it. After reading statements like this, returning to Jesus' creed that "God is One" is (we think) like breathing clean, fresh air. Let us briefly look at how central this creed was to Jesus' whole life and walk with his God and Father.

No One but God Is Good

One day a "rich young ruler" came to Jesus and asked him, "Good teacher, what must I do to inherit eternal life?" (Luke 18:18). Jesus replied, "Why do you call me good? No one is good except God alone" (v. 19). The traditional explanation I was taught is that Jesus stops this young man right in his tracks because he needed to realize that Jesus really was God. It is as if Jesus said, "Don't you realize who I am? I am God Himself. Don't call Me 'good' without remembering this. Recognize who it is you are talking to!" Sound a bit strained? Whilst admitting that Jesus' reply is difficult I think there is a better explanation. Jesus was saying that he himself is not God. This is the natural, obvious sense so let's look at it in more detail.

The word for "good" here is the Greek word *agathos*. It is an adjective which according to one lexicon properly refers to "inner excellence."[37] When used of God it refers to the fact that He is completely, perfectly, and essentially good.[38] Jesus says that only God is *agathos* or good. It refers to God's holiness, His "otherness," that which sets Him apart from all of His creation. On the practical level it means that God cannot help being good, God cannot sin, nor can He even be tempted to sin. God alone is "incorruptible" and immortal (1 Tim. 1:17).

On the other hand, *Jesus rejects for himself the description agathos,* that inner quality of perfection which belongs only to God. "*In essence he rejects this divine attribute of holiness* and, on the

---

[36] Bishop Beveridge, *Private Thoughts,* part 2, pp. 48-49, cited by Charles Morgridge, *The True Believer's Defence Against Charges Preferred by Trinitarians for Not Believing in the Deity of Christ,* Boston: B. Green, 1837, p. 16.

[37] G. Abbott-Smith, *A Manual Greek Lexicon of the New Testament,* third ed., Edinburgh: T & T Clark, 1950, p. 2.

[38] Joseph Henry Thayer, *A Greek-English Lexicon of the New Testament,* New York: American Book Company, 1889, p. 2.

negative side, *he rejects incorruptibility*."[39] This means that Jesus was a real human being and had the option of being either good or bad. Jesus' temptations were real; he could have succumbed and failed. For he was not *agathos*, not good, not God in the absolute sense of the word. This means that he was liable to corruption (Acts 2:27). But it also means that his victories were real. The Bible teaches that Jesus learned obedience (Heb. 5:8). God the Father has never had to learn goodness.

Truly, there was a certain goodness that Jesus did possess. His was a goodness unique in human history. We know that he "increased [grew] in wisdom, in stature, and in favour with God and with man" (Luke 2:52). This was the sinless goodness that had been possible for Adam, originally. This is the goodness that qualified him to be the Good Shepherd who gave his life as a sacrifice for us. But the word describing him as "the Good Shepherd" (John 10:11) is a different Greek word, *kalos,* meaning morally excellent and worthy of recognition.[40] This (second) type of goodness certainly describes our Saviour.

So what does all of this mean? Evidently when the young man addressed Jesus as "good teacher" Jesus took offence. His response indicates a rebuke in fact: "Why do you call me good? No one is good, except God alone." (The crucial phrase *ei me heis ho theos* may also be translated "but the one God," which is a strong unitary monotheistic affirmation from Jesus' lips: "No one is good but the one God.") As the Trinitarian Raymond E. Brown affirms, "the text strongly distinguishes between Jesus and God, and that a description of himself to which Jesus objected was applicable to God. From this text one would never suspect that the evangelist referred to Jesus as God."[41] Surely we do not honour the Lord Jesus when we attribute to him what he himself rejected and what belongs only to his Father in heaven? If confirmation that this is the correct interpretation is sought, then we need only turn to Revelation 15. After his resurrection and ascension into heaven Jesus is seen leading the worship directed to God his Father. All the victorious saints of God sing "the song of Moses, the bond-servant of God, and **the song of**

---

[39] Sidney Hatch, *Brief Bible Studies,* vol. 23, no. 1, 1992.

[40] *A Critical Lexicon and Concordance,* second ed., revised, London: Longmans, Green & Co. 1886, p. 336.

[41] Raymond Brown, *An Introduction to New Testament Christology,* New York: Paulist Press, 1994, p. 174.

the Lamb, saying, 'Great and marvellous are Your works, O LORD God, the Almighty...Who will not fear, O LORD, and glorify Your Name? For **You alone are holy**" (v. 3-4). Even now in heaven the Lord Jesus' confession is that his Father "alone" is holy. As the Lamb of God, Jesus still worships God his Father as the only one who is good! Only his Father, the Lord God Almighty, is the source of all moral excellence. How much better to agree with our Lord Jesus and confess that there is only one who is good, that is God. Jesus rejects the identification of himself with the one true and good God.

The Father Is the Only True God

Right at the end of his life, in the shadows of Gethsemane Jesus is praying to his Father. Listen to his own confession of faith: "And this is eternal life, that they may know You, the only true God, and Jesus Christ whom You have sent" (John 17:3).

Once again, according to the founder of Christianity, his Father is "the only true God." "Only" means single, solitary, unique, one of a kind. "True" means real, genuine. According to Jesus himself, his Father is the only genuine God. There is no other God in His class. As for himself, Jesus claims simply to be the Christ, that is the Messiah whom God has sent. It is a sad fact of history that Augustine found this verse so problematic that he proposed altering the text to read, "That they may know Thee *and* Jesus Christ, whom Thou hast sent, as the only true God." So with sublime and arbitrary authority Augustine shoehorns Jesus into being the second member of the Trinity! Commenting on John 17:3 Augustine wrote:

> Consequently, therefore, the Holy Spirit is also understood, because He is the Spirit of the Father and Son, as the substantial and consubstantial love of both. For the Father and Son are not two Gods, nor are the Father and Son and Holy Spirit three Gods; *but the Trinity itself is the one only true God.* And yet the Father is not the same as the Son, nor the Son the same as the Father, nor the Holy Spirit the same as the Father and the Son; for the Father and Son and Holy Spirit are three [persons], yet the Trinity itself is one God. If, then, the Son glorifies Thee in the same manner "as Thou hast given Him power over all flesh," and hast so given, "that He should give eternal life to all that Thou hast given Him," and "this is life eternal, that they may know Thee," in

> this way, therefore, the Son glorifies thee, that He makes Thee known to all whom Thou hast given Him.[42]

So, according to Augustine, Jesus did not have the right word order when he prayed. Augustine tragically takes it upon himself to correct our Lord Jesus! But on another occasion Augustine wrote: "If you believe what you like in the Gospel, and you reject what you like, it is not the Gospel you believe, but yourself." Pity he did not stick to his own convictions. Well, take your pick. Who will you follow? Augustine? Or Jesus your Lord and the founder of his Church? The Trinity is the one true God? Or the Father is the only true God? Jesus himself was not a Trinitarian, for to him the Father is "the only true God." This is not just a matter of semantics, for according to Jesus Christ to "know" his Father as the only true God and to know Jesus Christ whom that One God has sent is "eternal life." As for Jesus, he identifies himself as "Jesus Christ" whom God has sent. "Jesus Christ" is not a first and last name, as for example John Smith. It is a proper name and a title. It tells us that Jesus is the Messiah, for the title "Christ" is the Greek word for the Hebrew title "Messiah." Entrance into the life of the Age to Come hinges on knowing that Jesus is the Messiah whom the one true God the Father has "sent."

Some have argued that the word "sent" implies that Jesus existed in heaven prior to his coming. But the Bible also says that John the Baptist was "sent" from God (John 1:6). This does not mean that John came down from heaven or preexisted his birth in any form; just that he was commissioned by God. When Paul wrote, "when the fullness of the time came, God sent forth His Son, born of a woman, born under the Law" (Gal. 4:4) we are to understand the concept of sending as that of divine commissioning for his unique Messianic work. The sending of the Son:

> must be seen against the background of the prophets whom God sent before that. The idea is then that God is no longer satisfied with a prophet, but that he sends his own son who is greater than the prophets. Does he send him from heaven? This is not mentioned even once...On the contrary, the son who is sent was born under the law, i.e. at a moment when the Torah was already in force...What Paul writes about the

---

[42] *Homilies on John.*

> sending of the son can in no way be understood of a situation preceding the beginning of history.[43]

Thus Jesus is the Messiah, the anointed or commissioned Son sent to reveal the one true God. According to Jesus, entering the life of the Age to Come depends on this knowledge. Of course, it does not just mean a knowledge with no subsequent action and change of lifestyle. Not just a mental assent to the central truth that the Father of Jesus is the one true God and that Jesus is His commissioned Messiah who is destined to rule that new world order. No. It means to love this God with all our heart, to live for His glory alone, and to honour His Son by our faith and obedience.

What practical difference does it make to believe in the personal unity of God? According to Jesus himself it means we can love God with all our hearts. We can have a warm, personal, loving, true and intimate relationship with Him through Jesus the Messiah. It is hard to love a philosophical abstraction. Right here is the root cause of much of Christianity's practical failure over the last two thousand years. Theology has erected a barrier between God and His people. Surely there is the great need today to return to the simple creed, the unitary and uniting creed that God our Father is One, and that Jesus is His Messiah sent to bring us into the life of the Age to Come? This brings us to the second part of Jesus' discussion with that scribe in Mark 12.

• **There is clearly a very practical connection between loving the one God and loving our neighbour as ourselves.** The second part of the greatest commandment is "You shall love your neighbour as yourself" (Mark 12:31). The scribe is impressed with Jesus' answer and affirms it: "Right, teacher, you have truly stated that He is One; and there is no one else besides Him; and to love Him with all the heart and with all the understanding and with all the strength, and to love one's neighbour as himself, is much more than all burnt offerings and sacrifices" (v. 32-33). Jesus states that "There is no other commandment greater than these" (v. 31). This scribe who came to Jesus asked a straight question and Jesus gave him a straight, honest answer. To love the one true God is a unifying experience. But man-made theology has made it difficult to know God and love Him. To say that three are one, and one is three, is a philosophical abstraction which divides the unity of God. No man

---

[43] Kuschel, *Born Before All Time?* pp. 274-275.

understands it. Nor does God ask us to believe it. But we can love a personal God and we can love our fellow man. The sad history of not loving the Father as the only true God has been the Church's failure to properly love the world. There is a definite connection and divinely revealed sequence here. First, know that God is one. Second, love *Him* with our whole being. Third, love our neighbour as ourselves.

The Bible teaches that all forms of social injustice, such as murder, adultery, theft, lying and cheating, mistreatment of parents and of children, are the result of not loving the one God with all one's heart. To love and honour the true God is to have deep respect for His creation. One of the purposes stated in the book of Revelation for God's ultimate judgment to be meted out on this unbelieving world is to "destroy those who destroy the earth" (Rev. 11:18). The wise man observed that it is the righteous man who has regard for his animals (Prov. 12:10). And according to the apostle Paul our social ills are the result of our theological muddle and failure, because "ungodliness" always precedes "unrighteousness" (Rom. 1:18). Sin will always find opportunity when men do not remain faithful to the one true God of Israel. This is simply to say that man's worship of false gods, that is idolatry, is at heart unfaithfulness to the God of the Bible. The result will always be failure to love God's world and our fellow man. The history of our failure to do this is testimony enough as to how much we have misunderstood the first and the second great commandments. The worship of a false god has brought nothing but disunity all round.

• There is another Scriptural reason why believing that God is one is far more than just a matter of mental correctness. According to the Bible, this great truth will be **the fundamental doctrine in the Age to Come.** When the Lord Jesus returns to earth in the glory of his Father the world will experience sweeping changes of a spiritual (religious) nature, as well as physical (environmental) and political changes. According to a remarkable prophecy in Zechariah 14:9 there will be a universal recognition of the unity of God's person: "The LORD will be king over all the earth; in that day the LORD will be the only one [*echad*], and His name the only one."

In the day when the Lord Jesus comes back to earth Jehovah will be recognized as one, and His name one. *The Interpreter's Bible,* commenting on this passage, says that when the Kingdom of God is established over all the earth, "the Jewish confession of faith, the Shema of Deuteronomy 6:4, will become the universal creed."[44] As we have seen, Deuteronomy 6:4 is the foundation creed of the faith of Israel and of Jesus himself. Once again we come across the Hebrew word *echad* meaning "one." If we look at verse 7, just two verses before this remarkable prediction of verse 9, we have the word *echad* again. This verse is translated: "For it will be **a unique** day which is known to the LORD." Here *echad,* the word for "one," is actually translated "unique." Just two verses down in verse 9 it has exactly the same meaning when describing who will then be the unique God. We read that in that *unique* day "the LORD will be the only one, and His name the only one." In the Messiah's Kingdom the LORD who is Jehovah will be "unique," the only one of His kind.

Trinitarianism, the idea that God is three in one, is a post-Biblical development which finally became the creed of the fourth-century Church. It was a part of the apostasy that developed from the second century on, finally reaching creedal status under Constantine. But when Christ returns the world will return to the foundational doctrine that "God is One." Zechariah 14:9 predicts that the *Shema* will be the fundamental creed of the Age to Come. The other creeds of Christendom will be swept away!

One of the heroes of the Reformation, a truly great martyr of Christian history and a man who emphasized the oneness of God, was Francis David of Transylvania. Ordered by King Stephen Bathory, the prince of the land, not to preach again in his pulpit, Francis David defied the royal edict, and closed what turned out to be his final sermon by saying in effect, "Whatever men may say, some day it will become clear to all the world that God is one." Francis David was tried for heresy and condemned to "perpetual imprisonment." He died five months later in a nearby castle dungeon. One of the Calvinist ministers present at David's trial made a long speech urging the king to impose the death penalty, and threatening him with the wrath of God if he failed to do so.

Does it make any difference whether or not we confess the oneness of God today? Definitely, because by this faith we prove that we are the sons of that coming age. Those who claim to be seeking the glory of His coming Kingdom surely should be promoting the ideals of that age now. For there is coming a day

---

[44] *The Interpreter's Bible,* VI, p. 1112.

when the Lord Jesus "delivers up the kingdom to the God and Father...and then the Son himself also will be subjected to the One who subjected all things to him, that God may be all in all" (1 Cor. 15:24, 28). Most evangelical Christians have a keen interest in Bible prophecy. But I have heard little mention of the future worldwide recognition of the unity and uniqueness of God's Person. This is surely a neglected aspect of end-times prophecy!

• **For the sake of Christ's Gospel** we should remove this unbiblical doctrine. The world is deeply divided over who God is. The difficulties our human race faces are firstly religious. Millions of Jews and over a billion Muslims are repulsed by this strange teaching that God is three in one. It creates a barrier and a stumbling block to these precious folk coming to a true knowledge of the God of the Bible. One of the recurring themes in the Koran is that no "partners" should be set alongside Allah, for "your God is one God" (Sura 16:1, 22). The Koran holds up Abraham as "indeed a model, devoutly obedient to Allah, and true in faith, and he joined not gods with Allah" (Surah 16:120). Islam was a historical reaction to the idolatry of the Roman Catholic Church of the post-Nicene days. But Islam's main bone of contention was the Church's insistence that three co-equal Persons comprise the one God.

The same holds true for Jews. To them the belief that Jesus of Nazareth crucified and resurrected is not only the Messiah but also of the same substance as God "seems to be something radically un-Jewish; they feel it to be something which utterly contradicts strict monotheism, particularly as expressed in the 'Shema Yisrael' which pious Jews say every day, indeed to be blasphemy."[45] Surely there is urgent need to rethink how the Bible speaks of Jesus as the Son of God in order to remove valid Jewish objections to the Gospel. It is not surprising that the "fruit" of a theology presenting a multi-personal God is failure to gain an audience with millions whose fundamental belief is that God is one.

• Finally, under this heading as to whether it makes any difference whether we believe in the Trinity or not, I would say that the Bible very plainly teaches that **apostolic Christianity insists on a right understanding of God for salvation.** I cannot do any better than Buzzard and Hunting here:

---

[45] Kuschel, *Born Before All Time?* p. 514.

> One of the most devastating concepts to invade the modern Church is that a person's beliefs are insignificant as long as he loves God and his neighbour. After all, do not all versions of religion promote worship of the same God? The plain biblical fact is that Scripture insists on truth, as distinct from error, as the basis of worship and salvation itself. Paul expressly linked salvation to a correct understanding of the identity of God and Jesus: "This is good and acceptable in the sight of God our Saviour, who desires all people **to be saved and to come to the knowledge of the truth**. For there is one God and one mediator between God and men, the man Messiah Jesus" (1 Tim. 2:3-5). The connection between correct, i.e., biblically orthodox belief and salvation is inescapable here, as also in Paul's statements in which "belief in the truth" is starkly contrasted with being wicked, and where salvation depends on receiving "the love of the truth" (2 Thess. 2:10-13).[46]

One of the agonizing challenges I wrestle with, even long after coming to the knowledge that the God of the Bible is one, not three, is this: What about the vast majority of Christians who sincerely believe in the Trinity? I was once one of them, a committed believer in the Bible. I believed that Jesus Christ is co-equal and co-eternal with God the Father. More than that, I loved "the eternal Son." And anybody who did not so confess him, was, I sincerely believed, in a perilous position before God. So, how will God deal with those who are sincere, but sincerely deceived? I admit this is still a perplexing question to me. But according to the present light I have, what I can say is that "the Judge of all the earth" will do the right and the fair thing by every single person who has ever lived (Gen. 18:25). I can also say, on the authority of Scripture, that there is no salvation, no right standing before God and therefore no entrance into His everlasting Kingdom outside of Christ Jesus (Acts 4:12). Jesus the Messiah alone is God's authorized agent of salvation. All other names and authorities are deceivers, liars and thieves (John 10:1-15). There are "many false Christs" that can even work signs and wonders, "so as to mislead, if possible, even the elect" (Matt. 24:24) and there are other gospels whose exponents risk God's curse (Gal. 1:8-9).

---

[46] Buzzard and Hunting, *The Doctrine of the Trinity,* p. 299.

Evidently, more than sincerity is required. If sincerity is the criterion for entrance into the Kingdom of God, then those extremist Muslims who strap bombs to themselves and blow innocents up in the belief they are going straight to the paradise of God, will be saved. There are none more sincere in their belief in God than the martyrs. If sincerity is the criterion for salvation, then those devotees of idols in the Hindu faith will also be acceptable. It will, of course, be countered that these last two groups should not be compared with the Christian who believes that Jesus is the Way and that his blood and resurrection have secured everlasting redemption for them, even though they believe in an unscriptural "God-man" by the name of Jesus. What if that Jesus is "another Jesus" not commissioned by the Father? (2 Cor. 11:4). What if that Jesus is an idol, a creation of man's imagination, no different in essence from any other man-made likeness? What if that Jesus is, to use John's language, an "antichrist" (1 John 4:2-3)?

After all, the R.A. Torreys and the Martyn Lloyd-Jones and the J.I. Packers *et al* of the Church were all godly men, committed to the honour of God, and whose lives clearly demonstrate a holiness and beauty that reflects the glory of God. Surely these sincere people are saved? This is the point that causes me consternation. The only thing I can fall back on is that "the firm foundation of God stands, having this seal, 'The Lord knows those who are His,' and, 'Let everyone who names the name of the Lord abstain from wickedness'" (2 Tim. 2:19). God knows His own. And His own evidently are only the ones who, having learned the apostolic teaching, remain in it, for "anyone who goes too far and does not abide in the teaching of Christ, does not have God" (2 John 9).

There is the perception out there in "church world" that anybody who does not believe in the Trinity and anybody who does not confess that Jesus is the Lord God of the OT is lost forever, with no hope of ever entering the Kingdom of Heaven. Since writing the first edition of this book I have been often interrogated, "Do you seriously think unitarian monotheists will enter the Kingdom of God?" My answer is that I will be in very good company in that Kingdom. After all, Moses, a believer in the unitary Being of God, will be there (Deut. 6:4)! David, who knew the difference between the one Lord God and the Lord Messiah will be there (Ps. 110:1)! Isaiah, Jeremiah, Daniel and all the faithful prophets, who knew that the God of Israel was one Lord, not three, will be there! The apostles who knew nothing of a mysterious and unrevealed Trinity will be there in that Kingdom. And above all, Jesus himself, the founder of Christianity who confessed that his Father is "the only true God," will be there! (John 17:3). As a believer that God is one Person, one Lord, I will be in very good company.

If the believer is in the process of being saved, then we are all growing in our level of understanding. Thank God we will not be saved when we come to a full and perfect understanding of all doctrines. On that criterion none of us would enter that glorious Kingdom. We are all started on the journey of faith. We all now see only "dimly, but then face to face. Now we know in part, but then we shall know fully" (1 Cor. 13:12). However, there will be no Trinitarian believers in the Kingdom. They will have all been converted to see as Zechariah the prophet predicts, "The LORD will be king over all the earth; in that day the LORD will be the only one, and His name the only one" (Zech. 14:9). In Messiah's Kingdom, the LORD who is his God and Father will be universally recognized in His unique and matchless glory as the one and only true God. (Cf. 1 Cor. 15:28: "When all things are subjected to Him [i.e. God the Father] then the Son himself also will be subjected to the One who subjected all things to him, so that God may be all in all.")

Belief in the Trinity necessary for salvation? Hardly. If the doctrine of the Trinity were true, and required to be believed for salvation itself, it may be pointed out that it is utterly unique in the sense that all other essential Christian doctrines *are* taught plainly in the Bible, whereas the Trinity is somehow humanly constructed and "derived from all of what the Bible teaches." This means we are being asked to accept a teaching that would be the only non-articulated, unannounced doctrine of the Christian faith, based on a human construction of Scripture! Evidently, Trinitarians actually do believe, and ultimately have to defend, the idea that the Bible does not have to be specific about certain, essential Christian doctrines!

From cover to cover the unanimous revelation of the Bible is that truth matters. It is necessary to "receive the love of the truth so as to be saved" (2 Thess. 2:10). God is the God "who desires all men to be saved and to come to the knowledge of the truth. For there is one God, and one mediator also between God and men, the man Christ Jesus" (1 Tim. 2:4-5). For Paul, salvation is coming to know the truth — here defined as knowing the "one God" and the one mediator who is "the man Messiah Jesus." This is precisely the confession of Jesus himself that eternal life is to "know You, the only who is truly God, and Jesus Messiah whom You have sent" (John 17:3). Inextricably woven throughout Old and New Testaments is the united witness that we must know this One God and His Son Jesus the Messiah. There are not many different ways of being saved. There are not many roads that lead to the God of the Bible. The one God says that no matter how well-meaning we may be, we are not at liberty to invent our own path to His throne. Cain tried it in the very beginning and God rejected him (Gen. 4:5). To fail here is to invite division, paganism and polytheism which is the enemy of truth and freedom as history has shown.

Perhaps as you have read the last few pages you can see how I have agonized over this challenging question: "What about the vast majority of Christians who sincerely believe in the Trinity?" It has not been an easy one for me, but of one thing I am absolutely sure. Trinitarians who insist that the God of the Bible is a "Tri-Unity" *do not sound like Jesus who himself was not a Trinitarian!* God for Jesus was only and always the Father, the single Yahweh God of the OT. To speak of this Personal God in the Trinitarian language of being an "essence" or a "substance" is contrary to Jesus' language, not to mention being contrary to logic, for a substance is not a "he" but an "it"! "So," as Chang notes, "Trinitarianism has reduced 'God' to an 'it'...The church needs to return to Yahweh and put an end to all distortions of the concept of God. Only so can we be delivered from the evil of falsehood and return to the truth which can only be found in Yahweh."[47] Or, as Anthony Buzzard succinctly states in his latest book, if Jesus provides us with the only right definition of God then "Abandoning the creed of Jesus must amount to abandoning him."[48] Surely it is high time we abandoned our own theology and returned to the unitary monotheism of the one we say we follow? Or at least be honest enough to admit we have a different God from the One Jesus knew and loved!

If we may let our Lord and King have the final word here, he plainly says, "The **true worshippers shall worship the Father** in spirit and truth; for such people the Father seeks to be His

---

[47] Chang, *The Only True God*, p. 391-392

[48] Anthony Buzzard, *Jesus Was Not a Trinitarian,* Restoration Fellowship, 2007, p. 61.

worshippers. God is spirit; and those who worship Him **must worship in spirit and truth**" (John 4:23-24). Who does Jesus declare are the "true worshippers"? He insists, "The true worshippers shall worship the **Father**..." If we would be amongst the true worshippers we must with Jesus worship his Father. Evidently, those who worship "God the Father, God the Son and God the Holy Ghost, three Persons in one God," are not said by Jesus to be the true worshippers. Those who worship the Father as the "only true God" are. The worshipper of the One God, the Father, has Jesus' own affirmation that he is the true worshipper.

This is the Biblical pattern throughout. The so-called Lord's prayer, the model prayer, teaches us to "pray **in this way**: Our **Father** who art in heaven..." (Matt. 6:9). This pattern of prayer and worship prescribed by our Lord Jesus is followed and sanctioned by *every example given in Scripture.* See the following:

"Now may the God who gives perseverance and encouragement grant you to be of the same mind with one another **according to Christ Jesus**; that with one accord you may with one voice **glorify the God and Father** of our Lord Jesus Christ" (Rom. 15:5-6).

"For this reason, **I bow my knees before the Father**" (Eph. 3:14).

"Always giving thanks for all things in the name of our Lord Jesus Christ **to God, even the Father**" (Eph. 5:20).

"Now **to our God and Father** be the glory forever and ever. Amen" (Phil. 4:20).

"We give thanks **to God, the Father** of our Lord Jesus Christ, praying always for you" (Col. 1:3).

"Giving thanks **to the Father**" (Col. 1:12).

"And whatever you do in word or deed, do all in the name of the Lord Jesus [i.e. according to his teaching and authority], giving thanks through him **to God the Father**" (Col. 3:17).

This list is by no means exhaustive. But it is sufficient to show that we are, with our Lord Jesus, to worship and pray to the *Father*. This is the usual pattern of prayer and worship in the New Testament. They prayed to the One God through the name or authority of Jesus Christ. They evidently were not aware that the Holy Spirit was God (a third Person), for where in all the pages of the Bible do the saints pray to the Holy Spirit? And where in all the pages of Scripture do the worshippers of God sing to the Holy Spirit as is the general custom within Christendom today? Were the New

Testament worshippers ignorant Christians? Or were they perhaps better informed as to who the true worshippers are whom the Father is seeking? You might ask, what about those passages where the Lord Jesus is worshipped? Or where the Lord Jesus is prayed to? Surely this is proof positive that Jesus is God because only God is to be worshipped? (The words of Jesus are often used to substantiate this belief: "You shall worship the Lord your God, and serve Him only" (Matt. 4:10), as though Jesus meant: "I am the LORD your God, worship Me only." But this meaning is totally incongruous and has no parallel in the NT record.) Then, of course, there is God the Father's own directive to the angels concerning Jesus the Son of God: "And let all the angels of God worship him" (Heb. 1:6). The fact that Jesus is worshipped by Thomas as he falls at his feet and honours him with the confession, "My Lord and my God!" to many presents the final proof that Jesus is God (John 20:28).

To all of this there is a very simple solution. Once again it comes back to a failure to understand Bible culture; a failure to read the Bible through Hebrew eyes. In the Old Testament the main Hebrew word for worship is *shachah.* It occurs about 170 times but the surprising thing is that only about half this number relate to the worship of God as God. This fact is hidden in our English translations. The translators prefer to say "bow down to" or "revere" when *shachah* refers to homage paid to noble persons, whether angels or men, but say "worship" when God is the object. This is a false distinction the original text does not support. Here are just a few examples:

Lot "worshipped" the two strangers who looked like normal travellers as they entered Sodom (Gen. 19:1).

Abraham "worshipped" the Gentile leaders of the land where he lived (Gen. 23:7).

Jacob "worshipped" his older brother Esau (Gen. 33:3).

Joseph's brothers "worshipped" him (Gen. 43:26).

Ruth "worshipped" Boaz (Ruth 2:10).

David "worshipped" Jonathan (1 Sam. 20:41).

David "worshipped" King Saul (1 Sam. 24:8).

Mephibosheth fell on his face and "worshipped" David (2 Sam. 9:6).

Abigail "worshipped" David the outlaw (1 Sam. 25:23, 41).

The whole congregation "worshipped" the king (1 Chron. 9:20).

These are just a few instances of the many that could be cited to show the reluctance of the translators to consistently translate *shachah* as "worship" when worship of important persons was obviously a common feature of Hebrew culture. In Scripture worship is offered to God and to men. There is no special word in the OT for "worship" reserved exclusively for God. But there is a reluctance to translate this one word consistently. If you look up your English translations of the above verses you will find they do not use the "w" word. They prefer to say "bowed down" or "revered" or "paid homage to" instead of "worshipped." This inconsistency of translation has created the false impression that only God can be worshipped.

So then, how do we explain this in light of the clear command that we are to worship God the Father alone as both the first commandment and Jesus himself command? Is this a contradiction after all? No way. The answer is that whenever men "worshipped" other men it was a *relative* worship. In most of the examples above it is clear that the ones worshipped were God's representatives. Once again we are back to the principle of Jewish agency. The Israelites had no difficulty in offering this proportional or *relative* worship to the ones who came in God's Name, with God's message. It is obvious that the first commandment "You must not bow yourself down [*shachah*] to them nor serve them" is *not* a prohibition against a *relative* worship of those worthy of it. If this was the case then obviously all these OT godly men and women sinned greatly. God even promises a coming day when He will make our enemies "to come and worship at your feet, and to know that I have loved you" (Rev. 3:9). Such worship of the saints at God's decree is clearly a relative and proportional worship. It is perfectly legitimate to give honour to whom honour is due. This is why many Jews felt no impropriety in "worshipping" Jesus in the Gospels because they recognized him as a prophet of God, or the Messiah sent from God. But it is preposterous to think these good people believed Jesus was Jehovah God just because they worshipped him. When they saw and heard the mighty works of Jesus they glorified God through him (Matt. 9:8; 11:27; 28:18; Luke 7:16; 9:11; 10:22). This fits the whole of the New Testament teaching that it is God the Father who is to receive glory through His Son Jesus (Eph. 1:3, 6, 12; 1 Pet. 1:3; Heb. 13:15, etc.). Christ's exaltation is the means to a higher end. For through him all worship is ultimately directed to his God and Father. To worship him as the Lord Messiah is thus a divinely pleasing but subordinated or *relative* worship. It is instructive to read that in the coming Kingdom the Lord Jesus will orchestrate the worship of his brethren in the ultimate praise of his Father. He will "proclaim" the Name of God to his "brothers" and he will "in the midst of the congregation sing Your praise" (Heb. 2:12). There, in that glorious Kingdom, Jesus Christ will continue to be a joyful worshipper of God his Father. There he worships the Father as the LORD God who alone is good and holy (Rev. 15:3-4). Thus, the one God and Father is alone worshipped *absolutely.* All other divinely appointed worship is homage to persons who are not God Himself. Jesus is among those worthy of such worship for he is worshipped as the one Messiah, God's supreme Son and agent.

What the first commandment warns against is the worship of any rival gods or false representatives of those rival gods. This the LORD cannot tolerate. This is why Jesus refused homage to the Devil when he was offered the kingdoms of this world. This is why Jesus accepted Thomas' worship because Jesus knew God's decree respecting the Messiah. Jesus knew the prophecy: "Worship the LORD with reverence, and...do homage to the Son" (Ps. 2:11-12). Jesus knew God his Father had decreed "Let all the angels of God worship him" (Ps. 97:7). Jesus knew that the angelic messengers of Jehovah had in the past received *relative* worship from God-pleasing men and women. Jesus knew that agents of the one true God could be addressed as though they were God. And Jesus knew he was the Son and ultimate agent of God, so how much greater his dignity! As the "only begotten Son" whom the Father had "sealed" and commissioned he knew that whoever honoured him honoured the Father also. This was his Father's decree (see Ps. 2:11-12; 97:7). And Jesus said that he who had seen the Son had seen the Father.

Thomas' Worship of the Risen Jesus as "My Lord and My God"

This is why Jesus did not rebuke Thomas when he fell at his feet and worshipped the risen Lord. Not because Jesus knew himself to be Jehovah God and this fact had finally dawned on Thomas. Rather, it was homage proffered to Jesus as God's ordained Messiah. Jesus can be worshipped as the Lord Messiah. In fact, this is clearly what the writer John means by reporting this incident, for the very next two verses say that these things "**have been written**

that you may believe that Jesus is the Christ (Messiah), the Son of God; and that believing you may have life in his name" (John 20:31). To say that Thomas was worshipping Jesus as Almighty God is to directly contradict John's own stated purpose for writing his whole Gospel. When Thomas fell at Jesus' feet and worshipped him, Thomas was at last recognizing that the resurrected Jesus was the long-promised Lord Messiah. Thomas' language was steeped in OT concepts. Remember when David stepped out of the cave and called to king Saul, "My lord and my king" (1 Sam. 24:9)? In the same way King Messiah is to be worshipped and adored by his bride: "Then **the king** will desire your beauty; because he is **your Lord,** bow down to him" (Ps. 45:11). Thomas' language is in the same Hebrew tradition. He means the same thing. Thomas is addressing the rightful king of Israel, the now risen and victorious Lord. We just have to think like first-century Jews steeped in their OT prophets! "A saviour has been born for you who is **Messiah and Lord**" (Luke 2:11). The wise men believed the infant Jesus was the king of Israel. They brought their gifts of gold, frankincense and myrrh to worship him: "'Where is the one who has been born **king of the Jews**? We saw his star in the east and have come to **worship him'**...They bowed down and worshiped him" (Matt. 2:2, 11). "God has made him both **Lord and Messiah**, this Jesus whom you crucified" (Acts 2:36). Worship is offered to Jesus because he is the Messiah, the Son of God, the king of Israel. We have already seen that in Jewish understanding, the word "God" can refer to one who represents the Almighty God (Ex. 7:1, etc.). The king of Israel could be called "god" because he represented God to the people. Thomas knew the Old Testament prophecies that the Messiah was to be called "god," for he was to represent Jehovah perfectly. Thomas' worship was that of a Jew deeply grounded in the Old Testament faith that God is one Jehovah and that the Messiah is also called "god" in a relative and royal rather than an absolute sense. Psalm 45:7 says of the Messiah, "You have loved righteousness, and hated wickedness; therefore God, **your God**, has anointed you with the oil of joy above your fellows."

Evidently this anointed one has a God above him: Jehovah is his God. Come to think of it, isn't this what Jesus himself said just a few verses before he received Thomas' worship? "Stop clinging to me; for I have not yet ascended to the Father; but go to my brethren, and say to them, 'I ascend to my Father and your Father, and **my God** and your God'" (John 20:17).

Exalted in heaven right now Jesus *still* calls the LORD God Almighty "**my God**" and "my Father" (see Rev. 3:2, 5, 12). The LORD God is still called "**his God** and Father" (Rev. 1:6). In the Revelation there is always "our God" and "His Christ" (Rev. 12:10; 20:6) or "the Lord God, the Almighty, and the Lamb" (Rev. 6:16; 21:22; 22:1, 3). Yes, in good Hebrew understanding, Thomas' worship preserves this Biblical distinction:

Lord and Messiah = Lord and king = Lord and god

Therefore, it is perfectly legitimate for Christians who love the Lord Jesus as their Saviour and Messiah to pray to him. (He said, "If you ask me anything in my name, I will do it," John 14:14. And the apostle Paul appealed directly to the Lord Jesus in prayer for a pressing personal need in 2 Cor. 12:8.) It is perfectly legitimate for Christians in worship to sing and make melody "with your heart to the Lord; [for this is to] give thanks for all things in the name of our Lord Jesus Christ to God, even the Father" (Eph. 5:19-20).[49] But only the Father can be worshipped as the Almighty God. As Buzzard and Hunting so well put this:

> "Worship" may be offered to kings as representing God, and even to glorified saints (1 Chron. 29:20; Rev. 3:9). It is fallacious, therefore, to argue that because Jesus is "worshipped," he must be God. Jesus can be "worshipped" as Messiah. Only the Father is worshipped as God. The same Greek verb does service for both senses of "worship."[50]

And from the same authors:

---

[49] Some may ask how we know "the Lord" here is Jesus and not the Father. In 1 Cor. 8:6 Paul has already laid down for us that there is "one Lord, Jesus the Messiah." It stands to reason that thereafter in this book when Paul speaks of "the Lord" without any other qualification he is in fact speaking of the Lord Jesus. The same applies in Ephesians. Already in Eph. 4 Paul has told us there is "one Lord" and then there is "one God and Father of all who is over all and through all and in all" (v. 5-6). Again, it is clear that the "one Lord" who is Jesus is differentiated from "the one God, the Father." It is again reasonable to assume thereafter in Ephesians that whenever Paul speaks of "the Lord" without further qualification, he is referring to Jesus Christ and not the Father.

[50] Buzzard and Hunting, *The Doctrine of the Trinity,* p. 203.

> As Messiah, Jesus, the accredited representative of the Creator, is honoured in association with the One God, his Father (Rev. 5:12, 13). But he also joins the saints in the Lamb's song of praise to the Father (Rev. 15:3). He is the beginning and end of God's great plan of salvation (Rev. 1:17). Yet he died (Rev. 1:18), a fact which plainly means that he cannot be God since God cannot die. Only the Almighty God is God Himself. In Revelation 1:8 the Father is both the Alpha and Omega and the Lord God Almighty. The latter title ("the Lord God Almighty") is nowhere given to Jesus, despite the attempts of some red-letter Bibles to apply this verse to the Son, perpetuating the long-standing confusion of the Messiah with God.[51]

Yes, it does matter what we believe about the one God of the Bible and His Son. Jesus Christ the founder of his Church said it matters. His creed is that his Father is "the only true God" and that he himself is the Messiah whom that one God has commissioned. It matters because our relationship to God hinges on knowing this one true God and His Son. He defines this knowing as "eternal life." It matters because our world is lost and needs this one message that can unite all under the one God of the Bible. It matters because it determines whether we are accounted as true and acceptable worshippers in the Biblical pattern. It matters because on that great and unique day in the Age to Come, "Every knee will bow and every tongue will confess that Jesus the Messiah is Lord, to the glory of God the Father" (Phil. 2:10-11). The worship we give to our glorious Lord Jesus Christ is worship that is ultimately given to his God and our God, to his Father and our Father.

---

[51] *Ibid.*, p. 134.

Four
ANOTHER LORD

The LORD says to my lord:
"Sit at My right hand, till I make your enemies
a footstool for your feet" (Psalm 110:1, RSV).

At the beginning of this book I mentioned a fateful night and a life-changing meeting with a British professor of Bible now based at Atlanta Bible College in the States, Anthony Buzzard. Anthony asked me "Do you believe in the Trinity?" Without batting an eyelid I responded in the affirmative. Didn't everybody? Except, of course, that radical Arius and his modern-day descendants the Jehovah's Witnesses. But I grew up on the side of the majority. I belonged in the true and tried, fair-dinkum tradition of the Church on this one. What is more, I had never had one moment's angst as to the truth of the Trinity. I had preached on this doctrine from the pulpit with much assurance and conviction. I had no trouble confounding those who doubted it. I had never had a moment's intellectual or emotional consternation over it. Until that fateful meeting. So what was it that knocked me off my perch that night?

Quite simply, it was the verse quoted at the beginning of this chapter. Psalm 110 verse one. After all my Bible study and theological training Anthony hit me in a blind spot. Did I not know that in a key OT text there are *two* Lords? "**The LORD says to my lord**." The first LORD is Jehovah which in its 6800 occurrences always refers to the one supreme God. That one God is also called ***Adonai***, Lord God, 449 times. The second Lord (who is addressed by Jehovah in Ps. 110:1) is ***adoni***, which in all of its 195 occurrences *never* means the supreme God but *always* refers to a human (or occasionally angelic) superior. *Adonai* and *adoni* show us the biblical distinction between Almighty God and man.

That unforgettable night I learned that this Old Testament verse is the most often quoted verse in the pages of the New Testament. It must be a very significant verse then. Wherein does its significance lie? The Messiah in Psalm 110:1 is addressed by a human title, and not by a divine title! The Messiah is not an equal of Jehovah God.

He is the Lord Messiah, not the Lord God! According to the Hebrew Bible there are *two* Lords. No wonder I felt like a "stunned mullet"![1]

Let's have a look at a few Old Testament verses that show us the clear distinction alluded to here. In Genesis 15:2 Abraham prays to God and says, "O LORD God [*Adonai Yahweh*], what will You give me, since I am childless?" In another prayer Abraham's servant addresses God: "O LORD, God of my **lord** Abraham, please grant me success today" (Gen. 24:12). The second word for "my lord" here is *adoni* which according to any standard Hebrew lexicon means "lord," "master," or "owner." Another example is found in David's speech to his men after he had cut off the hem of King Saul's robe and his conscience bothered him: "So he said to his men, 'Far be it from me because of the LORD [here the word is *Yahweh,* Lord God] that I should do this thing to my lord [*adoni*]" (1 Sam. 24:6). One more example will suffice. It is a rather gory one. Two men had beheaded Saul's son Ish-bosheth thinking they had done David a favour. As they presented the severed head to David these two men announced: "Thus the LORD [*Yahweh* which is the equivalent of LORD] has given my lord [*adoni*] the king vengeance this day on Saul and his descendants" (2 Sam. 4:8).[2]

Here are the words of some of the very best Hebrew commentators: "*Adonai* and *Adoni* are variations of pointing to distinguish divine reference from human."[3]

"The form *Adoni* ('my lord'), a royal title (1 Sam. 29:8), is to be carefully distinguished from the divine title *Adonai* ('Lord') used of Yahweh. *Adonai* the special plural form [the divine title] distinguishes it from *adonai* [with short vowel] = 'my lords.'"[4]

"Lord in the Old Testament is used to translate *Adonai* when applied to the Divine Being. The [Hebrew] word...has a suffix [with special pointing] presumably for the sake of distinction...between divine and human appellative."[5]

"The Hebrew *Adonai* exclusively denotes the God of Israel. It is attested about 450 times in the Old Testament...*Adoni* [is] addressed

---

[1] *Stunned mullet* — a fish out of water in a new environment, with a hint of numbness.

[2] See Appendix 1 for more examples from the OT.

[3] Brown, Driver, Briggs, *Hebrew and English Lexicon of the Old Testament,* under *adon* (lord).

[4] "Lord," *International Standard Bible Encyclopedia,* p. 157.

[5] "Lord," *Hastings Dictionary of the Bible,* vol. 3, p. 137.

to human beings (Gen. 44:7; Num. 32:25; 2 Kings 2:19, etc.). We have to assume that the word *Adonai* received its special form to distinguish it from the secular use of *adon* [i.e. *adoni*]. The reason why [God is addressed] as *Adonai* [with long vowel] instead of the normal *adon*, *adoni* or *adonai* [short vowel] may have been to distinguish Yahweh from other gods and from human lords."[6]

"The form 'to my lord,' *l'adoni*, is never used in the Old Testament as a divine reference...The generally accepted fact is that the masoretic pointing distinguishes divine references (*adonai*) from human references (*adoni*)."[7]

Back to Psalm 110:1. If David the Psalmist had expected the Messiah to be the LORD God he would not have used "my lord" (*adoni*), but the term used exclusively for the One God, Jehovah — *Adonai.* On no occasion does *adoni*, "my lord," refer to the Lord God. This distinction is usually preserved in our English translations by writing *Adonai* as "Lord" and *adoni* as "my lord." Unfortunately, though, many English translations which faithfully preserve this distinction elsewhere capitalize the second "lord" only in Psalm 110:1. This is unwarranted. It gives the misleading impression that the word is the divine title, *Adonai*. It is not. A number of publications actually misstate the facts here and report that the second "lord" is from the Hebrew *Adonai*, which is not the case. Some, however, do maintain the correct distinction even here (knowing it is damaging to the Trinitarian position that Jesus is God). The Revised Version faithfully translates it: "The LORD saith unto my lord, Sit thou at my right hand" (also RSV and NRSV).

The eminent NT scholar George Eldon Ladd translates the verse this way: "The Lord [Yahweh] said to my Lord [Messiah], Sit at my right hand, till I make thy enemies a stool for thy feet."[8]

Dr. William Barclay states that Psalm 110 was universally accepted as Messianic and that "The first *Lord* is God, for God is the speaker; the second *Lord* is the Messiah, the conquering liberator and triumphant champion who is to come."[9]

Most, whilst recognizing the distinction, seem frightened to truly render it for fear of its implications for Christology. So they

---

[6] *Dictionary of Deities and Demons in the Bible,* p. 531.

[7] Wigram, *The Englishman's Hebrew and Chaldee Concordance of the Old Testament,* p. 22.

[8] G.E. Ladd, *A Theology of the New Testament*, p. 339.

[9] Barclay, *Jesus as They Saw Him,* p. 41.

half-translate, keeping the misleading capital on the second "lord": "The LORD says to my Lord, Sit at my right hand" (as per KJV, NASB, NKJV).

Both the Pharisees and Jesus knew that this inspired verse was crucial in the understanding of the identity of the promised Messiah. Jesus quoted it to show that the Messiah would be both the son (descendant) of King David and David's "lord" (see Matt. 22:41-46; Mark 12:35-37; Luke 20:41-44). If David had prophesied that the Messiah was going to be the Lord God, he would have used the word exclusively designating the one true God, *Adonai*. He did not. Instead, he used the Hebrew word designating human superiors but never the Lord God, *adoni*, meaning "my master," or "my lord." The Psalm therefore gives us an indispensable key as to who the Messiah is.

> It is on this bed-rock definition of Jesus' status that all New Testament Christology is built. Jesus is the lord whom David addressed prophetically as "my lord" (*adoni*). Jesus is indeed *kurios* (lord) but certainly not the Lord God. That title, *adoni,* invariably distinguishes a *human superior from the One God in the Old Testament. It is a distinction which is clear cut and consistent.*[10]

This key verse, then, quoted more than any other in the New Testament, authorizes the title "lord" for Jesus. Failure to understand this distinction has led to the erroneous idea that whenever the New Testament calls Jesus "Lord" it means he is the Lord God of the Old Testament:

> Jesus, on the basis of Psalm 110:1, is David's lord ("my lord") and thus "**our** Lord Jesus Christ." The Father of Jesus remains uniquely the one Lord God, who is also "the God of our Lord Jesus Christ" (Eph. 1:17). "God" and "lord" therefore point to a crucial difference of rank. The Messiah is not "coequal God."[11]

Occasionally, it will be objected that this distinction between *Adonai* and *adoni* was a late addition to the Hebrew text by the Masorites around 600 to 700 AD and therefore is not reliable. This objection needs to be considered in light of the fact that the Hebrew translators of the Septuagint (the LXX) around 250 BC recognized

---

[10] Buzzard and Hunting, *The Doctrine of the Trinity,* p. 48.

[11] *Ibid.*, p. 49.

and carefully maintained this Hebrew distinction in their work. They never translated the second "lord" of Psalm 110:1 ("my lord," *kyrios mou*) to mean the Deity. The first LORD of Psalm 110:1 (the LORD, *Ho Kyrios*) they always reserved for the one God, Jehovah. In the light of this incontrovertible evidence, the sincerely held (but false) view that Jesus is the Lord God of the Old Testament should surrender to the Biblical confession that he is the Lord Messiah, uniquely anointed by the Lord God of Israel. We note that the apostles regularly maintain this distinction.

1 Corinthians 8:6

Paul gives his definitive statement on the Godhead in the book of Corinthians. He draws a clear-cut distinction between the Lord God and the Lord Messiah: "There is no God but one...For us there is but one God, the Father, from [*ek*] whom are all things, and we exist for Him; and one Lord, Jesus Messiah, through [*dia*] whom are all things, and we exist through [*dia*] him" (1 Cor. 8:4, 6).

Notice how Paul here carefully distinguishes between the "one God, the Father" and the "one Lord," that is "Jesus Messiah." Paul has not scuttled his Jewish unitarian monotheistic creed. His confession is squarely based on the distinction of the two Lords in Psalm 110:1, the LORD God (*Yahweh*) and the Lord Messiah (*adoni*). Jesus is the divinely appointed Lord Christ as distinct from the Lord God. Unfortunately for those who hold the doctrine of the Trinity this creedal statement from the apostle's pen gives no support to the invented idea that the One God is three in one. Paul positively does *not* say that "for us Christians there is one God: the Father, Son and Holy Spirit."

This confession from 1 Corinthians 8:6 that "there is one Lord, Jesus Messiah" for first-century Christians:

> was a title Jesus received on his exaltation, by virtue of his resurrection...It was the exalted Lord who had supplanted all other "lords" and absorbed their significance and rule in regard both to the cosmos and to redemption...Paul is speaking primarily about the new understanding and the new state of affairs brought about for believers by Christ's Lordship, about the relations between God, Christ, believers and created things that now pertains. Paul is not making a

> statement about the act of creation in the *past,* but rather about creation as believers see it *now.*[12]

Kuschel concurs. He says that in Paul the "Lord Jesus Christ" is never a protological figure (who could then have been involved in the creation of the world at the very beginning) but is always already an eschatological figure. The Lord — on the basis of his resurrection — was appointed by God in power (Rom. 1:3ff). The confession "Jesus is Lord" became the universal confession after Jesus had been exalted by God (Phil. 2:11). Because of his resurrection and exaltation Christ now lives in God's mode of being, which is the mode of being in the Spirit (1 Cor. 6:11; 15:45).

> In other words, when Paul speaks in 1 Cor. 8:6b of the Lord Jesus Christ, he quite naturally means the exalted Lord, who in the mode of the Spirit is present here and now. What we have is a universal soteriology which embraces the whole creation. Christ's sphere of rule is now no longer limited.

That means "this passage is about the mediation of the new creation...The Christological formula in 1 Cor. 8:6b is thus not to be understood cosmologically and protologically, but eschatologically and in terms of the present." 1 Corinthians 8:6 tells us that God — the Father —is past and future, beginning and end, origin and goal, creator (*ek*) and fulfiller (*eis*) of the world and human beings. By contrast, Christ is the ruler over the earth, bringing liberation to the present, because he is mediator (*dia*) of a new creation (2 Cor. 5:7), of a new covenant (2 Cor. 3:6) and is therefore Lord of all those "gods and lords" that men commit to in the present. But as Kuschel says, "*this Lord Jesus Messiah himself exists for God and will ultimately and finally be subjected to the one God, the Father,* so that the Father God may be everything to everyone" (1 Cor. 15:28). "Here Jesus Christ is certainly the mediator of God in establishing the new creation, but he is evidently not the divine mediator of the Genesis creation, before time." This "forbids us to interpret 1 Cor. 8:6b as a divergence from Jewish monotheism."[13]

All NT saints maintained this distinction between the one God and the Lord Messiah. When the pregnant Mary visited her cousin Elizabeth she was met with the greeting, "And how has it happened that the mother of **my Lord** [i.e. the Messiah] should come to me?"

---

[12] Dunn, *Christology in the Making,* p. 181.

[13] Kuschel, *Born Before All Time?* pp. 289-290.

(Luke 1:43). To suggest that Elizabeth believed Mary was carrying the LORD Jehovah in her womb is to defy any sense of social and cultural history appropriate for this Jewess. Such a thought would have never crossed her Hebrew mind. Elizabeth's greeting is the first echo of Psalm 110:1 in the New Testament. This was the confession of the angels to the shepherds too, when they declared tidings of great joy because "today in the city of David there has been born for you a Saviour, who is **the Lord Messiah**" (Luke 2:11). Further in the same chapter the old man Simeon was told that "he would not see death before he had seen **the Lord's** [i.e. Yahweh's] **Messiah**" (Luke 2:26).

Jesus Called by Titles Given to God

What about those Old Testament verses that refer to the Lord God but are applied to Jesus in the New Testament? This is a good question and the answer hinges around the resurrection and glorification of Jesus at God's right hand.

Up until his resurrection Jesus was the Messiah but he was not officially "the Lord Jesus Messiah." The term "Lord" is almost never used by Matthew and Mark in narrative passages and only three such times by John (4:1; 6:23; 11:2), but some 15 times by Luke (e.g. 7:13; 10:1; 11:39). These fairly rare occasions when *the writer* calls Jesus "the Lord" are to be recognized as post-resurrection statements as the author recollects those events in the life of Jesus of Nazareth before he was crucified and raised. Dunn in a footnote illustrates the principle beautifully: In a somewhat similar way it could be said of one of Britain's prime ministers, "Prime Minister Wilson studied economics at Oxford." No one misunderstands the phrase to mean that Harold Wilson was already Prime Minister when he was at Oxford (though it is the most "natural" meaning of the sentence). Each one who reads it consciously or unconsciously interprets it as saying (in more precise language): "Harold Wilson, who later became Prime Minister, studied economics at Oxford."[14] In the same way, when the authors of the Gospels speak of Jesus in his pre-resurrection ministry they sometimes call him "the Lord."

Whilst many folk addressed Jesus as "Lord" in the Gospel narratives it was used as a polite form of address, equivalent to

---

[14] Dunn, *Christology in the Making,* p. 334, footnote 121.

"Sir." (Some English Bibles actually translate the word *kyrios* this way and capture the sense perfectly.) But the clue to the history of the word ("Lord" as a title for Messiah) is found in John's Gospel, where the word is used of Jesus in the narrative portions of the first 15 chapters only three times, but in the resurrection stories of the last two chapters it is used nine times. "The evangelist feels free to speak of Jesus as Lord *after his resurrection* but does not feel the designation is appropriate in the earlier ministry. This suggests that the title belongs primarily to Jesus as the Risen and Ascended One."[15]

Quite right. For Jesus has *become* Lord in a universal sense not recognized prior to his resurrection. The exaltation of Jesus to God's right hand means that "God has **made** him **both Lord and Christ**" in an all-embracing cosmic way not his before (Acts 2:36). Jesus is now "at the right hand of God" — a status he once did not enjoy — "having gone into heaven, **after** angels and authorities and powers **had become** subjected to him" (1 Pet. 3:22). In the days of his flesh Jesus had been anointed and yet had suffered even though he was Messiah, the Son of God. But now in his exaltation "Jesus becomes the Messiah in a new sense: he has begun his messianic reign as the Davidic king. So the exaltation of Jesus to the right hand of God means nothing less than his enthronement as messianic king."[16] This is the sense of Romans 1, where we are told that the Gospel of God concerns His Son "who was born of the seed of David according to the flesh, who was declared **with power** to be that Son of God by the resurrection from the dead...Jesus Messiah our Lord" (v. 3-4). Quite clearly, it is the resurrection that marks Jesus out "with power" to be the Son. He was already the Son before his resurrection (Matt. 1:20; Luke 1:35). He was a direct descendant of David "according to the flesh." He lived in true human weakness and limitations. But since his resurrection a definitive change has taken place. The power of his Sonship and royal status has begun to be felt. He now lives in the realm of God's power and glory. Thus the Christology of the apostolic church "must be formulated in terms of [these] Jewish expectations."[17]

---

[15] Ladd, *A Theology of the New Testament,* p. 338.
[16] *Ibid.*, p. 335.
[17] *Ibid.,* p. 337.

With this information we are in a position to answer our question: When the NT transfers from the OT titles and verses that clearly refer to Jehovah the One God over to Jesus Christ, are we not thereby entitled to say that Jesus is the Jehovah God of the OT? After all, it is a staggering thing to find, for example, that where the prophet Joel speaks of the Day of the Lord (Yahweh) and of calling on the name of the Lord (Yahweh) for salvation, Peter says this means calling on the name of Jesus of Nazareth (Acts 2:20-21; 4:10-12). Surely we can conclude that this means Jesus is the Yahweh of the OT? Not at all! The scriptural solution is that God the Father has always been LORD, but now Jesus has been "**made...Lord.**" This means that:

> Jesus, as Lord, has entered upon the exercise of certain divine functions. He has poured out the Spirit (Acts 2:33); he has become the object of faith (2:21; 3:16); he gives repentance and forgiveness (5:31); he is the Holy One (3:14); the author of life (3:15); the recipient of prayer (4:29); he will be the judge of the world (10:42); and he stands at the right hand of God to receive the spirit of the first martyr (7:55, 59).[18]

This is to say that the Lordship of Jesus is a divine prerogative *granted* to Jesus. God has *invited* him to share His very throne. Jesus has *become* the one by whom God will bring under control every rebellious power in the world and universe. This is why Peter cites Psalm 110:1 in his Pentecost sermon: "The LORD [Yahweh] said to my lord [Messiah], 'Sit at my right hand, till I make your enemies a stool for your feet'" (Acts 2:34). By his exaltation, Jesus stands so close to God that he exercises many of the divine prerogatives. To quote the words of another eminent scholar, because of his resurrection "the exalted Jesus will in the future fulfill functions which are really functions of God Himself."[19] All of which is to say that Jesus by his resurrection now exercises a full functional equality with God. This is why the NT uses OT verses that speak of the Lord God and transfers them over to Jesus Christ. He is the Son of God, the perfect agent and representative of his Father. And in Hebrew understanding, as we have already seen, "the agent is as the principal himself."

---

[18] *Ibid.*, p. 339.
[19] Kuschel, *Born Before All Time?* p. 269.

In the light of this what are we to make of the traditional claim that unless we believe that Jesus is the Lord God of the Old Testament we cannot be saved? Speaking on Romans 10:9, "that if you confess with your mouth Jesus as Lord, and believe in your heart that God raised him from the dead, you shall be saved," Martyn Lloyd-Jones asserts that the text teaches two essentials. The first is that Jesus is Lord, and the second is that God raised him from the dead. Those are the two absolute essentials of the Christian faith. There is no salvation unless we are clear about them. But right here Lloyd-Jones makes a fundamental and classic mistake. He claims:

> the word translated "Lord" is used in the Greek translation of the Old Testament to stand for the Hebrew word "YHWH" (Jehovah) — the name by which God wished to be personally known...so this statement, "that if you confess with your mouth Jesus as Lord," means, "If you confess with your mouth that Jesus is Jehovah (YHWH)!" Jesus is the Lord God Jehovah!...You say, "My faith rests upon Jesus, Jesus of Nazareth, but I say that He is God, He is Jehovah." This is the Christian confession.[20]

It is a sad thing for me to read such erudite scholars making such baseless, misleading claims. If they are to be consistent, what do they make of the confessions of the early New Testament Christians who called Jesus "Lord" but had no idea they were calling him Jehovah? An example or two will suffice. When Mary Magdalene found Jesus' grave empty, she wept with deep emotion, because she thought somebody had stolen the body. She did not recognize that the risen Jesus was standing right in front of her. Jesus said to her, "Woman, why are you weeping? Whom are you seeking?" Mary supposed Jesus was the gardener and said to him, "Sir [Greek *kurios,* "Lord"], if you have carried him away, tell me where you have laid him, and I will take him away" (John 20:15). Here Mary, thinking Jesus is no higher a dignitary than the gardener, calls him "Lord." No one in their right mind would believe for a moment that Mary thought the gardener was Jehovah, the Lord God! The translators rightly render the word *Lord* here as "Sir." The same appellation is given by the Philippian jailer to Paul and Silas, the prisoners under his charge. The jailer falls at their feet

---

[20] M. Lloyd-Jones, *Romans: Exposition of Chapter 10,* Saving Faith, Banner of Truth, Edinburgh, 1997, pp. 93-94.

and calls them *Lords,* that is, sirs. In John 4 the woman at the well has just met Jesus. Jesus has not yet even told her he is the Messiah. But she addresses him as Lord: "Sir [*kurios,* "Lord"], you have nothing to draw with and the well is deep" (v. 11). Martyn Lloyd-Jones is evidently unaware that the one Greek word for *Lord* may be applied to either God or man. In what sense then is the confession "Jesus is Lord" to be taken?

"Lord" in the Book of Acts

The safest answer is to see how the apostolic Christians understood it. A good place to turn is the book of Acts. This book presents us with a clear and unified testimony of the apostles' witness. It is significant that nowhere in Acts do the apostles say that believing that Jesus is Jehovah, the Lord God, is an essential requirement for salvation. Peter, who had been given the keys to the Kingdom, called Jesus "**a man** accredited to you by God" (Acts 2:22). The Bible states that after his sermon on the day of Pentecost about 3000 persons were saved. If Peter thought it was essential to believe that Jesus was Almighty God he did not say so in this first sermon. If it was necessary to believe in the Trinity to enter the Kingdom of God then Peter forgot to mention this essential fact on this definitive day. This proves it is not necessary to believe that Christ is God in order to be saved. When preaching to these Jews Peter presents a Messiah who is the descendant of King David (v. 30). He is one who would have rotted and decayed in the grave like any other man had not God raised him up again (v. 24-32). Because God authenticated "this Jesus" by resurrecting him (thus reversing the national verdict accusing him of blasphemy, that is, claiming to be God's Messiah), Jesus is now "exalted to the right hand of God" (v. 33). God has thus sealed "this Jesus whom you crucified" (v. 36) and declared him as "Lord and Messiah" to the nation of Israel and "for all who are far off" (i.e. the Gentiles as well, v. 39). The proof of his Messiahship is that the Holy Spirit has been poured out. Every Jew believed that the dawning of the new Messianic age would usher in a mighty outpouring of God's Spirit. This Jewish audience knew that Peter's statements meant that the God of their fathers, Jehovah, had raised Jesus in fulfilment of the Old Testament prophecies concerning the Christ. Their understanding that "Jesus is Lord" was governed by their understanding of the Messianic fulfilment of Psalm 110 as Peter quotes it in Acts here. No unitary monotheistic Jew would have taken Peter's statements in Acts 2 to mean that Messiah was Jehovah God. It must be interpreted with Hebrew eyes. This same pattern is followed throughout Acts.

In the next chapter, Peter calls Jesus anything but the Lord God. Jesus is called God's "servant" twice (Acts 3:13, 26); God's "Christ" (v. 18, 20); "the prince of life" (a title nowhere in the Bible applied to God, v. 15); the "prophet" whom Moses predicted (v. 22, 23). In fact, Peter is very careful not to confuse the identity of the Lord God and this Jesus who is the Lord Messiah. Note verse 13 where Peter says, "The God of Abraham, Isaac, and Jacob, the God of our fathers has glorified His servant Jesus, the one whom you delivered up, and disowned in the presence of Pilate, when he had decided to release him." This same expression "the God of Abraham, the God of Isaac, the God of Jacob" appears in Exodus 3:15 where God tells Moses to announce to the people that "The LORD [YHWH], the God of your fathers, the God of Abraham, the God of Isaac, the God of Jacob, has sent me to you" (Ex. 3:15). The God of Abraham, Isaac and Jacob equals the LORD (Jehovah). Here in Acts 3:13 it is "the God of Abraham, the God of Isaac, the God of Jacob, the God of our fathers" who has now "glorified His servant Jesus." Is Jesus then the God of Abraham, the God of Isaac, the God of Jacob, the God of our fathers? Absolutely not! This would make complete nonsense of the text. The God of Abraham glorified who? Himself? No: His servant Jesus. Jesus is not the God of Abraham. Jesus is not Jehovah, the LORD. He is God's anointed one, God's servant.

In Acts 10 the same distinction appears again. Peter says, "You know of Jesus of Nazareth, how God anointed him with the Holy Spirit and with power, and how he went about doing good, and healing all who were oppressed by the devil; for God was with him" (v. 38). Who anointed Jesus? God anointed Jesus of Nazareth. And the whole purpose of anointing somebody is so they might receive the power and the ability to fulfill their commission. If I said, "The king anointed the prince" you could not possibly think the prince was the king. In the same way Jesus is the "Prince of Life" (Acts 3:15) whom God anointed. Jesus applied the Messianic prophecy of Isaiah 61 to himself when he read these words in the synagogue: "The Spirit of the Lord God is upon me, because the LORD [Jehovah] has anointed me" (v. 61; Luke 4:16-21). The person who is anointed is not the LORD Jehovah. God does not need to anoint

God! Jehovah God anoints Jesus the Messiah. That is what Jesus claims for himself, and what Peter announces time and again.

We do not have the time nor space here to go through every chapter in the book of Acts to prove this. But I encourage you to do this for yourself. Take a coloured marker like I did when I first looked at this matter, and you may well be surprised at the frequency and consistency of this topic. What was the message that Paul preached after his dramatic conversion experience? That Jesus is Jehovah God? Of course not, for his message was consistent with the rest of the apostolic testimony: "Immediately he began to proclaim Jesus in the synagogues, saying, 'He is the Son of God'" (Acts 9:20). In fact, Paul kept increasing in strength "and confounding the Jews who lived at Damascus by proving that this Jesus is the Messiah" (v. 22). To be the Son of God is to be the Messiah: Same message! In fact, whilst you are at it, take the same coloured marker and go through the rest of the New Testament. You will be absolutely amazed, as I was (even after having read and studied seriously the Bible for decades!), at the distinction the Scriptures make between God the Father and the Lord Jesus Christ. (You could try 1 Cor. 1:3; 8:6; 2 Cor. 1:2; Phil. 1:2; 4:20; 1 Thess. 1:1; 3:13; 2 Thess. 1:2; 2:16; 1 Tim. 1:2; 2 Tim. 1:2; Titus 1:4; Gal. 1:3.)

In other words, there is no verse in the whole book of Acts (or any other New Testament book) that requires you to believe that Jesus is the Lord God, Jehovah, in order to enter the Kingdom and be saved. In all the book of Acts there is no preaching of the Trinity. Yet in Acts thousands were saved according to the Scriptural record. This should be conclusive proof that the Trinity was not a part of early apostolic doctrine. Nor should it ever be taught that unless we believe that "Jesus is the Lord Jehovah" we cannot be saved. What is essential to salvation — that is, essential to entrance into the Kingdom of God when it comes — is to confess that God has made this Jesus "both Lord and Christ [Messiah, King] — this Jesus whom you crucified" (Acts 2:36). And that confession must be in the same terms as the inspired oracle of David in Psalm 110:1 where the Lord Messiah is not the Lord God.

The confession "Jesus is Lord" must be understood in its Jewish environment and in the circumstances of a plainly dated historical period. There should be no argument about this. Unfortunately, as we have seen, through the pressures of culture and politics, the persona of Jesus has been reshaped into one neither he nor his apostles would recognize. There can be no reasonable doubt that the Jesus worshipped and believed in today is a myth of the same gigantic proportions as the idol in Nebuchadnezzar's dream (Dan. 2). Like Nebuchadnezzar's idol, the Jesus of today is a composite and contradictory figure, part gold, part silver, part bronze, part iron and part clay. It is still possible to extract the gold. But if we would hold it up unalloyed we must burn off the dross of Hellenistic thinking and again assert that Jesus is the Jewish Lord Messiah. Any other confession will result in "another Jesus."

We cannot say we were not warned. The apostle John, almost certainly the last living apostle, warned that false views of the person of Jesus Christ would bring disastrous consequences. He left us with a sure-fire test: "By this you know the Spirit of God: every spirit that confesses that Jesus Christ has come in the flesh is from God; and every spirit that does not confess Jesus is not from God; and this is the spirit of the antichrist that is coming, and now it is already in the world" (1 John 4:2-3).

Historically, the particular "antichristian spirit" John seems to have warned against was Docetism (from the Greek *dokeo* meaning to suppose or to seem). This form of Greek Gnosticism claimed that Jesus only seemed or appeared to have a human body. The Docetists said that the man Jesus was born of Mary but the "Christ" part of him descended on him from heaven at his baptism. Just before his crucifixion, this heavenly Christ left the man Jesus to die alone. The Docetists taught that the Son of God part of Jesus was an emanation or spirit being from God. To combat this dangerous doctrine John wrote (and this time let us render the translation a little nearer to what John actually wrote): "In this way you know the spirit of the God. Every spirit which is confessing Jesus Christ **in flesh** having come is from the [true] God. And every spirit which is not confessing **that** Jesus is not from God."

Notice two things in particular. Firstly, our English versions say Jesus Christ came "in the flesh" but the Greek text states simply "in flesh." It means that Jesus Christ was a real human being. He did not just seem to have, or appear to be, flesh and blood. He was fully human, 100% man. Secondly, every spirit that does not confess *that* (particular) Jesus is not of God. The definite article before Jesus has a demonstrative force and must not be overlooked. Every spirit which is not confessing that kind of Jesus — an "in flesh" or human

Jesus — is not from the true God. *John not only says "Jesus" was a human being. He also says "Christ" was a human being. It is Jesus Christ who is human!* (Keep in mind what was said earlier in the book: "Christ" is the Greek title meaning "Messiah." Christ is not a name. It is an office, a title.) There is not a God part and a man part. There are not two natures fused together here. The true NT apostolic confession is that Jesus (the) Christ is a real flesh and blood man.

The Docetists had created a different Jesus, a new "Jesus Christ." Their Jesus had two parts, two natures, one human and one divine — the latter being an emanation or spirit being from a remote God in heaven. This anti-Christ of theirs was a god *clothed* with a human nature. The Docetists could not accept that God could make a man to be the Messiah by creating him in the womb of Mary by a special act of creation. Nor could they believe that God could anoint this Jesus as the Messiah or the Christ and then raise him from the dead after he was crucified. Come to think of it, this Docetic idea does not sound at all unlike the modern notion of a two-natured Jesus, composed of 100% God and 100% man (which is 100% contradiction). Many Christians today confess a Jesus who is the Messiah, but more than that: They say he is God, too. The Jesus whom John confessed was replaced by a curious "double person," fully God and at the same time fully man. Mortal, yet immortal. Temptable and yet, as God, not temptable. Preexisting and yet coming into existence. While being God, he did not know what God knew (Mark 13:32). According to 1 John 4:2-3 this is the theology (spirit) of the opposition Christ. (This false spirit/doctrine will culminate in the final Antichrist who will pretend he is the incarnate God as 2 Thess. 2:4 predicts.) But the "Jesus Christ" (or "Jesus Messiah") John knew and believed was a human being. He was "in flesh." The Christ *is* the man Jesus as distinct from the one God (1 Tim. 2:5). Any other doctrine of Christ presents the spirit of an opposition Christ.

It is amazing to note what John wrote in his second letter. It is similar, but with one interesting difference: "For many deceivers have gone out into the world, those who do not acknowledge Jesus Christ as **coming** in the flesh. This is the deceiver and the antichrist" (2 John 7).

John has changed the verb from a past tense in 1 John 4:2-3 to a present participle here in his second letter. Possibly he is referring to the Second Coming of Jesus from heaven: "Jesus Christ is coming in flesh," that is, he is returning to earth as a human being! I like Sidney Hatch's comment:

> here we think of Hebrews 13:8, "Jesus Christ the same yesterday, and today, and forever." Yesterday that Man who died for us at Calvary and then rose from the dead. Today that Man who is ascended and glorified, seated at the right hand of his heavenly Father. Tomorrow the Man who is coming in power and great glory.[21]

The verse does *not* say, as many like to think it says, that Jesus Christ is the "same from *eternity*, today and forever." It positively states that Jesus the Messiah is the same "yesterday," and "yesterday" is a defined point of past history, not a timeless eternity. Besides, "Jesus" is the name given to the human at his birth. Even believers in the Trinity do not believe Jesus preexisted his human birth! It is quite clear that the human Jesus did grow physically and did mature mentally and spiritually. This is to say that Jesus the Messiah did change yesterday, which is proof positive that he cannot be the Eternal God! The comfort given us in this Hebrews text is that we are to imitate the victorious faith of Jesus the Messiah. The command in the previous verse 7 is that we must "Remember those who led you, who spoke the word of God to you; and consider the outcome of of their way of life, and imitate their faith." And of course, the ultimate example of the one whose example and faith we follow is the man Jesus.

Ah, the next time you go out on a starry night and look up into the heavens, remember that "up there" at God the Father's right hand is a Man in glory. And remember that this Man is the guarantee that all who faithfully confess him in this day will be conformed to his image when he comes again. That glorified Man is the Head of God's new creation. He is the guarantee of a New Age dawning. Psalm 110:1 has come to pass. The LORD (*Yahweh*) has set David's human lord (*adoni*) at His own right hand in heaven. Exalted there as our Lord Messiah, the man Jesus awaits the time when he will return to planet earth to reign on the throne of David over a renewed world. This is the Lord Messiah the Bible confesses. We should all embrace that Saviour and no other.

---

[21] Sidney Hatch, *Brief Bible Studies,* vol. 26, no. 2, 1966, p. 20.

Five
ANOTHER JESUS

For if one comes and preaches another Jesus whom we have not preached...you bear this beautifully (2 Cor. 11:4)

In his introduction to *The Passover Plot* Dr. Schonfield wisely sets the standard for the debate in relation to Jesus' identity and mission in these words:

> The only way in which we can hope to know the real Jesus is by first becoming conscious of him as a man of his own time, country and people, which necessitates an intimate acquaintance with all three. We have resolutely to refuse to detach him from his setting, and let the influences which played upon him play upon us. We have to mark the traits in him which were personal, individual, whether pleasing or unpleasing, which convey to us the attributes and idiosyncrasies of a creature of flesh and blood. Only when this Galilean Jew has made an impact upon us in the...(natural)...aspects of his mortality are we entitled to begin to cultivate him and estimate his worth, allowing him to communicate to us the imaginations of his mind and the motivations of his actions.[1]

Dr. Schonfield reported that many Christians he spoke with were not even aware that the term "Christ" was simply a Greek translation of the Hebrew title Messiah, and thought somehow that it referred to the Second Person of the Trinity. "So connected had the word 'Christ' become with the idea of Jesus as God incarnate that the title 'Messiah' was treated as something curiously Jewish and not associated." He wrote:

> I have often asked my Christian friends, "Is it not enough if you believe in One God, Lord of all spirits, and accept Jesus as his messianic messenger?" But it seemed that the Messiahship of Jesus in their view had only to do with the

---

[1] Hugh Schonfield, *The Passover Plot,* p. 12.

> Jews, and meant nothing in their experience. Many were not even aware that Christ was simply a Greek translation of the Hebrew title Messiah (the Anointed One), and supposed that it had to do with the heavenly nature of the Second Person of the Trinity. It took me a long time to appreciate that when we talked of God we were not speaking the same language, and that there was a serious problem of communication.[2]

N.T. Wright, the Bishop of Durham, agrees: "One of the most persistent mistakes throughout the literature on Jesus in the last hundred years is to use the word 'Christ,' which simply means 'Messiah,' as though it was a 'divine' title."[3]

Mashiach

In Jewish parlance, a "messiah" (Heb. *mashiach,* an "anointed one") could refer to a prophet, a priest or a king who was consecrated for service to God. The Hebrews believed that when God anointed that person, he or she was equipped to do God's work because he/she received a measure of the Holy Spirit. God appointed such agents to sacred office. Thus, in the Hebrew Bible, there are *various* "messiahs," numbers of "anointed ones," or "Christs." Twelve times King Saul is called *mashiach* (1 Sam. 12:3, 5; 24:6–twice, 10; 26:9, 11, 16, 23; 2 Sam. 1:14, 16, 21). David is so designated six times (2 Sam. 19:21; 22:51; 23:1; Ps. 18:50; 20:6; 28:8). A priest is called "messiah" four times (Lev. 4:3, 5, 16; 6:22). The reigning king is called "anointed one" three times (Lam. 4:20; Ps. 84:9; 89:38). The patriarchs are so designated twice (Ps. 105:15; 1 Chron. 16:22); Solomon once (2 Chron. 6:42); a prospective king once (1 Sam. 16:6). And even the pagan king Cyrus is once nominated "messiah" in Isaiah 45:1! The coming or promised one, the ultimate "Messiah," is so denominated nine times (1 Sam. 2:10, 35; Ps. 2:2; 89:51; 132:10, 17; Dan. 9:25, 26; Hab. 3:13). Thus, there were many "christs" who preceded Jesus, but he is the ultimate "Christ." In the NT Christians are designated as "anointed ones," that is, "christs" (see 2 Cor. 1:21). There is no hint that the title messiah designates the Deity. To be a messiah is to be an agent of the one God. As the ultimate and greatest *mashiach* Jesus combined

---

[2] *Ibid.,* p. 12.

[3] N.T. Wright, *Who Was Jesus?* p. 57.

in his person the offices of prophet, priest and king. Certainly, God the Father anointed him above all his predecessors, above his companions (Heb. 1:9). It never occurred to a Jew to think that Jesus as Messiah was also somehow a second member of the Godhead now incarnated, that God the Son was roaming around in human flesh, having Himself become man. According to its OT usage, the term Messiah, the Anointed One, indicates a call to office. Most certainly, "It was not the title of an aspect of the Godhead."[4] This is a later Gentile invention that came about by ignoring Jesus' Jewish context and inventing a doctrine called the Incarnation — the idea that a second member of the Trinity, God the Son, became a human being. As Lockhart says, Christianity ignored the "Messiah" and theologically worked the "Christ" up into the "God-Man." "Jesus as the 'Messiah' is a human being; Jesus as the 'Christ' is something entirely different. This doctrine has it that the two natures — the God-nature and human nature — were so intrinsically fused that Jesus was simultaneously *all* human and *all* divine, a combination of opposites quite impossible of explanation or understanding."[5] As Don Cupitt captures the problem of Jesus' double nature, "it is as if Jesus were at one moment Clark Kent and at the next Superman."[6] Or as Lockhart pithily says, to believe in the two natures as a literalism is "the equivalent of being asked to believe that Jonah swallowed the whale, and not the whale Jonah."[7]

When a sincere Roman Catholic believer calls Mary "the mother of God" Christians of the Protestant heritage cringe. We are amused at the impossible prospect that one day the Almighty God should have humbly approached the Jewish girl Mary with the request, "Mary, would you please be My mother?" From our "objective" and detached "outsiders'" perspective it is easy to see how this Mary-myth transgresses Scriptural bounds. We can spot a mile away how later tradition worked Mary up to being a perpetual virgin, who never subsequently enjoyed sexual intercourse with her husband Joseph (even though Scripture teaches she had children by Joseph after Jesus' birth). We can spot the second Mary-myth which says that Mary herself was immaculately conceived, meaning that

---

[4] Hugh Schonfield, *The Passover Plot,* p. 47.
[5] Lockhart, *Jesus the Heretic,* p. 44.
[6] D. Cupitt, *The Myth of God Incarnate,* quoted in Lockhart, *Jesus the Heretic,* p. 137.
[7] *Ibid.,* p. 45.

she was always without sin, and was allegedly — and without any Scriptural justification — without dying miraculously lifted up into the heavenlies to be glorified next to her Son as "co-redemptress" (the official Roman doctrine of the Assumption). However, it's much harder on "our" side of the fence to spot how the Christ-myth has also been created. When Jesus is called "God the Son" do we as readily see how this transgresses the Scriptural record? We will shortly see that in the Bible Jesus is nominated the Son of God, something quite different in meaning from God the Son. And when Jesus was in post-biblical times called "the God-man" we do not see the obvious blind spot in our Greek eyesight, for the Bible never once so describes him. Jesus calls himself "a man" (John 8:40) and the apostles call him "a man" (Acts 2:22; 1 Tim. 2:5). He is constantly contrasted with and distinguished from God, his Father. The Hebrew Bible predicted Jesus would be a man (Is. 53:3). But never does the Scripture use the term "God-man" to tell us who Jesus is. The Greek language of the day had a perfectly good word for "God-man" (*theiosaner*) but it never appears in the NT. So why do we persist with these extra-biblical terms? Why do we continue to employ non-biblical (i.e. unbiblical) language to describe Jesus? Or does it really matter?

That saying is true which says that we are very quick to spot the speck in the eye of another's theology, but how blind we are to the beam in our own. Mary is not the mother of God, according to the Scriptures. And neither is Jesus God the Son, nor is he the "God-man" according to the Bible. And he is nowhere called "God from God" as the later Nicene creed called him. Protestants who claim to be people of the Bible ought to know that the contentious extra-biblical word used at Nicea, *homoousios,* meaning "of equal substance," "did not come from Scripture but, of all things, from Gnostic systems."[8] The result was that such terminology introduced alien notions into the Christian understanding of God. In other words, "an epoch-making paradigm shift has taken place between scripture and Nicea."[9] In this chapter we ask how, in what sense, is Jesus the *Son* of God? Before we do that let me briefly say something about the second great traditional teaching I alluded to at the beginning of Chapter 3: namely, that there are "two natures"

---

[8] Kuschel, *Born Before All Time?* p. 500.

[9] *Ibid.,* p. 503.

found in our Lord Jesus. The Council of Chalcedon in AD 451 attempts to explain it this way:

> Our Lord is truly God and truly man, of a reasonable soul and body, consubstantial with the Father according to the Godhead, and consubstantial with us according to the manhood; in all things like unto us without sin; begotten before all ages of the Father according to the Godhead, and in these latter days for us and for our salvation born of the Virgin Mary, the mother of God according to the manhood; one and the same Christ, Son, Lord, only begotten, to be acknowledged in two natures, inconfusedly, unchangeably, indivisibly, inseparably, the distinction of natures being by no means taken away by the union, but rather the property of each nature being preserved and concurring in one person and one subsistence; parted or divided into two persons but one and the same Son, and only begotten, God, the Word, the Lord Jesus Christ.

Once again that noted preacher Martyn Lloyd-Jones says he stands in awe of this astounding statement, admitting that:

> it is beyond reason; it is beyond our understanding. As we have had to say in connection with the doctrine of the Trinity, and with many other doctrines, our business is to submit ourselves to the Bible...We must cease trying to span the infinite with our finite reason, indeed with our sinful reason, and we must receive the truth as it is given.[10]

Again I want to say that to stand before mystery clearly revealed in Scripture is one thing, but to stand before man-made contradiction is quite another. Just who is Jesus the Christ? There are at least one billion people in the world who flatly deny that Jesus is in any sense the Son of God at all. To Muslims it is outright blasphemy to call Jesus God's Son. The Koran states:

> They [Christians] say: "The Most Gracious has betaken a son!" Indeed ye have put forth a thing most monstrous! At it the skies are about to burst, the earth to split asunder, and the mountains to fall down in utter ruin, that they attributed a son to the Most Gracious. For it is not consonant with the majesty of the Most Gracious that He should beget a son (Sura 19:88-92).

---

[10] Lloyd-Jones, *God the Father, God the Son,* p. 283.

A large group claiming the name of Christian holds that Jesus *is* the Father Himself. In the Book of Mormon the chapter heading to the Book of Mosiah asserts, "Christ is both the Father and the Son": "And because he dwelleth in flesh he shall be called the Son of God, being the Father and the Son — the Father, because he was conceived by the power of God; and the Son, because of the flesh; thus becoming the Father and Son — and they are one God, yea, the very Eternal Father of heaven and earth" (Mosiah 15:2-4).

It may surprise some readers to learn that this doctrine, known as modalism, is held by some sections of the Pentecostal church today. It originated in the early post-apostolic Christological debates, and was also called "Patripassianism." For modalists, Christ was the Father Himself, come down to earth in human flesh. In fact, the Father Himself came down into the Virgin, was Himself born of her, Himself suffered, indeed was Himself Jesus Christ.

There are, however, speaking generally of the broader Christian Church, three views on the Sonship of Jesus: The Nicene or Athanasian view, the Arian view, and the third view which is sometimes called the Socinian view, after Faustus Socinus (1539-1604), an Italian religious reformer who ministered especially in Poland. In view of this history, which Son of God are we to confess? Who is the Biblical Son of God?

The Nicene View

Many church historians and theologians have tried to trace how the death of Jesus as he was abandoned by both God and man on the cross led, just 300 years later, to the confession that he was none other than the God who had created the universe and who now "upholds all things by the power of his word" (Heb. 1:3). For in 325 AD with the backing of the same Roman power that had crucified him, the Jew Jesus was officially proclaimed to be of the "nature" of God the Father, "God of God, Light of Light, Very God of Very God." Jesus is "begotten, not made," "of one substance with the Father" and through him all things in heaven and earth were made. A subsequent Church Council at Constantinople in 381 AD added that Jesus was "born of the Father before all time." Then in 451 AD at the Council of Chalcedon the famous formula was added that Jesus was "true God, true man," and was "consubstantial with the Father according to the Godhead, the selfsame consubstantial with us according to the manhood...Before all time he was begotten of the Father as to his Godhead, but in the last days the selfsame, for us and for our salvation, was born of Mary, the Virgin, the bearer of God, as to his manhood."

So, essentially formulated in the fourth century, this view speaks of "God the Father, God the Son, and God the Holy Spirit." Historically this "Catholic" interpretation has been promoted by decree and force. Those who did not so confess were threatened with ex-communication from the Catholic Church. And in the sixth century the Roman Emperor Justinian decreed that anybody who did not confess faith in this Trinity and in the "two natures" of Jesus Christ would be executed.

The belief that Jesus is "the eternally begotten Son," the second member of the Godhead, was championed by Augustine and prevails in the mainstream church, both Roman Catholic and Protestant, today. It is the view that Jesus the Son of God has existed from eternity as the "eternally generated Son."

Charles Swindoll is a well-known evangelical with a worldwide radio audience and readership through his many popular books. He is chancellor of the famous Dallas Theological Seminary. In his book *Jesus: When God Became Man* Swindoll typifies the universally accepted church belief in the Christmas story of the Incarnation:

> On December 25th shops shut their doors, families gather together and people all over the world remember the birth of Jesus of Nazareth...Many people assume that Jesus' existence began like ours, in the womb of his mother. But is that true? Did life begin for him with that first breath of Judean air? Can a day in December truly mark the beginning of the Son of God? Unlike us, Jesus existed before his birth, long before there was air to breathe...long before the world was born.

Swindoll continues with obvious enthusiasm:

> Jesus never came into being; at his earthly birth he merely took on human form...Here's an amazing thought: the baby that Mary held in her arms was holding the universe in place! The little newborn lips that cooed and cried once formed the dynamic works of creation. Those tiny clutching fists once flung stars into space and planets into orbit. That infant flesh so fair once housed the Almighty God...As an ordinary baby, God had come to earth...Do you see the child

> and the glory of the infant-God? What you are seeing is the Incarnation — God dressed in diapers...Imagine him in the misty precreation past, thinking of you and planning your redemption. Visualize this same Jesus, who wove your body's intricate patterns, knitting a human garment for himself...Long ago the Son of God dove headfirst into time and floated along with us for about 33 years...Imagine the Creator-God tightly wrapped in swaddling clothes.[11]

So here, in the traditional church interpretation, we have a Jesus who existed before his birth; a Jesus who never came into being; a Jesus who even as a baby continued to hold the universe (which he originally created) in his tiny clutching hands whilst cooing; a Jesus who is the infant-God needing his nappies to be changed in the very body which he had knitted like a garment for himself. The noted Anglican Dr. Jim Packer describes the Incarnation — when God became man, the divine Son became a Jew, the Almighty appeared on earth as a helpless baby, unable to do more than lie and stare and wriggle and make noises, needing to be fed and changed and taught like any other child. "He who had made man was now learning what it felt like to be man. He who made the angel who became the devil was now in a state in which He could be tempted — could not, indeed, avoid being tempted — by the devil."[12]

This Nicene understanding of Jesus Christ is the view that finally after much opposition triumphed over competing views. It is the "traditional" church view espoused to this day.

The Arian View

This is named after the priest Arius (died AD 336). Church history has so maligned Arius that his name has become a byword for despicable heresy. But it is difficult to locate exactly what Arius taught, because eventually his "heretical" works were destroyed. All we really have of his beliefs is what his enemies wrote about him. And it is well known that the victors write history from their winning position. But essentially this Arian view holds that Jesus preexisted his birth as a lesser "god." Jesus was generated by God the Father, sometime before the Genesis creation of the universe.

---

[11] Charles Swindoll, *Jesus: When God Became Man,* quoted in *Focus on the Kingdom*, ed. Anthony Buzzard, vol. 7, no. 3, Dec., 2004, p. 2.

[12] J.I. Packer, *Knowing God,* London: Hodder & Stoughton, 1973, p. 50.

The Jehovah's Witnesses, with their idea that Jesus was an archangel (Michael to be precise), are the major proponents of this idea today, though their view goes beyond the view of Arius. I will not spend time on this position here, because Scripture clearly teaches that the Son of God was not and is not an angel (Heb. 1:4-14).[13] In the third and fourth centuries Arius' understanding was quite pervasive (as already noted in chapter one).

The Socinian View

In this view Jesus' Sonship derives from an actual creation in the womb of Mary in history. Jesus did not personally preexist his own human existence. He is a true human being, although a unique human being. Jesus called himself "the only begotten Son." God the Father, by a special act of creation, brought him into existence. Jesus is the Son of God by a biological miracle.

Jesus came "out of" (Gk. *ek*) Mary and did not just pass "through" her from eternity into time and then proceed back to his former life in eternity. In a miraculous way God the Father created a human being, the Last Adam. Genetically speaking, Jesus is completely human, though a specially created human being.

In the light of these differing interpretations, it is appropriate to ask when we confess Jesus as the Son of God, *Which* Son are we actually professing? This is not merely an academic question. It is crucial because Jesus Christ himself came to build his Church on the solid rock of an informed and enlightened understanding of his true identity. "Who do you say that I am?" was his searching question to his disciples. It is this third view — the view that the Son of God came into existence in Mary by divine miracle — that I want to examine in some detail, because it is the view they never told me in church. It is a powerful view which makes excellent sense of the Bible, as I hope to show.

The Last Adam

The Bible tells the story of two men. The first man Adam ruined everything. The second man Jesus Christ came to put it all back together again, for God has "purposed...the summing up of all things in Christ, things in the heavens and things upon the earth" (Eph. 1:9-10).

---

[13] Please see Appendix 2: "Jesus and Michael."

It is evident that Adam, "the red earth-man" as his Hebrew name suggests, was originally genetically perfect. That is, he had no sin nature and lived in harmony with God, himself, his wife, and the world. Put on the earth by his Creator to be His agent, His representative, God's lord on earth, this man chose to rebel against God and so dragged himself and all his descendants down and away from the life and goodness of God. He who had originally reflected the glory of God was now a fallen being, only able to produce "disfigured" or "scarred" children in his own sinful likeness (Gen. 5:3). So the original Adam is the "one man" through whom sin and death entered this world (Rom. 5:12). Adam "wrecked it" for himself and everybody coming after him.

However, right there in the beginning when sin polluted the human species God proposed the solution. There was a prophetic announcement that one day a saviour, a redeemer would come on a giant rescue mission. "The seed" of the woman would come and crush the Serpent who had tempted Adam and deceived Eve (Gen. 3:15). But why would God call the coming Saviour a "seed"? When God created every kind of plant and animal he gave them the reproductive capacity to produce "after their kind." The Scripture says they had "seed in them" (Gen. 1:12). They were to "be fruitful and multiply" and fill the entire earth after their respective kinds. And if he had remained faithful to his LORD, Adam would have produced a race of genetically flawless and happy people living in beautiful harmony with the Creator and all creation. But alas, his rebellion meant that all his descendants, you and I included, would bear his fallen image. But thanks be to God, true to His promise, He has brought into the world another "Adam." Unlike the first Adam, this "seed" of Eve will generate a new humanity after his perfect image. Today Jesus is producing fruit "after his kind," a new body of humans who are doing what Adam should have originally done — loving God with all their strength and loving their neighbours as themselves. This new humanity, with Jesus as its Head, will enter the new Kingdom-Age to come.

Now it is right here that a critical point of difference between our two main views of who Jesus as the Son of God is, arises. Just exactly what kind of a man is this "Son of God"? The first view, the majority view, the view they told me in church, the Nicene view, is that the salvation of mankind could only have been achieved by God Himself becoming a man and paying the price for our redemption.

The concept that God must be born as a man in order for a valid sacrifice for sin to occur is called the doctrine of the Incarnation.

Without getting too academic and technical the doctrine of the Incarnation states that in some sense God, without ceasing to be God, was made man so that He could save mankind. The *New Bible Dictionary* summarises it this way:

> It appears to mean that the divine Maker became one of His own creatures...When the Word "became flesh," His deity was not abandoned or reduced or contracted, nor did He cease to exercise the divine functions which had been His before...The Incarnation of the Son of God, then, was not a diminishing of deity, but an acquiring of manhood.[14]

It is important to realize that although the "Incarnation" is assumed to be a basic tenet of Christianity, many scholars admit that the term and the concept it conveys do not appear anywhere in the Bible. One such scholar is James D.G. Dunn who says, "Incarnation, in its full and proper sense, is not something directly presented in Scripture."[15]

In other words it is a constructed doctrine beyond the boundaries of the Bible. It was formulated during several centuries of debate and massive upheaval in post-apostolic days. *The Oxford Dictionary of the Christian Church* verifies this fact:

> The doctrine, which took classical shape under the influence of the controversies of the 4th-5th centuries, was formally defined at the Council of Chalcedon of 451. It was largely moulded by the diversity of tradition in the schools of Antioch and Alexandria...Further refinements were added in the later patristic and medieval periods.[16]

The authors of *One God and One Lord* further explain:

> The reason the councils and synods took hundreds of years to develop the doctrine of Incarnation is that it is not stated in Scripture, and the verses used to support it can be explained without resorting to a doctrine that bears more similarity to pagan mythology than biblical truth. Teaching the Jews that God came down in the form of a man would have completely offended those living at the time of Christ

---

[14] *New Bible Dictionary,* Grand Rapids, MI: Eerdmans, 1975, p. 560.

[15] James Dunn, *Christology in the Making,* London: SCM Press, 1989, p. 4.

[16] *The Oxford Dictionary of the Christian Church,* p. 696.

> and the Apostles, and greatly contradicted their understanding of the Messianic Scriptures...This doctrine is derived most prominently from the Gospel of John, and in particular from the phrase in John 1:14 (KJV): "and the Word was made flesh." But was "the word" synonymous with "the Messiah" in Jewish understanding? Hardly. The Jews would have understood it to mean "plan" or "purpose," that which was clearly and specifically declared in Genesis 3:15 — a "seed" of a woman who would destroy the works of the Devil. This plan of God for the salvation of man finally "became flesh" in Jesus Christ. This verse is not establishing a doctrine of Incarnation contrary to all prophetic expectations, nor a teaching of preexistence. It is teaching of God's great love in bringing into existence His plan to save mankind from their sin.[17]

Many prophecies indicate that the Coming One would arise from the "seed," the stock of humanity, and in particular from Abrahamic and Davidic stock. The Messiah would be from the biological chain within the human family, specifically of Jewish pedigree: "The LORD your God will raise up for you a prophet **like me** from **among you, from your own countrymen** [literally, brothers]; you shall listen to him" (Deut. 18:15).

In this passage Moses predicts that the coming Messiah would be a person "like me," raised up from "among" the people of Israel, and that *God would not speak to the people directly*, because they were afraid that if God spoke without a mediator they would die (v. 16). The coming "prophet" would be a man of whom it is said that God would "put His words in his mouth, and he shall speak to them all that I command him. And it shall come about that whoever will not listen to My words which he shall speak in My name, I Myself will require it of him" (v. 18-19). To say that the Messiah is God *Himself* is to contradict the whole point of this prophecy. For it announces that the ultimate spokesman for God is expressly not God but a human being. The New Testament says that Jesus is the one who fulfilled this prophecy (Acts 3:22; 7:37).

---

[17] Mark H. Graeser, John A. Lynn, John W. Schoenheit, *One God and One Lord: Reconsidering the Cornerstone of the Christian Faith,* Indianapolis: Christian Educational Services, 2003, p. 353.

The very first verse of the NT says that Jesus Christ is "the son of David, the son of Abraham" (Matt. 1:1). On the day of Pentecost the apostle Peter confirms this Hebrew expectation that the Promised One would be a human being. Because David was a prophet he knew that "one of his descendants" would sit on the Davidic throne (Acts 2:30). Literally, Peter said that the promised Saviour would be "of the fruit of his loins." Understandably, no Jew who believed these Scriptures ever imagined that the baby born in Bethlehem was going to be Jehovah Himself come as a human baby. The central Christian doctrine of the Incarnation as taught today is thus alien to the Bible. We suggest that this fact demands urgent attention from all lovers of God, Jesus and the Bible.

In addition, Jehovah God says clearly that He is *not* a man (Num. 23:19; Job 9:32). The converse is therefore true: If a person is a man, then he cannot be God. Take another clear verse: "The Egyptians are men, and not God, and their horses are flesh and not spirit" (Is. 31:3). Notice here that the men and the horses are placed in the one category of "flesh." But God "the Holy One of Israel" (Is. 31:1) is in another realm altogether. To use Jesus' own words, "God is Spirit" (John 4:24). On the authority of Jesus himself we know that the categories of "flesh" and "spirit" are never to be confused or intermingled, though of course God's Spirit can impact our world. Jesus said, "That which is born of the flesh is flesh, and that which is born of the Spirit is spirit" (John 3:6). And "God is Spirit." The doctrine of the Incarnation confuses these categories. What God has separated man has joined together!

One of the charges that the apostle Paul levels at sinful man is that we have "exchanged the glory of the incorruptible God for an image in the form of corruptible man" (Rom. 1:23). Has it ever dawned on us as we sit in church listening to how the glorious Creator made Himself into a man that we could be guilty of this very same thing? The doctrine of the Incarnation has reduced the incorruptible God to our own corruptible image. We are made in God's image, not the other way round.

It is appropriate here to put this contrast in starker terms. The defining characteristic of the Creator God is His absolute holiness. God is utterly different from and so utterly transcendent over His creation that any confusion is forbidden. So here's the question. Is it possible that this eternal and holy God who is Spirit could make Himself into a dog or a cat? How about a flower or a tree? Or what about something inanimate like a rock? Even to pose the question is to be hit by its impossibility and absurdity. These are all created things which God has made. So how is it that we have become so conditioned as to be able to happily accept the equally dishonouring proposition that God could change Himself into a creature of flesh and blood?

One of the most famous names associated with this theory of the Incarnation is Athanasius. Athanasius was the priest who locked horns with Arius when the post-apostolic church was formulating the creeds confessed by mainstream Christianity even to this day. Athanasius said that God can choose to do anything He pleases and that for the sake of our salvation God chose to become a man. Athanasius insisted that Jesus Christ is not one of God's creatures but is rather God Himself incarnated in human form. It goes without saying that this kind of reasoning strikes at the very heart of Jesus' identity as a man by removing him entirely from our human kind.

In his book *When Jesus Became God* Richard Rubenstein presses the issue:

> Can God do anything He chooses to do? Of course — *except* those things that are inconsistent with being God. Can He choose to be evil or ignorant? Could He be the devil — or nothing at all? No, the Christian God is the Eternal God of Israel, Creator of the Universe. Athanasius maintains that this utterly transcendent God transformed Himself into a man, suffered, died, and then resurrected Himself! Doesn't this mixture of Creator and creature sound pagan? The bishop recognizes this, and tries to avoid its implications. For example, he insists that God did not create Jesus, as the Arians believe, or adopt him as His Son, but that he "begot" him out of His own nature. As he says, the idea of God fathering offspring with human beings by natural means is too disgusting for any Christian to contemplate. He therefore hastens to add that the Father's method of generating the Son is beyond human understanding.[18]

Rubenstein wryly adds:

> Indeed! Everything about this theory is beyond human understanding. The bishop ridicules the Arians for saying

[18] Rubenstein, *When Jesus Became God*, p. 118.

> that Jesus, being a creature of God, had the power to grow or decline in virtue, and that he *chose* to be virtuous through the exercise of his uniquely powerful will. No, Athanasius says, Christ being God was perfect by nature and could not change as humans do. But how can Jesus be called virtuous if he had not the power to choose? How can he be a model for human behaviour if he was incapable of change? The answer: this is a matter that is beyond human understanding![19]

Then Rubenstein rightly comments:

> The problem is not only that Athanasius' theory mixes God with His creation, but that it removes Jesus entirely from human society, from the universe of moral turmoil, and places him in the unchangeable heavens. If Christ is not a changeable, choosing creature at least *something* like us, how can we hope to imitate him? And if he is God Himself, not our representative and intermediary, how can he intervene on our behalf?...What, one wonders, would Jesus have made of that?[20]

Lockhart also rightly spots and expresses this dilemma: "If the Logos is inherently perfect and incapable of change, progress or suffering, he is no more able to mediate than the transcendent God himself."[21]

This is a huge difficulty for the theory of the Incarnation. The Bible clearly teaches that God cannot be tempted with evil things (James 1:13). God cannot sin. God is always true to His own unchangeable righteous character. He alone is good. So if Jesus Christ is fully God then his temptations that were "in all points like as we are" (Heb. 4:15) could not have been *real* temptations. If he was God then he *had* to win automatically. But the Scriptures clearly portray Jesus as a man limited by his human boundaries, gaining the victory through struggle by obedience to his Father.

Yet this confusing doctrine of the Incarnation of the eternal God is said to be essential to our salvation. Martyn Lloyd-Jones, the great reformed theologian, is typical of this approach. He says that the whole "doctrine of our redemption ultimately depends upon it

---

[19] *Ibid.*, p. 119.
[20] *Ibid.*, p. 119.
[21] Lockhart, *Jesus the Heretic,* p. 21.

[the Incarnation]. If He had not taken our human nature, He could not have saved us." This position reflects the mainstream position of the Church, namely that "the eternal Son of God, the second Person in the blessed Holy Trinity, took unto Himself human nature," so as to effect our salvation.[22]

The Adam Paradigm

It is our contention, however, that this theory of the Incarnation destroys the striking parallel between the first Adam and the last Adam and actually *disqualifies* Jesus from being our Saviour:

> Romans 5:12-19 clearly defines a critical, logical parallel between Adam and Jesus Christ in the context of the redemption of mankind. A major consequence of the doctrine that God became man is that it destroys this key parallel, for *Adam* is hardly comparable to an eternally preexistent being. Rather, he was a created being made in the image of the One who created him, God. Adam was not "fully man and fully God," "100 percent man and 100 percent God," "coequal with God the Father," or "of the same substance as the Father." Adam was a created, empowered being who chose to disobey a direct command of God, with dire consequences to himself and all mankind as a result.[23]

Shortly, I will show from the Scriptures that Jesus, like Adam, was a created man just as Adam before him was a created man. But for the moment it should be sufficient to see that one critical problem with this Incarnational view is that there are *no Old Testament predictions that indicate that God Himself would become a man.* (Later we will look at a few verses that are supposed to teach this.) But for the moment let us clearly understand that:

> Jesus could have no intrinsic advantage over Adam, or his qualification as Redeemer would be legally nullified. He was the Last Adam, not the first *God-man.* The differences between Adam and Jesus were circumstantial, not essential: Adam started tall with no navel; Jesus started short with a navel. Adam was created fully formed and fully able to

---

[22] Lloyd-Jones, *God the Father, God the Son,* p. 255ff.

[23] Graeser et al, *One God and One Lord: Reconsidering the Cornerstone of the Christian Faith,* p. 366.

> comprehend the voice of God. Jesus had to learn from his parents. Adam did not have to suffer the indignity of a humble birth and be considered illegitimate, the son of common folk. Adam had only to dress and keep the garden and care for his wife. He had to keep from eating the fruit, or die and bring death to all his descendants. Jesus had to drink the cup of suffering and die so he could be raised to conquer death and make it possible for others to eat of the "fruit" of eternal life.[24]

Trinitarians argue that Christ had to be the infinite God; otherwise how could the death of one finite man possibly save mankind? Surely one man can only die for or redeem one man, it is argued. I have to be honest and say I once sincerely believed this line of reasoning. I now see it represents a complete failure to understand the Bible's teaching regarding how the death of Jesus saves. Here is the testimony of another who also came to see the fallaciousness of this argument:

> The error of this kind of reasoning became evident to me when I perceived the truth in John 3:14-15, "as Moses lifted up the serpent in wilderness, so must the Son of man be lifted up, that whoever believes in him may have eternal life." This refers to the incident recorded in Numbers 21:7-9 in which the people were dying from the bites of the poisonous snakes. Moses was instructed by God to make a serpent of brass and set it on a pole for all to see; those who *believed* as they looked were saved from the poison of the snakes. Jesus compares this incident to *faith* in him: "And as Moses lifted up the serpent in the wilderness, so must the Son of Man be lifted up, that whoever *believes* in him may have eternal life" (John 3:14-15). The point here should be extremely clear: the saving of the thousands who looked to the brass serpent had nothing whatever to do with anything inherent in that serpent — they were saved by *God* through *faith* in His promise that whoever looked would be saved: "Yahweh said to Moses, 'Make a fiery serpent and set it on a pole, and everyone who is bitten, when he sees it, shall live'" (Num. 21:8). The next verse confirms that those who had the faith to look lived. The same is true for all those

[24] *Ibid.*, pp. 366-377.

> who are looking to Jesus for salvation through *faith* (Heb. 12:1-2); it is *God's* saving power in Christ which saves them from sin and death. It is, therefore, not something inherent in the constitution of Christ that saves, but it is God our Father (Yahweh) who saves us in and through Christ. For salvation is entirely God's work; it is by faith and through His grace alone...We fail to properly present Biblical soteriology (doctrine of salvation) if we fail to make it clear that God our Father is the ultimate or fundamental author of our salvation while Jesus is the mediating, or instrumental, agent for our salvation.[25]

We should, of course, not overlook the fact that Jesus was a sinless person, always and fully pleasing to God. Thus he is entirely adequate to the task of dying for every human person. He alone qualifies as the "one mediator between God and men" yet himself remains "the man Christ Jesus" (1 Tim. 2:5).

If Jesus was to satisfy the just requirements for redeeming us, whatever Adam was, Jesus Christ had to be also. This is why Jesus Christ had to be a created human being, with just one nature, a fully human one. He must have no unjust advantage of having "two natures." For this Adam clearly did not have.

And to push our point even further, how have we then accepted that this "Incarnate God" could *die* on the cross for our redemption? God cannot die. He is immortal (1 Tim. 6:16). To insist that Jesus was the "God-man" whose blood was of "infinite" value because of the Incarnation is to invite a huge difficulty and contradiction. To "explain" this impossibility Trinitarians maintain that Jesus actually had "two natures," the divine and the human, and that when he died it was only the human nature that died. But in the words of Anthony Buzzard:

> If Jesus were God, and God is immortal, Jesus could not have died. We wonder how it is possible to maintain that "Jesus" does not represent the whole person. Nothing in the Bible suggests that Jesus is the name of his human nature only. If Jesus is the whole person and Jesus died, he cannot be immortal Deity. It appears that Trinitarians argue that only Deity is sufficient to provide the necessary atonement.

[25] Chang, *The Only True God*, p. 173-174, emphasis his.

> But if the divine nature did not die, how on the Trinitarian theory is the atonement secured?[26]

All of which brings us full circle to our original question: How and in what way is Jesus the Son of God? What kind of a man is he? It is significant that he himself never claimed to be Jehovah God. But he did claim to perfectly represent God his Father, to be His agent.

As the NT teaches the first Adam is the type or the pattern for the Last Adam, Jesus Christ (Rom. 5:14). The coming Redeemer had to correspond in every way to *the original pattern, Adam.* Paul expressly states this in 1 Corinthians 15: "So also it is written, 'The first man, Adam, became a living soul.' The last Adam became a life-giving spirit. However, the spiritual is not first, but the natural; then the spiritual" (v. 45-46).

Trinitarians who identify "the man from heaven" in 1 Corinthians 15:47 with a pre-existent Christ fail to notice the context which is:

> focused on the resurrection and is built on a sequence of parallel contrasts — physical/spiritual, earthly/heavenly, first man/second man — where it is clear enough that the second half of each contrast refers to the resurrection state. This includes the description of the second man as "from heaven," for it is precisely his heavenly image which provides the pattern for the resurrection state of others (1 Cor. 15:49). Paul has already made this clear earlier in the same chapter: Christ in his resurrection is the "firstfruits of those who have fallen asleep"; *as risen* he is the archetype of resurrected humanity (15:2-23). And in the immediate context he has been at some pains (for whatever reason) to insist that the spiritual does *not* precede the physical (15:46). Hence in relation to (first) Adam, Christ is *last* Adam (15:45). It would throw his argument into complete confusion if he was understood to mean that "the *second* man from heaven" was actually the pre-existent one, and therefore actually first, *before* Adam.[27]

---

[26] Buzzard and Hunting, *The Doctrine of the Trinity,* p. 274.

[27] Dunn, *Christology in the Making,* Foreword to Second Edition, p. xviii, emphasis original.

It is worth noting that this quote appears in Dunn's foreword to the second edition of his book. It is his response to those who continued to challenge his exegesis that "the man from heaven" cannot be a reference to the apostle Paul's supposed belief in Jesus as the eternally existing Son of God. Dunn confesses that his critics' failure to take full note of the resurrection context in 1 Corinthians 15 is "astonishing"! I might add that I also fully relate to his frustration when such obvious exegetical rules of context are ignored to prop up an unsubstantiated theory.

The physical man precedes the spiritual man! Traditional theology has reversed the order. The Son of God did not precede Adam in time, according to Paul. Jesus is the Second Adam. In the post-apostolic book II Clement, written early in the second century, some were already starting to sabotage God's programme. II Clement 9:5 reads: "Christ, the Lord who saved us, *being first spirit became flesh.*"

Harnack, the well-known church historian, comments on this statement: "That is the fundamental, theological and philosophical creed on which the whole Trinitarian and Christological speculations of the Church of the succeeding centuries are built, and it is thus the root of the orthodox system of dogmatics."[28] Harnack went on to describe this fateful development as "the history of the substitution of the historical Jesus by the preexisting Christ, of the Christ of reality by the fictitious Christ in dogmatics, the victorious attempt to substitute *the mystery* of the person of Christ for the person himself." Or, as others have well expressed it:

> *In order for him to redeem mankind, Jesus had to be whatever Adam was before his fall.* Jesus Christ is the Last Adam, a man like Adam who could undo what Adam did. The Last Adam, by dying on the cross, sacrificed himself as an offering for the sin that the first Adam introduced into the world. This Adamic parallelism establishes one of the most foundational biblical truths regarding Christ, one that allows us to see the entire span of the Bible: two men, two gardens, two commands, two decisions, two deaths, two universal results, two races of people and two Paradises.[29]

---

[28] Harnack, *History of Dogma,* vol. 1, p. 328, italics original.

[29] Graeser et al, *One God and One Lord,* p. 27.

So the order of appearance is quite clear: Adam first, Christ second. Christ is the *last* Adam. Adam *precedes* Christ. Adam was not a copy of a heavenly, preexistent Christ, but "a type of him who **was to come**" (Rom. 5:17). *As a true man Jesus was patterned after the likeness of Adam!* In contrast to this biblical model, however, it will no doubt be a huge surprise for most who read this and believe that Jesus was born the Infant-God (as cited above in Swindoll, Packer, *et al*) that official Incarnational theology teaches that Jesus was *not "a man"* but was rather in fact impersonal *"man." That is official Trinitarian teaching. It proposes that Jesus the Son of God has human nature, but is not a human person!* At the Council of Chalcedon (451 AD) orthodoxy officially taught that God the Son united himself to a *personless human nature.* The "ego" of Jesus (i.e. his true centre of personality) is his Godhood because he is the second Person of the blessed Trinity. Because the Son of God had no beginning but simply came through Mary, he merely assumed impersonal human nature; therefore Jesus does not have a true human personal ego or centre. One commentator puts it this way:

> Now the doctrine of the Incarnation is that in Christ the place of a human personality is replaced by the Divine Personality of God the Son, the second Person of the Most Holy Trinity. Christ possesses a complete human nature *without a human personality.* Uncreated and eternal Divine Personality replaces a created personality in Him.[30]

Thus, the shocking truth of the official doctrine of the Incarnation is that Jesus is de-humanized. It turns out he really is not like the first man Adam, not like us after all, not a man, but "man" in a nebulous, generic sense. According to the Bible model this *disqualifies* Jesus from being the "seed of the woman," the genuine descendant of David, and means he cannot be our Saviour!

The traditional Christian idea that Jesus is God in the flesh also creates other unnecessary inconsistencies. It is to assume that in some way when he was growing up he became aware of being Deity within himself. For most of his youth and young adult life Jesus had to somehow conceal his status as Deity from everyone he met. He had to suppress his latent powers. He must perform no miracle, heal no sick, so that ordinary people around him — including his own

---

[30] Leslie Simmonds, *What Think Ye of Christ?* quoted in *Focus on the Kingdom*, ed. Anthony Buzzard, vol. 7, no. 3, p. 5.

family — would have no inkling of his real ego and identity as Jehovah God.

> If he was the same before his baptism as he was afterwards this could hardly fail to be manifest in his earlier years. After Jesus had been accepted as God it did not take Christians very long to appreciate this difficulty, and they produced a number of books purporting to relate authentically the prodigies he had performed as a boy...But quite evidently there had been no such exploits, and nothing to indicate that the young Jesus son of Joseph was other than he seemed.[31]

That is, Jesus was authentically human. Let us turn now to see how this man Jesus the Christ came into being.

The Origin of Jesus Christ

I remember a sincere man once telling me the story of how Jesus came to save us. Apparently Gabriel the archangel had become concerned. He noticed that the "eternal Son of God" was missing from heaven. Where had he gone? Anxiety quickly sprang up amongst all the angels. Rumours were rife. So Gabriel presented himself before the throne of God to ask where the Son of God was. Jehovah then let Gabriel in on the secret. Because of their great love for lost humanity, His Son had agreed in their eternal counsels to leave heaven. He was about to be born as a human baby so that men could be redeemed. And Gabriel had better make haste to announce this mind-blowing mystery to the virgin Mary!

It struck me at the time this man told me this bit of make-believe how easily genuine Bible lovers can swallow such lolly-coated myth as though it were gospel truth. To mainstream church people Jesus Christ is the second member of the Godhead. There never was a time when the "eternal Son" did not exist. He is God. Before He became man He was the Creator of the heavens and the earth.

The official explanation is that Jesus is "the eternally begotten Son of God." We shall soon see that this is a contradiction in terms, for by definition to be begotten means to have a beginning. It is impossible to have a beginningless beginning. Even worse, it is a flat contradiction of the Scriptures. Speaking of His Son in that

---

[31] Schonfield, *The Passover Plot,* pp. 70-71.

wonderful Messianic Psalm God says, "Thou art My Son; **today** I have **begotten** thee" (Ps. 2:7). God states that His Son was begotten "today," i.e. in time. But church tradition says Jesus is "eternally begotten," outside of time, and there never was a time when Jesus did not exist! We may well ask, then, if no verse in the Scripture calls Jesus the *eternal Son* of God, where did this teaching come from? And why are there no Bible verses that speak of Jesus being begotten by the Father in *eternity*? It must be important, because without it there is no doctrine of the Trinity! The Bible's silence on this subject is deafening.

This kind of "forked tongue" explanation has its roots way back in the church tradition of the early post-apostolic days. Athanasius wrote:

> Nor again is it right to seek how God begets and what is the manner of His begetting. For a man must be beside himself to venture on such points; since a thing ineffable and proper to God's nature and known to Him alone and the Son, this he demands to be explained in words. It is better in perplexity to be silent and believe than to disbelieve on account of perplexity.

This dreadful attempt to cover up a direct contradiction of the Bible should alert us to how Scripture has been severely mishandled. Indeed, it is not only Athanasius who confesses his inability to adequately expound this complex doctrine, but he acknowledges that the council fathers at Nicea were also troubled over the fact that they could not answer Arius in purely biblical categories (!).[32]

So we trace how Athanasius and the council at Nicea set the tone. Since then Church tradition has dictated that "God, Whose nature and existence are above time, may not engender in time" (John of Damascus). So by the decree of these men, tradition has subsequently forbidden God to act in time and history within His own world! They told God what He could not do! Another, Gregory of Nazianzen, is equally lost in a fog of feeble explanation: "But the manner of the Son's generation we will not admit that even angels can conceive, much less you. Shall I tell you how it was? It was in a manner known to the Father who begat, and to the Son who was

---

[32] Athanasius, *Letters Concerning the Decrees of the Council of Nicaea,* 5.18-21; NPNF Series 2, 4.161-164.

begotten. Anything more than this is hidden by a cloud and escapes your dim sight."

One of the first great proponents of this mainstream and traditional view was Origen (we have already noted Origen's connections with Platonism). Let's see how he also prevaricates on the clear testimony of Scripture. He disposes of the obvious meaning for the word "today" to make way for his own theology:

> Christ as Son. When the words are addressed to Him, "Thou art My Son, this day have I begotten Thee," this is spoken to Him by God, with whom all time is today, for there is no evening with God, as I consider, and there is no morning, nothing but time that stretches out, along with His unbeginning and unseen life. The day is today with Him in which the Son was begotten, and thus the beginning of His birth is not found, as neither is the day of it.[33]

How easily do these men explain away the clear meaning of words. And the Church has revered such men. I do not believe God talks such nonsense. God cannot lie. I also believe that the Scriptures are the inspired words of God (2 Tim. 3:16). Jesus also believed this. He said the Scripture cannot be broken. What is written is written and we are to listen intelligently to that. We are therefore not free to make up our own private interpretations (2 Pet. 1:20). Which will you believe? "Today" refers to time or eternity? "Begotten" means to be originated or does it mean to have no beginning? Are we to believe that the day of his birth is not to be found?

Matthew and Luke on the Begetting of Jesus the Son of God

More importantly, what did the apostles believe? Matthew begins like this: "The book of the genealogy of Jesus Christ, the son of David, the son of Abraham" (Matt. 1:1). The KJV translates it "The book of the generation of Jesus Christ." The Greek word translated "genealogy" here is the word "genesis." And the word "genesis" means "origin." The first words of the Bible in Genesis 1 read "in the beginning."

Matthew tells us that this is the book of the *origin — or genealogy — of Jesus Messiah.* It reminds us of Genesis 2:4: "This is the account [literally, These are the generations, the origins] of

---

[33] *Commentary on John*, Book 1, 32.

the heavens and the earth when they were created, in the day that the LORD God made earth and heaven." Just as the material universe is not eternal but has a point of beginning, so too Jesus the Son of God has a beginning.

Matthew goes on to explain the lineage of Jesus Christ: "To Abraham was born Isaac." Wait a minute. Although this is a reasonable translation of what Matthew wrote, it is not precise enough and clouds something vitally important. At least the old KJV is accurate here when it translates, "Abraham **begat** Isaac; and Isaac **begat** Jacob; and Jacob **begat** Judas."

There is no doubt as to the meaning here. Abraham fathered Isaac. Abraham generated Isaac. Isaac did not exist before being begotten. Then Isaac "begat" Jacob. Same meaning. Isaac sired a son. And so Jacob came into being. In fact, Matthew uses this "begat" word throughout his genealogy before he gets to the human birth of Jesus a total of 39 times. And in every single case we know exactly what Matthew means. The father procreated, generated, brought into being a son.

The same word "begat" is used of the coming into being, the origin of Jesus Christ. Is it not curious that our translations do not reflect this? In verse 16 the KJV says that of Mary "**was born** Jesus, who is called Christ." An equally valid translation of what Matthew wrote is "Mary, of whom **was begotten** Jesus, who is called Christ," though the natural sense in this instance is probably that Jesus was born of Mary. According to Matthew Jesus was born and came into existence, was procreated, had his origin in the same way as we understand all the others in this genealogy did. Well, actually not quite in the same way! For Matthew goes on to explain something unique about Jesus' procreation: "Now the birth of Jesus Christ was as follows..." Whoa! That's not what Matthew wrote. He wrote this: "Now the **genesis** of Jesus Christ was as follows..."[34]

There it is again — the origin of Jesus! This is the "today," the point in history when Jesus begins, comes into being. Unlike all the other human babies in Matthew's list this baby does not have a human father begetting him. No. The angel appears in a dream to a worried Joseph who wonders how Mary has gotten herself into such

---

[34] I am aware that this is a disputed text. But this is not the place to enter into a matter of textual criticism. Currently the consensus amongst textual critics is that Matthew wrote *genesis*. For a scholarly discussion of this disputed text see Bart Ehrman's *The Orthodox Corruption of Scripture*.

a fix as to be pregnant when he knows perfectly well that he has not had sexual relations with her. The explanation is given in verse 20: "for that which has been conceived in her is of the Holy Spirit." Once again we must protest at the way the translators have handled what Matthew wrote. What he wrote was this: "for that which has been **begotten** in her is of the Holy Spirit." *It is the same word Matthew has used throughout this chapter to indicate procreation.* We could translate it accurately this way: "For that which has been **generated** in her is of the Holy Spirit." This is the action of God the Father who begets His Son.

Here then is the begetting of the Son of God in history on earth. But there is even more to what Matthew tells us. Four women's names appear in the list before we come to Mary: "Zerah **by** Tamar," (v. 3) "Boaz **by** Rahab," (v. 5) "and Obed **by** Ruth" (v. 5); "Solomon **by** her who had been the wife of Uriah" (v. 6). Once again we have no trouble understanding what this means. The Greek word rendered "by" in these four instances is *ek* and means "out of." The mother produces the egg out of which comes her baby. Now the same explanation is given for Mary's baby Jesus. Verse 16: "Mary by [Greek *ek:* out of] whom was born Jesus." So we note that Jesus came out of Mary, not *through* Mary. Again Jesus originated from true human stock, so to speak. In other words, there is no personally preexisting Son who enters Mary's womb from eternity and passes into time. He comes "out of" Mary, as all babies originate in their mothers. (It is interesting that certain Gnostics made the claim that Christ did not come *from Mary, but came through her "like water through a pipe*."[35])

This begetting or beginning of the Son of God is even more precisely described, if this is possible, in Luke's account. Gabriel announces to the virgin Mary: "The Holy Spirit will come upon you, and the power of the Most High will overshadow you; and for that reason the holy offspring shall be called the Son of God" (Luke 1:35).

Gabriel tells us that Mary's son is to be conceived in a miraculous way. "Holy Spirit" power will overshadow her. (There is no definite article before "Holy Spirit" in the Greek.) This indicates that God's presence, His initiating power is the cause of Jesus' conception and begetting. Raymond E. Brown says this "would be

[35] As quoted by Irenaeus in his *Against Heresies* I, 7, 2.

consonant with a theology of a new creation wherein God's Spirit, active in the first creation of life (Gen. 1:2) was active again."[36] Let us not miss the import of what is being said here, by either Gabriel through Luke or by Brown. The virgin Mary conceived by "the power of the Highest." Brown goes on to say it is not that we are to understand this begetting in a "quasi-sexual" way as if God takes the place of a male principle in causing Mary to conceive. There is more of a connotation of creativity. Mary is not barren; rather she is a virgin who has not had sexual relations with a man, and therefore the child is totally God's work — a new creation. The Spirit that comes upon Mary is directly parallel to the Spirit of God that hovered over the waters before the creation in Genesis 1:2. The earth was void and without form when that Spirit appeared; just so Mary's womb was a void until through the Spirit God filled it with a child who was His Son. In the annunciation of the birth of John the Baptist we heard of a yearning and prayer on the part of the parents who very much wanted a child; but since Mary is a virgin who has not yet lived with her husband there is no yearning for or human expectation of a child — it is the surprise of a staggering new creation. No longer are we dealing with human request and God's generous fulfilment; this is God's initiative going beyond anything man or woman has dreamed of.[37]

In contrast to the creeds of Christendom which tell us to believe that our Lord was eternal and uncreated, Gabriel says otherwise — the Son of God began in Mary's womb. We are dealing with the begetting of God's Son in the womb of Mary through God's creative Spirit. As Brown says, it is only in second-century writings that we find the Lucan and (misunderstood) Johannine concepts combined into an Incarnation of a preexistent deity in the womb of the virgin Mary.[38] Luke does not think of a preexistent Son of God. Luke therefore did not believe in the Trinity and would be excluded from membership in almost all churches today.

---

[36] Raymond Brown, *The Birth of the Messiah: A Commentary on the Infancy Narratives in the Gospels of Matthew and Luke,* New York: Doubleday, 1993, p. 299.
[37] *Ibid.*, p. 314.
[38] *Ibid.,* p. 314, footnote 48.

Two Begettings?

It is true that there is *possibly* another occasion in Jesus' life where he is said to be "begotten." The day of his resurrection/coronation is said by some commentators to be a begetting. The prophetic decree of Psalm 2 ("You are My Son; this day I have begotten you") is applied not to his conception/birth, but to his resurrection/exaltation to the Father's right hand. The NT evidence for this claim is slim and dubious at best. The only passage I can locate that may give this impression is Hebrews 1:3-5. Here, after stating that Jesus rose from the dead and "sat down at the right hand of the Majesty on high" (Heb. 1:3), the begetting of Jesus is cited from Psalm 2. Some allege that on this basis the begetting of the Son into heaven by resurrection is a symbolic begetting. Therefore, since Jesus' resurrection did not initiate his personal beginning why should Luke's birth account of the begetting of Jesus not also be taken metaphorically? Taken this way, it would indicate that Jesus (who had supposedly existed from eternity) now only entered a new phase of his existence via Incarnation. His conception is therefore not a real personal beginning. His birth is symbolically important, but does not mark his personal origin. Jesus' virginal conception is merely metaphorical language for adoption. Is this a valid proposition?

On at least two separate occasions the Father spoke from heaven saying, "This is My beloved Son." These public declarations — one at his baptism, and one at his transfiguration — did not establish Jesus' Sonship; they rather confirmed openly what was already fact, namely that Jesus indeed was God's Son. Neither baptism nor transfiguration gave to Jesus a new status. The purpose of these public announcements was not to show the world that the Father was adopting Jesus as His Son. These events only revealed a sonship already real from his conception. But can this reasoning be applied to the announcement by God at the coronation of Jesus ("You are My Son; today I have begotten you") if indeed it was a post-resurrection announcement? When God set Jesus down at His own right hand in heaven, it was a confirmation — in the same vein as the Father's announcements at the baptism and Mount of Transfiguration — to all in heaven and on earth that this one who had been rejected by men was indeed His Son. But is more intimated than just universal recognition of Jesus as His now-resurrected Son? Is his resurrection a (metaphorical) begetting? If so, how can there be two begettings — one at conception and one at coronation? Fortunately, we can turn to other parallel passages in the NT for light.

Psalm 2 is also quoted in the NT in Acts 13:33. Here there is no doubt at all that the Father's decree, "You are My Son; today I have begotten you" is a reference to Jesus' conception/physical beginning and to his life's ministry. As the apostle Paul announces "the good news of the promise made to the fathers" (Acts 13:32) he tells how God the Father "raised up Jesus" (v. 33) in fulfilment of His decree in Psalm 2. This clearly refers to Jesus' physical begetting, because only in the next verse is the *resurrection* of Jesus introduced: "And as for the fact that He raised him up from the dead, no more to return to decay..." (v. 34). (This point is lost to readers of the King James Version where there is an unfortunate mistranslation. The word "again" appears in verse 33 where it has no right to be. This gives the impression that the Psalm 2 citation refers to Jesus' resurrection when it reads, "God hath fulfilled the same unto us their children, in that He hath raised up Jesus *again*." The original Greek does not introduce the word "again" until verse 34 where, as we have noted, the resurrection first comes into view.)

Earlier in Paul's sermon we find the same expression that God "raised up David to be their king" (Acts 13:22). Just as God raised David up to royal service God has raised Jesus up for ministry as David's literal descendant. This also finds an OT echo where God promises to "raise up" a descendant after David "who will come forth from you, and I will establish his kingdom" (2 Sam. 7:12). Once again God's decree to raise up Jesus as a real flesh and blood descendant of David is a reference not to the resurrection, but to his actual physical birth and life. Our conclusion is that in view of both OT background and other NT references to God's decree, the begetting of the Son always refers to Jesus' physical beginning.

Perhaps another key in helping us to answer our question is found in the introduction to the letter to the Romans. Here we are told the Gospel concerns: "His Son, who was born of the seed of David **according to the flesh**; declared with power to be the Son of God **according to a spirit of holiness** by the resurrection from the dead" (Rom. 1:3-4).

There are *two* "according to's" here which throw light on our question. The first says that "according to the flesh" God's Son was born (literally, *came into existence*) of Davidic descent. He is a real human being. As Paul states in Galatians 4, God sent forth (commissioned) His Son "born [again literally, *coming into existence*] of a woman" (Gal. 4:4). (If Jesus always existed as the eternal Son before his birth, these statements are false.) The second "according to" says that Jesus is "declared with power to be the Son of God according to a spirit of holiness by his resurrection." Note that the resurrection does not constitute Jesus as the Son of God, it announces — "with power" — an already established Sonship. Jesus Christ is the only man so far to have experienced two realms of existence. As God's Son "according to the flesh" Jesus lived in weakness and humility on this earth. Not many knew his true identity. But after he was resurrected, and taken to the right hand of God, this Son entered *a new phase of existence*. His coronation ushered him — for the first time — into the realm of the Spirit and immortality. Jesus' resurrection is a powerful confirmation that his claims to be the uniquely begotten Son of God were true. It is a major enhancement of a sonship already enjoyed; as Son of God his status is intensified. His resurrection *may* be spoken of as a "spiritual begetting," which marks him off "**with power** to be the Son of God." But it came after the Son was literally and physically begotten in Mary. That conception in Mary marks the physical begetting that begins his actual existence as Son of God; his coronation though may be spoken of as a "spiritual begetting" which begins a new *phase* in his Sonship. Raymond Brown is quite adamant that Jesus' begetting as Son of God in Mary's womb is to be taken literally. His rationale is that the "coming" of the Holy Spirit in Luke 1:35b (which explains why the child is called "holy" in 1:35d) and the "overshadowing" by the power of the Most High in 1:35c (which explains why the child is called Son of God in 1:35d) "*really* beget the child as God's Son — there is no adoption here."[39]

Professor Anthony Buzzard further underscores this:

> We are presented in these verses [Luke 1:35], on the authority of God's emissary, with a plain statement about the origin of Jesus as Son of God. The miraculous conception in Mary, according to Luke, was the immediate cause of the divine Sonship of Jesus. It is *"for that reason"* (Luke 1:35) — the conception by Mary through the power

[39] *Ibid.,* pp. 313-314.

> of God's Holy Spirit — that Jesus was to be called the Son of God. A French commentator on this passage nicely renders the Greek, *dio kai*, as *"c'est précisément pourquoi"* ("that is precisely why," "for that reason indeed") he shall be called the Son of God. It is not difficult to see that Luke's view of Jesus' Sonship is at variance with the traditional idea that one who already existed as God and Son of God had entered the womb of Mary. If this were so, the conception of Jesus would not be the cause of Jesus' divine Sonship. He would have been the Son of God already.[40]

In another article Anthony Buzzard drives home this point even more tellingly:

> The message is simple and clear. The Son of God of Gabriel's announcement is none other than a divinely created Son of God, coming into existence — begotten — as Son in his mother's womb. All other claimants to divine Sonship and Messiahship may be safely discounted. A "Son of God" who is the *natural* son of Joseph could not, on the evidence of Gabriel, be the Messiah. Such a person would not answer to the Son who is son on the basis of a unique divine intervention in the biological chain. Equally false to Gabriel's definition of the Son of God would be a son who *preexisted* his conception. Such a son could not possibly correspond to the Messiah presented by Gabriel, one whose existence is predicated on a creative act in history on the part of the Father. Gabriel does not present a Son of God in transition from one state of existence to another. He announces the miraculous origin and beginning of the Messiah...Conception and begetting mark the point at which an individual *begins* to exist, an individual who did *not* exist before![41]

So Gabriel informs us that God's creative power initiated into history His uniquely born Son. Here is no metaphorical begetting. As another scholar puts it: "He [God] was creating a human being, the Last Adam, not a second God or second person of a triune God. In this way our Lord's humanity, by special creation, came from

---

[40] Buzzard and Hunting, *The Doctrine of the Trinity,* pp. 68-69.

[41] Anthony Buzzard, *Focus on the Kingdom,* vol. 5, no. 7, p. 1.

both God and Mary and he was completely, entirely, and purely human."[42]

When God breathed into the lifeless body of Adam he became a living soul. The fact that God's spirit or breath animated Adam did not mean that Adam became a man with two natures, that he was fully God and fully man. No, he was purely, entirely human. Just so, when God overshadowed Mary and by His power created Jesus out of her maternal ovum, Jesus did not become a man with two natures. He too was purely, entirely human, *just like Adam*. For those who object to this striking Adam parallel it is informative to note that Luke draws this very lesson just a few verses later. He traces the lineage of Jesus the Son of God all the way back to Adam who likewise is called "the son of God" (Luke 3:38)! God who had created the first "son of God" — Adam — now by special miracle also creates the last Adam — Jesus — who is also designated "Son of God."

In Nicene Christology this conception/begetting of Jesus does *not* bring the Son of God into being. In the traditional scheme the conception of Jesus is merely the beginning of his earthly career. But for Gabriel the miracle is the reason and the basis for the Son's very existence. Jesus is the Son of God for "*this precise reason*" taught so beautifully by none other than the archangel in Luke 1:35:

> *At stake here is the whole nature of the Saviour. Is he really a human being, or did he have the benefit of billions of years of conscious existence, before deciding to become a man?*...The Son of God, Messiah and Saviour, is defined in precise theological terms by Gabriel, laying the foundation of the whole New Testament and fulfilling the promises of the Old...Jesus is the Son of God on one basis only, his miraculous coming into existence in Mary's womb. This was God's creative act, initiating His new creation and providing the model of Christian Sonship for us all. Though obviously we are not, like Jesus, brought into existence supernaturally, nevertheless we, like him, are to receive a supernatural birth from spirit by being born again under the influence of the Gospel...A Son of God who is *already* Son of God before his conception in his mother is a personage essentially non-human. Under that revised scheme what

---

[42] Sidney Hatch, *Brief Bible Studies,* vol. 25, no. 2. p. 10.

> came into existence in Mary was not the Son of God at all, but a created *human nature* added to an already existing Person.[43]

A definitive book, *The Virgin Birth in History and Faith*, was written in 1941 by Douglas Edwards. Edwards was himself a Trinitarian, which means that he believed Jesus was the second member of the eternal Trinity. However, he refuses to use the virgin birth for this belief. He categorically says that:

> The New Testament never connects the Virgin Birth with the Divinity of Christ...The nativity narratives...connect the Virgin Birth not with the Deity of Jesus Christ but with His Christship and His Manhood...so far from marking Him out *as God* — His birth "of the Spirit" empowers Him to be *the Man for whom the Kingdom is a visible reality.*[44]

Nothing could be plainer, according to Edwards:

> The apostles did not believe that Jesus was God because he was born of a virgin, nor did they expect others to believe in his Divinity on this ground...It was not the *Godhead* of Christ that the miraculous birth attested. Nor would it have occurred to the early Christians to appeal to the Virgin Birth as a proof of the Divinity of Christ. Nor do they so appeal to it.[45]

J.O. Buswell concurs:

> The notion that the Son was begotten by the Father in eternity past, not as an event, but as an inexplicable relationship, has been accepted and carried along in the Christian theology since the fourth century...We have examined all the instances in which "begotten" or "born" or related words are applied to Christ, and we can say with confidence that the *Bible has nothing whatsoever to say about "begetting" as an eternal relationship between the Father and the Son.*[46]

Raymond Brown goes so far as to say that Luke 1:35 is a positive embarrassment to mainstream belief: "Luke 1:35 has

---

[43] Anthony Buzzard, *Focus on the Kingdom,* vol. 5, no. 7, p. 3.

[44] Douglas Edwards, *The Virgin Birth in History and Faith,* London: Faber & Faber Ltd., 1941, p. 191.

[45] *Ibid.,* p. 190.

[46] J.O. Buswell, *A Systematic Theology of the Christian Religion,* Zondervan, 1962, p. 110.

embarrassed many orthodox theologians, since in preexistence theology a conception by the Holy Spirit in Mary's womb does *not* bring about the existence of God's Son. Luke is seemingly unaware of such a Christology; conception is causally related to divine Sonship for him."[47]

The New Testament scholar and textual critic Bart Ehrman says, "In point of fact, there is nothing in Matthew's narrative, either here or elsewhere throughout the Gospel, to suggest that he knew or subscribed to the notion that Christ had existed prior to his birth."[48]

For the moment let us press the issue home. To "beget" means to bring into existence, to cause to be. To say the Son was "eternally begotten" is like talking about square circles. You cannot begin and not begin at the same time! As Anthony Buzzard has pointed out, it is doubtful if this expression contains any more meaning than "hot ice cubes."

Where then is the "traditional" doctrine of the eternal begetting of the Son to be found in Scripture? *The traditional view says the Son was begotten, but was never given existence* — he was eternal. Such Church-speak is illogical nonsense. *If there is no eternal begetting of the Son then there is no eternal Son. Orthodoxy would have us believe that the Father is unbegotten and had no beginning, but the Son was begotten, and he also had no beginning!* Surely it is clear that it is crooked to assign meaning to words which no lexicon supports. This is just playing with words and making them mean whatever one claims they mean.

Other "explanations" are offered to justify the traditional creed. Christ is the Son of God "begotten, not created" and "begotten before all worlds," but this destroys the meaning of "beget" which is a form of creation or procreation. The well-known C.S. Lewis champions the traditional cause and asks what these words mean:

> One of the creeds says that Christ is the Son of God "begotten, not created"; and it adds "begotten by his Father before all worlds." Will you please get it quite clear that this has nothing to do with the fact that when Christ was born on earth as a man, that man was the son of a virgin? We are not now thinking about the Virgin Birth. We are thinking about something that happened before Nature was created at all,

---

[47] Raymond Brown, *The Birth of the Messiah,* p. 291.

[48] Ehrman, *The Orthodox Corruption of Scripture,* p. 76.

> before time began. "Before all worlds" Christ is begotten, not created. What does it mean?
>
> We don't use the words *begetting* and *begotten* much in modern English, but everyone still knows what they mean. To beget is to become the father of; to create is to make. And the difference is this. When you beget, you beget something of the same kind as yourself. A man begets human babies, a beaver begets little beavers and a bird begets eggs which turn into little birds. But when you make, you make something of a different kind from yourself. A bird makes a nest, a beaver builds a dam, a man makes a wireless set — or he may make something more like himself than a wireless set: say, a statue...Now that is the first thing to get clear. What God begets is God; just as what man begets is man. What God creates is not God; just as what man makes is not man. That is why men are not Sons of God in the sense that Christ is. They may be like God in certain ways, but they are not things of the same kind. They are more like statues or pictures of God.[49]

Lewis gets into the usual Hellenistic/philosophical tangle here, but at least we can begin by endorsing his statement that "to beget is to become the father of." We are working from the same definition. Jesus had a beginning, albeit a beginning "that happened before Nature was created at all, before time began." However, there are at least two problems with Lewis' explanation. Firstly, *without any Scriptural warrant* for doing so, he places Jesus' begetting as Son way back into a timeless eternity past. As we have just seen, Matthew and Luke place Jesus' begetting in time — in first-century Palestine, three months after Elizabeth's pregnancy — and in place — in the womb of Mary. There is not one word in the Bible anywhere that teaches Jesus was begotten in eternity. Not one.

Secondly, Lewis makes the arbitrary statement that God begets God. This would mean that the unbegotten God begets an unbegotten person. This directly contradicts the meaning of "beget" and the Scriptural fact that Jesus was the begotten Son of God. Lewis fails to account for the Bible's understanding of what it means to be the Son of God. His distinction between "begetting"

---

[49] C.S. Lewis, *Mere Christianity*, New York: Macmillan Publishing Co., 1943, p. 138.

and "creating" might be quite valid — if we were working in the realm of Greek philosophy and metaphysics. But we are not now working in that realm. We are now thinking with Hebrew minds. For in the begetting of Jesus by the miraculous overshadowing of the Spirit of God, God is working a new creation. In the Hebrew mind, the begetting of Jesus was the creation of the Son of God, as we have seen. And here is the key we need to gain clarity. It is found in the Bible's own definition and background to the description "Son of God" and it is to this particular understanding we now turn.

Son of God

One of the world's leading (and at the time of writing still living) systematic theologians is Dr. Colin Brown of Fuller Seminary. Dr. Brown is a leading contributor to the *International Standard Bible Encyclopedia.* Dr. Brown speaks of "a systematic misunderstanding of Son-of-God language in Scripture." Indeed, Brown says, "One may ask whether the term 'Son of God' is in and of itself a divine title at all. Certainly there are many instances in biblical language where it is definitely not a designation of deity." He then illustrates this point from the Bible. This term is used to describe Adam the created vice-regent of God on earth (Luke 3:38); it is used to designate the nation of Israel and the king of Israel (Ex. 4:22; Hos. 11:1; Ps. 2:7; 2 Sam. 7:14, etc.); and in its plural form to designate even angels (Job 1:6; 2:1; 38:7). He then says:

> In the light of these passages in their context, the title "Son of God" is not in itself a designation of personal deity or an expression of metaphysical distinctions within the Godhead. Indeed to be "Son of God" one has to be a being who is *not* God! It is a designation for a *creature* indicating a special relationship with God. In particular, it denotes God's representative, God's vice-regent. It is a designation of kingship, identifying the king as God's son.[50]

Indeed to be "Son of God" one has to be a being who is *not* God! This is easily demonstrated by the way the Bible uses the term "son of God." But in none of these instances is it a title designating Deity in the "traditional" or "orthodox" sense. It is clear that

[50] Colin Brown, "Trinity and Incarnation: In Search of Contemporary Orthodoxy," *Ex Auditu* 7, 1991, p. 88.

Sonship of God meant something quite different to the Jewish mind of the writers of the Bible than to the later Gentile mind.

When Jesus asked his disciples, "Who do you say that I am?" Peter replied, "You are the Christ" (Mark 8:29). Luke expands Peter's confession to "You are the Christ of God" (Luke 9:20). And Matthew has the fullest description: "You are the Christ, the Son of the living God" (Matt. 16:16). It is quite evident that these two titles Christ (Heb. Messiah) and Son of God are interchangeable. The one defines the other. Matthew's "Son of God" is a synonym for "Christ."

This confession of Peter's must be understood in its Jewish setting. Peter's frame of reference was his Hebrew Bible. And in that Bible the titles "Christ" and "Son of God" refer to Israel's king. For instance, we see this clearly in Psalm 2, a widely regarded Messianic Psalm. In this Psalm we have "the LORD" who is Jehovah God. We also have "His **Anointed** [Messiah]" (v. 2). God declares this prophetic word: "But as for Me, I have installed My **King** upon Zion, My holy mountain" (v. 6). The next verse has God calling this Messianic King "**My Son**" (v. 7). To the Jews who awaited the fulfilment of God's promise of the Messiah, the promised one was to be both King and Son of God. These three descriptions meet in the person of Jesus of Nazareth. The Anointed (Hebrew *Messiah;* Greek *Christ*) *is* the King, *is* the Son. "The title 'Son of God' used for Jesus has its origin in the Israelite royal ideology."[51] And when Peter acknowledged this, Jesus commended him as blessed. The Father has revealed it to him. "Jesus' sonship to God is not described as a 'divine nature,' but as a result of divine creation/election and is fully worked out in Jesus' obedience to the Father." As Schonfield is at pains to point out again and again, "Jesus is the Archetypal Man, the archetypal Son of God." And as Frances Young so astutely observes, "When Paul wrote: 'God was in Christ reconciling the world to himself,' he is unlikely to have envisaged a Nicene conclusion.'"[52] To sum up so far we have:

Son of God = King = Messiah = Christ

---

[51] Kuschel, *Born Before All Time?* p. 236.

[52] Lockhart, *Jesus the Heretic,* pp. 172-173.

The Blasphemy of Jesus

Since the titles "King of Israel," "Messiah/Christ" are synonymous with "Son of God" what do we make of John 10 where the Jews are about to stone Jesus for "blasphemy"? Our Bible reads, "The Jews answered him, 'For a good work we do not stone you, but for blasphemy; and because you, being a man, make yourself out to be God.'"

To our tradition-bound ears this sounds as if Jesus was claiming to be God. But was he? Would it make sense in that land and time for Jews who were strict unitarian monotheists to accuse Jesus of being Jehovah Himself? Unfortunately, once again we have to clear up a simple matter of translation. The Greek here does not have the definite article before the word "God." They did not accuse Jesus of claiming to be "the God," that is, the LORD God. Nor does the Greek text capitalize the "G" for God. No Jew would for a moment believe this. To make them say that Jesus claimed to be God (the Supreme Being) is simply to read back into the text what is historically anachronistic and absurdly out of context. When we read the word "God" our Western minds immediately think of the Supreme Deity. But in the ancient world the word "God" was much more ambiguous and context always determined its meaning. What the Jews in fact accused Jesus of was that he was claiming an unprecedented authority to speak directly for God. They did not recognize him as the Messiah and thought his claims outrageous and false.

The apostle Paul gives us a good clue to this widespread and popular use of the word "god" when he tells us that in his society there were "many gods and many lords" so-called (1 Cor. 8:6). On one occasion Paul himself had to dissuade the adoring crowds who wanted to worship him and Barnabas. The crowd called out, "The gods have become like men and have come down to us" (Acts 14:11). Later in his life Paul was bitten by a poisonous snake. The locals expected Paul to swell up and die but when he showed no ill effects the same people changed their minds and began to say that Paul was "a god" (Acts 28:6). The translators know that the natives did not think that Paul was "God" so they wrote Paul was "a god." Another instance: In Acts 12 King Herod gave a moving oration and the people cried out, "The voice of a god, not of a man!" (v. 22). The translators did not write "The voice of God..." because it is self-evident those pagans did not say that Herod was speaking with the very voice of God. This is very plain to anybody.

We could cite many more examples where context determines which "God/god" is intended. Evidently the Bible, reflecting the common idiom of its day and age, calls several beings "God/god." Whenever the Bible speaks of the one Supreme Deity who is the uncreated God it usually uses the definite article. The Father of Jesus is normally called "the God" (Greek: *ho theos*). In fact, some 1350 times in the NT whenever the Supreme Deity, the Father, is referred to He is called "the God" with the definite article.

Before we return to our passage in John 10 where the Jews accuse Jesus of blasphemy, saying that he is claiming to be "God," let us lock this fact clearly into our minds by using a simple illustration. If I said to you that the minister was going to visit you today, you might think I meant a government minister. Then again, you might think I meant the local church minister. Or you might even think I intended to say the (Prime) Minister of our country was coming to speak to you. Only the context would help you fix in your mind which minister I meant. The word "minister" by itself is quite ambiguous. Just so, in the ancient world the word "God" was a flexible word whose meaning was determined by the wider context.

Back in John 10:24 the context is clear. The Jews say to Jesus, "How long will you keep us in suspense? If you are the Christ [the Messiah], tell us plainly." Jesus lays out the credentials that mark him out as the long-promised Messiah. His works that are done by the Father's authority prove his claim to be the anointed one, the Messiah. But these hardened Jews who refuse to believe that he is the Messiah will not listen because they are not his sheep (v. 26). His true sheep who hear his voice are safe (v. 28). In this matter, says Jesus, "I and the Father are one" (v. 30). That is, one in purpose and mission. The Greek word for *one* here is neuter (*hen*) and refers to the works or purpose that Jesus is talking about: keeping the sheep safe. (Compare 1 Cor. 3:8 where "he who plants and he who waters are one," that is, one in purpose, or one in mission.) The Catholic exegete Karl-Josef Kuschel says of this verse:

> Even Catholic exegesis now sees that John did not intend metaphysical statements about the unity of Father and Son...We need to be careful not to press the verse about unity, as Christians of later centuries did in the controversy

> over the Trinity...Positively, John is concerned with a unity of revelation between Father and Son...Essentially we have a unity of will and action between God and Jesus...a unity of activity...So in defining the unity, John is not concerned with either mythological speculations or metaphysical conceptualizations of Jesus' Godhead, divine being or divine nature...He is not concerned to know that before the Incarnation there were two preexistent divine persons who were bound together in the one divine nature. This way of conceiving things is alien to John...The statement has nothing to do with any dogmatic-speculative statements about the relationship of the natures within the Godhead.[53]

Quite right. Whenever God Himself is called *one* the masculine (*heis*) is used (see for instance, Gal. 3:28; Eph. 4:6 in the Greek). Sufficient then to say that those who try to make Jesus mean that he and the Father are one in *essence* or *nature* are reading into the text not out of it. This is to impose Greco-Western categories back onto the Hebrew mind which never thought of God in terms of essence.

At this point the Jews are ready to stone Jesus for blasphemy "because you, being a man, make yourself out to be..." ("the God" or "a god"? Which is it to be?) With other commentators I suggest that it should be translated to mean that Jesus is making himself out to be "a god" (just as they translated Acts 28:6 and 14:22 that we looked at earlier). This is because there is no definite article and in the very next two verses the translators follow common sense: "Jesus answered them, 'Has it not been written in your Law, "I said, you are **gods**"? If he called them **gods**, to whom the word of God came...'" (John 10:34-35).

Here is another reason why the translators are incorrect to say that Jesus was claiming to be "God." Look at verse 36: "Do you say of him, whom the Father sanctified and sent into the world, you are blaspheming because **I said I am the Son of God**?"

If Jesus was claiming to be "God" then surely he would have come right out and said "I said I am (the) God"! But no. He says, "I **said I am the Son of God**." As was discussed earlier, to be the Son of God means you are *not* God! Jesus' whole point is that if God in the OT called the human judges who were commissioned to act on His behalf "gods," then how much more should the one who is

---

[53] Kuschel, *Born Before All Time?* pp. 388-399.

"sanctified" and "sent" in the Father's authority be called the Son of God. This interpretation that the Jews accuse Jesus of being "a god" — i.e. of being the representative or agent of the one true God of Israel — fits the whole context. Remember, the Jews had asked Jesus not to keep them in suspense but to tell them plainly if he was the Messiah (v. 24). Jesus does exactly that. He tells them he is the Son of God. And as we have already seen, in the Bible the titles "Son of God" and Christ (Messiah) are virtually synonymous. In John 10:22-36 the Jews accuse Jesus of claiming to represent God and to be His spokesman. Jesus explicitly denies that he is God. It is a pity the translators have obscured all this by injecting their own theology into the text, thereby giving the impression that Jesus was claiming to be God Himself, the Yahweh of the OT.

I Am

But what about the great "I am" statements of Jesus? Especially that classic one in **John 8:58** where Jesus says, "Truly, truly, I say to you, before Abraham was born I AM"? Surely here Jesus makes the same claim for himself that Jehovah God made back in Exodus 3 where the LORD says to Moses at the burning bush "I AM WHO I AM." Surely Jesus is claiming to be the I AM of the Old Testament as Trinitarian belief asserts?

Now here is something very obvious that they never told me in church (or at theological college). This expression from Jesus' lips "I am" (Greek *ego eimi*) occurs throughout the Gospel of John and in no other text in John can it mean I AM the God of the Old Testament. Go back to John 4:25-26 for instance. The woman at the well said to Jesus, "I know that Messiah is coming (he who is called Christ); when that one comes, he will declare all things to us." And Jesus said to her, "I who speak to you am *he*." You will notice that in most Bibles the word *he* is in italics. This means that the translators have correctly supplied a word in English that is not in the Greek but that nevertheless makes the intended sense quite clear. Here Jesus says to the woman — in the context of her question about the Messiah — that he is the Messiah, the Christ. "I who speak to you am *he*." In the Greek it reads *ego eimi.* Jesus simply says I am he, the Messiah. Definitely not "I AM is the One speaking to you!"

In John 9 Jesus heals the blind man. But is this really the beggar who used to sit groping in the dark? Some people said, "Yes, it's him all right." Others said, "No, just looks like him." But the beggar says, "*ego eimi*"! And the translators have no trouble writing, "I am the one." So why aren't the translators consistent? Why not capitalize what this man says as I AM? Because it is clear that he is not claiming to be the God of the Old Testament. Saying "I am" (*ego eimi*) does not make somebody God in the Bible!

Or look at John 8:24, 28 where the exact phrase "I am" appears and the translators supply the true meaning by adding in italics the little word *he* because it is clear that it simply means "I am the Messiah." Verse 28: "When you lift up the Son of Man, then you will know that I am *he,* and I do nothing on my own initiative, but I speak these things as the Father taught me." Jesus cannot be saying that the Son of Man who can do nothing apart from the Father will be seen to be the I AM when he dies. God cannot die. The consistent and natural explanation is that Jesus is claiming to be the Messiah. He is the duly authorized agent of God.

Actually, the I AM of Exodus 3 is introduced as I AM WHAT I AM or I WILL BE WHAT I WILL BE. Jesus did not say this! Anthony Buzzard explains:

> It is important to notice that Jesus did not use the phrase revealing God's name to Moses. At the burning bush the One God had declared His name as "I am who I am" or "I am the self-existent one" (Ex. 3:14). The phrase in the Greek version of the Old Testament reads *ego eimi ho hown,* which is quite different from the "I am he" used by Jesus.[54]

What Jesus is saying to these Jews is simply "Before Abraham was born, I am *he,*" that is, "I am the Messiah." Notice the context in John 8:56 where Jesus says, "Abraham rejoiced to see my day." That is, by faith Abraham looked forward and saw the coming Messiah before he came in history. He believed the promise that God would send the Promised One. On the other hand these Jews did not believe that Jesus was their Messiah. They were claiming to be Abraham's descendants. Jesus said that this was impossible for they did not recognize him as their Messiah. But Jesus asserts that even before Abraham was born, he is the One who was always in God's plan. This Abraham believed and saw. The Messiah preexisted in God's plan and therefore in Abraham's believing

---

[54] Buzzard and Hunting, *The Doctrine of the Trinity,* p. 220.

mind, because he trusted the promise of God. Jesus positively did *not* say, "Before Abraham was, I was." Also, Jesus did *not* say, "Before Abraham was, I AM WHAT I AM."

The conclusion is inevitable. Jesus' claim "Before Abraham was born, I am *he*" is the straightforward claim that he is the long-promised one, the Messiah, the One in question. Jesus is the Saviour in God's promise even before Abraham was born. In each of the other examples cited, the translators supply the word "he" to the phrase "I am." Why not be consistent here in John 8:58 as well? The only reason not to is because of traditional bias. What Jesus said is this: "Before Abraham was born, I am *he,*" meaning, I am the Messiah that Abraham looked forward to. This is a very reasonable statement from one who thinks that God had the Messiah in mind from the beginning.

I Am the Way, the Truth and the Life

At this point it is appropriate to mention another of the "I am" statements of Jesus often used to support the notion that Jesus claimed to be God. Jesus says, "I am the way, the truth, and the life" (John 14:6). Surely this is a claim to be the Supreme Deity?

The first thing to note is that this statement is not the whole statement. The rest of what Jesus says is that because of his unique mediatorial status as the Son, "no one comes to the Father, but **through** me." Jesus is simply announcing that he is God's mediator, God's only authorized agent of approach. Elsewhere the Scripture clearly teaches this: "There is one God, and one mediator between men and God, the man Christ Jesus" (1 Tim. 2:5).

By definition a mediator has to be a separate person from the other two parties who are seeking terms (see Gal. 3:20). To qualify as the mediator between God and men, one has to himself be a *man*! God cannot be the mediator. John 14:6 teaches this truth precisely. It says nothing about Jesus being God. Just that he is God's mediator for all who would come to the Father through his Gospel announcement.

The second thing to note in these "I am" statements is that the whole context of the Gospel of John tells us how and why Jesus is "the way, the truth, and the life," namely because this authority has been *given* to him by the Father. The Father "has **given** all judgment to the Son" (John 5:22).The Father "**gave** to the Son to have life in himself" (John 5:26). Jesus' own confession is quite clear: "I live

because of the Father" (John 6:57). Jesus said, "I can do nothing of my own initiative" (John 5:30). It is on "the Son of Man" that "the Father, even God, has set His seal" (John 6:27). We could multiply these sayings of Jesus many times over. His testimony is that he is subordinate to the Father. His testimony is that all this has come to him from his Father's hand. His works, his words, his very life are all the result of God's initiative. And precisely because these things are given to him, Jesus can say that he is the way, the truth, and the life, and that nobody can come to the Father but through his mediation. The "I am" statements do not prove his Deity; they demonstrate that God is the source of it all. Jesus has been given these things and therefore cannot be God Himself. By definition, the Father of Jesus possesses all things and can be given nothing.

One scholar shows that to take these I AM statements to mean that Jesus is claiming to be Almighty God borders on the ridiculous. Referring to John 8:28 (where Jesus says, "you will know that I am *he,* and I do nothing on my own initiative") Barrett writes: "It is intolerable that Jesus should be made to say, 'I am God, the supreme God of the OT, and being God I do as I am told.'"[55]

And on John 13:19-20 where Jesus says "I am telling you before it comes to pass, so that when it does occur, you may believe that I am *he*...He who receives me receives Him who sent me," the same author ironically points out it would be equally intolerable that Jesus should be made to say, "I am God, and I am here because someone sent me."[56] Perhaps it would be wise to stop saying that these "I am *he*" statements of Jesus mean that he is claiming to be God.

John Chapter One

Ah, I can hear an objection. What about John 1 (theologians call this the prologue) where we read, "In the beginning was the Word and the Word was with God and the Word was God. He was in the beginning with God. All things came into being through Him, and apart from Him nothing came into being that has come into being" (John 1:1-3)?

---

[55] Barrett, quoted in *Focus on the Kingdom,* ed. Anthony Buzzard, vol. 6, no. 1, p. 2.
[56] *Ibid.,* p. 2.

The first thing to be said is that the apostle John is not going to contradict anything Matthew and Luke (or the OT) have said about the origin and person of his beloved Lord Jesus. Scripture is a beautifully woven and harmonious testimony to God's Truth. If Matthew and Luke tell us unequivocally that Jesus had a beginning by the miraculous power of God in the womb of Mary, then John is not going to tell us that Jesus the Son had no beginning, that he always personally preexisted as God and was the second member of the eternal Trinity. Such a contradiction would destroy apostolic unity and the testimony of Scripture which Jesus said cannot be broken.

With this principle in mind, we should observe first what John's Prologue does *not* say. John did not write, "In the beginning was *the Son* and *the Son* was with God and *the Son* was God." (Some translations make this bold claim even though it is totally unwarranted from the text.) But our inherited tradition automatically makes our eyes run in that groove. One of the reasons we tend to read *into* it this meaning is the very fact that our translations have put a capital "W" for "Word." The capital W subconsciously dictates that we think John means a person when he speaks of "the Word." But for those not familiar with NT Greek rest assured that this is not the case. Every single letter in the earliest Greek manuscripts is capitalized. (These manuscripts are called uncials. Other manuscripts are written in all lower case.) So it is a matter of what the translator decides to do in his translation that will have a big bearing on how we will read it. Did John write "the Word" or "the word"? We will determine this after discussing a few other details first.

The next technical point we need to clear up is that in NT Greek, like many modern languages such as French, German and Spanish, all nouns are given gender. We do not have this in English because objects are neuter. But in these foreign languages a pronoun must always agree with the noun it refers to in gender, number and case. Anybody with any knowledge of French, Spanish or German is very familiar with this. For example, in German the word for "table" is a masculine noun. But no German when he talks about a table for a moment thinks it is a person when he says, "Help me shift this table because *he* is heavy." In NT Greek an object can be either masculine, feminine or neuter.

Now in NT Greek "the word" (*logos*) happens to be of the masculine gender. Therefore, its pronoun — "he" in our English translations — is a matter of interpretation, not translation. Did John write concerning "the word" that "he" was in the beginning with God? Or did he write concerning "the word" that "it" was in the beginning with God? As already stated, in NT Greek the *logos* or word is a masculine noun. It is OK in English to use "he" to refer back to this masculine noun if there is good contextual reason to do so. But is there good reason to make "the word" a "he" here?

It is a fact that all English translations from the Greek before the King James Version of 1611 read this way: "In the beginning was the word, and the word was with God, and the word was God. **It** was in the beginning with God. All things came into being through **it** and apart from **it** nothing came into being that has come into being. In **it** was life; and the life was the light of men." In fact, there are many English translations since the KJV that refer to the *logos* as "it." Churches of Christ people will be no doubt surprised to learn that their esteemed Alexander Campbell translated John 1:1 as:

> In the beginning was the Word, and the Word was with God, and the Word was God. **This** was in the beginning with God. All things were made by **it**, and without **it** not a single creature was made. **In it** was life, and the life was the light of men. And the light shone in darkness; but the darkness admitted it not.[57]

To read it this way means, of course, that "the word" is not a person. This is a very acceptable translation. Indeed, I will now show that it is in fact preferable for the following reasons.

The word *logos* appears many, many more times in this very Gospel of John. And nowhere else do the translators capitalize it or use the masculine personal pronoun "he" to agree with it! They know the context will not stand for this. Take John 2:22 which reads, "When therefore he was raised from the dead, his disciples remembered that he said this; and they believed the Scripture, and **the word which** Jesus had spoken." "The word" here is clearly not Jesus the person himself, but rather his message. Another instance: John 4:37 translates *logos* as a "saying": "For in this case **the**

---

[57] Alexander Campbell, *The Sacred Writings of the Apostles and Evangelists of Jesus Christ, Commonly Styled the New Testament, Translated from the Original Greek,* Brooke County, VA, 1826.

saying is true." Another one: "The man believed **the word** that Jesus spoke to him" (John 4:50). Or take John 6:60 which reads, "Many therefore of his disciples, when they heard this said, 'This is a difficult **statement**.'" And so on for the many other cases in this very Gospel.

The rest of the New Testament is the same. *Logos* is variously translated as "statement" (Luke 20:20), "question" (Matt. 21:24), "preaching" (1 Tim. 5:17), "command" (Gal. 5:14), "message" (Luke 4:32), "matter" (Acts 15:6), "reason" (Acts 10:29). So there is absolutely no reason to make John 1 say that "the word" is the person Jesus himself, unless of course the translators are wanting to make a point. *In all cases* logos *is an "it."*

There is even strong evidence to suggest that John himself reacted to those who were already misusing his Gospel to mean that Jesus was himself the Word who had personally preexisted the world. When he later wrote his introduction to 1 John he clearly made the point that *what* was in the beginning was not a "who." He put it this way: "**What** was from the beginning, **what** we have heard, **what** we have seen with our eyes, **what** we beheld and our hands handled, concerning **the word of life**..."

Four times John says that which was from the beginning was a "what"! Here the relative pronouns are neuter, not masculine. And to avoid all confusion as to his meaning he even says it was *the word of life* which was in the beginning with God. Surely John is his own best interpreter as to what he means. His introduction in 1 John is his answer to the misunderstanding that was even then being promoted by the Gnostics, namely the error that made Jesus into a preexisting heavenly redeemer, a mixture of flesh and spirit, human and divine, rather than a 100% human being.

These arguments, significant as they are, begin to take on strong proportions when we consider the next vital piece of information. That is, the apostle John's background was in the Hebrew Scriptures. It is surely better exegesis to read the prologue to John's Gospel with his Hebrew background in mind. And if we go back to the OT we can easily discover the framework for John's understanding of "the word." In the Hebrew Bible "word" is *never a person.* "Word" always means "promise" or "decree" or "proposal" or "plan" or "message" or just plain "word." (See for example Gen. 41:37; Jud. 3:19; Dan. 9:25; Ps. 64:5-6; Is. 8:10.) In fact "the word" is used about 1450 times in the Hebrew Bible this way. Not once does it refer to a preexisting Son of God. Not once does it mean a person. Not once!

The Hebrews certainly understood God's word to be the equivalent of His personal presence and power. What is announced is as good as done (Gen. 1:3, 9, 11, etc). He watches over His word to perform it and fulfill it (Jer. 1:12). God's word carries the guarantee that He will back it up with action (Is. 55:10-11). Not one word of His will fail. His word carries His power. His word is as His deed. God's word *is* God in His activity in Hebrew understanding. When "**the word of the LORD** came to Jonah" instructing him to go to the city of Nineveh and preach there, Jonah "ran away **from the LORD**" (Jonah 1:1-3). Here the word of God, which is His revealed will, equals God Himself expressing Himself. When God told Jonah His plan or His will and Jonah disobeyed, to the Hebrew mind Jonah ran away from God *Himself.*

The writer of the Gospel of John must be allowed to use his native categories and thought-forms. We must respect his Hebrew background. At the time his Gospel was composed, the Aramaic commentaries on the Hebrew Scriptures known as the *targums* used the term *memra* (the word) to describe God's activity in the world. The *memra* (word):

> performs the same function as other technical terms like "glory," "Holy Spirit" and "Shekinah" which emphasised the distinction between God's presence in the world and the incomprehensible reality of God itself. *Like the divine Wisdom, the "Word" symbolised God's original plan for creation.* When Paul and John speak about Jesus as though he had some kind of preexistent life, they were not suggesting that he was a second divine "person" in the later Trinitarian sense. They were indicating that Jesus transcended temporal and individual modes of existence. Because the "power" and "wisdom" that he represented were activities that derived from God, he had in some way expressed "what was there from the beginning." *These ideas were comprehensible in a strictly Jewish context, though later Christians with a Greek background would interpret them differently.*[58]

---

[58] Karen Armstrong, *A History of God: From Abraham to the Present: The 4000-year Quest for God,* p. 106, emphasis added.

The fact that John introduces "the word" of God to us in personified terms is very much in keeping with his Hebrew culture. For instance, John's prologue shows obvious parallels with Proverbs 8:22-30 where Wisdom is personified (but never hypostatized, never turned into a real person). Another example perhaps more in keeping with John's imagery is found in Psalm 147:15 where we read, "He [God] sends forth His command to the earth; His word runs very swiftly." Here the command/word of God is indeed personified, but not hypostatized.

Also worthy of note is that many commentators are of the opinion that John 1:1-14 is poetic in its literary style. And a basic rule of interpretation is that poetry contains metaphorical language which must not be over-literalized. Thus John's poetic introduction must be allowed to make use of figurative language in keeping with such personification. A personified *logos* is not a revolutionary idea to John! Roger Haight endorses this sentiment when he writes, "One thing is certain, the Prologue of John does not represent direct descriptive knowledge of a divine *entity or being* called Word, who descended and became a human being. To read *a metaphor* as literal speech is misinterpretation."[59]

Nor is this interpretation of a non-personal "word" a "Johnny-come-lately" understanding in the Church. Some of the early church fathers shared this view. Origen's commentary on John states: "*logos* — only in the sense of the utterance of the Father which came to expression in a Son when Jesus was conceived." Similarly Tertullian: "It is the simple use of our people to say [of John 1] that the word of *revelation* was with God."[60] To these church fathers the "word" was not yet understood as a personally preexistent Son.

Or as eminent professor of New Testament T.W. Manson beautifully summarizes:

> I very much doubt whether John thought of the *Logos* as a personality. The only personality on the scene is Jesus the son of Joseph from Nazareth. That personality embodies the *Logos* so completely that Jesus becomes a complete revelation of God. But in what sense are we using the word

---

[59] Roger Haight, *Jesus: Symbol of God,* Maryknoll, NY: Orbis, p. 210.
[60] *Ad Praxeus* 5.

> "embodies"?...For John every word of Jesus is a word of the Lord.[61]

In the light of this background it is far better to read John's prologue to mean that in the beginning God had a plan, a dream, a grand vision for the world, a reason by which He brought all things into being. This word or plan was expressive of who He is. We humans who are made in God's likeness understand this idea exactly. Let us illustrate. Here is a man who loves to go fishing. He dreams about fishing all day long. By profession, however, he is a plumber. The thing that keeps him going during the week when he is digging trenches and fixing pipes is that the weekend is coming up. This is what revs him up and inspires him. He will escape all this hum-drum and soon be driving to the coast and fishing. This goes on for years. But then one day this man has one of those moments in life that we call a brain explosion. Why not buy a little beach shack right on the water's edge? And why not own his own boat? A dream is born. From then on, he works like a man possessed. He works extra long hours to bring in the money needed to make his dream come true. In fact, he even foregoes most of his weekends of fishing so he can earn extra to buy his dream house and boat. Oh sure, every once in a while he will take time off to go and drop the line in. He is keeping the dream alive. When the fish aren't biting his mind drifts off. He can "see" his beach shack. He can visualize his own boat. And all the years at work plumbing he can "see" the goal. He tells everybody and anybody who will listen to him about his beach shack and about his boat and about his life of fishing. Nobody doubts his intention. But one day to everybody's amazement our plumber is gone. Where is he? "Oh," they say, "Don't you know? He has moved to the coast. He is living in a beach shack and fishing out of his own boat." His dream — which till now has been *with* him, or *inside* his mind — has come true. It was, we may say, "his baby," his favourite preoccupation, and it became reality!

The Word Was *with* God

There is good evidence in the Hebrew Scriptures that the prepositions "with" (*im* and *et*) often describe the relationship between a person and what is in his heart or mind. We have a

---

[61] T.W. Manson, *On Paul and John,* SCM Press, 1967, p. 156.

common expression in English when we say, "What's *with* him?" or "What's the matter *with* her?" Something is going on *inside* somebody. Here are a few examples of this use of the Hebrew preposition "with."[62]

"Im (with), alone = in one's consciousness, whether of knowledge, memory or purpose"

Num. 14:24: "He had another spirit with him" (operating in his mind).

1 Kings 11:11: "This is with you [Solomon]" (what you want).

1 Chron. 28:12: "The pattern of all that was in the spirit with him" (in his mind).

Job 10:13: "I know that this was with you" (hidden in your heart).

Job 23:10: "He knows the way which is with me" (the way of which I am conscious).

Job 23:14: "He performs the things which are appointed for me and many such things are with Him" (He has many such purposes).

Job 27:11: "That which is with the Almighty I will not conceal" (His purposes).

Ps. 50:11: "Wild beasts of the field are with Me" (known to Me, in My thought and care).

Ps. 73:23: "I am continually with You" (in your thoughts).

"Et: a dream or word of Yahweh is said to be *with* the prophet."

Gen. 40:14: "Keep me in mind when it goes well with you" (literally, "remember me with yourself"). The word was what God had in mind.

2 Kings 3:12: "There is with him the word of the Lord" (2 John 2: truth is "with us"; Gal. 2:5: truth "remains with [*pros*] you").

Isa. 59:12: "transgressions are with us" (in our consciousness). (Cp. John 17:5, the glory which Jesus had with God — present to God's mind, as His purpose.)

Jer. 23:28: "The prophet with whom there is a dream" (the prophet who has a dream).

Jer. 27:18: "If the word of the Lord is with them."

---

[62] I am indebted to Anthony Buzzard for these examples, cited from *Brown, Driver and Briggs Lexicon,* Oxford: Clarendon Press, 1968, p. 768, 86.

Job 14:5: "His days are determined. The number of his months is with you" (known to you).

Prov. 2:1: "Treasure my commandments within you" (= with you).

Prov. 11:2: "Wisdom is with the humble."

In view of this Hebrew usage and background, Anthony Buzzard suggests an accurate translation of John 1:1, 14 as follows: "In the beginning God had a Plan and the Plan was fixed as God's Decree and the Plan was fully expressive of God's mind...and the Plan became embodied in the Man Messiah Jesus."

The Bible says "As a man thinks in his heart, so he is" (Prov. 23:7). God is no different. For before He created a thing He had this dream with Him. This word was fully expressive of Himself. And when He created the universe and the purpose of the ages He worked according to His master plan, His dream. As Peter says, "**by the word of God the heavens existed** long ago, and the earth was formed out of water and by water" (2 Pet. 3:5). A similar idea is expressed by John in Revelation 4:11: "for You did create all things, and because of Your **will** they existed, and were created." This agrees with the OT. For example in Psalm 33:6, 9 we are told that "by the LORD's word the heavens were made." God spoke and it was done. He commanded and the world stood fast. There was divine power in God's spoken word. All of this is simply to say that the Greek word for *logos* is masculine in gender but is not referring to a personally preexisting Son of God. "The word" for John is an "it," not a "he." On one occasion Jesus is given the name "the Word of God" and this is in Revelation 19:13. This name has been given to him after his resurrection and ascension, but we will search in vain to find it before his birth.

It is not until we come to verse 14 of John's prologue that this *logos* becomes personal and becomes the Son of God, Jesus the human being. "And the word became flesh." The great plan that God had in His heart from before the creation at last is fulfilled. Be very clear that it does *not* say that *God* became flesh. Not at all. It says "the word" became flesh. God's master plan is now reality in the man Jesus. Jesus is the final and full expression of all that God's wisdom planned "in the beginning."

This is the conclusion also of the definitive study of the Incarnation *Christology in the Making*. Listen to James Dunn's finding:

> The conclusion which seems to emerge from our analysis thus far is that it is only with v. 14 that we can begin to speak of the *personal* Logos...Prior to v. 14...we are dealing with personifications rather than persons, personified actions of God rather than an individual divine being as such. The point is obscured by the fact that we have to translate the masculine Logos as "he" throughout the poem. But if we translate the masculine Logos as "God's utterance" instead, it would become clearer that the poem did not necessarily intend the Logos in v. 1-13 to be thought of as a personal divine being. In other words, the revolutionary significance of v. 14 may well be that it marks...*the transition from impersonal personification to actual person.* This indeed is the astounding nature of the poem's claim. If it had asserted simply that an individual divine being had become man, that would have raised fewer eyebrows. It is the fact that the Logos poet has taken language which any thoughtful Jew would recognize to be the language of personification and has *identified* it with a particular person, *as* a particular person, that would be astonishing: the manifestation of God become a man! God's utterance not merely come through a particular individual, but actually become that one person, Jesus of Nazareth![63]

There are some NT Greek scholars who note that John was very specific in what he penned back in verse 1. He wrote "and the word was God." He did *not* write "and the word was *the God.*" In other words these scholars take God (Greek *theos*) *here in the adjectival sense.* The word was expressive of God, had the character of God, was divine in its character. It is the difference between "The teacher was the man" and "The teacher was man." The New English Bible captures this adjectival sense beautifully: "and what God was the word was." Moffat's translation also does well with "the logos was divine." As Dunn definitively says, "Nowhere either in the Bible or in the extra-canonical literature of the Jews is the word of God a personal agent or on the way to become such."[64] "The *logos* of the

[63] Dunn, *Christology in the Making,* p. 243.
[64] *Ibid.,* p. 219.

prologue becomes Jesus; Jesus was the *logos* become flesh, not the *logos* as such."[65]

It may well be that John actually mentions the virgin birth — that is, the beginning of Jesus' existence — in his prologue, before verse 14. The verses under consideration are normally read in the following way: "But as many as received him, to them he gave the right to become children of God, even to those who believe in his name, who **were** born not of blood, nor or the will of the flesh, nor of the will of man, but of God" (John 1:12-13).

As this reads in our modern Bibles, it refers to the new birth that Christians experience through faith in Christ: Our relationship with God through Christ is not something of human origin, or human will-power, or human genius; our salvation is all of God's doing through His Son. However, one day I read that this may not have been what John originally wrote. According to a number of Bible scholars, these verses have more than likely been tampered with. There is no doubt that they were the subject of much early debate. For example, Tertullian accused the Valentinian Gnostics of having altered the text to read as I have just quoted it, and as we find it in most modern translations. According to Tertullian the plural verb "were" should actually be the singular verb "was." In this case the verse would read like this: "But as many as received him, to them he gave the right to become the children of God, even to those who believe in his name, who **was** born not of blood, nor of the will of the flesh, nor of the will of man, but of God."

As can be seen, this singular verb changes the sense completely. Instead of it being the Christians who are born by God's will, it is now Christ himself who is born by God's initiation. Tertullian thus accuses the Gnostics of trying to eliminate the idea of Jesus' miraculous birth ("who was born") by making it relate to their own experience ("who were born"). In support of this understanding, Irenaeus and Justin Martyr argue for the singular, in order to maintain that Jesus was not a mere man, born in the natural way, but was miraculously conceived by the action of God. A strong point in favour of this reading is that these three references *antedate* any of our extant NT manuscripts. However, in all honesty, it must still be said that the jury is either still out on this one, or currently leans

---

[65] Kuschel, *Born Before All Time?* p. 382.

slightly in favour of the plural verb as appears in our modern Bibles (but not the Jerusalem Bible).

I confess, however, that whenever I read these verses with the plural they seem a little incongruous, just a little out of place, even though the plural meaning is quite in keeping with the Bible's teaching that our salvation is entirely of God's grace. To my mind, the more natural sense is to understand a reference to the birth of Jesus without human will. If we take it as plural (that is, that it speaks of the new birth of Christians) it points out in a puzzling manner the blatantly obvious: that the believers' spiritual birth "of God" has nothing to do with sexual intercourse, fleshly craving, or male will! On this reading, we must ask who would have supposed it did anyway? The more it is pondered, the more baffling it becomes that John should have three times over differentiated spiritual regeneration from physical generation! Read naturally, in the singular, the passage is an exact statement of the virgin birth, for Jesus was born "of God" without human agency, will, or natural craving. The verse would then be a strong statement of the virginal begetting of Jesus and would confirm that John did not intend to introduce a preexisting Son, as was later mistakenly thought. Without stronger textual evidence the point remains undecided, though this nuance appears the more natural and convincing.

1 John 5:18

There is, however, one verse that John wrote which clearly does speak of the begetting of Jesus in time. Unfortunately, the King James Version is based on a corrupted text and reads: "We know that whosoever is born of God sinneth not; but he that is begotten of God keepeth himself, and that wicked one toucheth him not" (1 John 5:18, KJV).

This reads as though the Christian who is born of God keeps himself from Satan's schemes. With Douglas Edwards, and modern translations, we reject this variant reading because:

> nowhere in either Testament is a creature of God, whether Jewish or Christian, said absolutely to keep *himself*. A Christian may be bidden to "keep himself pure" (1 Tim. 5:22), or Christians to "keep themselves in the love of God" (Jude 21); but, whether in the Old Testament or in the New,

> never is a man regarded as his own keeper, nor is anyone but God ever said to "keep" another.[66]

Quite right. It is always the LORD who is your keeper (Ps. 121:4-8). In the NT the phrase is only ever used of God and of Christ (John 17:11, 12, 15). However, the meaning is entirely altered if we read it as more accurately preserved in the Greek original: "We know that no one who is born of God sins; but he who was born of God keeps him and the evil one does not touch him" (1 John 5:18).

Read this way, the text tells us that the Christ who was born or begotten of God keeps the Christian safe. Jesus did promise that this keeping would be proof of his care for his sheep (John 10:27-28). Let us analyse this point in more detail. The first part of the verse, "We know that no one who is born of God sins" literally reads in the original text, "no one who has been born of God" and refers to an event of the past with present consequences (this is in the *perfect tense* in the Greek text). It clearly refers to the new birth every Christian has experienced. The new birth, having begun at a point in the past, has ongoing consequences for the believer — he/she does not habitually practise sinning. This phrase is used of the Christian six times previously in John's letter, and on each of these six occasions John uses the Greek perfect tense. However, here in the second part of 1 John 5:18 we come to a unique turn of phrase. This second part of the verse correctly reads "but he who was born of God keeps him." (This time John changes his tenses and uses what is called the *aorist tense.*) This is a reference to a once and for all and never to be repeated event of the past, that is, the supernatural begetting of Jesus Christ himself. He was brought into existence at a defined moment of past history. John states that Jesus "was begotten of God."

What is the significance of this for our present discussion? Quite simply, to show that John is consistent with Matthew and Luke in maintaining that Jesus' existence began from the moment of his conception. Jesus was begotten by a divine creation. Instead of being born, like other men, of sexual intercourse, of fleshly craving, or of a husband's will, Christ was begotten by God. This is consistent with our interpretation of John's *logos* in his Gospel prologue. John does not contradict himself, saying in one place that

---

[66] Edwards, *The Virgin Birth in History and Faith,* p. 129.

Jesus was the eternal Son of God with no beginning, and then in another place forget what he wrote and say that Jesus Christ began at a definite point in history.

The World Was Made Through Him

Perhaps I can hear you objecting at this point: Surely verses 10 and 11 of this prologue seem to cause a great problem for this interpretation? These verses read: "He was in the world, and the world was made through him, and the world did not know him. He came to his own, and those who were his own did not receive him."

Does not this imply that the world was made by Jesus the Son? If he made the world he had to be alive before the world began. Does it not show that the *logos* was in fact a preexisting Person after all? We must remember what John has already written, i.e. his (Hebrew) context. We must not let our Western eyes start reading other ideas into the text. The *logos,* God's master plan, His wisdom is behind the creation of all things. Perhaps John had this OT verse from Proverbs 3:19 in mind: "The LORD by wisdom founded the earth; by understanding He established the heavens."

Nothing exists that was not in His mind from the very beginning. Through His word, His "understanding" all things have come into being (John 1:3). What an amazing and comforting thought to know this universe is founded upon a purpose and a wisdom that is grounded in the very Being of our Eternal God! Just as all of creation evidences an Intelligent Mind and design, so too all of history is not haphazard. And what is the purpose of history? According to John it is Jesus Christ. God made the world with him in the centre of his mind and plan. Jesus is as one commentator puts it the "diameter" of the ages.[67] Let's explore this thought briefly before answering the question from John 1:10-11 as to whether Jesus was personally existing before the creation of the world, and so was its Creator.

Where is our world heading? What is the purpose of history? Indeed is there any pre-determined end? The Scripture rings out loud and clear, yes! God has "made known to us the mystery of His will...which He purposed in him" namely, "the summing up of all things in Christ, things in the heavens and things upon the earth" (Eph. 1:9-10). So when God the Father brought the universe into

---

[67] Graeser et al, *One God and One Lord,* p. 63.

being He did it with His Son at the centre of His plan. God has purposed the drawing together, the summing up of all creation in Christ. He is the Lord of the ages. One day the goal will be accomplished. Every knee will bow and every tongue will confess that Jesus Christ is Lord "to the glory of God the Father" (Phil. 2:11).

> And then comes the end [Greek *telos*: goal, consummation, closing act], when he [Jesus Christ] delivers up the kingdom to the God and Father, when he has abolished all rule and all authority and power...and when all things are subjected to him, then the Son himself also will be subjected to [the Father], so that God may be all in all (1 Cor. 15:24, 28).

To be a Christian means you know that our Lord Jesus is the diameter, the purpose of the universe. His Kingdom is coming! This is God's purpose and it will not be frustrated. Another verse saying the same thing is Hebrews 1:2. It says God has "appointed" His Son to be the "heir of all things" and that it was "through him that He made the world(s)." Here our translations are unfortunately not quite accurate and miss the author's impact. What the author wrote was not that through Jesus God made the "world(s)," but "*ages*." We get our English word *eon* from this Greek word. We will shortly examine this in more detail, but it is sufficient for now to know that God planned to complete His purpose for all creation *through the agency* of His Son Jesus. The preposition that is used in relation to Jesus and the world, or the ages, is "through" (Greek *dia* from which you will see comes our English word *dia*meter). Those in the know tell us that *dia* is the "preposition of attendant circumstances" and signifies instrumental agency. Put simply, this means that *dia* denotes the means by which an action is accomplished. And Scripture tells us that God the originator is bringing His purpose, His *logos* to fulfilment through Jesus Christ. Jesus is the Agent, the Mediator of God's master plan. Jesus is always seen as secondary, or subordinate to the Father.

So we see in his introduction to Hebrews the author says God now speaks through Jesus (Heb. 1:1). God redeems through Jesus and He saves the world through Jesus (Heb. 1:3). This was Jesus' own clear testimony throughout (e.g. John 5:19-27). Jesus is the channel through whom God comes to us. Jesus is the bridge between God and us.

There are occasional exceptions to this general use of the preposition *dia.* Sometimes blessings are said to come to us through God (e.g. 1 Cor. 1:9; Heb. 2:10). But usually there is a clear distinction made between God's initiating activity and the means through which God brings that activity to pass. The prepositions used of God's action are *hypo* and *ek* which point to primary causation or origin. Let's cement this idea in our minds by looking at one or two verses that highlight the difference: "Yet for us there is but one God, the Father, from [*ek*, 'out from'] whom are all things, and we exist for [*eis*, 'to'] Him; and one Lord, Jesus Christ, through [*dia*] whom are all things, and we exist through [*dia*] him" (1 Cor. 8:6).

Prepositions are the signposts that point out the direction of a passage. The authors of *One God and One Lord* caution us to:

> Notice the distinct and separate use of the Greek prepositions *ek* in relation to God and *dia* in relation to Christ. This should arrest our attention and keep us from speeding past these important signs on our way to a preconceived idea (and maybe getting a ticket for violating the laws of logic). *Ek* indicates something *coming out from* its source or origin, and indicates *motion from the interior.* Remember this last phrase, because it is central to understanding the precision of this verse. In other words, *all things came out from* the loving heart of God, or God's "interior," so to speak. This agrees with Genesis 1:1 which says, "In the beginning, *God* created the heavens and the earth." Both verses say that *the source* of "all things" is the one true God, the Creator of the heavens and earth and the Father of the Lord Jesus Christ.[68]

In contradistinction to this "one God and Father" out of Whom all things originate, the "one Lord, Jesus Messiah" is given the preposition *dia* which means "through." In other words, Jesus is God's agent *through* whom God accomplishes His plan for our lives. This is the consistent pattern all the way through the New Testament. God the Father is the source, the origin of all blessings, and Jesus His Son brings those blessings of salvation to us:

"Now all these things are **from** God, who reconciled us to Himself **through** Christ" (2 Cor. 5:18).

---

[68] *Ibid.*, p. 67.

"God the Father of our Lord Jesus Christ...has blessed us...in Christ. He predestined us to adoption as sons **through** Jesus Christ **to Himself**" (Eph. 1:3-5).

"For **God** has not destined us for wrath, but for obtaining salvation **through** our Lord Jesus Christ" (1 Thess. 5:9).

"**God** will judge the secrets of men **through** Christ Jesus" (Rom. 2:16).

"For **God**...has saved us, and called us...according to His own purpose and grace which was granted us **in** Christ Jesus from all eternity" (2 Tim. 1:9).

"Blessed be **God the Father** of our Lord Jesus Christ, who **has caused** us to be born again to a living hope **through** the resurrection of Jesus Christ from the dead" (1 Pet. 1:3).

"**To the only God** our Saviour, **through** Jesus Christ our Lord, be glory, majesty, dominion and authority, before all time and now and forever. Amen" (Jude 25).

"Jesus the Nazarene, a man attested to you by **God** with miracles and wonders and signs which God performed **through** him in your midst" (Acts 2:22).

Texts could be multiplied. Always God the Father is the source and origin of all works, deeds and salvation which come to us through the mediatorship of His Son. *From* Him comes all to us *through* our Lord Jesus Christ so that *to* God the Father may all the praise be directed. Kuschel also observes the critical function these prepositions perform in the NT's understanding of the essential distinction between the one God — the Father — and the one Lord — Jesus the Messiah. Commenting on 1 Corinthians 8:6 where Paul says that for us Christians "there is but one God, the Father, from whom are all things, and we exist for Him; and one Lord, Jesus Messiah, through whom are all things, and we exist through him," he says:

> God, the Father, is past *and* future, beginning *and* end, origin *and* goal, creator (*ek*) and fulfiller (*eis*) of the world and human beings. By contrast, Christ is the present, the centre, life; he is the ruler over the earth who brings liberation in the present, and who as mediator (*dia*) of a new creation (2 Cor. 5:17), of a "new covenant" (2 Cor. 3:6), can also be the Lord of all those "gods and lords" who rule in the present. Accordingly, the theological *ta panta* ["all things"] might refer to the very first creation of the world;

> by contrast, the Christological *ta panta* refers (as is usual in Paul) to the prevailing circumstances in the present.[69]

Armed with this vital information we can turn to our original question under this heading. When we read in John 1:10 that "he was in the world, and the world was made **through** him, and the world did not know him" does Scripture indicate that after all Jesus himself created the world? Not at all if we consider the whole uniform context we have been considering. The Father is the sole origin and Creator of "all things." In contrast, Jesus is the Father's commissioned Lord Messiah through whom God's plan for the world is coming to completion. The whole Bible from cover to cover categorically states that God created the universe and all the ages with Jesus Christ at the centre of His eternal purpose. Jesus is the *dia*meter running all the way through. And the tragedy that this verse highlights is that although Jesus the promised Messiah came to the Jews who knew God's intention, they did not recognize him when he appeared. The Jews longed for, prayed for, yearned for the One who would come according to God's promise and usher in this glorious hope for the world, but they were blinded by their man-made religious traditions. The Jews who craved for the promised Kingdom of God and the promised Lord Messiah who would finally unite all the world's history under God, missed it. "The world was made **through** him," i.e. with Christ in mind. Everything will be gathered up, summed up in him, yet even to this day our world does not see this nor know the One who in God's purpose will bring the goal of creation to pass at his Second Coming.

It is this message which the apostles preached with such telling effect. Take Acts 2:23 for instance: "This man, delivered up by the predetermined plan and foreknowledge of God, you nailed to a cross by the hands of godless men and put him to death."

What God determined by His will from before time began has come to historical actuality in Jesus Christ. Jesus of Nazareth is the one who from the beginning had been pre-ordained for this role.

> At the same time this may not be understood as an affirmation of Christ as himself preexistent. It is the divine *purpose* for Christ which "existed" from the beginning, not the one in whom it should be fulfilled; just as Paul can speak of the divine purpose similarly determined for those

---

[69] Kuschel, *Born Before All Time?* p. 290.

> who believe in Christ (Rom. 8:28-30). No thought of the personal preexistence of either Christ or believers is involved.[70]

Did Jesus Exist Before John the Baptist?

As we continue through John's introduction, we come across another statement often used to justify faith in the eternal Son of God. John the Baptist testifies in verse 15, "This was he of whom I said, 'He who comes after me has a higher rank than I, for he existed before me'" (John 1:15). Here — according to many of our translations — we plainly read that Jesus existed before John the Baptist. And we know that John the Baptist was conceived six months before the angel Gabriel told Mary she would have a miraculous conception by God's Holy Spirit. Since John the Baptist was six months older than Jesus and yet his inspired word — according to some English renditions — is that Jesus existed before he did, surely the Baptist believed that Jesus preexisted his own birth because he was the second member of the Godhead?

What is the answer to this? Can the Son of God, who is the individual Jesus, be both older and younger than his cousin John the Baptist? Once again it is an issue of translation. The Greek may equally read — and is so translated in some English versions such as the Revised Version, Rotheram and the Geneva Bible — "because he is first [Greek *protos*] in regard of me," (RV), meaning, "he is better than me," my superior, my chief. Jesus' superiority over John the Baptist lies in the fact that he is the long-promised Messiah, and is destined to rule the world when God inaugurates his Kingdom. The Greek is ambiguous and "first" may refer to either rank or time. Just a little later in verse 30 the Baptist again states: "This is he on behalf of whom I said, 'After me comes a man who has a higher rank than I, for he..."

Same difficulty. "For he existed before me" or "for he is before me in rank"? The Greek of this verse is the same as verse 15, so does not need to be translated differently. It is my conviction that the sense is, "he has gone ahead of me because he is my superior." Some might feel we cannot be dogmatic on this point, so let's examine more evidence.

---

[70] Dunn, *Christology in the Making,* p. 235.

Jewish "Ideal" Preexistence

In the English language, and certainly the way young people speak in Australia, we often speak about something that happened in the past as though it is happening in the present. For instance, a witness to a bank robbery may say, "And here I am standing in the queue minding my own business, when bursting through the door comes this hooded bank robber. He tells us all to get on the floor. He waves his gun around and threatens us. Then he goes up to the teller and yells, 'Give me the money!'" We understand the events described occurred in the past, even though the narrative is in the present. Speaking of past events in the present is a peculiarity of the English language.

Most languages have peculiarities. The Hebrew mind and language has a peculiarity that English speakers are not accustomed to. They do the opposite of what I have just described. They often use the past tense or the present tense to speak of events yet future. The reason is that the Jews believed that whatever was determined in the mind of God existed before it came to be in history. God is the God who calls the things which do not exist as (already) existing (Rom. 4:17). God promised Abraham that He would give him the promised land and that he would be the father of many descendants: "Go...to the land that I will show you; and I will make you a great nation" (Gen. 12:1-2). God repeated this promise to Abraham a number of times: "Now lift up your eyes and look from the place where you are, northward and southward and eastward and westward; for all the land which you see, I will give it to you and to your descendants forever" (Gen. 13:14-15). Now here is an amazing thing. So sure is the fulfilment that sometimes this predictive language is in the past tense, as though it were already accomplished: "To your descendants I **have given** this land" (Gen. 15:18). It came to be a common feature of Hebrew thinking that whatever God had decreed already preexisted (in plan and purpose) before it materialised on earth. "When the Jew wished to designate something as predestined, *he spoke of it as already existing in heaven.*"[71]

In the verse alluded to above, where God "calls the things which do not [yet] exist as [already] existing" the context refers to Isaac

---

[71] E.G. Selwyn, *First Epistle of St. Peter,* Baker Book House, 1983, p. 124, emphasis added.

who was "*real in the thought and purpose of God before he was begotten.*"[72] Scripture tells us that Jesus Christ "was foreknown before the foundation of the world, but has appeared in these last times" for our sakes who believe in God's word (1 Pet. 1:20). This does not mean that Jesus personally preexisted his appearance on earth, because in the same chapter we find that Christians have also been in the "foreknowledge of God the Father" (1 Pet. 1:2). The words "foreknowledge" and "foreknown," noun and verb, are exactly alike. Peter uses precisely the same idea to refer to both Christians and Jesus. Christians do not preexist in heaven before our birth on earth. Nor did Jesus. "It is the divine purpose for Christ which 'existed' from the beginning, not the one in whom it should be fulfilled; just as Paul can speak of the divine purpose similarly predetermined for those who believe in Christ (Rom. 8:28-30)."[73]

Similarly, the Bible speaks of Jesus as the Lamb of God who was crucified before the world began (see Rev. 13:8). Every Bible reader of course knows that Jesus was crucified under Pontius Pilate in Palestine in the first century. But God ordained his crucifixion to happen before He even created the universe. Therefore, in God's mind, and in Hebrew understanding, that which came to be had already been. The prophetic future was spoken of in the past tense. We may call this the "prophetic past tense." What God has decreed, He says is as good as done.

One day the Lord Jesus at his Second Coming will say to his own people, "Come, you who are blessed of my Father, inherit the kingdom prepared for you from the foundation of the world" (Matt. 25:34). In Paul's language this hope is "laid up for you in heaven" which means it is in God's promise and plan and is certain of fulfilment (Col. 1:5). This hope is so certain that Paul can even speak of Christians as *already* glorified (Rom. 8:29-30, noting the past tenses). Indeed, this plan hatched in God's mind "according to His own purpose and grace which was granted us in Christ Jesus from all eternity" (2 Tim. 1:9). "The gift was *purposed* 'ages ago,' unless we are to take it that the actual giving and receiving, 'us' and 'Christ Jesus' were all alike preexistent."[74] This hope of Christians

---

[72] Everett F. Harrison, *Romans, Expositor's Bible Commentary,* Zondervan, 1976, p. 52, emphasis added.
[73] Dunn, *Christology in the Making,* p. 235.
[74] *Ibid.,* p. 238.

entering into the life of the Age to Come was "promised long ages ago" (Titus 1:2):

> Here it is even clearer that what is thought of as happening "ages ago" is God's promise; and it is that promise of eternal life which has been manifested. Indeed, the text says it is his word that he has manifested — that is, not Christ the Logos, but the word of promise, fulfilled in Christ and offered now in the *kerygma* [message]. In other words, we are back where we started — Christ as the content of the word of preaching, the embodiment of the predetermined plan of salvation, the fulfilment of the divine purpose.[75]

A classic example of this way of thinking is the tabernacle that Moses built in the wilderness. Moses was instructed to build it according to a "pattern" that God showed him on the mount (Num. 8:4). Then Moses was told to ordain priests according to God's clear directions. The high priest too was to follow this blueprint from God. The NT says that these servants and this tabernacle serve as "a copy and shadow of the heavenly things" (Heb. 8:5). And the fact that Jesus has now taken his seat at the right hand of God in the heavens as our High Priest, proves that he is serving on our behalf "in the true tabernacle, which the Lord pitched, not man" (Heb. 8:2). The idea is that the institutions God revealed to Moses were mere copies of the real and true ones that existed long before in heaven. That is to say, they existed in heaven because they existed in the mind and planning of God before God revealed them on earth.

In fact, the Jews applied this thinking to many of their great national treasures. They developed:

> the idea of a Jerusalem, divine, preexistent, prepared by God in the heavenly places, there from all time, and prepared some day to come down among men. The old house is folded up and taken away, and a wonderful new house which the Lord has built comes and takes its place (1Enoch 90:28, 29). The preexistent Jerusalem was shown to Adam before he sinned.[76]

And in the same Jewish vein John speaks of the new Jerusalem, the holy city, "coming down out of heaven from God" (Rev. 21:10).

---

[75] *Ibid.*, p. 238.

[76] William Barclay, *Jesus as They Saw Him*, Amsterdam: SCM Press, 1962, p. 136.

What John conveys is not that there is a literal city already built somewhere up in heaven that will be transplanted from outer space (no more than Jesus had been crucified in heaven before he died on earth). Rather, in good Jewish tradition, John is saying that there will be a renewed city of Jerusalem on earth when Messiah returns. This will indeed "materialize" and it is certain of accomplishment because God has promised it. God's plan is so absolutely sure, and cannot be thwarted by anything man might do, that John can "see" it already coming down. The city preexists in an "ideal" state, that is, in God's promise, but not yet in time-space actuality.

Thus, if we apply all of this to John the Baptist's statements, "He who comes after me has a higher rank than I, for he existed before me" (John 1:15), and "After me comes a man who has a higher rank than I, for he existed before me" (John 1:30), we will see him meaning, not that Jesus is a preexistent heavenly being, "but as the one who fulfilled God's predetermined plan of salvation, as the one predetermined by God to be the means of man's salvation through his death and resurrection."[77] John the Baptist was only the forerunner, preparing the way for Jesus the Christ. The Baptist's role was to point men to "the Lamb of God who takes away the sin of the world." Jesus, therefore, has greater rank than John, and in this sense was "before" John. Given the two possibilities of translating the Greek here, we must prefer that nuance of meaning that best fits the Jewish context of John the Baptist, that best dovetails with the wider context of Scripture, and so suggest the better translation: "He who comes after me has a higher rank than I, for he was above me in God's plan [to save the world]." Jesus did not personally preexist John the Baptist, nor did he consciously exist in heaven before he appeared in history on earth. He existed "ideally" in God's decree and purpose so sure. It is the preexistence "more of an idea and purpose in the mind of God than of a personal divine being."[78] The Messiah:

> is present in the mind of God and chosen before the creation, and from time to time revealed to the righteous for their consolation; but he is neither divine nor actually preexistent. He is named and hidden from the beginning in the secret thoughts of God, finally to be revealed in the Last

---

[77] Dunn, *Christology in the Making,* p. 178.

[78] *Ibid.*, p. 56.

Times as the ideal Man who will justify God's creation of the world.[79]

The Son of Man Already in Heaven Before

This line of thought naturally takes us to two other difficult expressions spoken by Jesus himself in the Gospel of John: "And no one has ascended into heaven, but he who descended from heaven, even the Son of Man" (John 3:13). And "What then if you should behold the Son of Man ascending where he was before?" (John 6:62).

If we read these statements with our traditional (Greek) glasses on, we will again run into difficulty, thinking Jesus said he lived with the Father in heaven before transferring his existence into the womb of Mary on earth. In order to understand what Jesus is saying, we must again look at its "Jewishness." It is significant that Jesus here calls himself "the Son of Man." This title occurs about 82 times in the NT and with two exceptions all occurrences are in the Gospels. And in all but the two exceptions (Acts 7:56 and Rev. 1:13) this title comes from the lips of Jesus himself. We understand then that it held a dear place in his heart. We are under an obligation to discover why Jesus delighted to call himself "the Son of Man." The OT supplies the background, and when we examine this we can see that Jesus did not just invent the title out of thin air.

In the OT "son of man" simply means a human being and often appears as strictly parallel to the word "man" (see Num. 23:19; Is. 56:2; Jer. 49:18; Ps. 8:4; Ps. 146:3, etc.). In Ezekiel there is a slightly more specialized use of the phrase "son of man." Here it occurs more than 90 times, and always as an address by God to Ezekiel. "Son of man," says God to Ezekiel, "stand on your feet and I will speak with you" (2:1). "Son of man, eat what you find; eat this scroll, and go, speak to the house of Israel" (3:1). "Then He said to me, 'Son of man, go to the house of Israel and speak My words to them'" (3:4). In Ezekiel the title points to Ezekiel's humanity, with all its attendant ignorance, frailty and mortality, in contrast with the glory and strength and knowledge of God.

Some commentators have latched onto this usage and have suggested that when Jesus called himself "the son of man" he was speaking in terms of the human part of his nature, and that when he

[79] Schonfield, *The Passover Plot,* p. 256.

used the term "son of God" he was speaking in terms of the divine side of his nature. This cannot be for two obvious reasons. First, it is in fact when he uses the term "son of man" that Jesus makes many of his greatest and most divine statements and claims. Second, to partition Jesus' life into times when he spoke humanly as Son of Man and divinely as Son of God is to leave him a split personality.

Other commentators suggest the title means Jesus was thinking of himself as the Representative Man, the Man in whom humanity finds its peak and its example. William Barclay quotes F.W. Robertson: "There was in Jesus no national peculiarity or individual idiosyncrasy. He was not the son of the Jew, or the son of the carpenter; not the offspring of the mode of living and thinking of that particular century. He was the Son of Man." William Barclay debunks this immediately by saying:

> this theory falls on two grounds. First, it is too abstract to have emerged at all in the world of New Testament thought. It is a violence to just rip Jesus out of his cultural context. Second, once again we have to note that it was precisely in terms of Son of Man that Jesus made many of his most superhuman claims and statements.[80]

A third group of commentators suggest that the title Son of Man is used by Jesus to deliberately contrast himself with the national visions the Jews had of a Messiah who was a supernatural figure of power and apocalyptic wonder-worker. This picture of the identity of the Son of Man as the divine agent through whom God would establish His worldwide government of righteousness and peace is drawn from Daniel 7:

> I kept looking in the night visions, and behold, with the clouds of heaven one like a Son of Man was coming, and he came up to the Ancient of Days and was presented before Him. And to him was given dominion, glory and a kingdom, that all the peoples, nations, and men of every language might serve him. His dominion is an everlasting dominion which will not pass away; and his kingdom is one which will not be destroyed (v. 13-14).

Some suggest that when Jesus called himself Son of Man he was pointing to himself as a humble, unpretentious human with no aspirations for such a prophesied greatness as Daniel saw. He was

---

[80] Barclay, *Jesus as They Saw Him,* p. 70.

not claiming, they contend, to be this heavenly warrior-king, for whom the nation of Israel hoped and prayed. Again William Barclay explodes this line of thought when he says:

> The one fact which makes that suggestion impossible is that it appears that in fact Son of Man was a Messianic title, and a title involved in one of the most superhuman pictures of the Messiah in all Jewish thought. If the title Son of Man had any contemporary Messianic meaning at all, it was the precise opposite of a simple, humble, human figure.[81]

There is no doubt that the ultimate origin of the title Son of Man is in the book of Daniel. In Daniel 7 the seer has a vision of the great empires which up until then had held sway over the Mediterranean world. He sees these empires under the symbolism of beasts; they are so callous, so cruel, so bestial that they cannot be typified in any other way. There was the lion with eagles' wings; there was the bear with three ribs in its mouth; there was the leopard with four wings and four heads; there was the fourth nameless beast with iron teeth, dreadful, terrible, irresistibly strong. These stood for the empires which up to that time had held sway, all of them of such savagery that beasts were the only picture of them. But their days were ended and their power was broken. Then the world power is given by God into the hands of a power which is not bestial and savage but gentle and humane and can be typified and symbolised in the figure of a man. Daniel predicts that the saints, God's people of both the Old and New Testaments, will possess the Kingdom. This is to say that at last the dream of Israel will be realized. That nation has gone through unspeakable things. They have been brutally treated. But the long-awaited Messianic age will dawn. And, naturally according to Daniel's vision, there grew in Israel's national consciousness the hope that this New Age would be brought into being by their national hero, the Messiah, the Son of Man. The title Son of Man becomes a title for the Messiah.

Jesus took this title for himself. When he called himself the Son of Man he was saying "I, myself." Compare his question "Who do men say that the Son of Man is?" (Matt. 16:13) with the parallel in Mark 8, "Who do men say that I am?" (v. 27). A look at the contexts will show that Jesus used this title to make some of his greatest claims and declarations. The Son of Man is the saviour of

---

[81] *Ibid.*, p. 71.

the world (Luke 19:10). The Son of Man will rise from the dead (Matt. 17:9). The Son of Man will inherit the glory of the Kingdom of God (Matt. 19:28) and will come to earth and raise the dead for judgment (Matt. 24:30; Mark 13:26; Luke 17:26, 30). The Son of Man will come to earth with all the power of the angels of God (Matt. 13:41; 16:27-28).

However, there was an amazing twist to the plot that both the disciples and his listeners could not at that stage grasp. It was the fact that the Son of Man would suffer and be shamefully treated by the leaders of Israel and by the cruel Gentiles. The Son of Man would die. He used the title in this connection of humiliation and suffering more than any other connection (Matt. 17:12, 22; Mark 8:31; 10:33; 14:21, 41; Luke 9:44; 18:31; 22:22, etc.). It was after Jesus revealed this twist of a suffering Son of Man that Peter rebuked Jesus, "God forbid it, Lord! This shall never happen to you" (Matt. 16:22). For Peter and his fellow disciples the whole Jewish consciousness of the majestic, divine glory of the Son of Man had nothing to do with rejection and humiliation and *crucifixion as a common criminal.* This was an impossible contradiction of terms. Statements like this left Jesus' followers bewildered. But from the beginning he knew he faced a double destiny. He was indeed the Son of Man, the Messiah destined for ultimate triumph over all God's enemies. But he was also the Suffering Servant, who must get to the glory by way of the cross. Jesus therefore "took this title Son of Man and re-minted it...The Son of Man is the title which contains within itself the shame and the glory of Jesus Christ."[82]

With this brief background we are now in a position to interpret John's puzzling statements that "no one has ascended into heaven, but he who descended from heaven, even the Son of Man," and "What then if you should behold the Son of Man ascending where he was before?" (John 3:13; 6:62). It is clear Jesus did not use the title Son of Man in a vacuum. His whole life was based on what was written in the OT Scriptures, that is, prophecy. "The Son of Man is to go, just as it is written of him" (Matt. 26:24; Mark 14:22). "And yet how is it written of the Son of Man that he should suffer many things and be treated with contempt?" (Mark 9:12).

---

[82] *Ibid.*, p. 92.

How then can Jesus have said that the Son "has ascended to heaven"? Simply because this is what had been forecast about him in Daniel. Following a well-established principle of Hebrew thinking, God's acts may be said to have happened already, once they are fixed in the divine counsels. The unexpected past tense "has ascended" may be explained as a past tense of determination in the divine plan. Thus "No one [as it is written in the book of Daniel] is destined to ascend to heaven except the one who came down from heaven, the Son of Man who [in Daniel's vision of the future] is in heaven." The final phrase "who is in heaven" (omitted from some versions) is well-attested and may well be original; its omission from some manuscripts was due to the difficulty of understanding how Jesus could say he was in heaven during his ministry on earth. The difficulty disappears when the special reference to Daniel's prophecy is taken into account. The Son of Man is identified with the figure who in the book of Daniel is seen in heaven. He is there not because he is actually alive prior to his birth, but because God has granted a vision of his future destiny. At the time of speaking, Jesus had not yet ascended to heaven; but the ascension is so certainly prophesied by Daniel that Jesus can say he has ascended, i.e., he is destined to do so.[83]

When Jesus asks, "What then if you should behold the Son of Man ascending where he was before?" we believe he is seen in Daniel's heavenly vision of the Messiah in future glory. This is the glory that Messiah, destined to rise from the dead and sit at God's right hand of power, will have. Jesus is grasping by faith God's picture of his ascension glory, in what was written. A further consideration that proves these verses do not support the doctrine that Christ is the "eternal Son of God" in heaven before his birth is that the "Son of Man" is a *human person* who preexists (in God's decree in vision form) in heaven. Even Trinitarians do not claim that the Son of Man, the human Jesus, existed prior to his conception. Thus we establish again the very Hebrew understanding and background to these sayings of Jesus, namely, that God calls those things which do not yet exist as though they do. Like Father, like Son!

---

[83] Buzzard and Hunting, *The Doctrine of the Trinity,* pp. 198-199.

John 6:62

In particular reference to Jesus' question in John 6:62, "What then if you should behold the Son of Man ascending where he was before?" the relevant discussion begins back in verse 22. After Jesus miraculously feeds the multitude they ask him for a sign that they might believe he truly is God's Messiah. Jesus berates the multitude for seeking him from purely temporal motivation. He admonishes the crowd to rather seek the food which endures to eternal life. This bread that "endures to eternal life" comes through the one upon whom the Father has "set His seal" (v. 27). The crowd wonders how they may do the works that please God, and Jesus tells them they must believe "in him whom He [the Father] has sent" (that is, commissioned) (v. 29). To be "sent" is to have God's "seal." From this point on, the issue at hand is whether Jesus fits this requirement: Is he the one "sent" from God? He demonstrates that he does "fit the bill," so to speak, because just like the manna God sent "out of heaven" Jesus also has "come down from heaven" (v. 38).

Is Jesus referring to the common belief that he personally preexisted in heaven before his birth as a man in Bethlehem? Or is there a better contextual explanation?

It is noteworthy how many times in the following verses the interchangeable phrases "out of heaven," "from heaven," "of God," "from God," "from the Father," and "sent" occur. Both the manna in the OT and Jesus are "from heaven" or "from God." So what did Jesus mean by this expression?

We are not left to conjecture because this is classic Hebrew phraseology/imagery. This expression "from heaven" is quite common in Hebrew idiom. John's baptism is also said to be "from heaven" (Lk. 20:4). Our resurrection bodies are said to be "from heaven" (2 Cor. 5:2). Every good and every perfect gift is said to "come down from heaven" (Mal. 3:10; James 1:17; 3:17). All of which is to say that whatever is "from heaven" is given and wrought by God and by His authority. Neither the manna, the gifts and blessings, John's ministry, nor our resurrection bodies literally preexisted in heaven before coming down to earth. Exist in God's purpose they did/do. Exist in God's plan, yes. Exist in His promises, certainly. But not literally in eternity past before materializing on earth in history.

Now, in the same vein, when Jesus says he has come down "from heaven" he surely intends that his person and his ministry are commissioned by God, sanctioned by the Father, and are the LORD's miraculous provision for hungry men. Personal preexistence is not the topic. The issue under discussion is whether Jesus is the authorized agent (Son) of his Father or not; is he an imposter or really from God? Is God's seal upon him? What sign will he give to prove his credentials?

In this context Jesus states the ultimate sign that he is "from God" or "from heaven" is that he will at the last day "raise up" all who "eat and drink" of him. The resurrection will prove his credentials, so to speak. Again and again in this very passage Jesus mentions the resurrection from the dead as the great sign:

> And this is the will of Him that sent me, that of all that He has given me I lose nothing, but **raise him up on the last day**. For this is the will of my Father, that every one who beholds the Son, and believes in him, may have eternal life; and I myself will **raise him up on the last day**...No one can come to me, unless the Father who sent me draws him; and I will **raise him up on the last day**...He who eats my flesh and drinks my blood has eternal life; and I will **raise him up on the last day**...As the living Father sent me, and I live because of the Father, so he who eats me, he also shall live because of me. This is the bread which came down out of heaven, not as the fathers ate, and died, he who eats this bread shall live forever (John 6:39, 40, 44, 54, 58).

With this context of the resurrection of the last day for all who have believed in Jesus the Son of God in mind, we come to the critical verse 62: "What then if you should behold the Son of Man ascending where he was before?" Most modern-day readers take this to mean that Jesus is saying he will ascend back up to heaven to enjoy the kind of preexistent glory he had with God the Father before his Incarnation. In view of the entire context of resurrection from the grave this appears an out-of-context, indeed foreign idea that Jesus is not addressing.

The word in verse 62, "ascending" in the Greek simply means "going up."[84] Given the previous context of resurrection from the dead, and the whole Hebrew understanding we have been considering, Jesus may simply be asking if they would be offended

---

[84] The word for "go up" is found in Matt. 5:1; 14:23; 3:16; 13:7; Mark 1:10; 4:7, 8, 32; Luke 19:4, etc.

if they saw him "come up" (from death out of the ground), that is, be resurrected, and be where he was before, which is to say, alive again on the earth. Jesus may possibly be announcing that his own resurrection from the dead would be proof that he is indeed "from God."

To some interpreters this may be stretching the import since Jesus' resurrection is not termed an ascension. Fair enough. But I am not so sure that the context of resurrection throughout this chapter as already highlighted disqualifies this nuance out of hand.

There is one other piece of relevant information here that proves Jesus was not speaking of his personal preexistence before Bethlehem. In verse 51 Jesus defines the bread which came down from heaven as "my flesh." *It is his flesh that preexists in heaven!* This tells us that it is the human Jesus, the son of man, who preexists. Furthermore, note that Jesus states they will "behold the **Son of Man** ascending where he was before." The "Son of Man" is a *human being* and even Trinitarians do not claim that the Son of Man, the human Jesus, the man of flesh and blood existed prior to his conception! Thus, to claim that John chapter 6 shows Jesus personally existing in heaven prior to his coming to earth proves too much for the Trinitarian position. It is much better to stick with the explanation already given, namely that Jesus' preexistence was "ideal."

The bottom line according to context seems clear: Jesus is *not* announcing that he has come down from a conscious personal existence in heaven prior to his own human coming. Nor is he saying he will re-take any pre-incarnate or pre-human glory when he "ascends" again. He firmly believes in the prophetic word that "the Son of Man" will rise from the dead and sit in the promised glory of the future Messianic Age, just as the prophetic word has foretold.

The Glory Jesus Had with the Father Before the World Was

In John 17 Jesus prays just before his arrest in the garden, "I glorified You on the earth, having accomplished the work which You have given me to do. And now, glorify me together with Yourself, Father, with the glory which I had with You before the world was" (v. 4-5)

If ever there was a statement that proved the personal preexistence of Jesus with the Father in heaven before he came to earth, surely this is it. Once again, we must caution against haste, for "In biblical ways of speaking and thinking one may 'have' something which is promised in God's plan before one actually has it."[85] We have already seen this principle in operation, where God's plan and promises are spoken in the "prophetic past tense." God promised Abraham, "I **have given** you this land." God says to Christians, "You **are** seated with Christ in the heavenlies; you are **already** glorified" (Eph. 2:6; Rom. 8:30). We have these things already in the plan and purpose of God — even though we do not (yet) have them! Scripture tells us that we have eternal life as a present possession, even though clearly we await the day of our entrance into the life of the Age to Come, whether by resurrection for those already dead, or the rapture of the living, when Christ returns. God calls the things that are not as though they already exist (Rom. 4:17). Clearly, in Hebrew thinking, the glory which Jesus had *with* God before the world was, is the glory that was present in God's mind and purpose from the beginning. (Please refer again to the earlier section under the heading **John Chapter One** to see how common this is in Hebrew usage.)

When we examine the rest of Jesus' prayer, it becomes quite clear that the glory Jesus claims to have had "with the Father before the world was" is a *glory in prospect.* Jesus is using the peculiar Hebrew way of thinking and speaking by which the past tense is employed to speak of the future. To confirm this all we need to do is follow Jesus' prayer through. Jesus speaks as though he has already accomplished his work: he says I have "accomplished the work which You gave me to do" (v. 4). Quite obviously he has not actually finished the work because his crucifixion has not yet happened, and his cry from the cross, "It is finished," has not yet been uttered. Next, Jesus speaks as though the disciples have *already* fully glorified him (through their preaching ministry) even though the resurrection has not yet happened: he prays, "I have been glorified in them" (v. 10). Jesus also says "I am no more in the world" (v. 11) even though he clearly is still in the world. In his own mind, he is already, by faith in his Father's promise, sitting in heaven having been resurrected. Jesus says he has already sent the disciples into the world to preach: he prays, "I have sent them into the world" (v. 18), even though this did not fully happen until after the resurrection. Jesus prays for his disciples, and "for those also

---

[85] *Ibid.,* p. 201.

who [will] believe in me through their word" (v. 20). That is, he prays for subsequent generations of Christians who will come to faith in Christ down the track. He prays that "the glory which You have given me I **have given** to them" (v. 22). He prays that all these believers "which You **have given** me" (the whole future community of faith) "may behold my glory, which You have given me; for You did love [choose] me before the foundation of the world" (v. 24). *The very same glory promised to Jesus has already been given to generations of believers not yet born!* The glory that the Father gave to Jesus in promise before the world began *has already been given* to those who will *in the future* trust in his Name. The promise of God is equal to the possession. Just as Jesus had promised his persecuted disciples that "your reward in heaven is great" (Matt. 5:12), even though they had not yet received it, so Jesus in the shadow of his cross was laying hold of the promise of God for himself. God had promised Jesus that after his suffering the glory would come. Knowing that he would be raised again, Jesus "endured the cross, despising the shame" for he would soon sit "down at the right hand of God" (Heb. 12:2). This glory that his Father had promised to him from before the world began, Jesus now prays to the Father to make good.

> The use of the past tense in John 17 needs to be examined carefully. There are clear indications in this chapter that past tenses may indeed describe not what has actually happened but what is *destined to happen,* because God has already decreed it...Clearly, divinely planned future events may be described in the past tense.[86]

The great Bible commentator Henry Alford notes that "our Lord stands by anticipation at the end of his accomplished course and looks back on it as past."[87] In other words, throughout this prayer, Jesus is employing classic Hebrew thought. God's predetermined plan is as good as already completed.

It really is quite incredible how deeply entrenched the notion is that Jesus Christ consciously lived in heaven before coming to earth. Some English translations have been quite biased here and add to this deep-seated misconception. Take for instance the following

---

[86] *Ibid.*, pp. 294-295.

[87] Henry Alford, *Greek New Testament,* London: Rivingtons and Deighton, Bell & Co., 1861, p. 823, quoted in *The Doctrine of the Trinity,* p. 205.

verses (quoted from the New International Version): "Jesus knew that the Father had put all things under his power, and that he had come from God and was returning to God…" (John 13:3). The only problem is, the Greek text does not say that Jesus was *returning* to God. It simply reads that Jesus was *going to* God. The word "returning" has been substituted by the translators for no textual reason at all.

The same unfortunate impression is found in John 16: "I came from the Father and entered the world; now I am leaving the world and going *back* to the Father" (v. 28). Here again we encounter the same problem: the word "back" does not appear in the Greek text at all. What Jesus really said is this: "I came from the Father and entered the world; now I am leaving the world and going to the Father." In John 20:17 Jesus did not say, "I have not yet returned to the Father," as the NIV reports. Once again we see the bias of preconceived ideas about the origin of Christ.

When Jesus says that he "came forth from the Father" we must not read into this that he meant he was alive with God before coming to earth. It was quite common for the Jews to say that something came forth "from God" or "from heaven" if God was its source. Thus, John the Baptist was a man "sent from God" (John 1:6). When God told Israel that He would bless them He promised to "open the windows of heaven and pour out a blessing" (Mal. 3:10). This is plainly a figure of speech. Nobody expected God to literally pour out things from heaven. It simply means that God was the source of every blessing they would receive. Similarly, we are told that every good and perfect gift is "from above" and "comes down from the Father" (James 1:17). One of the clearest examples of this typical Jewish manner of speaking occurs when Jesus was challenged by his opponents, "By what authority are you doing these things, and who gave you this authority?" (Matt. 21:23). Jesus cleverly answers this interrogation by asking them a question: "The baptism of John was from what source, from heaven or from men?" (v. 25). "This verse makes the idiom clear: things could be 'from heaven,' i.e., from God, or they could be 'from men.' The idiom is the same when used of Jesus. Jesus is 'from God,' 'from heaven' or 'from above' in the sense that God is literally his heavenly Father and thus his origin."[88]

---

[88] Graeser et al, *One God and One Lord*, p. 190.

"The Only Begotten God"?

As we continue through John's introduction to his Gospel we come across verse 18. It is a verse that has also generated a lot of discussion, because there has been a dispute as to what John originally wrote. Did he write as some of our translations have it, "No man has seen God at any time; the only begotten **Son**, who is in the bosom of the Father, he has explained Him"? Or did he write "the only begotten **God**, who is in the bosom of the Father..."?

One of the best contemporary textual critics, Bart D. Ehrman, discusses this in his important book *The Orthodox Corruption of Scripture.* Ehrman is able to show convincing reasons why the reading "the only begotten God" represents a corruption of what John wrote. (For those interested, this variant text is found only in the Alexandrian tradition, and has not fared well in virtually every other representative of every other textual grouping, whether Western, Caesarean, or Byzantine. And even within the Alexandrian group there is evidence for "the only begotten Son.") Nevertheless, Ehrman argues that it is on internal grounds that the real superiority of "the only begotten Son" shines forth:

> The problem, of course, is that Jesus can be the *unique* God only if there is no other God; but for the fourth Gospel, the Father is God as well. Indeed, even in this passage the *monogenes* [only begotten] is said to reside in the bosom of the Father. How can the *monogenes Theos* [only begotten God], the unique God, stand in such a relationship to (another) God?[89]

Not only so, but Ehrman wonders what "the only begotten God" would have meant to its first-century audience? It would have made no sense within its Jewish-Christian context. Furthermore, Ehrman says the reading "the only begotten Son" is no doubt the genuine one, because it "coincides perfectly well with the way *monogenes* [only begotten] is used throughout the Johannine literature. In three other Johannine passages *monogenes* serves as a modifier, and on each occasion it is used with *huios* [son] (John 3:16, 18; 1 John 4:9)."[90] This is a powerful point that even those who prefer the reading "the only begotten God" (because of theological bias!)

---

[89] Ehrman, *The Orthodox Corruption of Scripture,* p. 80.
[90] *Ibid.,* p. 80.

concede. The conclusion? "There seems little reason any longer to dispute the reading found in virtually every witness outside the Alexandrian tradition. The prologue ends with the statement that 'the unique Son who is in the bosom of the Father, that one has made him known.'"[91] For Ehrman then, this variant reading, "the only begotten God" represents a corruption of the text. As already discussed earlier in this chapter, God cannot be begotten for He has no beginning. If Jesus were called God here, he is an only begotten God, and someone who is begotten is *not* God. We may be sure that Jesus is not here called the eternal God.

Is Christ "Over All, God Blessed Forever" (Romans 9:5)?

A verse frequently appealed to justify belief that Jesus Christ is God reads in most modern translations this way:

> For I could wish that I myself were accursed, separated from Christ for the sake of my brethren, my kinsmen according to the flesh, who are Israelites, to whom belongs the adoption as sons and the glory and the covenants and the giving of the Law and the temple service and the promises, whose are the fathers, and from whom is the Christ according to the flesh, who is over all, God blessed forever. Amen (Rom. 9:3-5).

So translated it does sound very much as though Paul is teaching that Jesus the Christ is God because he "is over all, God blessed forever." It is a particularly moving passage because Paul is appalled that his Jewish brothers with all the advantages of their heritage have rejected Jesus as their Messiah. Paul goes so far as to say that he would rather be accursed, cut off from all the blessings of Israel and her Messiah, if only he could convince the Jews to turn and be saved. In the midst of this emotional passage, Paul breaks out into deep praise. But praise to whom? To Christ as God? Or to God the Father of Christ? "To whom this praise is directed is one of the most disputed questions in the exegesis of Pauline Christology."[92] The reason for this dispute is that there are two ways of translating the Greek text, depending on where the translator places the punctuation. It may read: "they [the Israelites] have the patriarchs, and from them according to the flesh comes the Christ

---

[91] *Ibid.,* pp. 81-82.
[92] Kuschel, *Born Before All Time?* p. 301.

who stands over all as God, he is praised for ever. Amen." Taken this way, this is obviously an unambiguous praise of Christ as God Supreme. Alternatively, and equally legitimately, the text may be read: "And from them [the Israelites] comes Christ according to his physical origin. God, the Lord over all, be highly praised forever. Amen." This interpretation directs the praise to the God the Father. Clearly, in light of both possibilities, we are going to have to appeal to wider considerations.

Exegetes who prefer to ascribe the praise to Christ as God (a Christological interpretation), admit this view suffers from the problem that Paul nowhere else calls Christ God. Kuschel notes that "in our analysis of the text so far we, too, have not come across a single saying in Paul which points in this direction (not even in Phil. 2:6). In Paul Jesus Christ is essentially the exalted Lord, who after his resurrection is appointed by God to his divine dignity." Paul never loses sight of the fact that God the Father is always and ultimately the superior of Messiah (1 Cor. 15:28). In other words, Kuschel maintains that "the wider context of Pauline theology already makes a theological rather than a Christological interpretation of Rom. 9:5 more probable."[93]

But what of the more immediate context here in Romans 9? I believe it is this closer context that proves decisive in which way we are going to lean. In a passage where Paul is justifying his Christian position against the majority of Jews who reject Jesus as Messiah, it would seem odd to be saying that Jesus is Jehovah God. This would be like waving the proverbial red flag to a bull. Frankly, it would be a tactic that would not work, given the culture and context in which Paul operated. To appeal to Christ as God in a passage where Israel is the focal point is anomalous. As Dunn notes, "a doxology to Christ as god at this stage would be even more unusual within the context of Paul's thought than an unexpected twist in grammatical construction. Even if Paul does bless Christ as 'god' here, the meaning of 'god' remains uncertain" (particularly in view of our earlier discussion on the various ways "god" is used in Scripture).[94]

Anthony Buzzard observes that "more remarkable is the fact that during the whole Arian controversy, this verse was not used by Trinitarians against the unitarians. It clearly did not attest to Jesus as

---

[93] *Ibid.*, p. 302.

[94] Dunn, *Christology in the Making*, p. 45.

the second member of the Godhead."[95] Regardless of which way the reader may prefer to read Romans 9:5 — as praise to Christ as Almighty God, or as praise to God the Father — it must be thought an astounding thing that such a critical doctrine as the Trinity should depend on such fine points of grammar. (This same reasoning applies to other exegetically "doubtful" verses such as Titus 2:13 and 2 Peter 1:1.) Wherever else Paul ascribes praise to God in the same formula, it is always praise to God the Father "to whom be the glory forevermore. Amen" (Gal. 1:4-5). Come to think of it, even at the conclusion of this very book of Romans, Paul maintains his unitarian praise: "to the only wise God, through Jesus Christ, be the glory forever. Amen" (Rom. 16:27). It is highly unlikely that he so soon, in the space of a few chapters, would contradict himself!

Is God the Only Saviour?

I imagine by now you may be arguing with me and saying something like this: Well, if Jesus is not God in human flesh what do you say to the Scriptures that say only God can save? If Jesus is not God how can we possibly be saved? After all, God says, "I, even I, am the LORD; and there is no saviour besides Me" (Is. 43:11). If Jesus is not God then there are two saviours! And this is something the Bible here clearly excludes.

We have already seen that a strong argument against the idea that God became man in order to redeem us is that there is not one single OT prophecy that supports it. Not one verse foretells that God Himself was going to become a man in order to save us. The opposite is the case. The prophets predict a *human being who would under God's anointing Spirit rescue us.*

Wherein lies the solution? Ah, let's now read this through our Hebrew eyes and see what a difference it makes. Remember that dictum the Jews had about the law of agency where "the agent is as the principal himself"? It applies right here.

Let's go back to Exodus 23. You remember that we used this chapter earlier to illustrate the Hebrew law of agency. We saw that the angel of the Lord acted in God's stead. What the angel did and said was really what God Himself did and said, for "My name is in him" (v. 21). In verse 23 Jehovah explained, "For **My angel** will go before you and bring you in to the land of the Amorites, the Hittites,

---

[95] Buzzard and Hunting, *The Doctrine of the Trinity,* p. 269.

the Perizzites, the Canaanites, the Hivites and the Jebusites; and **I will completely destroy** them." The angel was the instrument through whom God destroyed the enemies.

Now let's proceed on in the chapter. God says to the Israelites, "**I** will send My terror ahead of you...**I** will make all your enemies turn their backs to you. And **I** will send hornets ahead of you, that they may drive out the Hivites, the Canaanites, and the Hittites before you" (v. 27-28).

To our understanding this sounds as if the LORD Himself is going to do the work. But then we come to verse 31: "**I will deliver** the inhabitants of the land into your hand, and **you will drive them out** before you." So God expects *the Israelites* to drive their enemies out. Is there a contradiction here? Will God Himself drive out their enemies or will the Israelites do it? We note the principle again and again. God says He will act when in fact He is going to empower His angels and His people to do the work.

This kind of talk has a thorough Hebrew feel about it. Actions that are directly ascribed to God are in fact carried out by his commissioned agents. Take another instance: "And the LORD...He saved them by the hand of Jeroboam" (2 Kings 14:27).

Once again we observe the clear distinction between God who is the ultimate *Author* of deliverance and His appointed *agent* who in this case was King Jeroboam. Or take this verse: "Therefore You did deliver them into the hand of their oppressors who oppressed them. But when they cried to You in the time of their distress, You did hear from heaven, and according to Your great compassion You did give them **deliverers** who delivered them from the hand of their oppressors" (Nehemiah 9:27).

Commenting on this the authors of *One God and One Lord* make this pertinent point:

> God, Christ and others are referred to as "savior," but that clearly does not make them identical. The term "savior" is used of many people in the Bible. This is hard to see in the English versions because, when it is used of men, the translators almost always translated it as "deliverer." This in and of itself shows that modern translators have a Trinitarian bias that was not in the original languages. The only reason to translate the same word as "Savior" when it applies to God or Christ, but as "deliverer" when it applies to men, is to make the term seem unique to God and Jesus

> when in fact it is not. This is a good example of how the actual meaning of Scripture can be obscured if the translators are not careful or if they are theologically biased.[96]

It has often been argued that the very name Jesus, which means "Yahweh saves," proves Jesus is Jehovah because "he will save his people from their sins" (Matt. 1:21). But the logic is not consistently applied because the OT name Joshua means "Yahweh saves." I have never yet heard someone who believes in the Deity of Christ argue that Joshua was God in the flesh. We know that in the OT Joshua was God's appointed man to deliver Israel. As Joshua and Israel went forth in obedience to His word God saved them. Just so, in the matter of our salvation, God sent forth His Son into the battle. Through Jesus God has saved us. This is why both God and Jesus are called Saviour. But the Bible never loses sight of the fact that God the Father is the ultimate *Author* of our salvation *through* His Son.

This same line of reasoning applies to the healing of the paralytic in Mark 2. This is one of the most commonly appealed to Scriptures that allegedly proves that Jesus must be God, because "only God can forgive sins" (v. 7). When Jesus pronounces the man forgiven/healed, the Pharisees say that Jesus is "blaspheming" because he is claiming to be God. But a little careful attention to detail will show that Jesus is not claiming Deity. He is rather claiming "authority." He says, "But that you may know that **the Son of Man has authority** on earth to forgive sins..." (v. 10). The parallel account in Matthew's report is that once the people saw Jesus heal the paralytic, "they were filled with awe, and glorified God, **who had given such authority to men**" (Matt. 9:8). *We note that Jesus is claiming to be "the Son of Man," that is, the human Messiah, with a God-given right to pronounce forgiveness.* Not too much later Jesus invests other men — his apostles — with the same authority to forgive sins: "**If you forgive** the sins of any, their sins have been forgiven them; if you retain the sins of any, they have been retained" (John 20:23). If only God can forgive sins, then God and Jesus *and the apostles* are all God! Besides, there is no teaching anywhere in the Bible that says only God can forgive. Even Christians are commanded to forgive each other's sins (Eph. 4:32;

---

[96] Graeser et al, *One God and One Lord,* p. 363.

Col. 3:13). The fact that the Pharisees say that only God can forgive sins does not make this an established Bible doctrine. The Pharisees often had wrong doctrine and were often corrected by our Lord Jesus. This was one such occasion.

It is traditionally argued that because Jesus is called "Immanuel, which translated means, 'God with us'" Jesus is God in the flesh. But a little further reflection will debunk this reasoning very quickly. Elijah's name literally means "God is Jehovah" but nobody says the prophet was really Jehovah. Bithiah means "daughter of Jehovah" but nobody argues that she must be the sister of Jesus (1 Chron. 4:18, KJV). Eliab's name means "my God is my Father" but nobody would argue that Eliab is the Messiah. The prophet Joel's name means "the LORD God" and Elihu means "my God Himself." Eli means "my God." Ithiel means "God is with me" but nobody argues that he must be God in the flesh. If Jesus' name "Immanuel" proves his Deity then Elijah, Joel, Eliab, Eli, Elihu and Ithiel are also God Himself. Here, rather, is a place where Jewish practice must be understood. To those of us who love the Lord Jesus, his name is significant and beloved and brings great joy because it communicates to us the wonderful truth that as God's Son he is the appointed Saviour. Through him God is with us and saves us.

Those who believe that Jesus can only be our Saviour if he is God sometimes appeal to the prophecy from Jeremiah 23: "In his days Judah will be saved, and Israel will dwell securely; and this is his name by which he will be called, 'The LORD our righteousness'" (Jer. 23:6).

Does this not say that the coming saviour will be "the LORD our righteousness," that is, God Himself? This is easily answered when we note that a few chapters later we have this prophecy in Jeremiah 33: "In those days Judah shall be saved, and Jerusalem shall dwell in safety; and this is the name by which she shall be called: the LORD is our righteousness" (v. 16).

Here the city of Jerusalem is given the very same title as the coming redeemer earlier. I have never yet heard anyone argue that the city of Jerusalem must also be God Himself because it bears the same title as Jehovah. Hebrew eyes are needed to avoid confusion. This is why it is fallacious to reason that because Jesus is called the "King of Kings and the Lord of Lords" (Rev. 19:16) he must necessarily therefore be Almighty God Himself. The fact that Artaxerxes is called "king of kings" and that God Himself calls

Nebuchadnezzar "king of kings" does not put these men in the same league as Messiah Jesus, nor mean they have the same nature as him. The designation "king of kings" is obviously a very Hebrew way of speaking that has nothing to do with equivalency of nature. The Hebrews could also speak of a "servant of servants," which simply means the lowest of the low (Gen. 9:25). In the book of Daniel God addresses Nebuchadnezzar: "You, O king, are the king of kings, to whom the God of heaven has given the kingdom, the power, the strength, and the glory" (Dan. 2:37).

In the same Hebrew fashion, when Scripture designates Jesus Christ as "the king of kings, and Lord of Lords" the message conveyed is that God has also given him the Kingdom, the power, the strength, and the glory of the Age to Come. Equality of being with the God who gives the Kingdom does not come into the equation, for either Nebuchadnezzar or Jesus. If, as already noted, to share the same nomenclature as God does not prove literal identity with God Himself, the same holds true for a sharing of the same titles. Whilst Jesus may share the title "king of kings and Lord of Lords" with God his Father, there is one title reserved uniquely for the Father God. No other individual, including the Lord Jesus, is ever called by the title "God of gods" (cp. Deut. 10:17). This title, as well as "the Lord God" (e.g. Rev. 1:8), is always reserved for the one true God, who is the Father.

In Zechariah 14 we have a remarkable prophecy that Christians eagerly anticipate. It concerns a day yet future when God Himself will go out and fight against the nations of the world that will be gathered against Israel and the holy city of Jerusalem. This is popularly known as the Battle of Armageddon. On that day, just when the enemies appear ready to strike the knock-out blow God Himself will intervene in the world's history and "His feet will stand on the Mount of Olives, which is in front of Jerusalem on the east; and the Mount of Olives will be split in its middle from east to west by a very large valley, so that half of the mountain will move toward the north and the other half toward the south" (Zech. 14:4). The feet that cause this earthquake in the Hebrew Bible are the LORD's feet. However, Christians believe this to be a reference to Jesus Christ himself returning at the Second Coming to inaugurate the Kingdom of God on earth. The argument is that since Jesus' feet are spoken of as God's feet, then Jesus must be God Himself. In the light of what we have seen so far, this cannot be. If we keep in mind the principle of Jewish agency, we will have a right understanding that "Jesus' feet are spoken of as God's feet in exactly the same way Aaron's hand is spoken of as the LORD's hand in Exodus 7:17-19."[97]

The Philippians Hymn

Most Christians read Philippians 2:5-11 as if it teaches that Jesus Christ always preexisted as God, but out of love humbled himself even to the point of becoming man so that through his Incarnation he could die on the cross to redeem lost humanity. After this astounding mission of self-denial Jesus returned to his Father in the glory of heaven, where he always was before. Few are aware that this traditional church interpretation is like a river that has jumped its banks and long ago left its original course. Over the centuries the channel of tradition has cut deep to the point where the original intent and meaning has long been restricted to the bottom of the Grand Canyon of "orthodoxy." Only one whose heart and mind is open is prepared to consider other possibilities. Perhaps these words from Karl-Josef Kuschel might help us to explore other sound options in interpretation. Few, says Kuschel, seem to be aware that:

> present-day exegetes have drawn the radically opposite conclusion that the Philippians hymn does not speak of the preexistence of Christ at all. Indeed, an increasing number of present-day New Testament scholars with good reason question the premises of exegesis hitherto and cannot see preexistence, let alone Incarnation, in the Philippians hymn.[98]

Evidently we need to take a fresh look at these verses. They read:

> Have this attitude in yourselves which was also in Christ Jesus, who, although he existed in the form of God, did not regard equality with God a thing to be grasped, but emptied himself, taking the form of a bond-servant, and being made in the likeness of men. And being found in appearance as a man, he humbled himself by becoming obedient to the point of death, even death on a cross. Therefore, also God highly

---

[97] David Burge, in private correspondence, 27-03-2005.
[98] Kuschel, *Born Before All Time?* p. 250.

> exalted him, and bestowed on him the name which is above every name, that at the name of Jesus every knee should bow, of those who are in heaven, and on earth, and under the earth, and that every tongue should confess that Jesus Christ is Lord, to the glory of God the Father (Phil. 2:5-11).

Before looking at the specifics let's just take a step back and view the setting. Let's get the big picture first. There are essentially two different traditions that will colour our understanding. Once again we are confronted with the fact that we can view this passage through Greek eyes or through Jewish eyes. Traditionally, the "Greek eyes" have it! For since the fourth century the Church has adopted the preexistence Christology of Hellenistic syncretism, which simply stated means that Jesus was a divine being who came to earth to set us free. Some scholars call this the Gnostic Redeemer myth. Historically, however, and long before this Greek view prevailed, the "Jewish eyes" — in the early apostolic church — had it. There is strong evidence to suggest that the apostolic church interpreted the Philippians hymn in the light of Old Testament tradition: Specifically Christ is presented "in good Jewish fashion as a human counterpart to Adam."[99] Or, as James Dunn in his monumental work says, this passage is best understood as an expression of "the Adam Christology which was widely current in the Christianity of the 40s and 50s."[100] Here is a thought worth further exploration.

There are other New Testament passages that compare and contrast Adam and Christ (e.g. Rom. 5:12-21; 1 Cor. 15:21-22, 45-47). It is possible that Philippians 2:6-11 is "one of the fullest expressions that we still possess" of Adam Christology from this very early church period.[101] Though the hymn is of course about Christ, it highlights and defines him against the background of Adam's failure. The passage presupposes Adam's disastrous choice, his attempt to "be like God" and his rebellion. But where Adam grasped and failed, Christ "did not regard equality with God a thing to be grasped" but surrendered to God's will, even to the point of humiliating crucifixion, and so was glorified by God. So then, let us see if the language of the passage itself supports this idea that

---

[99] *Ibid.*, p. 251.

[100] Dunn, *Christology in the Making,* p. 114.

[101] *Ibid.*, p. 114.

Genesis chapters 1-3 form the background to what is being said. Read in the light of this traditio-historical background we can observe the contrasts and comparisons between Christ and Adam. We will look at the individual words and phrases soon enough, but just for the moment let us paint the big picture first.

The first comparison is that Christ "existed in the form of God" just as Adam also was "in the image of God." Many scholars point out that the expressions "form [*morphe*] of God" and "image [*eikon*] of God" are "near synonyms."[102] Or, "*Morphe* and *eikon* are equivalent terms that are used interchangeably in the LXX."[103] So the first line of the hymn tells us that Christ shared the image and glory of God just as Adam did before his fall.

The next parallel is a contrast between Adam and Christ. "Form of a slave" is evidently an allusion to Adam's fate after the fall. When he sinned Adam became a slave to the curse of nature and to death. Christ, however, voluntarily accepted the "form of a slave." There is another contrasting pair that points in the same direction: "likeness of God" probably alludes to Adam's temptation when he wanted to be "like God" (Gen. 3:5), and "likeness of men" points in turn to Adam's state after sinning. Some feel these comparisons that Dunn makes draw too long a bow, but if we continue to follow them through, I think they will be seen to have certain merit.

If we view the Philippians hymn as a comparison in some sense of Adam and Jesus, the passage is a piece of Adam Christology of the same kind found elsewhere in the NT. It:

> would be a further example of the widespread two-stage Christology of the earliest Jewish-Christian communities...and thus would not be in the context of mythical [i.e. Hellenistic] tradition, but of Old Testament tradition. So there is no question here of a preexistent heavenly figure. Rather, Christ is the great contrasting figure to Adam. To be specific, was it not Adam who wanted to become even more like God and thus succumbed to...the primal sin? Was it not Adam who then as punishment had to live a kind of slave's existence? And is not Christ of this hymn precisely the opposite? Did he not give up his being in the image of God voluntarily? Did he

---

[102] *Ibid.*, p. 115.

[103] *Expository Times,* vol. 70, no. 6, March 1959, pp. 183-184.

> not take on the form of a slave, not as a punishment, but voluntarily and obediently, so that he was then appointed by God to his heavenly dignity?[104]

So, is this a compelling way of looking at this hymn? We should not be surprised that it draws on solid Jewish pictures. Viewed this way, the great antithesis of the hymn is the contrast between Christ and Adam: Adam the audacious man; Christ the man who humbled himself. Adam the man who was forcibly humbled by God; Christ the man who voluntarily humbled himself before God. Adam the rebellious man finally cursed by God; Christ the obedient man finally exalted by God above all. Adam who wanted to become like God was made into dust again; Christ descended to the dust, even the cross and has become Lord of the world. Thus, the Philippians hymn shows us how Christ is the new Adam who has reversed all the old Adam did. In short:

> There is no question of a preexistence of Christ with the scheme of a three-stage Christology: preexistence, humiliation, post-existence. Instead of this, the author celebrates the whole earthly-human life of Christ as a life of voluntary self-surrender to lowliness...to the existence of a slave and a shameful death.[105]

By his victory over the sin of pride which brought Adam down, Christ is now exactly as God intended man to be. He is now treated as if he were God! He now enjoys the incorruptibility that Adam was meant to enjoy. And to achieve this he did not use his privilege as God's Messiah and King (v. 5). He claimed no special advantage because he was the Son of God. If we understand the hymn with this Jewish background we see "the original hymn represents an attempt to define the uniqueness of Christ considered precisely as man."[106] It teaches not a preexistent Deity, but an obedient humanity.

> *The Christ of Phil. 2:6-11 therefore is the man who undid Adam's wrong*: confronted with the same choice, he rejected Adam's sin, but nevertheless freely followed Adam's course as fallen man to the bitter end of death; wherefore God bestowed on him the status not simply that

---

[104] Kuschel, *Born Before All Time?* pp. 251-252.
[105] *Ibid.,* p. 252.
[106] *Ibid*., p. 252.

> Adam lost, but the status which Adam was intended to come to, God's final prototype, the last Adam.[107]

This big-picture interpretation fits the context beautifully. For does not the apostle begin the hymn with this exhortation to "Have this attitude in yourselves which was also in Christ Jesus" (Phil. 2:5)? How can I relate to one who supposedly was Almighty God before his existence as a man and who during his sojourn here was the "God-Man"? That kind of a (Greek) Christ is no model for me. Martyn Lloyd-Jones who trumpets that traditional idea that this hymn presents the "God-Man" to us lifts Jesus right away from us. He writes:

> It was not merely the case that it was possible for Him not to sin, but rather, it was not possible for Him to sin. And that is the essential difference between Christ and Adam; ...The first Adam was perfect. He had not sinned, but sin was possible. It was possible for Adam not to sin, but you could not say of him that it was not possible for him to sin, because he did sin. But of the Son of God we say that not only was it possible for Him not to sin...it was also not possible for Him to sin…because He is the God-Man. Not only human but also divine. But still, because human, subject to temptation, and the devil did tempt Him. And so we see the importance of asserting at one and the same time the doctrine of His true humanity and yet also the doctrine of His complete sinlessness...The devil tempted Him with all his might, in a way that nobody else has ever been tempted. It was a real temptation, but He at the same time was entirely free from sin, and it was not possible that He could or should fall. God sent Him to be the Saviour, and because of that there could not be, and there was no failure.[108]

Once again, it is hard not to imagine that Lloyd-Jones is bogged down to his theory of the Trinity and the Incarnation. Read his quote again. He says "it was not possible" for Jesus to sin "because He is the God-Man." It was "not possible that Jesus could or should fall." Yet confusingly Jones says Jesus' temptation was "a real temptation." If it "was not possible for him to sin" because he was

---

[107] Dunn, *Christology in the Making,* p. 119.
[108] Lloyd-Jones, *God the Father, God the Son,* pp. 275-276.

the "God-Man" then Christ was not like Adam at all. The Biblical parallel is smashed. And how can it be "real temptation" if there is no possibility of sin? The Bible, on the other hand, indicates that the possibility for failure was very real indeed. At the climax of his life in Gethsemane, for instance, Jesus is sweating great drops of blood, as he is struggling for the victory. But Douglas Lockhart in *Jesus the Heretic* points out that if we start from a position of later Incarnational "orthodoxy" Jesus' prayer in the garden is full of doctrinal errors, mistakes in self-interpretation which would have earned him the stake a few hundred years later! He says this biblical Jesus is distinctly unorthodox by our traditional standards. For here in the garden of Gethsemane it is obvious Jesus does not consider himself God. The Messiah he certainly is, the one to offer the supreme sacrifice, but for all that he is tempted flesh and blood. "All things are possible to You," he prays, implying that all things are not possible to him. And then, "not what I desire, but what You desire," indicating submission to God, and not the completion of a purpose of his own making. Here is the Son of God submitting to God, not God submitting to God. Jesus Christ then faced the same archetypal choice that confronted Adam.[109]

His words on the cross, "My God, my God, why have You forsaken me?" further divorce him from the philosophic creation that he was wholly God, for how could Jesus as God forsake himself? (Martin Luther is said to have struggled with this "cry of dereliction" for days. Luther locked himself up in his study searching for the meaning. At last he jumped up and exclaimed, "God forsaken by God!") Sound confusing?

I repeat what I said earlier in this chapter: *If Jesus was to satisfy the just requirements of redeeming us, whatever Adam was, Jesus Christ had to be also. This is why Jesus Christ had to be like Adam, a created human being, with just one nature, a fully human one. He must have no unjust advantage of having "two natures." For this Adam clearly did not have.*

The Form of God

With this big picture in mind we can now turn to some of the problematic words and phrases in this passage. The two key phrases which have been very important to those who teach that Jesus Christ

---

[109] Lockhart, *Jesus the Heretic.*

was God before his Incarnation are "he existed in the form of God" and "emptied himself" (in order to be "made in the likeness of men"). Let's take a closer look.

Martyn Lloyd-Jones is representative of the mainstream belief that these verses teach that Jesus always existed as God before he took on human flesh. He says:

> Well, take this word *form* — "Who being in the form of God" — what is this? Form is the sum total of the qualities that make a thing what it is. Take, for instance, a piece of metal; that piece of metal can be either a sword or a ploughshare, though it is the same metal. And when I talk about "the form" of a sword I mean the thing that makes that piece of metal a sword rather than a ploughshare. So if I take a sword and smelt it down and turn it into a ploughshare, I have changed its form. That is a most important point.[110]

Evidently the great preacher expects us to believe that because Jesus existed "in the form of God" he was always God because "form is the sum total of the qualities that make a thing what it is." However, we may ask: If Paul wanted to tell us that Jesus was God, why did he not just plainly write that Christ "*was God*" instead of "he existed in the form of God"? The verse does *not* say of Jesus Christ, "who, being God," for the simple reason that Paul is telling the Philippians that Jesus represented God the Father in every possible way.

As can be seen by Lloyd-Jones' statement the word "form" (*morphe*) is critical to the position of Trinitarians who believe Jesus always was God before becoming man. It is true that the lexicons offer contrasting meanings for this word. *Vine's Lexicon* tells us that *morphe* refers to an "inner, essential nature." In his *Expository Dictionary of New Testament Words* Vine quotes with approval Gifford:

> *Morphe* is properly the nature or essence, not in the abstract, but as actually subsisting in the individual, and retained as long as the individual itself exists...Thus in the passage before us *morphe theou* ["form of God"] is the Divine nature actually and inseparably subsisting in the Person of Christ...For the interpretation of "the form of God" it is

---

[110] Lloyd-Jones, *God the Father, God the Son,* p. 285.

> sufficient to say that (1) it includes the whole nature and essence of Deity...(2) that it does not include in itself anything "accidental" or separable, such as particular modes of manifestation, or conditions of glory and majesty, which may at one time be attached to the "form."[111]

On the other hand many lexicons disagree with this idea that "form" means the inner, essential nature. They say that "form" means "outward appearance, shape." Representative of this definition are the *Theological Dictionary of the New Testament* edited by Gerhard Kittel, the lexicon by Walter Bauer, translated and revised by Arndt and Gingrich, and Robert Thayer's lexicon. The latter notes that whilst some scholars try to make *morphe* refer to that which is intrinsic and essential, in contrast to that which is outward and accidental, "the distinction is rejected by many." So it is evident that Greek scholars are in some disagreement as to whether "form" means "inner, essential nature or essence" or whether it simply means the "outward, external appearance or shape." How may we resolve this difference? It is not as difficult a problem as it may seem. All we need do is turn to the writers of the New Testament period and see how they invariably use the word. For the following five examples I acknowledge my indebtedness to the authors of *One God and One Lord.*[112]

From **secular writings** we learn that the Greeks used *morphe* to describe when the gods changed their appearance. Kittel points out that in pagan mythology the gods change their forms, and notes Aphrodite, Demeter and Dionysus as three who did. This is clearly a change of appearance, not nature. Josephus, a contemporary of the apostles, used "form" to describe the shape of statues.

Second, in other places where *morphe* is used in **the Bible** it is clear it means outward appearance. In Mark 16:12 Jesus appears to the two disciples who are on the road to Emmaus "in a different form." Jesus did not have a different "inner, essential nature" but simply a different outward appearance.

Third, the Greek translation of the Old Testament, the **Septuagint** (LXX) was written around 250 BC for Greek-speaking Jews. The Septuagint uses *morphe* several times and without

---

[111] W.E. Vine, *Expository Dictionary of New Testament Words,* Virginia: Macdonald Pub. Co., pp. 463-464.

[112] Graeser et al, *One God and One Lord,* p. 504ff.

exception refers to the outward appearance. In Job 4:15-16 Job says, "A spirit glided past my face, and the hair on my body stood on end. It stopped, but I could not tell what it was. A form [*morphe*] stood before my eyes." "Form" here clearly refers to the outward appearance of this spirit. In Isaiah 44 the word *morphe* refers to the outward appearance of man-made idols: "The carpenter measures with a line and makes an outline with a marker; he roughs it out with chisels and marks it with compasses. He shapes it in the form [*morphe*] of man" (v. 13). It would be absurd to suggest that "form" here refers to the inner, essential nature of the idol, for the idol is physically shaped to look like the appearance of a man. In Daniel 3 the lads Shadrach, Meshach and Abednego refused to bow down to Nebuchadnezzar's image and we are told "the form [*morphe*] of his countenance" changed (v. 19). The NASB Bible says, "his facial expression" changed. Nothing in his nature changed, but all who saw him knew his outward appearance had.

Fourth, the inter-testamental writings of the Jews called the **Apocrypha** were written between the last OT book of Malachi and the NT book of Matthew. Roman Catholics have these books in their Bibles today, but they do not appear in Protestant Bibles. These books use *morphe* in exactly the same way that the Septuagint does — that is, to mean "outward appearance." For instance, in "The Wisdom of Solomon" we have: "Their enemies heard their voices, but did not see their forms" (18:1). The word *morphe* in the Apocrypha shows that it always refers to the outer form, not the inner essence.

Fifth, *morphe* is the root word of some **other New Testament words** and is also used in compound words. These also add weight to the idea that *morphe* refers to outward shape or manifestation. In 2 Timothy 3:5 the Bible speaks of men who have a "form [*morphosis*] of godliness." Their insides, their inner natures were evil, but they had an outward appearance of being godly. On the Mount of Transfiguration Christ was "transformed" (*metamorphoomai*) before the apostles (Matt. 17:2; Mark 9:2). They did not see Jesus get a new inner nature, but they did see his outward appearance change profoundly. 2 Corinthians 3 tells us that Christians will be "changed" (*metamorphoomai*) into the image of Christ (v. 18). We will look like Christ and reflect his glory.

Kenneth Wuest notes that in Koine *Greek* morphe had come to refer to "a station in life, a position one holds, one's rank. And that is an approximation of *morphe* in this context of Philippians 2."[113]

What are our conclusions so far? All these ancient uses of the word "form" speak of outward appearance or likeness and not inner, essential essence. To argue that because Jesus "existed in the form of God" he had the inner nature of God is to clutch at a straw to try to prove a pre-conceived point. All Philippians 2 is teaching is that Jesus the Messiah was the true representative of God. When men looked at him they saw what God looks like. As Jesus said, "he who has seen me has seen the Father" (John 14:9). Taken this way, we may interpret "the form of God" and "the form of a slave" to mean role or status. Note the equivalence:

Jesus was in the form of God in the sense that he stood in the place of God in much the same way as we saw earlier (in chapter two) that Moses stood before Pharaoh as God (Ex. 4:16; 7:1). Moses stood before Pharaoh "in the form of God," that is, in the role of God, but this status did not mean he was *actually divine in essence*. Just so, Jesus walked before men "in the form of God" as his Father's fully authorized agent. Of course Jesus' position and status as the Messiah is far superior to that which Moses enjoyed. But even so, Jesus did not claim this likeness with God something to be exploited for his own advantage. Whether or not Philippians 2 is drawing an OT parallel with Adam may be a moot point for some. But one thing is absolutely certain. The passage is stressing the enormous status Jesus enjoyed as the man Messiah (as v. 5 introduces him). The lesson is that despite his role as God (agency!) Jesus behaved as a servant. In response to walking in "the form of a servant" God has now elevated him to His right hand of glory as Lord Messiah.[114]

Before we pass onto the second main problematic expression in this hymn, a brief word is in order about the word "existed" in our phrase, "who *existed* in the form of God," or as the King James Bible translates it, "who, *being in the form of God*." Trinitarians have often said that the word here for "existed" or "being" proves that Jesus Christ preexisted as God before he came into this world. It is a simple matter of fact that the verb "was" here frequently

[113] *The Practical Use of the Greek New Testament*, Moody, 1982, p. 84.
[114] See Appendix 3: "Divine Agency."

occurs in the New Testament and by no means carries the sense of "existing in eternity." It was the philosopher Justin Martyr who for the first time applied the distinctive word "to preexist" to Jesus (Greek *prohyparchein*). But the New Testament never uses this word. It is certainly not the word used here in Philippians 2:6. The following more technical explanation from Kuschel is noteworthy:

> The phrase "being like God" (Greek *isa theou*), too, may not simply be translated with terms like "equality to God," "being like God," as often happens. That would require the form *isos theos.* What we have in the text is the adverb *isa,* and that merely means "as God," "like God." So there is no statement about Christ *being* equal to God, and this in turn tells against an interpretation in terms of preexistence. So, on both traditio-historical and linguistic grounds...there is no justification for interpreting the phrase of the hymn in terms of being of Christ.[115]

As Kuschel observes elsewhere in his marvellous book:

> I have found that the word preexistence is not a biblical expression but a problematical term used in post-biblical reflection...It seeks to systematize what for the New Testament is not a theme of systematic thought. In other words, a Christology today which heedlessly uses the dogmatic theme of "preexistence" and introduces it into the New Testament foists on the New Testament an idea which it does not contain in this form.[116]

In fact, we may even speak more strongly here of this word for "existing" (*hyparchon*) or "*being* in the form of God." Kuschel says that far too little attention is paid to the fact that the verb *hyparchon* contains within it the word *arche,* origin. So, "if we translate this literally as well, we could say, 'He who has his *origin* in God's "world."' So the disputed 'in form' is not a statement about essence but a statement about origin."[117]

Emptied Himself

Now to the second phrase in Philippians 2 that causes difficulty. It is the one that says Jesus Christ "did not regard equality with God

---

[115] Kuschel, *Born Before All Time?* p. 251.
[116] *Ibid.*, p. 394.
[117] *Ibid.*, p. 259.

a thing to be grasped, but emptied himself" (v. 6-7). It is unfortunate that the old King James Version of the Bible translated this verse completely wrong. It reads that Jesus "thought it not robbery to be equal with God" and gives the impression that as the preexistent God Jesus did not think there was anything wrong in being considered equal with God.

It ought to be clear by now that this is the exact opposite of what is meant. The whole context of the passage is about being humble, putting God's will and glory first, and serving others' interests above one's own interests. Although he was in "the form of God" Jesus did not reckon his God-given status as something to be exploited. This meaning contrasts well with the conduct of Adam who unfortunately did consider equality with God a thing to be grasped at. Adam *wanted* to be like God as Genesis 3:5 teaches. Adam tried to grasp at equality with God. But Jesus would not usurp God's authority for selfish advantage. He said, "I came to serve" (Matt. 20:28), not to snatch! At his arrest in the garden he said, "Do you not think that I cannot appeal to my Father, and He will at once put at my disposal more than twelve legions of angels?" (Matt. 26:53). As the Messiah, God's appointed King, he had every right to call for divine protection. He "emptied himself" of all such Messianic privileges.

Therefore, it can be categorically stated that Philippians 2:5-11 has nothing to do with Jesus Christ being God in a preexistent state. The import is really very simple and very practical: how are Christians to conduct themselves in this world? Not by imitating the man Adam who forfeited everything by a grab for power and glory, but by imitating Jesus the Messiah (v. 5) who through humility and obedience to God gained it all and more. After all, if Jesus was already God, then verses 9 to 11 are nonsensical. There is no "**Therefore** also God highly exalted him, and bestowed on him the name which is above every name, that at the name of Jesus every knee should bow, of those who are in heaven, and on earth, and under the earth," for if he was already God he had this before his birth! No. It is clear that God has given him a new position, a new name (authority), a new rank that he did not previously possess. The Greek is very clear here: *dio kai* means (as in Luke 1:35) "for this reason precisely." Why has God exalted Jesus to His right hand? "Therefore, God has highly exalted him and given him the name above every other name because he is back where he was before as

God"? Not at all! He is given this status as a reward for the *precise reason that he humbled himself and died.* His exalted status is a *reward.* If we follow the last Adam's pattern we too will be exalted by God when Christ returns. It is evident, then, that "this hymn does *not* contain what numerous interpreters seek and find in it: an independent statement about preexistence or even a Christology of preexistence...No preexistence of Christ before the world with an independent significance can be recognized even in Phil. 2."[118]

The Colossians Hymn

Insofar as it is used by the "traditionalists" to justify belief in a personally preexistent Christ, the passage in Colossians 1:15-19 ranks right up there with John 1 and Philippians 2. It is easy to see how this conclusion is reached, when the passage is read in the gridlock of "orthodoxy." Paul wrote:

> And he is the image of the invisible God, the first-born of all creation. For by him all things were created, both in the heavens and on earth, visible and invisible, whether thrones or dominions or rulers or authorities — all things have been created through him and for him. And he is before all things, and in him all things hold together. He is also head of the body, the church; and he is the beginning, the first-born from the dead; so that he himself might come to have first place in everything. For it was the Father's good pleasure for all the fullness to dwell in him (Col. 1:15-19).

We must carefully examine both the overall context and the particular phrases before rushing to the conclusion that the apostle is teaching that Jesus the Son of God created the heavens and the earth, and that he is therefore co-equal with God the Father, the second member of the Trinity. Everything we have looked at so far would indicate that Paul has not suddenly done a back-flip from his clearly stated belief that there is "one God, the Father...and one Lord, Jesus the Messiah" (1 Cor. 8:6; Eph. 4:5-6, etc.).

The overall context must be clearly borne in mind. The apostle is "giving thanks to the Father" because He "has qualified us to share in the inheritance of the saints in light," which is to say that God the Father has "delivered us from the domain of darkness, and transferred us to the kingdom of His beloved Son" (v. 12-13). Paul

---

[118] *Ibid.*, p. 262.

is thus speaking of the *new creation* that God has effected through His Son Jesus. He is speaking of things that relate to "redemption, the forgiveness of sins" (v. 14) and "the church" (v. 18) and how through the Son the Father God has "reconciled all things to Himself, having made peace through the blood of his cross" (v. 20).

As Kuschel says, "The direct context of the Colossians hymn is itself of an eschatological kind and represents the 'shift of the ages.'"[119] In other words, "the New Testament does not merely picture the resurrection of Jesus as the resuscitation of a corpse, but as *the emergence within time and space of a new order of life*."[120] When the Father raised Jesus to life again it was not only an isolated historical event. It was more importantly the injection into history of the beginning of "the eschatological resurrection."[121] Eternal life — the life of the Age to Come — is guaranteed in Christ who is "the first fruits" of all who will follow (1 Cor. 15:23). Jesus is the first of a whole crop of new-lifers to come! A new order of things now exists. A new age in prospect has already begun. If "anyone is in Christ, he is a new creation; the old things [have] passed away; behold, new things have come" (2 Cor. 5:17). To be baptized into Christ is to already in prospect be "in the likeness of his resurrection" (Rom. 6:5). We are already "seated with Christ in the heavenlies" (Eph. 2:6). Because Christ has been raised to the glory of the Father, we are already in promise "glorified" (Rom. 8:30). We have been transferred into "the kingdom of His beloved Son" (Col. 1:13).

It is this tectonic shift in the ages that is the context of this hymn of praise. We are looking at a whole new order of things. The waves of this continental shift from the resurrection of Christ are rolling towards the distant shore-line of the coming Kingdom of God with tsunami-like power. Old authorities and structures have been rattled, for Christ is now the head of God's new creation. A new dynasty in God's universe has been inaugurated. This is the cosmological context of the individual phrases we will now examine.

---

[119] *Ibid.*, p. 331.
[120] G.E. Ladd, *A Theology of the New Testament,* Grand Rapids, MI: Eerdmans, 1974, p. 323, emphasis original.
[121] *Ibid.*, p. 324.

Christ the Image of God

Speaking of "His beloved Son" who has brought us "redemption, the forgiveness of sins" (Col. 1:13-14), the apostle tells us that "he is the image of the invisible God, the first-born of all creation" (v. 15). An image, as we know, is a visual representation or copy of an original. This word "image" intimates that there is a difference in identity between the copy and the original. When we look in the mirror we understand that we do not see our "real" selves, only an image of ourselves. I know that I am not the person behind the glass, but really the person in front of the glass. This word "image" is a very strong pointer to the fact that Christ the Son is *not* God. For the image cannot be the original, who in this case is God the Father. The first phrase, "he [the Son] is the image of the invisible God" reminds us of Jesus' own word that "he who has seen me has seen the Father" (John 14:9). Jesus is the face and voice of God, so to speak (1 Cor. 4:6). As Kuschel rightly points out, "the expression 'image' does not relate to 'the essence of a thing' but to 'Christ's revelatory function'...Talk of the 'image' is a statement about revelation."[122]

As the image of God, Christ reveals the Father to us. But what exactly is revealed? Kuschel is quite clear here. In the light of the eschatological resurrection of the Son, God and his image Christ must be thought of as belonging inseparably together. From now on:

> one can now (after the eschatological shift) no longer speak of God without having to speak of Jesus Christ and *vice versa.* Anyone who speaks of Christ at the same time speaks of God Himself. In relation to creation, this means that one cannot really know the new creation as a work of the Creator except in Christ. So there are two sides: God makes himself known in the image of Christ, and the creation cannot be known as the work of *this* creator without Christ.[123]

Christ the First-Born of All Creation

The next phrase — the Son is "the first-born of all creation" — has been hotly debated in theological circles. If "first" in the word "first-born" means only precedence in time, and if "creation" means

---

[122] Kuschel, *Born Before All Time?* p. 333.
[123] *Ibid.*, p. 333.

the original creation of Genesis 1, then the case for Christ's personal preexistence is strong. Christ must have abandoned a previous heavenly existence and become a human being. But does the phrase "first-born of all creation" fit this view? This interpretation, as we will now see, does not suit the context when we again keep the Old Testament background in mind.

The word "first-born" comes to the NT with a rich Hebrew heritage. The Hebrews had a custom of conferring special birth-right privileges on their oldest sons. The eldest son of a father would receive the "double portion" of the family's inheritance. The well-known story of Jacob tricking his father Isaac into conferring on him — rather than on the first-born Esau — the family blessings is typical of this culture (Gen. 27:32).

But there is a further nuance of meaning to this word "first-born." The Greek word for "first" can mean either first in time or first in status, regardless of birth position. The "first-born" may designate one who is given the honour of chief rank, that is, first place. This usage can also be found in the Hebrew Bible, as when Jacob summons his sons to bequeath his patriarchal blessings on them, he designates Reuben as "my first-born...**preeminent in dignity and preeminent in power**" (Gen. 49:3). Although Reuben is first-born in time, the prominent idea is his superior status and dignity. This is clearly the meaning in Jeremiah 31:9 where God calls Ephraim his "first-born" even though Ephraim's brother, Manasseh, was the elder of the two. Or when God calls Israel His first-born son in Exodus 4:22 and commands Pharaoh to "Let my son go that he may worship me" (v. 23) the concept has to do with Israel's precedence in importance over Egypt as far as God's plans were concerned. The classic instance of this idea of pre-eminence of rank is in the Messianic Psalm 89 where God, in glowing words, speaks of the coming promised Davidic king, the Lord Messiah:

> He will cry to Me, "You are my Father, my God, and the rock of my salvation." I also shall make him My first-born, the highest of the kings of the earth. My lovingkindness I will keep for him forever, and My covenant shall be confirmed to him. So I will establish his descendants forever, and his throne as the days of heaven (Ps. 89:26-29).

In the spirit of prophecy, God announces that this king's superior position is a matter of appointment, not time of birth. Furthermore, God makes His appointed King "the highest [in status and rank] of the kings of the earth." Thus, when the apostle applies the term "first-born" to the Son of God in Colossians 1, he is using a well-known OT Messianic description. In fact, the expression is repeated a few verses later, where Paul writes, "He is also head of the body, the church; and he is the beginning, the first-born from the dead" (v. 18). The different qualifier here is noteworthy. Whereas in verse 15 the Son is the "first-born of **all creation**," here the Son is the "first-born **from the dead.**" If we take into account the Hebrew literary style of parallelism, where the same idea is repeated but in slightly modified form, it is quite reasonable to suggest that the qualifiers "of all creation" and "from the dead" mean the same thing.

The thought, then, is clearly that Jesus the Son of God is the first Man of God's new creation, because he is the first man ever to be raised to immortality. Christ's resurrection is the beginning of the eschatological resurrection. His resurrection is the promise and the guarantee that God's new order of reality has begun. The Church is that new community in prospect. This confirms that the subject matter under discussion is not the Genesis creation of the heavens and the earth, but rather the creation of the Church, the body of believers who constitute God's new humanity, the New Man(kind). For this reason "he is the beginning" (*arche* which has an ambivalence, and can mean either the ruler or chief, or origin or beginning, v. 18). Either way, Jesus as the first-raised from the dead is the origin of God's new creation, and he is in consequence of this priority in resurrection also the highest in rank "so that he himself might come to have first place in everything" (v. 18). However, whether we take the term "first-born" to mean first in relation to time or first in relation to rank, this much is at least clear, that "taken in its natural sense, the expression first-born excludes the notion of an uncreated, eternal being. To be born requires a beginning."[124] In order to verify our findings so far, we must look at the second part of this phrase that the Son is "the first-born **of all creation**."

Christ the Head of the New Creation

The various popular English translations are at odds as to whether the Son is "the first-born **over** all creation" (as in the NIV

---

[124] Buzzard and Hunting, *The Doctrine of the Trinity,* p. 104.

and NKJV), thus first in rank, or whether he is "the first-born **of** all creation" (which reflects a literal translation of the genitive case, as in the KJV, RV and NASB), meaning first in time, which would refer to Christ being the first-created being of creation.

We evidently need the wider context to determine which nuance fits best. It is clear that Paul continues his line of thought in the next verse, as he uses the conjunction "for": "For in him all things were created, both in the heavens and on earth, visible and invisible, whether thrones or dominions or rulers or authorities — all things have been created through him and for him" (v. 16).

Jesus never claimed credit for the original Genesis creation of the heavens and the earth. He was in no doubt that the universe was God's handiwork (Matt. 19:4; Mark 13:19). Observe here in Colossians 1 that the "all things" created are *not* "the heavens and the earth" as per Genesis 1:1, but rather "all things **in** the heavens and **[up]on** the earth." These things are defined as "thrones or dominions or rulers or authorities." Evidently, Jesus has been given authority to restructure the arrangements of angels as well as being the agent for the creation of the body of Christ on earth, the Church. This is the thought as we soon shall see in Hebrews 1 where the angels are told to worship the Son. It is also the thought that Peter mentions in 1 Peter 3:21-22 where, after "the resurrection of Jesus Christ, who is at the right hand of God, having gone into heaven, after angels and authorities and powers had been subjected to him," it is the new Messianic order that God has brought in through Christ the Son that is under discussion. Just before his ascension into heaven at the Father's right hand of power, Jesus declared that "all authority in heaven and on earth has been given to me" (Matt. 28:18). His resurrection has brought Jesus a new status, "far above all rule and authority and power and dominion, and every name that is named, not only in this age, but also in the one to come" (Eph. 1:21).

All of this is to reiterate that this hymn of praise concerns the *new order* of things that now exists since the resurrection of the Son. An eschatological shift of the ages has begun with Christ's exaltation to the Father's right hand. God has "put all things in subjection under his [the resurrected Christ's] feet" (Eph. 1:22). Paul repeats this thought in the next chapter of Colossians: "and he is the head over [or of] all rule and authority" (Col. 2:10). In the words we looked at in Philippians 2, God has rewarded Jesus' obedient death on the cross by highly exalting him, and bestowing on him "the name which is above every name, that at the name of Jesus every knee should bow, of those who are in heaven, and on earth, and under the earth, and every tongue should confess that Jesus Christ is Lord, to the glory of God the Father" (Phil. 2:8-10).

It is highly significant that in verse 18 Jesus attains to a supreme position, meaning that he did not have it already. Thus he cannot have preexisted as God. If he did his final status would be more of a demotion than the promotion described by Paul.

The phrase "first-born of all creation" is "to be understood in terms of a thoroughgoing eschatology...Because God acted like this in the end in Christ, He was already able to create the whole creation in him, through him and for him."[125] Kuschel is quite clear that "first-born of all creation" is a statement about the rank of Christ before (over) all that is created.[126] Christ is the head of a new dynasty, a new Kingdom.

These ascriptions of supreme authority to Christ, under God, suggest that when Christ came to be seated at the right hand of God, he — in turn — set up, or created, a new system of rulership among the angelic beings as well as preparing a place of honour and service within his Father's household for all his faithful people, both in this age and in the age to come (John 14:2-3). All of this is then part of "the new creation." It is this *new* creation that I understand to be the subject of Colossians 1:15-17. If this view is correct, the personal preexistence of Christ is not at all the subject of our text, contrary to popular interpretation.[127]

It is worth highlighting at this juncture an important point of (mis)translation that has led to the erroneous idea that Jesus created the heavens and the earth in Genesis 1. The King James Version says in verse 16 that "**by** him all things were created." This is not what Paul wrote. The correct translation is the one we have given above, namely that it is "**in** him [*en auto*] all things were created." The difference in intention is huge. The old KJV version would have us believe that Christ was the agent of the Genesis creation of the heavens and the earth, that he was the instrument of creation,

---

[125] Kuschel, *Born Before All Time?* p. 335.
[126] *Ibid.*, p. 335.
[127] William Wachtel, "Colossians 1:15-20 — Preexistence or Preeminence?" a paper presented at the Atlanta Bible College Theological Conference, April 2004, p. 4.

that he was personally present before the world began. Reputable Greek scholars such as J.H. Moulton in *Grammar of New Testament Greek* say that Colossians 1:16 should be rendered "for **because of** him [Jesus]."[128] The *Expositor's Greek Commentary* says on this verse: "*en auto*: This does not mean 'by him.'"[129] By wisdom, which later "became" Christ Jesus, all things were created. This is simply to say that Jesus is the reason for creation. The end of verse 16 says as much again: "all things have been created through him and for him," that is, with a view to him. Christ the Son of God, now exalted, is the agent or mediator of the new creation that God is bringing into being.

This is why "he is **before all things**, and in him all things hold together" (v. 17). But what does "before" mean here: "He is **before** all things"? The Greek word *pro* can mean before in the sense of place, meaning "in front of," or it can mean before in the sense of time, meaning "prior to," or it can mean before in the sense of "above all," meaning most important of all. The NASB translation has a marginal note here that would encourage us to believe Christ's preexistence is alluded to; its margin reads, "Or, *has existed prior to*" all things. But is this correct? This very same phrase "before all things" (Greek *pro panton*) occurs in other places such as in 1 Peter 4:8 where Peter writes, "Above all [*pro panton*], keep fervent in your love for one another." Here "above all things" has nothing to do with time or place, but everything to do with how Christian love is preeminent above all other virtues. So, before we settle on which meaning best fits "before" here in Colossians 1:17, we should note the present tense of the verb "is." This must not be rushed over. It does *not* say Christ "*was* before all things"! Personal preexistence is not under discussion here. This is confirmed in the next verse: "He is also head of the body, the church; and he is the beginning, the first-born from the dead; so that he himself might come to have **first place** in everything" (v. 18).

The theme is preeminence of rank in the new creation. Christ *is* before all things in the defined sense of having *first place* in everything. Just so the point is not missed on the reader, Paul doubly emphasizes this new position of power over all by adding

---

[128] J.H. Moulton, ed., *Grammar of New Testament Greek,* T & T Clark, 1963.

[129] Nicoll Robertson, *The Expositor's Greek Commentary,* Grand Rapids: Eerdmans, 1967.

the personal pronoun to the verb: "so that **he himself** might come to have first place in everything."

I love the Old Testament story of how Joseph was taken after years of suffering and humiliation and exalted by Pharaoh to the first place in Egypt. The story suggests a beautiful type/parallel with Christ being exalted by his God and Father to being His righthand man in His Kingdom. Pharaoh announces to Joseph:

> "You shall be over my house, and according to your command all my people shall do homage; only in the throne I will be greater then you." And Pharaoh said to Joseph, "See, I have set you over all the land of Egypt." Then Pharaoh took off his signet ring from his hand, and put it on Joseph's hand, and clothed him in garments of fine linen, and put the gold necklace around his neck. And he had him ride in his second chariot; and they proclaimed before him, "Bow the knee!" And he set him over all the land of Egypt. Moreover, Pharaoh said to Joseph, "Though I am Pharaoh, yet without your permission no one shall raise his hand or foot in all the land of Egypt" (Ex. 41:40-44).

What a beautiful picture of the kind of prominence and place of honour God has exalted the Lord Jesus to. This was not a position Christ had by always being God from eternity. Jesus is "the first-born from the dead; **so that** he himself might **come** to have first place in everything." His is a conferred authority, given to him by the Father as Scripture everywhere attests. "Christ only gained the status as 'pre-eminent in all things' as a consequence of his resurrection...When it talks about Christ's primacy in relation to 'all things' we are to think first and foremost of the risen and exalted Christ [not a previously existing Christ before creation in time]."[130]

As the supreme Lord of God's new creation order, as the "*chief*-born" from the dead, there is a day coming when his voice will awaken the dead and call all of God's faithful ones to enter the life of the New Age to come. Only in the throne is God his Father greater than the Son. No wonder the author can say "it was the Father's good pleasure for all the fullness to dwell in him" (v. 19). There is no limit to the measure of the working of God's Spirit and plan being executed through him. God's love and wisdom is so totally identified with Jesus, and particularly in the cross through

---

[130] Dunn, *Christology in the Making,* p. 191.

which God has reconciled all things to Himself (v. 20), that in Christ we actually see the very power and wisdom and love by which God created and by which He sustains the world. Christ represents what God is. He "embodies without remainder the outreaching love of God, reflects as clearly as is possible the character of the one God."[131] Exalted to the right hand of God's very throne Christ now exercises the practical functions of the Deity. As Dunn says, this Colossians hymn tells us that "*Christ now reveals the character of the power behind the world...*Christ defines what is the wisdom, the creative power of God — he is the fullest and clearest expression of God's wisdom (we could almost say its archetype)."[132] And perhaps even clearer:

> Once again then we have found that what at first reads as a straightforward assertion of Christ's preexistent activity in creation becomes on closer analysis an assertion which is rather more profound — not of Christ as such present with God in the beginning, nor of Christ as identified with a preexistent hypostasis or divine being (Wisdom) beside God, but *of Christ as embodying and expressing (and defining) that power of God which is the manifestation of God in and to his creation.*[133]

In conclusion, the Colossians hymn is not making a statement about the act of creation in the *past,* but is rather about creation as believers are to see it *now* in the light of Christ's new status as resurrected Lord. "The hymn is not concerned to make either a statement about preexistence or a statement about the earthly life of the Son, but a statement about the significance of the Son for the community in the present."[134]

Hebrews Chapter One

One other NT passage is readily appealed to in order to prove that Jesus Christ is Almighty God. It is Hebrews 1. In this chapter, when isolated from its context, individual phrases seem to justify this Trinitarian interpretation. These phrases are: "through whom also He made the world" (v. 2); "And let all the angels of God worship him" (v. 6); "But of the Son He says, 'Your throne, O God,

---

[131] *Ibid.*, p. 195.
[132] *Ibid.*, p. 191.
[133] *Ibid.*, p. 194.
[134] Kuschel, *Born Before All Time?* p. 356.

is forever and ever'"(v. 8); "You, Lord, in the beginning laid the foundations of the earth, and the heavens are the works of your hands; they will perish, but you remain...You are the same, and your years will not come to an end" (v. 10, 12). Read in isolation — out of context — these verses seem to say that Jesus is (Jehovah) God. Is this interpretation justified? Many expositors think not. Kuschel is adamant that we do not have to "interpret the Christology of Hebrews in such extremely ontological terms (in the light of Nicea!)."[135] (Ontology is the study of metaphysics dealing with the nature of being.) Kuschel comments that "the majority of exegetes" do not now assume "an extremely developed Hellenistic-syncretistic Christ-myth as a background to Hebrews, nor are dilemmas foisted on the text. *Material from the Hellenistic Jewish tradition is thought enough to explain the Christology of Hebrews.*"[136] In other words, we are cautioned not to read back into the text what later traditions have taught us.

Although debate has centred around who the actual author to the Hebrews is, we note that his whole literary skill and theological argumentation is indebted to the world of Old Testament ideas. The reason why the book of Hebrews was first written was to encourage believers who were undergoing fierce persecution to remain loyal to Christ. These believers were Jewish converts to Christ and they must be encouraged to see the superiority of Christ over the old Jewish system of things. Christ is superior to the angels (who had mediated the old covenant); he is superior to Abraham, Moses and Joshua. Christ is superior to the Levitical priesthood and Temple rituals and sacrifices. This superiority rests in the fact that Jesus is the resurrected Son of God, not that he is Almighty God. If Jesus is the Almighty in human form, then the author could have saved himself a lot of ink and papyrus. All he needed to do was write that Jesus is superior to all because He is God. End of argument. But the opening verses of Hebrews allow no such interpretation. They run like this: "God, after He spoke long ago to the fathers in the prophets in many portions and in many ways, in these last days has spoken to us in His Son, whom He appointed heir of all things, through whom also He made the world" (v. 1-3).

---

[135] *Ibid.*, p. 354.

[136] *Ibid.*, p. 355, emphasis added.

Dunn believes Hebrews 1:1-3 is parallel to Colossians 1:15-17, which as we have just seen is written with eschatology in mind, not protology. This contention is justified because it is explicitly stated that the end-time has already dawned; it is "these last days" that are in view. We are again looking at the eschatological shift of the ages with the appearance of Christ. Under the old covenant God spoke in various portions and in various ways to the fathers in the prophets. In contrast, He now speaks through a Son. One of the ways God spoke in those days was also through the mediation of angels (see Heb. 2:2). This means, amongst other things, that God's message to Israel was not through a preexistent Son who was an angel, as Jehovah's Witnesses believe (they teach that Jesus was Michael the archangel). Nor can it mean — as many Trinitarians think — that Jesus was the "the angel of the LORD" who appeared on numerous OT occasions. Nor indeed can it mean, according to later Nicene "orthodoxy," that God spoke to the fathers in Old Testament days through a preexistent Son. For the opening verses of Hebrews testify that before the birth of Jesus there was no Son of God as God's messenger to men. It is axiomatic that in the Old Testament God did not speak through the Son. Bluntly then: "What emerges from the first two verses of the book of Hebrews is that Jesus was not God's agent to Israel in Old Testament times."[137]

The Son — through whom God has in these end-times spoken — has been "**appointed** heir of all things" (v. 2). This language of the delegation of all authority to Jesus as Son reminds us of the many times Jesus said that his authority was given to him (John 5:22, 26-27). And just when was this authority, this appointment given to him? It was given to him after his resurrection as the reward for his obedience (see Acts 2:36; Phil. 2:9-11; Rom. 1:4; Acts 17:31).

Then comes the statement that through this appointed heir of all things God "made the world" (v. 2). The old KJV translation has "through whom He made the worlds." Again, the way this is translated predisposes our tradition-bound minds to run along a well-worn rut. We tend to immediately think of the Genesis creation at the beginning of the universe. But the word used for "worlds" here is the word for "ages" (it is the word from which we get our English word *eon/s*). The writer is not speaking of the Genesis

---

[137] Buzzard and Hunting, *The Doctrine of the Trinity,* p. 73.

creation of the heavens and the earth. He is speaking about time periods, epochs. In Jewish thinking there were classically two great ages. The first is the present and evil age. The next will be the Messianic age to come. And Hebrews 1:2 is speaking of the world — or more precisely — the Messianic age to come. He goes on to tell us that through Jesus' sacrificial death on the cross a new way has been opened up for us to enter the new earth and the new heavens of the future Messianic Kingdom when it dawns.

This "appointed heir of all things" is the agent, the mediator *through* (*dia*) whom God has — in prospect — brought about the new Messianic age. The eschatological Son "is the radiance of His glory and the exact representation of His nature" (v. 3).

> The eschatological context and the present participles used in these statements (literally: he, being reflection and stamp) make it clear that here there can be no question of any protological statement about preexistence or a statement about the earthly life of the Son, but a statement about the significance of the Son for the community in the present.[138]
>
> The Christology of the immediate context...[indicates] *the author is thinking primarily of the exalted Christ:* Christ is the Son who is the eschatological climax ("in these last days") to all God's earlier and more fragmentary revelation (v. 1-2a); that climactic revelation focuses on his sacrifice for sins, and exaltation to God's right hand (v. 3d-e).[139]

In other words, there is not any intimation here in this end-time context that Christ is seen as the preexistent God the Son, second member of the Trinity. True, this Son now "upholds all things by the word of his power" (v. 3b). But it is the new creation — the Messianic age — that is held together by his (authorized and delegated) power. In the Messianic Kingdom everything will be based on Christ's word and teaching (note that whoever in this present and adulterous generation is "ashamed of me **and my words**" will not share in the glory when Jesus comes as per Mark 8:38). Without Christ and his word of the Kingdom there is no Messianic Age to uphold.

And in that new age even the angels will worship the Son, for he has "**become** as much better than the angels, as he has **inherited**

---

[138] Kuschel, *Born Before All Time?* p. 356.

[139] Dunn, *Christology in the Making,* p. 208, emphasis original.

a more excellent name than they" (v. 4). This is what the Father had decreed through the prophets long ago (v. 5). If there is any doubt that Christ the Son will be worshipped in that glorious new age the author dispels such a question by promising that "when He [God] again brings the first-born into the world, He says, 'And let all the angels of God worship him'" (v. 6). At the Second Coming the Father's decree will become history. Every knee, whether in heaven or on earth, will pay homage to the Son (see Ps. 2:12). Jesus will then "sit on the throne of his glory" (Matt. 25:31). This worship of Jesus the Son does not make him Almighty God: Later in Hebrews 2 Jesus is seen leading his "brethren" — the redeemed church — in the (ultimate) worship of God the Father (Heb. 2:12-13). This act of (relative) worship of Jesus by the angels will honour the Father, for it is His will they do this (Phil. 2:9-11). Then the ultimate act of Jesus' own worship of God the Father will be "when he delivers up the kingdom to the God and Father, when he has abolished all rule and all authority and power" (1 Cor. 15:24). When all things are subjected to Christ, including the angelic hosts, "then the Son himself also will be subjected to the One who subjected all things to him, that God may be all in all" (1 Cor. 15:28). "As representing the divine majesty of the Father, the messianic title 'god' will be applied to Jesus, as it once was to the judges of Israel who foreshadowed the supreme Judge of Israel, the Messiah (Ps. 82:6)."[140]

Jehovah's designation of His Son as "God" in the quotation from Psalm 45, "Your throne, O God, is forever and ever" (v. 8) "is not speculation about divine nature from preexistence theology, but an interpretation of the statements which relate to the exalted Christ ('reflection' and 'stamp')."[141] In other words, the Christology of Hebrews is not really a preexistence Christology but primarily a Christology of exaltation. The author is not concerned with primal time, but with the status of Christ as regent in the present which ensures our salvation. The foundations of the new Messianic age — the new heavens and the new earth — will be firmly laid on Messiah's throne:

---

[140] Anthony Buzzard, *Who Is Jesus? A Plea for a Return to Belief in Jesus, the Messiah,* Restoration Fellowship, p. 24.
[141] Kuschel, *Born Before All Time?* p. 356.

> You, Lord, in the beginning laid the foundations of the earth, and the heavens are the works of your hands; they will perish, but you remain, and they all will become old as a garment, and as a mantle you will roll them up. As a garment they will also be changed. But you are the same, and your years will not come to an end (v. 10-12).

It has been argued that since these words quoted from Psalm 102 where their original reference is to Jehovah are now applied to the risen Son, then Jesus must be Jehovah. If we are not careful to follow the original intention of the writer it would be easy to see how these verses can be misread to mean that the Lord Messiah is the one who originally created the universe. But if we turn back to Psalm 102, the author's reference point, we will quickly understand that the Psalmist is also speaking about the coming Messianic age of the Kingdom which is to be centred in Jerusalem. This is a prophecy that "will be **written for the generation to come**; that **a people yet to be created** may praise the LORD" (Ps. 102:18).

The Psalmist anticipates the day when Jerusalem will be restored under Messiah. This will be an age when "the nations will fear the name of the LORD, and all the kings of the earth Your glory" (Ps. 102:15). It will be a day "when the peoples are gathered together, and the kingdoms, to serve the LORD" (Ps. 102:22). This Messianic agent through whom God will speak will be the one "to establish [literally, 'plant'] the heavens; to found the earth, and to say to Zion, 'You are my people'" (Is. 51:16). The *Word Bible Commentary* says of these verses:

> This makes no sense if it refers to the original (Genesis) creation...In other instances God acts alone using no agent (Isa. 44:24). Here the one he has hidden in his hand is his agent. Heavens and land here refers metaphorically to the totality of order in Palestine. Heaven means the broader overarching structure of the empire, while "land" is the political order in Palestine itself.[142]

All of which is to emphasize again that the series of truths being mentioned in these verses in Hebrews 1 refer to the time when God re-introduces His now glorified Son, His "first-born into the world" (Heb. 1:6). If there is still any doubt that this is the correct interpretation the writer states in Hebrews 2: "For He did not subject

---

[142] *Word Bible Commentary.*

to angels **the world to come, concerning which we are speaking**" (v. 5).

All of the prophetic announcements of Hebrews 1 relate to the Messianic age to come! His concern is not with the old Genesis creation but with the new world in mind. Hebrews 1 speaks about the Son being the king of Israel, and mentions a throne, a scepter and a Kingdom with no end. He is speaking of "the good things to come...that is to say, **not of this creation**" (Heb. 9:11)! In that Messianic age when the Son sits on his throne, he still has One above him whom he calls his "God": "Therefore God, **your God**, has anointed you with the oil of gladness above your companions" (Heb. 1:9).

Putting it another way, to make Hebrews 1:8-10 mean that Jesus is Jehovah God just because he is called God, is to create massive problems for Trinitarians. The reason is that it specifically states that the Son *has a God* who anointed him. If Jesus is (Almighty) God and has a God above him, then there are two Gods! This is an utter impossibility to the writers of the Scriptures.

Once again, we note that eschatology is the great factor in properly understanding the truths set forth in Hebrews 1. The writer to the Hebrews, and indeed all the writers of the New Testament, understand that by his exaltation, Jesus now stands so close to God that he exercises many of the divine prerogatives. Furthermore, the writer to the Hebrews is able to hold both the present age and the future age together in a present, unresolved tension. Although we do not now see all things subjected to the New Man we do by faith see Jesus as the Lord of that new day (Heb. 2:8-9). We are exhorted to hold this confession firmly to the end (Heb. 4:14). One day, on that Day, we shall enter into his inheritance as co-rulers with him. In the meantime, the tension between imminence and delay in the expectation of the end is characteristic of the entire biblical eschatology. This may not be the thought pattern of the modern scientifically trained mind. But unless we seek to think with the first-century Hebrew mind behind this book, we will do it violence by forcing into it modern analytical categories that miss the point altogether. As Anthony Buzzard challenges us with these words:

> The writer must be allowed to provide his own commentary. His concern is with the Messianic Kingdom, not the creation in Genesis. Because we do not share the Messianic vision of the New Testament as we ought, our tendency is to

look back rather than forward. We must attune ourselves to the thoroughly Messianic outlook of the entire Bible.[143]

Mighty God, Everlasting Father

The evidence so far considered — particularly from John 1, Philippians 2, Colossians 1 and Hebrews 1 — leads us to state with confidence that the united witness of the New Testament does not justify the traditional belief that Jesus the Messiah existed consciously in heaven as God the Son before his birth in time on earth. What they do show is that the Messiah promised in the Old Testament would be a human being so anointed by the Spirit of God that through him God would usher in a new age of redemption and glory. So radical is this salvation that it is thought of in terms of a new creation affecting the whole sphere of existence on earth and indeed in heaven. The Messiah's coming would be the fulcrum of history, so pivotal that it could be spoken of as a shifting of the ages. This Coming One would combine in his person the offices of prophet, priest and king. He would represent the one God perfectly and fully. The fullness of God's wisdom and power would dwell in him bodily. To have seen him would be to have seen God whose Spirit he possessed in full measure. This, of course, is nothing other than what the prophets had predicted long before.

In this light, two great OT predictions from Isaiah 9 and Micah 5 must now be examined as we bring this chapter to a close. It will become evident that these texts have been traditionally mishandled when used to teach the full Deity of Christ. To do them justice, we must discover the meaning the original authors intended.

The first reads thus: "For a child will be born to us, a son will be given to us; and the government will rest on his shoulders; and his name will be called Wonderful Counsellor, Mighty God, Eternal Father, Prince of Peace" (Isa. 9:6).

Written about 750 to 800 years before Jesus was born, this prophecy tells of a child to be born and a son to be given. Traditional Christian theology wants us to believe he is the second member of the Godhead because he is called "Mighty God, Eternal Father." A number of difficulties present themselves if this traditional interpretation is to hold. Firstly, the appellation "Mighty God" (Hebrew *el gibbor*) is defined by the leading Hebrew lexicon

---

[143] Anthony Buzzard, *Who Is Jesus?* p. 124.

as "divine hero, reflecting the divine majesty."[144] It refers to "men of might and rank, as well as to angels." It is instructive to observe that the Jewish translators of the Septuagint (LXX) described the Messiah simply as the "messenger of mighty counsel." Another recognized Hebrew authority defines *gibbor* as warrior, tyrant, champion, giant, valiant man, mighty man.[145] These authorities tell us that *gibbor* when used in association with God means a regal warrior with the attributes of God. In Ezekiel 31:11 where the NASB translates the word as "a despot" the margin says, "or, *mighty one.*" In Ezekiel 32 the phrase pops up again but the translators of our English Bibles wisely translate it as "the mighty ones" because it refers to men (v. 21). Again in Ezekiel 17 God says He has taken away "the mighty of the land" (v. 13).

The term "Mighty God" is a royal title. The next verse in Isaiah 9 agrees with this definition. Messiah will reign on David's throne. He will rule with justice and righteousness forever because of the zeal of the LORD of hosts. Isaiah carefully distinguishes between this Messiah and his God, not only in these verses but throughout the rest of his book (e.g. Is. 49:5 where Messiah calls the LORD "my God"). In any case, Isaiah did not write — as many misquote him — that the child to be born, the son to be given would be called **Al-**mighty God! That would have been a different Hebrew word altogether — *el shaddai* — used exclusively of Jehovah.

Isaiah's next description of the coming Son is "everlasting Father." If Trinitarians are to be consistent when saying that the term "mighty God" proves Jesus is God, then this appellation "everlasting Father" proves Jesus is God the Father, an argument which proves too much! (Some actually say this. They are called modalists. This simply cannot be for it would mean that Jesus is the father of himself!) But once again, this kind of literalism proves too much and is not in keeping with the Jewish author's mind or culture. Here is a common idiom in Hebrew thinking, as a little reflection will show. Kings were called fathers of their nation. A few chapters later in Isaiah God calls His servant Eliakim "a father to the inhabitants of Jerusalem and to the house of Judah" (Is. 22:20). God promises to invest Eliakim the king with a royal robe and entrust

---

[144] Brown, Driver and Briggs, *Hebrew and English Lexicon of the Old Testament,* p. 42.

[145] *Strong's Hebrew Dictionary.*

him with kingly authority (Is. 22:21). Abraham is called "our father Abraham" (Rom. 4:1, 12, 16) because he is the progenitor of the Hebrew race.

The word "eternal" here does not necessarily mean what it does to us moderns either. "Eternal" to our ears means eternity past, present and future, forever and forever. But to Hebrew minds it may carry the idea of being related to the (future) age. In accordance with its Hebrew usage, Isaiah's promise is that the future Son will be the progenitor of the coming age of the Kingdom of God. According to the Hebrew Lexicon the word "eternal" in Isaiah 9:6 means "forever (of future time)."[146] According to Strong's *Dictionary* the word is defined as "duration, in the sense of advance or perpetuity," and Strong's *Concordance* gives the primary definition as "perpetuity, for ever, continuing future."[147] In harmony with these meanings, the Septuagint (in the Alexandrian version) gives Messiah's title as "father of the age to come."[148] The Catholic Douay-Rheims Version of the Bible interestingly calls Messiah here "the father of the world to come."[149] The same word is used in Psalm 37: "The righteous will inherit the land and dwell in it **forever**" (v. 29). This cannot mean that the righteous existed from eternity, never having a beginning. The clear intention is that the righteous will never have an end. Clearly, the promised Messiah is the "everlasting father" of the world to come, since both he and the righteous (children) will live forever.

A Ruler from Eternity

The second well-known OT prophecy traditionally used to indicate that Jesus is the eternal God reads: "But as for you, Bethlehem Ephrathah, too little to be among the clans of Judah, from you one will go forth for Me to be ruler in Israel. His goings forth are from long ago, from the days of eternity" (Micah 5:2).

Many Trinitarians allege that this is clear proof that Jesus is the eternal God. Certainly, this is a remarkable prophecy of the coming

---

[146] Brown, Driver, Briggs, *Hebrew and English Lexicon of the Old Testament.*

[147] *Strong's Concordance.*

[148] *Codex Alexandrinus*, as translated by Sir Lancelot C.L. Brenton and Septuagint translation by Archimandrite Ephrem Lash.

[149] See also *The New International Dictionary of New Testament Theology,* vol. 1, p. 326.

birth of Messiah. But does it teach that a personally preexistent Jesus is God Himself because it says "his goings forth are from long ago, from the days of eternity"? Someone who steps out of "the days of eternity" into history must surely be a member of the Godhead? The phrase "days of eternity" (Heb. *y'may olam*) occurs just a few chapters later in Micah 7. Here God's people are promised they will "feed in Bashan and Gilead as in the days of old" (v. 14). Nobody would understand the same phrase to mean God's people used to feed well in eternity. The same expression is found in Deuteronomy 32: "Remember the days of old; consider the years of all generations. Ask your father, and he will inform you; your elders, and they will tell you" (Deut. 32:7).

The phrase "remember the days of old" (*y'may olam*) cannot mean remember from eternity, for it is instructing the Israelites to recall days that their fathers and leaders knew. This same meaning is found in Isaiah 45:21; 63:9, 11; Amos 9:11, etc. In none of these instances can it mean "eternity." Those translations which say that the coming ruler of Israel's "goings forth are from the days of eternity" are quite unfortunate. The prophet did not suggest that Jesus was going to step out of a personal preexistence from eternity past, but simply that *the promise* of the Messiah's emergence in Bethlehem is from "the days of old," that is, it can be traced to remote antiquity — way back to the very beginning of human history in fact, when God promised Eve that her "seed" would crush the tempter's head (Gen. 3:15).

Conclusion

I remember as a lad of 17 years of age travelling to Hong Kong. I have a beautiful uncle and aunty who generously paid for my mother, my brother and me to travel overseas for the first time. The culture shock in that oriental place blew my young mind away. Of the many images that confronted me, there is one I shall never forget. On a church wall high up on a mountain in the New Territories, near the Chinese border, was painted Jesus the Christ. He was Chinese — with full pig-tail and traditional Chinese dress!

It strikes me that we humans are quite adept at constructing Jesus in our own image. Not only has the historical Jesus of Nazareth been metamorphosed under the influence of Hellenism into the "God-man," but his own mother Mary has been promoted to the status of "Mother of God" and "co-redemptress," and the saints have become intercessors. But of the greatest consequence has been the invented doctrine of the Incarnation, where the Eternal God Himself is supposed to have taken on flesh and become man. This development has had disastrous consequences for the Biblical testimony to the unity and uniqueness of God. Don Cupitt remarks that once this doctrine of the Incarnation of a preexisting Son of God was created, the cult of the divine Christ actually put the Deity Himself into the background, for when God the Father was affirmed, He was envisaged in anthropomorphic terms. The door to paganism had been unwittingly reopened. However well-intentioned, the focus of worship had been shifted from God to man. This shift would eventually legitimize the cult of humanism. Deity would slide into the background. The "otherness" of God would be lost — or as the theologians call it, the transcendence of God. His "holiness," His "awesomeness" would become manageable and comfortable. God is now a man![150]

The correct Christology — "the rock" on which his true Church is founded according to Jesus himself — is Peter's confession that he is the Messiah, the son of the living God (Matt. 16:16). Luke records Peter's confession with a slight, but powerful, variation; he says that Jesus is "the Christ of God" (Luke 9:20). In the Greek NT there is a definite article before "God." To be boldly literal, Peter confessed that Jesus is "the Messiah of the [one true] God."

Does it follow that the failure to maintain the Biblical confession that Jesus is the Lord Messiah — and not the Lord God — has fostered in some kind of an inverted way the rampant secularism of our age? For now the Almighty and Everlasting God has assumed human form and the ultimate mystery and unity of God has collapsed into a concept of agreeable human proportions, namely, our little "self." In making Jesus fully God, did we make man God? This trend can be observed in the development of art from the fourth century onwards. The Jewish-Christian taboo against depicting God in any shape was forgotten. The result was a focusing of attention on Jesus and away from God's "otherness." Our sense of awe in worship, that which should take our breath away so to speak, was severely compromised. Christian art prior to Constantine was hesitant, but after Constantine it became quite elaborate. The Church made Jesus more than he ever was meant to

---

[150] Don Cupitt, *The Myth of God Incarnate.*

be, and in the process demoted the Father God he came to reveal. Jesus himself would very well ask us today, as he did the young man long ago, "Why do you call me good? There is none good but God" (Luke 18:19). And even now, exalted by his Father's throne in heaven, Jesus *still* worships the Father as the One who "**alone** is holy" (Rev. 15:4). It is these who so worship the Father through His Son who are the "true worshippers" (John 4:23).

The evidence of both Old and New Testaments, when interpreted with the Hebrew background in mind, does not lend any support to the traditional belief of a personally preexisting (Nicene) Christ, who is "God of very God" or the eternally generated Son. Nor does the evidence lend any support to the Arian Christ who was created by God back somewhere in eternity before the world began. Jesus is the man who was born in time. His origin or genesis was in the virgin Mary's womb, begotten by special creative act of God the Father. For *this reason precisely*, Jesus is the Son of God (Luke 1:35), the King whom God authorizes. The Hebrew prophets predicted that Messiah would be born of human "seed" or stock and under God's anointing would bring about a new, redeemed and glorified order. The New Testament announces that the risen and exalted Lord Jesus has inaugurated the promised shift of the ages. In short, these results prove that "a deep hiatus between the biblical evidence and classical dogmatics can no longer be concealed."[151]

The Jewish scholar Hugh Schonfield in his book *Those Incredible Christians* summarizes our chapter beautifully. He writes that the doctrine of the Deity of Jesus Christ:

> is diametrically opposed to the Jewish concept of God at the time Jesus lived, and no one being a Jew, subscribing to the Hebrew Scriptures, and seeking acceptance by Jews, would be likely to present himself in such a contrary character. Taken with the evidence that the doctrine was agreeable to current heathen notions the obvious inference is that it was an intrusion from Gentile sources and not fundamental...It was alien in its derivation and Jesus himself could not have entertained it. Early Gospel material shows him exercising all the extreme care of the devout Jew in guarding the name

[151] Kuschel, *Born Before All Time?* p. 39.

> of God from profanation and representing Him as the sole Being to be worshipped and described as good.[152]

To object to this conclusion is not just a matter of doctrinal nuance. The witness of history confirms it. As late as the second century the advocates of this view (that Jesus was the human Lord Messiah and not the eternal Son, second member of the Triune Godhead) could still point out that this was the original belief held "by all the first Christians and by the Apostles themselves."[153] It was fatal to the doctrine of the Deity of Jesus that his own apostles and the Christian members of his family had held that he was no more than a man uniquely anointed from birth by the Spirit of God, thus being the Messiah. What also counts for so much is the witness of the ecclesiastical historians that these original apostles and elders and relations of Jesus were the spokesmen of the Jewish Christianity with jurisdiction over the whole Church (before the destruction of Jerusalem in AD 70). "It was not, as its proponents alleged, Jewish Christianity which debased the person of Jesus, but the Church in general which was misled into deifying him."[154]

The authors of *The Jesus Mysteries* support Hugh Schonfield's conclusion by making the shocking claim that failure to account for this foreign take-over of the Church's doctrine of Jesus the Christ has left the Church unwittingly in the midst of a pagan mythology. They thoroughly document the many instances of peoples and cultures of antiquity surrounding the Mediterranean who had a plethora of beliefs in supposed god-men who had come to earth to redeem mankind. Every single one of these redeemer-godmen myths predates Christianity. Osiris of Egypt was believed to be of divine origin. "He represented to men the idea of a man who was both God and man." In fact, "The Egyptian myth of Osiris is the primal myth of the mystery god-man and reaches back to prehistory. His story is so ancient that it can be found in pyramid texts written over 4,500 years ago!"[155] The Greeks also had their god-man in Dionysus, who predates the Christian era by hundreds of years. In one ancient Greek play Dionysus explains that he has veiled his

---

[152] Hugh Schonfield, *Those Incredible Christians,* New York: Bantam Books, 1968, p. 50.
[153] *Ibid.,* p. 124.
[154] *Ibid.,* p. 124.
[155] Freke and Gandy, *The Jesus Mysteries: Was the Original Jesus a Pagan God?* pp. 27, 30.

Godhead in a mortal shape in order to make it manifest to mortal men. He tells his disciples, "That is why I have changed my immortal form and taken the likeness of man."[156] The Persians' god-man was called Mithras. The Babylonians, the Romans, the Syrians and many other ancient peoples all had their own pagan god-man mysteries. As already indicated, these god-man myths were ubiquitous long before Jesus of Nazareth appeared. Christians who are of the opinion that Jesus is the God-man Redeemer who is unique among the faiths are simply ill-informed.

Such history adds great weight to our contention that the Church abandoned its Hebrew foundation and quickly absorbed paganism into its teaching about the nature of Jesus of Nazareth. At the Council of Nicea in 325 AD Christianity adopted its own version of a "God-man" who was modeled on these already existing pagan myths. Now it is time for those wishing to remain faithful to the Bible to drop the use of the term "God-man" and its attendant teaching. The word "God-man" and all that goes with it does not appear in the New Testament. We must insist on the Biblical understanding of Jesus as the uniquely begotten/created man of God who belongs to the same family as Adam and Abraham, Moses and David. This man by his righteousness has been raised to immortality and exalted to God's right hand as the first glorified *man.* This is something totally unique and different from all other beliefs about god-men.

By remaining faithful to the Biblical pattern we have discussed throughout this chapter the uniqueness of Jesus of Nazareth will be preserved. Here is the wonder of our faith: At God's right hand is a true man, a real man, a man just like you and me! He is the perfect demonstration of all that God the Father can do through a man totally yielded to His will and filled with His Holy Spirit.

---

[156] *Ibid.*, p. 35.

Six
ANOTHER SPIRIT

When the Jehovah's Witnesses used to knock on our door I found that one of the best ways to challenge them was not to go down their well-worn path that Jesus is/is not God. I would take them down a track they were not used to, namely what the Bible had to say about the Holy Spirit. If I could show them from the Bible that the Holy Spirit was indeed a Person, then the conclusion was inescapable: the Holy Spirit was God Himself and we had proved there is a Blessed Trinity. And I found, so I thought, irrefutable proof that the Spirit of God was a Person because "he" had all the qualities of personhood that we people have. Did he not have a mind? (Romans 8:7 says, "And he who searches the hearts knows what the mind of the Spirit is, because he intercedes for the saints according to the will of God.") Did not the Spirit of God have emotions, feelings, temperament? (Eph. 4:30 says, "And do not grieve the Holy Spirit of God, by whom you were sealed for the day of redemption.") Did not the Spirit have volition, a will? (Acts 16:6 states the apostles were "forbidden by the Holy Spirit to speak the word in Asia.") Surely the Holy Spirit is more than a power or a force like mere electricity, for he has the essential traits of personality: mind, emotions, will? Added to these traits of personality, there are many verses that teach that the Holy Spirit speaks, sends, prays, leads, etc. And is not the Holy Spirit called "He" in our Bibles? Surely, in the light of these facts we are entitled to say the Holy Spirit is a Person, therefore is God, and therefore the *third* member of the Trinity? I thought I had a water-tight position, one that was honouring to God. Now, however, I realize I was simply reading the Bible with the eyes of my Western heritage, and not through Hebrew eyes.

One of the biggest problems for those holding that the Holy Spirit is the third member of the Godhead is the Old Testament itself. As we said at the very beginning of our journey, the Old Testament is the foundation of our Bibles, the first 75% in fact. And an incontrovertible fact is that the Hebrew Bible does not support the idea that the Spirit of God is a distinct member of the Godhead at all. Even committed Trinitarians like George Eldon Ladd admit:

> The *ruach Yahweh* (Spirit of the Lord) in the Old Testament is not a separate, distinct entity; it is God's power — the personal activity in God's will achieving a moral and religious object. God's *ruach* is the source of all that is alive, of all physical life. The Spirit of God is the active principle that proceeds from God and gives life to the physical world (Gen. 2:7). It is also the source of religious concerns, raising up charismatic leaders, whether judges, prophets, or kings. The *ruach Yahweh* (Spirit of God) is a term for the historical creative action of the one God which, though it defies logical analysis, is always God's action.[1]

This is indeed the consensus of the vast majority of scholars, from one end of the theological spectrum to the other.

> The continuity of thought between Hebraic and Christian understanding of the Spirit is generally recognized...There can be little doubt that from the earliest stages of pre-Christian Judaism "spirit" (*ruach*) denoted *power* — the awful, mysterious force of the wind (*ruach*), of the breath (*ruach*) of life, of ecstatic inspiration (induced by divine *ruach*)...In particular, "Spirit of God" denotes *effective divine power*...In other words, on this understanding, *Spirit of God is in no sense distinct from God,* but is simply the power of God, *God himself acting powerfully in nature and upon men.*[2]

Thus, for instance, the cause of King Saul's sad state can either be described as "**the Spirit of the Lord** departed from Saul" (1 Sam. 16:14) or "**the Lord** had departed from Saul" (1 Sam. 18:12). And in Isaiah 30:1 and 40:13 "My Spirit" and "the Spirit of the Lord" are synonymous with the divine "I." Especially noteworthy in Ezekiel "the Spirit" is interchangeable with "the hand of the Lord" (Ezek. 3:14; 8:1-3; 37:1). Thus, we are to understand that God's Spirit is His own operational activity and power directed towards His world. It makes a big difference — to our Western minds at least — right at the start of the Bible, whether we translate "the Spirit of God was moving over the surface of the waters" or "a wind

---

[1] G.E. Ladd, *A Theology of the New Testament,* p. 287.

[2] Dunn, *Christology in the Making,* pp. 132-133.

[breath] from God swept over the face of the waters" (Gen. 1:2). The first possibility conveys to our modern minds the impression that the Spirit is an individual in "His" own right. Many Trinitarians read it that way. The second possibility suggests — in this case correctly — that God's energetic and creative presence was active. That well-loved Psalm 139 expresses this Hebrew parallelism beautifully: "Where can I go from **Your Spirit**? Or where can I flee from **Your presence**?" (v. 7).

Thus, the Spirit of God is a synonym for God's personal presence with us. "Spirit of God" means God in effective relationship with (and within) His creation. To experience the Spirit of God is to experience God as Spirit.[3] "The *ruach-adonai* [Spirit of the Lord] is the manifestation in human experience of the life-giving, energy-creating power of God." And, "The Spirit of the Lord is the medium through which God exerts His controlling power."[4]

A brief look at a few more Old Testament verses will show this Hebrew parallelism, where the Spirit of God (Heb. *ruach*) can mean breath, life, spirit, presence, and — most particularly — a word of Yahweh:

"To whom have you uttered **words**? And whose **spirit** [or breath] was **expressed** through you?" (Job 26:4).

"For as long as **life** [literally, breath] is in me, and the **breath** [or spirit] of God is in my nostrils, my lips certainly will not **speak** unjustly" (Job 27:3-4).

"But it is a **spirit** in man, and the **breath** of the Almighty gives them **understanding**" (Job 32:8).

"The **Spirit** of the LORD spoke by me, and His **word** was on **my tongue**" (2 Sam. 23:2).

"Behold, I will pour out my **spirit** on you; I will make my **words** known to you" (Prov. 1:23).

"The grass withers, the flower fades, when **the breath of the LORD** blows upon it; surely the people are grass. The grass withers, the flower fades, but **the word of our God** stands forever" (Isa. 40:7-8).

It is vital not to rush over this. Many other OT examples could be cited to show that *spirit* and *breath* are interchangeable.

---

[3] *Ibid.*, p. 133.

[4] N.H. Snaith, *The Distinctive Ideas of the Old Testament,* pp. 152-153.

Translators also recognize the obvious connection between spirit/breath and the *word* that comes from that source. There is a key connection between the spirit/word of God and the expression of that word in speech. This nexus is never lost sight of in either the OT or the NT as we shall see. We already know this connection between mind/spirit/word instinctively anyway. You cannot know me, what my thoughts and dreams are, unless I express them to you, in either conversation or written words. You cannot know my spirit/mind until I tell you. My words reveal to you who I am. Just so, God's Spirit — that is, His innermost mind and being — can only be known when He speaks. The Spirit of God is known and given verbal expression by the word of God.

Whenever the Spirit of God came upon the prophets, they spoke the word of God. "Men moved by the Holy Spirit spoke from God" (2 Pet. 1:21). Zechariah complained that the people "made their hearts like flint so that they could not hear the law and **the words** which the LORD of hosts had sent **by His Spirit through the former prophets**" (Zech. 7:12). God's Spirit comes via the words of His prophets. "All Scripture is given by inspiration of God" (2 Tim. 3:16). That is, the words of Scripture are the expression of God's mind to us. Scripture is God's breath, as it were, coming to us from His innermost being and mind in life-changing power. The same is true for our Lord Jesus, for when the Spirit of the Lord came upon him, he preached the anointed words of God (Luke 4:18-19). Jesus' testimony concerning himself was that "he whom God has sent speaks **the words of God**, for He gives **the Spirit** without measure" (John 3:34). The same goes for his apostles when "they were all filled with the Holy Spirit and began to speak with other tongues [languages], as the Spirit was giving them utterance" (Acts 2:4).

Whenever the word of God is proclaimed the effect is like a sharp two-edged sword cutting deep into our minds (Heb. 4:12). In fact, "the sword of **the Spirit *is* the word** of God" (Eph. 6:17). This is why we cannot be "born again" (literally, "born from above," "born of the Spirit") without hearing the word of the Gospel (John 3:1-8). To receive that word into our souls is to receive the Spirit of God (Luke 8:11; 1 Pet. 1:23; James 1:18). To listen "to the message of truth, the gospel of your salvation" is to be "sealed in Him with the Holy Spirit of promise" (Eph. 1:13). To receive from the apostles "the gospel of God" is to receive "the word of God's message" and know the power of God operating within the soul (1 Thess. 1:9, 13). All of this proves that in both the OT and NT the way to receive God's Spirit is to listen to His inspired word(s). There is no other way. As already pointed out, this key is set right at the very beginning of the Bible, for when "The Spirit [breath/wind] of God was moving over the surface of the waters" it was then that God spoke and said, "Let there be..." (Gen. 1:2-3).

"The fact that 'spirit' and 'breath' are translations of the same Hebrew and Greek words points to the root meaning of spirit as God's creative power, the energy behind His utterance."[5] Spirit is the mind and energy behind the words and works of God. The *ruach* of the Lord "is the medium through which God exerts His controlling power." The Spirit of the Lord "is the manifestation in human experience of the life-giving, energy-creating power of God."[6] These evident facts explain why committed Trinitarians frankly acknowledge that the doctrine of the individual Personhood of the Holy Spirit is not a doctrine found in the pages of the OT. Well-known Australian Anglican Leon Morris openly admits as much when he writes:

> It must be recognized that this is a New Testament revelation, and that with no more than the Old Testament in our hands we should never have risen to this knowledge of God (as Triune)...Here it must be confessed that there is nothing that compels us to regard the Spirit in a Trinitarian fashion...Devout and learned Jews make a very close study of the Old Testament with a reverent acceptance of what it says as the very Word of God, yet do not come to a belief in a Spirit in any way separate from the Father. The Spirit as distinct from the Father is a New Testament doctrine.[7]

Another world-renowned Anglican, J.I. Packer (also a committed believer in the Trinity) acknowledges that the doctrine of the Holy Spirit's "distinct personhood is not expressed by the Old Testament writers."[8] By what reasoning then do these learned commentators come to the conclusion that the Holy Spirit is the third Person of the Godhead? They admit that they step outside the

---

[5] Buzzard and Hunting, *The Doctrine of the Trinity,* p. 217.
[6] Snaith, *The Distinctive Ideas of the Old Testament,* pp. 152-153.
[7] Leon Morris, *Spirit of the Living God: The Bible's Teaching on the Holy Spirit,* London: Inter-Varsity Press, 1974, p. 29.
[8] J.I. Packer, *Keep in Step with the Spirit,* Inter-Varsity Press, p. 59.

bounds of the Old Testament. They would have us believe that it is a doctrine newly revealed only in the NT. Theirs is a confession that they admit goes beyond the Hebrew Bible which formed the very basis of what Jesus and the apostles strictly adhered to. Let's follow their process: Having stated that "*Historical exegesis* assures us that Old Testament statements about God's almighty breath [the *ruach Yahweh*] were not intended by their writers to imply personal distinctions within the deity," J.I. Packer can justify the New Testament's apparent change of mind (!?) by saying, "Christian *theological interpretation* requires us to follow the Lord Jesus and his apostles in recognizing that the third person of the Godhead was active in Old Testament times and that Old Testament statements about God's almighty breath do in fact refer to the personal Spirit's activity."[9]

This is a dodge to justify his tradition. Let us not miss this sleight of hand trick. Packer is prepared to step outside the sound method of Biblical interpretation known as "historical exegesis" for another method. This should raise warning bells in our ears and flashing amber lights before our eyes. The historical exegetical method is concerned to faithfully determine what the original writers intended their original readers to understand. Whilst the message God is communicating through the writer/s is eternal and unchanging, and is as relevant to the 21st century as when it was first revealed, the historical exegetical method posits that we can only determine that word by being faithful to grammatical and cultural context. However, in order to validate his belief in the personhood of the Spirit, J.I. Packer is prepared to scuttle "historical exegesis" for what he calls "Christian theological interpretation" — in other words, what traditional and "orthodox" interpretation has determined. We may well ask, which stream of "theological interpretation" will we follow? Nicene? Arian? Socinian? Mormon?

We are now sailing on the wavy seas of human speculation. Protestants who deplore tradition-bound Roman Catholics because they revere Church tradition above the Scriptures fail to see that in some areas they are just as bound to tradition, i.e. to long-held interpretations of Scriptures. "Christian theological interpretation" can be extremely helpful and enlightening, it is true. But traditional interpretations are not necessarily inspired. Only the Scriptures

---

[9] *Ibid.*, p. 60.

remain inspired. We must ever remain free to re-examine what the Scriptures say. And on the question of the Personhood of the Spirit, it is our contention that the NT remains true to its OT foundations, that the Spirit of the Lord is still equivalent to God's personal creative power operative in the world, and is not intended to imply personal distinctions within the Deity. We contend that "historical exegesis" has not moved, but rather that "Christian theological interpretation" has shifted and needs re-examining, indeed needs re-attaching to its Hebrew roots.

The New Testament does not alter the Hebrew concept of "spirit" as we will now see. The distinguished Bible scholar N.H. Snaith states that:

> The New Testament *pneuma* (spirit) is used in all the ways in which the Hebrew *ruach* (breath, wind, spirit) is used. It is used of the wind (John 3:8), of human breath, both ordinarily (2 Thessalonians 2:8) and of the breath which means life (Revelation 11:11). It is used of the vital principle in man (Luke 8:55, etc.), as opposed to "flesh."[10]

Luke writes concerning the ministry of John the Baptist that: "It is he who will go as a forerunner before him in **the spirit and power of Elijah**, to turn the hearts of the fathers back to the children, and the disobedient to the attitude of the righteous; so as to make ready a people prepared for the Lord" (Luke 1:17). The virgin Mary is told that "[the] **holy spirit** will come upon you and **the power of the Most High** will overshadow you" (Luke 1:35). And concerning the promise of the coming of the Holy Spirit the risen Jesus predicts that the disciples are to wait in Jerusalem where they "shall receive **power** when **the Holy Spirit** has come upon you" (Acts 1:8).

In these three Lukan passages we observe the interplay of the concepts of "power" and "spirit" precisely as found in the Old Testament. I cannot improve on Alan Richardson's commentary on this phenomenon as it is quoted in Buzzard and Hunting's *The Doctrine of the Trinity: Christianity's Self-Inflicted Wound*:

> To ask whether in the New Testament the spirit is a person in the modern sense of the word would be like asking whether the spirit of Elijah is a person. The Spirit of God is of course personal; it is God's *dunamis* [power] in action.

[10] Snaith, *The Distinctive Ideas of the Old Testament*, p. 179.

> But the Holy Spirit is not a person, existing independently of God; it is a way of speaking about God's personally acting in history, or of the Risen Christ's personally acting in the life and witness of the Church. The New Testament (and indeed patristic thought generally) nowhere represents the Spirit, any more than the wisdom of God, as having independent personality.[11]

This Hebrew concept is further seen in a famous passage where the apostle Paul bursts out in praise to God. He does this by quoting from Isaiah 40:13: "Oh, the depth of the riches both of the wisdom and knowledge of God! How unsearchable are His judgments and unfathomable His ways! [Now his Old Testament quotation] For who has known **the mind** of the LORD, or who became His counsellor?" (Rom. 11:33-34).

But when we compare his source in Isaiah we note that Paul has changed it slightly. Isaiah actually wrote, "Who has directed **the Spirit of the LORD**, or as His counsellor has informed Him?" What we see here is a typical Hebrew understanding: To have the mind of the Lord *is* to be directed by His Spirit. There are many NT examples of this interplay between "mind" and "spirit." In Philippians 2 Paul wants the Christians to be "of the same mind," which is to be "united in spirit, intent on one purpose" (v. 2). On a personal level, how may I know that I am filled with the Holy Spirit? Answer: when I have the mind of God, the attitudes that He has, the values that His word espouses and above all the truth which it teaches!

Another passage of interest in this vein is 1 Corinthians 2:

> For to us God revealed them through the Spirit; for the Spirit searches all things, even the depths of God. For who among men knows the thoughts of a man except the spirit of the man, which is in him? Even so the thoughts of God no one knows except the Spirit of God. Now we have received not the spirit of the world, but the Spirit who [Greek neuter "which"] is from God, that we might know the things freely given to us by God (v. 10-12).

Here "the spirit of the man which is in him" is paralleled with "the Spirit of God" which is from God. It is quite clear that a person's spirit is not a separate person from himself, but is rather

---

[11] Buzzard and Hunting, *The Doctrine of the Trinity,* p. 218.

his/her own mind and inner thoughts (just as we saw earlier that "the spirit of Elijah" is not another Elijah, but the power and ministry of Elijah). Just so, "the Spirit of God" refers to God's inner and personal centre, His mind and word, even His self-consciousness.

In this passage Paul mentions another "spirit" which is "the spirit of the world." But we Christians have not received this spirit. We display a different mindset from that which pervades the world. Our thoughts and attitudes now reflect those of God Himself. Once again, if we may apply this on a personal level we may ask: How may I know whether God's Spirit dwells in me? Answer: I have His thoughts, His mind, His truth, His Gospel, His attitudes displayed in my life. This is what it means to be "led by the Spirit"; it is to "walk not according to the flesh, but according to the Spirit" (Rom. 8:4). Which is to say, we have "set our **minds** on the things of **the Spirit**" (Rom. 8:5). Once again these passages make the equation of "spirit" and "mind."

In Ephesians 4 Paul wants all Christians to "be renewed in the spirit of your mind" (v. 23). My mind is not another me, it *is* me! The Spirit of God is not another member of the Godhead, it *is* God! Therefore, the only way I have access to God is by receiving His mind, His revealed message, His Word, which is His Spirit as given through His Son Jesus. When the Bible says "the Spirit says" it is exactly *the same* as saying "God speaks." Our Western difficulty is that we turn divine attributes into personality. The Spirit of God possesses all the qualities of God, therefore may be spoken of in personal terms, such as His good Spirit, His gracious Spirit, His faithful Spirit or His Spirit of Truth. However, this does not prove separate personality any more than saying the city weeping or rejoicing proves Jerusalem is a person (e.g. Jer. 31:15; Is. 65:18). Putting this together so far we see that:

Spirit = Power = Mind = Presence = Breath = Wind = Word

Failure to understand this principle has led theologians and preachers and therefore churches into error. Take that great Baptist writer/preacher W.A. Criswell as representative of such basic misunderstanding. Criswell makes this statement:

> There never was a time when the early Christian disciples did not confess the Deity and the saving work of all three Persons of the Godhead. Doxologies to the Father, to the Son, and to the Holy Spirit were in use everywhere in the

> early churches. This is clearly seen in 2 Corinthians 13:14: "The grace of the Lord Jesus Christ, and the love of God, and the fellowship of the Holy Spirit, be with you all. Amen." The naming of the Trinity is also seen in Revelation 1:4, 5: "John to the seven churches which are in Asia: Grace be unto you, and peace, from Him who is and who was and who is to come; and from the seven Spirits who (which) are before His throne; and from Jesus Christ, the faithful witness, the firstborn of the dead, and the ruler of the kings of the earth."[12]

This logic is severely flawed. The fact that God and Jesus and the Holy Spirit are in the same sentence does not make them the same essential being. That would be akin to saying that just because Paul mentions Jesus Christ and God and Timothy in the greetings to the church at Colossae, Timothy is suddenly included in the Godhead (Col. 1:1). Exactly the same kind of reasoning! But worse than the flawed logic is the poor Bible exposition. The expression "fellowship of the Spirit" is found in Philippians 2 and Paul tells us exactly what this phrase means: "if there is any fellowship of **the Spirit**, if any affection and compassion, make my joy complete by being of **the same mind**, maintaining the same love, **united in spirit**, intent on **one purpose**" (v. 1-2).

The "fellowship of the Spirit" is here defined as the church being united in affection, in love, and sharing the spirit and purpose of God. The "fellowship of the Spirit" happens when Christians are so united in beautiful, loving harmony that they experience the very presence of God actively working in their midst. "The fellowship of the Spirit" occurs when the church is in agreement; everyone is "of the same mind." There is nothing here about the Holy Spirit being the third Person of the blessed Trinity. That 2 Corinthians 13:14 is a doxology to the Trinity is clearly not true. What Paul desires for the Corinthians is that the church may enjoy God's love through the grace of Christ in a common and harmonious fellowship of like-mindedness.

Another verse often appealed to in the same vein is the baptismal formula of Jesus in Matthew 28: "Go therefore and make disciples of all the nations, baptizing them in the name of the Father

---

[12] W.A. Criswell, *The Holy Spirit in Today's World,* Grand Rapids, MI: Zondervan, 1966, pp. 13-14.

and the Son and the Holy Spirit" (v. 19). That famous 19th-century "prince of preachers" Charles Haddon Spurgeon once said that he needed no other verse in the Bible to prove that God is a Trinity than this one. He was convinced that the Father, the Son and the Holy Spirit were each fully God because they were all subsumed together under the one (singular) name. Spurgeon noted that the text does not say we are to be baptized in the "names" of the Father, Son and Spirit, but "name," thereby proving God is a blessed three in one. How mighty a doctrine is hung on such a slender thread! To start with, the verse says nothing about God being three in one. To be baptized into the name of Father, Son and Spirit is the equivalent of being immersed into the authority or character of — or indeed, the attributes and knowledge of — the Father, Son and Spirit.

And "the Spirit" here means the body of truth that introduces believers into the Church's fellowship (1 Cor. 12:13). In Ephesians 4 Paul says as much: "There is one body and one Spirit, just as you were called in one hope of your calling" (v. 4). We may thus paraphrase Jesus' command this way: "Go out into the world and introduce them into the knowledge and thus the fellowship of the Father, the Son and of the Holy Spirit." We have already seen that "the fellowship of the Spirit" is equivalent to the church body dwelling in the harmony of the doctrine and the mind of the Gospel of God. (Just as a matter of interest, there are considerable concerns from the textual critics as to whether this verse is genuine to Matthew's original pen. Some textual critics believe it has been tampered with, and there is evidence to suggest they are right. For instance, Eusebius in the third century quotes the verse as, "Go ye therefore, and teach all nations, baptizing them in my name" — that is, in Jesus' name — and this agrees with the apostles' invariable baptismal formula. In the book of Acts, every single time a new convert was baptized, he or she was baptized "in the name of Jesus Christ" (see Acts 2:38; 8:16; 10:48; 19:5). In other words, Matthew 28:19 is the only verse in the entire NT that has the unique baptismal formula, "in the name of the Father, and the Son and the Holy Spirit." This is out of harmony with the rest of the NT and is somewhat suspicious.) However, even if we conclude that Matthew's baptismal formula is original (which it may be), the verse by no means proves that God is a three-in-one Being.

With You in Spirit

There is a classic example of this Jewish mindset in a pastoral setting in connection with the church at Corinth. There is a member of that church who has been sleeping with his step-mother, a situation even outsiders found repulsive. Yet the church seems to be tolerating such wickedness. Paul wants the man immediately removed from fellowship. He writes to tell the church his mind, because he is unable to be there in person and deal with him personally:

> For I, on my part, though absent in body but **present in spirit**, have already judged him who has so committed this, **as though I were present**. In the name of our Lord Jesus, when you are assembled, and **I with you in spirit**, with **the power of our Lord Jesus**, I have decided to deliver such a one to Satan for the destruction of his flesh, that his spirit may be saved in the day of the Lord Jesus (1 Cor. 5:3-4).

Paul cannot be bodily present to handle the discipline needed. But the next time the church meets together he will be "present in spirit." This is "as though I were present," which is as good as Paul's bodily presence. That is to say, the church now knows Paul's mind, his judgment. The assembly now has no excuse for failure to act decisively. Procrastination by the church at Corinth is now inexcusable because he has written to them. It is now *as if* Paul will be personally there because they know his mind. (Furthermore, to have Paul's mind on the matter is to have "the power of our Lord Jesus" present as well.) Once again, to have one's spirit is to have one's mind. The spirit of Paul is not a separate person. And just so, the Spirit of God is not a distinct Person. It means God's active presence and His mind at work in our lives through His revealed word.

You Have Lied to the Holy Spirit

One of the passages I used to use to convince folk that the Holy Spirit is God Himself is found in Acts 5. This well-known and graphic story concerns a husband and wife team, Ananias and Sapphira, who tried to deceive the church by pretending to be more pious in giving than they actually were. Peter said to the man, "Ananias, why has Satan filled your heart to **lie to the Holy Spirit**, and to keep back some of the price of the land?...Why is it that you have conceived this deed in your heart? You have not **lied** to men, but **to God**" (v. 3, 4). So how does one lie, it might be asked, to an impersonal force? Here we have an instance where lying to the Holy Spirit is equated with lying to God. However, on closer examination the difficulty disappears:

> The Holy Spirit here means the power and authority invested by God in Peter. Those who lie to Apostles speaking in the name of God and by His Spirit are rightly said to lie to the Spirit and to God. The point is confirmed by a comment from Paul: "He who despises us despises not men but God, who has given us His Spirit" (1 Thess. 4:8). There is a striking parallel in the Old Testament when the Israelites rebelled against Moses and Aaron. Moses told them that their rebellion was "not against us, but against God whose messengers we are." The "equation" of Moses and Aaron with God does not, of course, make the former part of the Godhead (Ex. 16:2, 8). The Spirit of God did, however, reside in Moses and it may be that the Israelite rebellion mentioned in the Psalms was directed against "Moses' spirit" (Ps. 106:33, AV, RV, RSV), or possibly against the angel of God's presence who was invested with the authority and power of Yahweh (Isa. 63:9-11).[13]

Another Helper

One of the most challenging series of teachings on the Holy Spirit is the group of five sayings by Jesus that have to do with the coming Holy Spirit, called the "comforter" (Greek *parakletos*). These are found in John's Gospel, chapters 14 to 16. Even the essential meaning of "paraclete" has been hotly debated. For some it suggests a power to make strong and to fortify. But most scholars seem to think this nuance comes more from the Latin *confortare* which found its way into early English translations. There is a famous mural where King William's troops are marching in battle array. The king is behind his troops, prodding them onward. The caption reads: "King William comforteth his troops." He is fortifying them for the coming conflict, so there is not much of our modern understanding of comfort in this meaning! Be this as it may however, there is certainly no ambiguity in the New Testament Greek meaning of *parakletos*. It has a forensic sense meaning

[13] Buzzard and Hunting, *The Doctrine of the Trinity,* p. 224.

"advocate." This comes out clearly in the only other place the word occurs in the New Testament, also from John's pen, in 1 John 2:1: "And if anyone sins, we have an advocate with the Father, Jesus Christ the righteous."

Here it is Jesus himself who is the advocate (*parakletos*) before the Father in heaven on behalf of his disciples on earth. As we will shortly see, this reference gives us the strongest clue as to what John means in his Gospel when he says: "But the helper [*parakletos*], the Holy Spirit, whom the Father will send in my name, he will teach you all things, and bring to your remembrance all that I said to you" (John 14:26). "When the helper [*parakletos*] comes, whom I will send to you from the Father, that is the Spirit of Truth, who proceeds from the Father, he will bear witness of me" (John 15:26). "But when he, the Spirit of Truth, comes, he will guide you into all the truth; for he will not speak on his own initiative, but whatever he hears, he will speak; and he will disclose to you what is to come" (John 16:13).

When Jesus first uttered these sayings to his disciples in the upper room, he was encouraging them by telling them they would not be left alone once he left them. Jesus had already been a paraclete to them; now "another helper" would instruct and be alongside, indeed even live within them, to help and guide.

To prepare our minds to accept that the NT goes beyond the OT revelation of the Spirit as God Himself in personal action, many Trinitarian commentators point out that there are two Greek words for "another." One word is *allos*, meaning "another of the same kind." The second Greek word for "another" is *heteros*, meaning "another of a different kind." Jesus promised "another [Greek *allos*] helper" rather than "another [*heteros*] helper." Many Trinitarians who want to see the helper as a third Person within the Godhead make much of this, alleging that Jesus promised "another-of-the-same-kind helper." That is, Jesus promised that the coming Spirit would be another just like himself, that is, another person. However, this is a very weak point. Leon Morris who himself believes in the Spirit as a third Person agrees that this is not strong exegesis: "The only catch in the reasoning is that not all Greek writers used the two words for 'other' strictly. Some did; some did not. It is not completely certain that John did (he uses *heteros* so rarely that we cannot be sure)."[14]

However, traditional Trinitarianism has understood this "other" helper to be a person, the third member of the Godhead, the Holy Spirit. It is not hard to see how this conclusion is reached, given the centuries of entrenched dogma that we have inherited. George Eldon Ladd is representative of this "orthodox" position that the Spirit here really is a separate person:

> The idiom John employs suggests that the Paraclete is a separate personality, more than the divine power in Old Testament thought. The word for spirit, *pneuma*, is grammatically neuter, and we would expect pronouns and adjectives, following the rules of grammatical agreement, to be in the neuter gender (so 14:17, 26; 15:26). Such correct agreement bears no witness either for or against the personality of the Holy Spirit. But where pronouns that have *pneuma* for their immediate antecedent are found in the masculine, we can only conclude that the personality of the Spirit is meant to be suggested. "But the paraclete, the Holy Spirit, which [*ho*] the Father will send in my name, he [*ekeinos*] will teach you all things" (14:26). The same language is found in 15:26: "the Spirit of truth which [*ho*] proceeds from the Father, he [*ekeinos*] will bear witness to me." The language is even more vivid in 16:13: "When the Spirit of truth comes, he [*ekeinos*] will guide you into all truth." Here the neuter *pneuma* stands in direct connection with the pronoun, but the masculine form rather than the "normal" neuter is employed. From this evidence we must conclude that the Spirit is viewed as a personality.[15]

Ladd's explanation that we "must" conclude that the Spirit is a personality seems to be very strong. Leon Morris would agree with Ladd for he states that the word *parakletos* "was applied to persons...in the first century it would be understood of a person. Certainly nobody then would have imagined that the word would denote a vague influence, a power flowing from God. Its use marks the Spirit as a Person."[16] (By the way, we applaud Morris' insistence on the method of "historical exegesis" here!) But let's

---

[14] Leon Morris, *Spirit of the Living God*, p. 36.

[15] Ladd, *A Theology of the New Testament*, p. 295.

[16] Morris, *Spirit of the Living God*, p. 35.

take a closer look.

Firstly, notice at the beginning how Ladd, in company with Morris and Packer, also prepares our minds to go beyond the Old Testament understanding of the Spirit of God: "The idiom John employs suggests the Paraclete is a separate personality, more than the divine power in Old Testament thought." So Ladd also wants us to believe that Jesus is now about to step outside all the parameters of the prophets and the Scriptures which he came to fulfill. This is a common assumption, namely that there is "progressive revelation," for in the Old Testament we have the New Testament concealed, and in the New Testament we have the Old Testament revealed. We do not deny that our Lord Jesus did come to bring fulfillment, even greater light and some "new wine for new wine skins," so to speak. But does "the idiom John employs suggest that the Paraclete is a separate personality" (a thought foreign to the Hebrew Bible)? Ladd recognizes that the Old Testament "Spirit of the Lord" is a metaphor for the power and word of God at work. But should we be so ready to assert that when we come to Jesus and the New Testament "the Spirit" means something essentially different and more?

Perhaps "the idiom" is just that, a particular form of expression called "personification." After all, the Hebrew mind was very good at personification. We often read of trees clapping, the sun running its orbit, the stars praising, the heavens talking, etc. in the Old Testament. In Proverbs 8:30 "Wisdom" is personified as "a master workman" and is said to have helped God to create the universe. No one would think for a moment that a real person named "Wisdom" is implied, except perhaps the Jehovah's Witnesses who say this was Jesus in his pre-human existence. One day I was talking to a Jehovah's Witness who said he believed that "Wisdom" really was Jesus with God in the beginning of the world. I then showed him Proverbs 8:12: "I, wisdom, dwell with prudence," and I asked him, "If Wisdom is Jesus then who is Prudence?" Quick as a flash and with a big smile on his face he said, "Ah, his dog!"

One can get into problems when one fails to understand the propensity of the Hebrew mind for personification. This acknowledged, it must be recognized that there are indeed instances where the Spirit of God is given personal traits. Take the instances where the Spirit is called the "hand" or "the finger of God" (see Ezek. 3:14; Luke 11:20). As what a man's hand performs is done by the man himself, just so what is done by the Spirit of God is done by

God Himself. But it must be asked: Was Jesus here using this regular Hebrew figure of speech called personification when he referred to the coming Spirit as the helper?

It would appear to me and certainly to Leon Morris, J.I. Packer, G. Ladd *et al* that more than mere metaphorical language is being employed when Jesus calls the coming Spirit the helper. Ladd's strong assertions that masculine pronouns which refer to the neuter Spirit (*pneuma*) mean "we can only conclude that the personality of the Holy Spirit is meant to be suggested" appear very convincing. And certainly in the popular mind it is considered a very strong argument, for whenever this topic comes up in discussion it is one of the very first "proof" texts offered: "But didn't Jesus say the Holy Spirit is a person by calling 'it' a 'he'?"

A little closer examination will, I think, clear up this popular misconception. Once again, we must keep the big picture in mind. Overall context is crucial. Jesus has just told the disciples he is leaving them. Nevertheless, he assures them "**I** will come to you" (John 14:18) in the form of the helping Spirit. It is appropriate, then, to rightly translate the masculine (*ekeinos*) as "that one," the "he" who is coming, when referring to the Spirit which is the helper: "When the helper comes...**that is** the Spirit of Truth...he..." (John 15:26). *There is an obvious interchange in Jesus' speech between Spirit and helper.*

If we keep this in mind and if for a moment we can divorce ourselves from the long hand of church tradition by not assuming this helper (also called "the spirit of truth" by Jesus) is a separate person from the Father and Jesus, we may equally faithfully translate these texts as follows:

> I will ask the Father, and He will give you another helper to remain with you unto the [new] age, the spirit of the truth, which the world cannot receive, because it does not see it or know it [neuter *auto* to agree with spirit]. But you know it [*auto*] because it [*auto*] remains with you and will be in you. I will not leave you orphans; I will come to you...But the helper, the holy spirit, which the Father will send in my name, it [masculine *ekeinos* to agree with the masculine subject *parakletos* but only translated "he" if the translator assumes a person is meant] will teach you all things and remind you of all things I spoke to you (John 14:15-18, 26).

Trinitarian scholars readily admit that here and "in the Greek text of John 16:13, the Holy Spirit (neuter) is assigned a masculine pronoun, possibly to emphasize the personal reality of the Spirit or the identification of the Spirit with the Paraclete."[17] We see then that the Spirit may be thought of equally as an influence, the Spirit of truth (cp. "the spirit of error" in 1 John 4:6 and "the spirit of the world" in 1 Cor. 2:12), or as the personal reality of Jesus himself behind the influence. Hence the interchange between the Spirit and the helper.

Given then the dilemma the translators face (will they say "it" or "he" when referring to the helper [masculine], which is the Spirit of truth [neuter]?) it all comes down to personal preference. Or does it? Perhaps the translators would be well advised to take the rest of the Scriptural evidence into consideration and not just rely on this one section in the Gospel of John. It would seem that the particular idiom used by Jesus here, i.e. "the helper," is a personification of the spirit of truth, and not a person *per se,* so that wider context ought to be the deciding factor. It is instructive that the fifth and only other occurrence of *parakletos* defines him as Jesus himself (1 John 2:1)! This suggests it is Jesus himself via his ministry from heaven who is projected to us in the power of God. The Trinitarian James Denny plainly acknowledges this to be so: "In 1 John 2:1 it is Jesus who is the Paraclete [Comforter], even after Pentecost, and even here (John 14:18), he says, 'I come to you.' *The presence of the Spirit is Jesus' own presence in Spirit.*"[18]

This wider Scriptural context must be taken into account when determining whether "the helper," that is, "the spirit of truth" is a separate person or a personification. *The language of the rest of the Bible does not fit the traditional notion of the Spirit as a third Person.* The Spirit is said to be given in different amounts or quantities. Jesus received it "without measure" (John 3:34) but individual believers receive a "supply" or a "provision of the Spirit of Jesus Christ" (Phil. 1:19). God is said to "provide you with the Spirit" (Gal. 3:5). This language has OT pedigree. One time God took of His Spirit from Moses and distributed it: "Then the LORD came down in the cloud and spoke to him; and He took of the spirit which was upon him and placed it upon the 70 elders. And it came

[17] *This Is My Name Forever: The Trinity and Gender Language for God,* ed. Alvin Kimel Jr., Downers Grove, IL: InterVarsity Press, 2001, p. 66.

[18] James Denny, "Holy Spirit," *Dictionary of Christ and the Gospels,* Edinburgh, T & T Clark, 1917, p. 742.

about that when the Spirit rested upon them, they prophesied" (Num. 11:17, 25). This has obvious implications and parallels for our interpretation of the events of Pentecost, which we will draw on shortly, after looking at one more OT story.

The Elijah story from 2 Kings also provides a background for understanding the Jewish significance of Pentecost and the coming of the Spirit. In the Hebrew Scriptures Elijah ascended bodily via a fiery chariot drawn by fiery horses (2 Kings 2:11). The prophet had promised to bestow on his disciple Elisha a "double share" of his enormous spirit. The test for Elisha would be whether he could actually witness his master's ascension. The narrative proclaimed that this "seeing" was accomplished, so Elisha walked away from that scene in the spirit and power of Elijah. The sons of the prophets affirmed this, for when Elisha returned to them they proclaimed, "the spirit of Elijah rests upon Elisha" (2 Kings 2:15). Elijah was known for his power to call down fire from heaven. He did this in a contest with the prophets of Baal on Mount Carmel (1 Kings 18:20-39). He had also prayed fire down on "a captain of fifty men with his fifty," and a second captain of fifty and his men, who had been sent to inquire about the status of the first group (2 Kings 1:9-12). In the folklore of Israel this fiery power belonged uniquely to Elijah.

The background and the obvious parallels to the ascension of Jesus and the Pentecostal outpouring of the Spirit in wind and fire are obvious. On the day of Pentecost God the Father took of the Spirit of the resurrected Lord Jesus and it came like a "rushing wind" and appeared like "tongues as of fire distributing themselves, and it rested on each one" of the disciples (Acts 2:2-3). As the elders received of Moses' spirit and prophesied, and as Elisha received a "double portion" of Elijah's spirit and went out in his master's power, just so — after Pentecost — do the disciples preach and go out in the spirit and power of their resurrected Lord to carry on his Gospel work.

In Jewish thought, then, Luke is saying that the risen Lord Jesus is greater than Moses and greater than Elijah. God's locus of activity is now on a new Israel, the body of believers. The Spirit of Christ now rests on the disciples and they will prophesy and go in power as they proclaim "the word." In Jewish parlance, there is no thought here that the Holy Spirit that Christ sends is the *third* member of the Godhead, any more than the spirit that God took from Moses, or the spirit that Elijah sent on Elisha, was a third member of the holy Trinity. In this same Hebrew way of understanding, we are to know that "to each one is given the manifestation of the Spirit for the common good" (1 Cor. 12:7). The helper which is the Holy Spirit of God describes the combined activity of the Father and the Son through their personal presence operating for our benefit. Jesus will not leave his disciples alone as orphans. But whereas they were used to him being with them personally, a new development is about to happen. God's presence and activity will be mediated to them through the resurrected Jesus as they preach his word. When the apostles set about preaching the word of the Gospel of the Lord Jesus they will know God's activity and presence working with them, helping them. In reality, when the apostles minister the word of Christ, it will be Christ himself being mediated through that Gospel-word to the world. Later, the apostle Paul will make this same identification of "the Spirit" with the risen Jesus: "Now **the Lord is the Spirit**...the Lord who is the Spirit" (2 Cor. 3:17-18), and "if someone comes and preaches another **Jesus** whom we have not preached, or you receive a different **spirit** which you have not received, or a different **gospel** which you have not accepted, you bear this beautifully" (2 Cor. 11:4). These verses make it quite clear that as far as Paul is concerned "the Spirit" describes the presence and activity of the risen Jesus, which is continuously mediated through the Gospel-word.

We might put it this way: The teaching of Jesus is backed by a guarantee that it will be continuously active in the lives of those who understand, believe and act on it. The words of Jesus will never pass away and they are, so to speak, heaven's permanent guarantee of God's and Jesus' presence with us day by day. Jesus has not become inactive but he is no longer with us visibly on earth. His Spirit, however, is an extension of himself to us in the interim until he comes back to earth when we will be able to see him literally.

Be Filled with the Spirit=Let the Word of Christ Dwell in You

One of the clearest places this parallelism between "spirit" and "word" is highlighted is in the well-known passages of Ephesians 5 and Colossians 3. In the first, the apostle instructs Christians to:

> **Be filled with the Spirit**, speaking to one another in psalms and hymns and spiritual songs, singing and making melody with your heart to the Lord; always giving thanks for all things in the name of our Lord Jesus Christ to God, even the

> Father; and be subject to one another in the fear of Christ. Wives, be subject to your own husbands, as to the Lord (Eph. 5:16-21).

The very same instructions and phrases appear in Colossians 3, except for the one obvious exception:

> **Let the word of Christ richly dwell within you**, with all wisdom teaching and admonishing one another with psalms and hymns and spiritual songs, singing with thankfulness in your hearts to God. And whatever you do in word or deed, do all in the name of the Lord Jesus, giving thanks through him to God the Father. Wives, be subject to your own husbands, as is fitting in the Lord (Col. 3:16-18).

It is quite evident that in the apostle's mind to be filled with the *spirit* is precisely *the same* thing as letting the *word* (teaching, message) of Christ direct our lives. This is simply to say that in John chapters 14 to 16 "the Spirit" that will come to help the apostles will be the post-resurrection revelation of Christ's message directed by the risen Christ to the world through the apostles. Their work is that of proclaiming the Gospel message of the risen Christ to the whole world (John 16:8-11). As in the Old Testament where being filled with "the spirit of wisdom" is equivalent to being filled with "the Spirit of God" (Ex. 31:3; 28:3), so in the New Testament to be filled with the Spirit of God is to have the mind or the word of Christ dwelling in us in "all wisdom" (Col. 3:18).

Earlier in this very Gospel of John, Jesus has already indicated that the work of the Spirit is identical to the "words of God": "For he whom God has sent speaks **the words of God**; for he gives **the Spirit** without measure" (John 3:34). Again Jesus says, "It is **the Spirit** that gives life; the flesh profits nothing; **the words** that I have spoken to you **are spirit** and are life" (John 6:63).

Commenting on these verses, Robert Hach says:

> The New Testament Jesus sees no dichotomy between the work of the Spirit and the work of language...Just as the Spirit (Greek *pneuma*, which literally means "breath") inspired the prophets and the apostles to speak the word of God (Eph. 3:5; 1 Thess. 5:19-20; 1 Pet. 1:10-12; 2 Pet. 1:20; 1 John 4:1-6), so to believe the words of the prophets and the apostles is to receive the Spirit (Gal. 3:2). The Spirit of God is, then, the *gospel-at-work,* the *gospel-come-to-life* within believing minds and hearts (2 Cor. 3:2-3, 17-18;

Eph. 4:21-24). The life which is "led by the Spirit" (Gal. 5:18) is a life that is governed by persuasion.[19]

These words appearing earlier in the Gospel of John (John 3:34 and 6:63) are the background and context of what Jesus says concerning "the helper...that is the spirit of truth" just before leaving the disciples. To receive the words of the Lord Jesus is to receive the Spirit of God, "for whoever is ashamed of **me and my words** in this adulterous and sinful generation, the Son of Man will also be ashamed of him when he comes in the glory of his Father with the holy angels" (Mark 8:38). *To receive and live by the words of Jesus is to receive Jesus himself.* It is often taught today that to become a Christian, all one must do is "receive Jesus into your heart" and you will be saved. The acid test as to whether I have "Jesus in my heart" is whether I have his *words* informing and empowering my life. If his Gospel-word is the motivating principle in my life, then I have the Spirit of God dwelling in me; indeed, I have the Father and the Son. Hence Paul's vigorous warning that if anyone fails to demonstrate the presence of the words of Christ in his life, he is devoid of understanding (1 Tim. 6:3).

We have only to read subsequent descriptions of the Spirit to verify this interpretation. A good example is found in Romans 8. Here Paul contrasts "the law of the Spirit of life" with "the law of sin and death" (v. 2). To walk (live) "according to the flesh" is to have one's "mind" set on death; but to have one's "mind" set on the "things of the Spirit" is to have God's peace (v. 5-6). If "the Spirit of God" dwells in us then we have "the Spirit of Christ" which is "Christ" (himself) in us (v. 9-10). Thus we have the equation: the Spirit of God *is* the Spirit of Christ *is* Christ himself *is* the "mind" controlled by the "law of the Spirit of life." When Paul elsewhere states that "God has not given us the spirit of fear, but of power and of love and of a sound mind" he is talking about a state of mind (2 Tim. 1:7). This is exactly what Jesus is talking about when he mentions the helper, which is the Spirit present in us. When we "keep his word" the Father and he himself will "make our abode with you" (John 14:23). All these are interchangeable ways of describing the same condition which all believers are meant to enjoy, and surely speak of the personal activity of God and of Christ in the believer, through the message/word of the resurrected Christ.

---

[19] R. Hach, *Possession and Persuasion,* p. 111.

Jesus says to the disciples, "When they deliver you up, do not be anxious beforehand about what you will say. Whatever will be given you at that time, speak, for **it is not you who speak but the Holy Spirit**" (Mark 13:11). Luke's version makes it clear that the Spirit speaking in the disciples is Christ himself: "Settle it therefore in your hearts not to meditate beforehand how to answer, for **I will give you speech and wisdom** which your adversaries shall not be able to resist or refute" (Luke 21:14, 15). In the third parallel passage in Matthew 10:20, it is "not you who speak, but it is **the spirit of your Father who speaks in you**." It is illuminating to find that "the Holy Spirit" of Mark 13:11 is "the spirit of your Father" in Matthew, and in Luke is Christ himself speaking. Simply put: [The] **Holy Spirit = "I"** (Jesus) **= the spirit of your Father**.

This wider context makes it unmistakably clear that *when Jesus speaks of the Holy Spirit he is speaking of the Father and himself in united action through the word.* This conforms to the exact statements of Jesus in John chapters 14 to 16: "**the Father** abiding in me does His works...He who believes in me, the works that I do shall he do also...**The Spirit of Truth**...abides with you, and will be in you...**I** will come to you...In that day you shall know that I am in my Father, and you in me, and I in you" (John 14:10, 17, 18, 20). Should not these verses in the Gospel of John be read in the wider context we have been considering? I am firmly convinced that they dovetail harmoniously with the rest of the Scriptural testimony concerning the Spirit of God as being the power and word and mind of God in action. Or to put the question even more pointedly, "Should the plain evidence of almost every part of Scripture be disturbed by a handful of verses in John's Gospel?" (as read out of harmony with the rest of Scripture).[20]

In sum so far then, there is no reason to divorce the statements of Jesus about "the helper" from the Old Testament foundational meaning of the Holy Spirit. Jesus' words and works were all performed by the anointing of God's Spirit. This is to say that his miracles were performed not because he was God but because God's wisdom and grace were fully operational through him. One would not argue that because Moses performed great signs and wonders he was therefore "God in the flesh." Why then must Jesus be God because he performs mighty miracles by the anointing of

---

[20] Buzzard and Hunting, *The Doctrine of the Trinity,* p. 222.

God's Spirit? The Old Testament prediction is that the Spirit of God would rest mightily on the Messiah: "And the Spirit of the LORD will rest on him, the spirit of wisdom and understanding, the spirit of counsel and strength, the spirit of knowledge and the fear of the LORD" (Is. 11:2).

Jesus the Messiah walked this earth with the Father's full authority and delegated power. God's Spirit, His Word, His breath, His life and His presence were mediated through His authorized Son. How wonderful to know that in Jesus of Nazareth we see a man fully indwelt by the Spirit of God. How much more so now that he is exalted and glorified in heaven at the Father's right hand should we not see his power at work in this world wherever his word is proclaimed? In this dark world we are "made partakers of the Holy Spirit" (Heb. 6:4-5) by sharing his word. Both the word of God and the Spirit are said to be the truth (cp. John 17:17 with 1 John 5:6). Thus, the helper which is the Spirit *is* Christ himself who says "**I** will come to you" (John 14:18).

If we recall the problem that existed in the Corinthian church and how Paul could not be personally there to deal with it, but could only be there "in spirit," we have the exact parallel with Jesus' promise of the helper. Jesus Christ is no longer with his disciples bodily, but now they have his word, his mind, his heart fortifying them, guiding them, because he is directing them from the Father's throne in the very power of God Himself.

Conclusion

A serious difficulty for those who believe the Holy Spirit is the third member of the Trinity, co-equal and co-eternal with the Father and the Son, is that the earliest post-apostolic church fathers say *nothing* of the Spirit as a distinct Person within the Godhead. Even the Trinitarian authors of *Jesus: A Biblical Defense of His Deity* acknowledge that "the last paragraph [of the Nicene Creed] was added in AD 381."[21] (This is the paragraph that says, "I believe...in the Holy spirit, the Lord and giver of life; who proceeds from the Father; who with the Father and the Son together is worshipped and glorified; who spoke by the prophets.") So, why did it take so long for the Church to formally declare that the Holy Spirit was the third Person in the Godhead?

---

[21] McDowell and Larson, *Jesus: A Biblical Defense of His Deity,* p. 84.

These authors make much of the fact that the early church fathers call Jesus "God" and therefore this is proof that Christians always believed in the Deity of Christ. They list Ignatius (died c. AD 110), Irenaeus (c. AD 125-200), Justin Martyr (AD 110-166) and Clement (died c. AD 101) in this group. They say that the burden of proof rests with those who deny Christ's full Deity to show that such testimony is not a telling argument in favour of the Trinity. I have already addressed this issue of silence earlier, and pointed out that later Trinitarian "orthodoxy" — in alliance with the Empire's political machinery — ruthlessly hunted out all "heretics" and erased their writings. We recall the story of the Nag Hammadi library. But for the defiance of one brave soul, we would never have known of the massive variety of positions within the Christian churches of the first few centuries. We also recall that various church councils following Nicea which did not support the line that eventually triumphed are not recognized and often not documented. We all know about Nicea, but what about the council of Rimini-Seleucia in AD 359 that reversed the earlier vote? So successful was "orthodoxy" that only the winners' story (their own "orthodox" story) survived. The writings of Arius himself do not survive; we have only fragments quoted by his opponents of what he is alleged to have taught. Yes, there are strong historical reasons as to why statements of others at the time are no longer extant. They were successfully expunged from the record.

However, for the moment, let us agree with the McDowells and Larsons *et al* who want us to believe in the Deity of Christ because the church fathers make clear statements to that effect. On their own reasoning, where is the personal Deity of the Holy Spirit? They will search in vain for any witness to the person and full Deity of the Holy Spirit in the early Fathers. These same church fathers do not call the Holy Spirit God. It is a damning piece of evidence that "No formal Trinitarian definition of the Holy Spirit appears until AD 381 at the Council of Constantinople...There is...no unbroken Trinitarian tradition linking us with the writings of the Apostles."[22] The only response in answer to this eloquent silence is to allege that "the early Fathers had no occasion to debate, defend, or define the deity and the personality of the Holy Spirit."[23] Thus, stunning silence is

---

[22] Buzzard and Hunting, *The Doctrine of the Trinity,* p. 227.

[23] Criswell, *The Holy Spirit in Today's World,* p. 14.

supposed to convince us that everyone believed in the Holy Spirit as a third member of the Godhead. This argument is circular. It sets out to prove its own assumptions, namely: If only the positive statements (in the absence of other recorded positions) of the church fathers prove they always believed that Jesus is God, why (on their own reasoning) does not the total silence of the church fathers that the Holy Spirit is God prove to Trinitarians that he does not exist as a third member of the Godhead?! As N.T. Wright correctly states:

> There are a great many things that we don't know in ancient history. There are huge gaps in our records all over the place. Only those who imagine that one can study history by looking up back copies of the London *Times* or the *Washington Post* in a convenient library can make the mistake of arguing from silence in matters relating to the first century.[24]

The Trinitarian assertion that the Holy Spirit is God Himself is surely impossible to maintain when we note that *nowhere* in Scripture is the Holy Spirit prayed to or worshipped (as in today's churches), *nowhere* is the Holy Spirit praised in song (as is typical in today's "worship" meetings), *nowhere* is the Holy Spirit said to send his personal greetings with those of the Father and the Lord Jesus to the churches when the apostles write their letters, and *nowhere* is the Holy Spirit given a personal name.

At the end of the last book in the Bible when the redeemed saints are in the presence of God and of Jesus Christ in glory is it not a strange omission that the third member of the Godhead has no seat of authority on the final throne? Some may point to "the seven Spirits who are before His throne" (Rev. 1:4). Criswell proffers this as a Trinitarian formula, or "doxology."[25] But a moment's reflection will dissolve this idea. Just a few verses later, Scripture defines the seven spirits as "seven lamps of fire burning before the throne" (Rev. 4:5), and again as the seven horns and seven eyes of the Lamb who had been slain (Rev. 5:6). In other words, the seven spirits do not refer to the Holy Spirit as a separate and full member of the Trinitarian Godhead at all. They are metaphorical descriptions of the qualities that the risen Lord Jesus now possesses at the Father's right hand. The Hebrew background to this shows that the Lord

---

[24] N.T. Wright, *Who Was Jesus?* p. 89.

[25] Criswell, *The Holy Spirit in Today's World,* p. 14.

Jesus is the Spirit-anointed Messiah who had been prophesied in the OT. In Isaiah the Messiah is prophesied to have a seven-fold anointing when the Spirit of the LORD rests on him, producing wisdom, understanding, counsel, strength, knowledge, righteousness and the fear of the LORD (Is. 11:2).

How strange that one who is alleged to be Almighty God Himself, a co-equal and co-eternal member of the "adorable Trinity" is not once prayed to, worshipped, or even given a personal name in either the NT Scriptures or the early church fathers! Serious omissions indeed. Some might counter that the Spirit's ministry is not to draw attention to himself "for he will not speak of himself." Even assuming the personality of the Spirit for the sake of argument, this reasoning is flawed, for Jesus also stated that his own ministry was to glorify his Father and yet this did not stop him from speaking about himself. Also, Paul says the apostles "do not preach ourselves but Christ Jesus as Lord, and ourselves as your bond-servants for Jesus' sake" (2 Cor. 4:5), but once again this stated goal of not proclaiming himself but only Jesus Christ did not stop Paul from giving heaps of personal biography throughout his writings. So, even assuming for argument's sake that the Spirit is God Himself, the third member of the Godhead, such biographical omission is rather odd.

Surely, it is much better to understand the language of the Spirit as helper in terms of personification, as this chapter has suggested. When Jesus says the Spirit will not speak out from himself, Jesus is using language of personification to convey the truth that any other message, any other word or spirit that purports to come from God will be immediately detected as false: All other gospel-testimony independent of Jesus and his apostles is unauthorized by God. In the same line Paul writes that "no one speaking by the Spirit of God says, 'Jesus is accursed'; and no one can say, 'Jesus is Lord,' except by the Holy Spirit" (1 Cor. 12:3). John warns concerning the "many false prophets" that "have gone out into the world" that "by this you know the Spirit of God: every spirit that confesses that Jesus Christ has come in the flesh is from God; and every spirit that does not confess Jesus is not from God" (1 John 4:2-3). All of which is to say that the evidence that the Spirit of God is at work after Jesus has ascended to the Father in heaven will be seen in the loyalty of Christians to the doctrine of the Father and the Son (1 John 2:22-23; 2 John 9). N.H. Snaith goes so far as to say that "the spirit of truth" should rather be translated "spirit of reliability, faith," or even "spirit which creates faith." "This involves translating *aletheia* [truth] in its Septuagint sense as equivalent to *emeth*, and not its Greek sense of truth as against a lie, or of reality as against appearance."[26] That "Spirit of Loyalty" is the spirit that is true and faithful to Christ and in this sense is said "not to speak of (i.e. independently) himself." This is not to say that the Bible never contrasts truth with error. It often does. Snaith is highlighting that there can be another dimension which helps our understanding of "the spirit of truth" — the idea that God's Spirit as helper will always be detected in that teaching/message true to Jesus' Gospel.

The second and third centuries shifted Jesus' and the apostles' understanding of the Spirit to "the third Person of the Godhead." This doctrine was a further radical paradigm shift away from Biblical monotheism. It is now time for radical re-evaluation and restoration to the Biblical concept of Spirit. If the terms "God the Son" and "the God-Man" currently used to describe our Lord Jesus are found in no Bible verse, just so the term "God the Spirit" represents a third- and fourth-century paganization of the Biblical teaching on the Spirit of God. Our modern Western understanding of the Holy Spirit as being a person in his own right is a classic case of the great difference between Church theology and Biblical theology.

When I look back on those days when I reasoned that the Spirit is a third member of the Deity because the Scripture shows the Spirit having personal qualities such as mind, emotion and will I feel ashamed. If only I had understood that the Bible is a Hebrew book my eyes would not have been so blurred. We must stop deifying "the Spirit" as a third person, co-equal and co-eternal God, and repent of our worship of a false god. This Nicene, un-Hebrew, extra-biblical doctrine of the Spirit as "the Lord and giver of life; who...with the Father and the Son together is worshipped and glorified" as the third member of a triune God is a distraction at best, and a false god at worst.

---

[26] Snaith, *The Distinctive Ideas of the Old Testament,* p. 181. Truth as the opposite of falsehood is also very much part of the NT witness.

Seven
ANOTHER HOPE

And the LORD God formed man of the dust of the ground, and breathed into his nostrils the breath of life; and man became a living soul (Genesis 2:7).

I clearly remember a certain definitive day when I was a little boy of just four years old. My father was a travelling salesman for Chandlers-AWA and was just leaving for work. He had just kissed my mum goodbye. As he was about to get in his car and drive off, I yelled out, "Daddy!" He had his hand on the car door and turned to me and said, "What?" I said, "Daddy, don't crash!" I remember his big smile and his assuring words. "No, Greg, I won't crash." It was just a few short weeks afterwards that my father was killed in a terrible car accident. It was not until years later that I learned from friends of the family that when not long after my dad's death they came to visit my mum, I was in the front yard swinging on the gate. The first thing I said to these visitors was, "My daddy is with Jesus in heaven!"

Children are often told that at death the soul is like a balloon whose string is cut so it can soar up into the sky and be with God. As a boy of four my theology was already aligned with the mainstream idea of the dead being alive in heaven as disembodied "spirits." My theology was already in agreement with W.A. Criswell, well-known American Baptist, who asks:

> Which is actually you? The house of clay in which you live or the spirit, the personality, that inhabits your body? When you die and we look upon your still, silent face in the casket, is that you we are looking upon? Are you dust? Is a corrupting corpse you? Do we bury you in the open grave? Surely not; you are something more than dust, corruption and decay. You are spirit, personality, quickening life.[1]

Are you a human being having a spiritual journey? Or are you a spiritual being having a human experience? To listen to the modern

---

[1] W.A. Criswell, *The Holy Spirit in Today's World*, p. 61.

consensus it is the latter. It is common-place to hear grieving relatives who are missing their loved ones say "So-and-so is up there in heaven now, looking down on us, and having a beer for us." As I write this the world has just witnessed what is alleged to have been the biggest ever funeral in history, that of the late Pope John Paul. The officiating cardinal Ratzinger made the statement that just as he had done from the Vatican window in life, the Pope is now standing at the window of heaven and pronouncing the blessing on all. This comment was repeated again and again in our media.

Author of *The Dying Experience and Learning How to Live* Mike Agostini relates the stories of those who have what are being called ADC's or after-death communications. He tells how Aussie singer/actress Olivia Newton-John asked her mum before she died to send her a message beyond the grave to indicate she really was all right. "Make the candles move, or flicker, or something," Olivia urged her still living mum. Olivia recalls how she sat with the body of her mum and felt "an incredible presence" in the room. The candles started to move enough to reassure her that her mum was there communicating. But suddenly, Olivia was called to the living room where family and friends were gathered. "You'll never believe what happened," they said. A candle in that room had just exploded with a fizzing sound right under the picture of Newton-John's mother.[2]

On a TV interview the same author told the story of a mother whose 16-year-old son had cancer but who wanted to assure his mother that once dead he would be fine and would prove it by communicating to her. After his funeral, the mother when entering her son's bedroom found the lights would often switch on and off, and she took this as a sign that her dead son was communicating with her that he was alive and well. She found that after some time, this mysterious phenomenon became less frequent. She took this as a sign that her boy knew he had gotten his message of reassurance through, and now he did not need to visit as frequently because he was off on other more necessary tasks in his after-life world.

As a pastor I once conducted a funeral for an old man who was adored by his family. He had been quite a character. Loved his football. One of his grandsons, who is a very sincere Christian

---

[2] Mike Agostini, *The Dying Experience and Learning How to Live,* Vaucluse Press.

believer, told me that he now imagined his grandfather up there in heaven youthfully kicking a football. I wondered how a spirit being can kick a footy. At least the tackles from the other players wouldn't hurt! No "hospital passes" to jolt up there!

How much of this understanding of the nature of man and what happens at death is biblical and how much is mythical, pure fantasy? One of the great German theologians of the last century was Rudolf Bultmann. Bultmann describes how Greek or Platonic influence infiltrated the early Church's understanding of the nature of man and death. Summarizing how Hellenism and Christianity united, Bultmann refers to the myth of the primal man. It goes like this:

> The primal man, a heavenly figure of light, had fallen under the power of demonic forces in pre-time. These powers had ultimately torn him apart and divided him up — dissolved into countless heavenly sparks of light. Now the human soul consisted of these preexistent heavenly sparks of light, which were imprisoned in human bodies. In other words, for the Gnostics the soul...was preexistent, of divine origin. But the demons here on earth watched zealously to see that human beings did not recall this divine origin. The demons endeavour to stupefy them and make them drunk, sending them to sleep and making them forget their heavenly home. Sometimes their attempt succeeds, but in other cases the consciousness of their heavenly origin remains awake. They know that they are in an alien world, and that this world is their prison. Hence their yearning for deliverance.[3]

It is easy to see then how the Greeks (and others like the Egyptians) believed that only at death could a man be free, for death returns the once preexistent spark of men's souls to its eternal home of light. Most of the mainstream church has great sympathy for this view today. Ask believers where their dead loved ones now are and they will say, "With the Lord in heaven, for 'to be absent from the body is to be present with the Lord.'" But is this the Biblical understanding? Has Gnostic myth replaced Biblical truth in our understanding of man and his destiny?

---

[3] Quoted in Kuschel, *Born Before All Time?* p. 137.

Man *Is* a Soul

In order to clear up the uncertainty regarding whether man has an "immortal soul" we turn to the Bible's account of our origins. The book of Genesis lays out the Hebrew understanding regarding man's original creation, his nature, his rebellion and his destiny. If man by nature has an immortal soul that cannot be destroyed but must escape the body at death to live on, either in fellowship with God or in eternal separation from God, then we will be given "the good oil"[4] here in the beginning. But it is right here that we come up with a big "snag." The stubborn fact is that there is not one passage to be found anywhere in the Bible that teaches that man has an immortal soul. True, many feel it is implied and we will shortly look at some of the passages that are used to formulate this impression. But from the start, let's see what the Hebrew Bible teaches concerning the nature and constitution of man.

Two verses in Genesis describe the creation of man. The first reads: "And God created man in His own image, in the image of God He created him; male and female He created them" (Gen. 1:27).

The words "image of God" used to describe man here have been subjected to curious manipulations throughout the centuries. Various meanings have been imported into the text. For instance, some who believe that God is a Trinity have assumed that man created in God's image must also be a tri-partite being of body, soul, and spirit (cp. 1 Thess. 5:23 where Paul speaks about Christian believers being preserved "body, soul and spirit"). Other commentators believe the words "image of God" must mean that since God is immortal, therefore man who is in God's image must also be immortal. Still others have seen "image of God" to mean that like his intelligent Creator, man has the ability to reason and he possesses moral values and conscience. And others develop this thought by saying that "in the image of God" means man has an eternal spirit capable of communion and fellowship with his Creator. It ought to be obvious that all these ideas, whilst appealing to our Western minds, are imported assumptions, for the text itself says nothing as detailed as these proposals. We need the light of other Scriptures to help us to understand exactly what man is.

---

[4] *The good oil* — the truth, with a hint of receiving it in confidence.

Fortunately we are not left to conjecture for too long, for in the next chapter we read: "Then the LORD God formed man of dust from the ground, and breathed into his nostrils the breath of life; and man became a living being [Heb. *nephesh,* soul]" (Gen. 2:7).

Here is God's definition of exactly what man is. Man became a "living soul" when God did two things. First, He formed (Hebrew *yatzar* means to form, shape, fashion, or mould) man's physical body from the dust (Hebrew *'aphar* means dry earth or fine crumbs of the earth) of the ground (Hebrew *'adamah* means red soil). Second, God breathed into Adam's body the breath of life and man became a living soul. Here then is the Hebrew Bible's explanation of what makes a man a "living soul": Body + breath of life = living soul. As this is the very first Bible verse containing the word "soul" as applied to man, its importance cannot be overstated. Notice that it does *not* say that man *has* a soul. Also, it does *not* say that God *gave* man a soul. Rather it says: Man *is* a soul. *It is the unique combination of the body and the breath of life which makes man a "living soul."* Any notion that man is made up of body *and* soul is ruled out. God did not put something of His immortal Self into man so that man became divine. Man is not part of God, not divine by nature. He is a living creature because God put into his nostrils the breath of life; that is, God animated him. Genesis 2:7 tells us that man came from the red soil of the earth. He is an earth-being, not a spirit-being from a distant star as Plato taught, nor a spark from the bottom of the pond as evolution teaches. His life force is direct from God, a sacred gift. Man is not a spirit being enjoying a human experience. Man is a human being on a spiritual journey.

Now readers of our English translations will perhaps be surprised to learn that the Hebrew word for "soul" (*nephesh*) in Genesis 2:7 has *already occurred four times* in the Hebrew Bible *before* this verse where it speaks of man:

"Then God said, 'Let the waters teem with swarms of living creatures [Heb. *nephesh*], and let birds fly above the earth in the open expanse of the heavens'" (Gen. 1:20).

"And God created the great sea monsters, and every living creature [Heb. *nephesh*] that moves, with which the waters swarmed after their kind, and every winged bird after its kind; and God saw that it was good" (Gen. 1:21).

"Then God said, 'Let the earth bring forth living creatures [Heb. *nephesh*] after their kind: cattle and creeping things and beasts of the earth after their kind'; and it was so" (Gen. 1:24).

"And to every beast of the earth and to every bird of the sky and to every thing that moves on the earth which has life [Heb. *nephesh*] I have given every green plant for food'; and it was so" (Gen. 1:30).

These verses distinctly say that fish, birds, animals and reptiles are "souls" as far as the Hebrew use of the word is concerned. (If the reader is interested to follow this a little further, then Gen. 2:19; 9:10, 12, 15, 16; Lev. 11:46; 24:18 will confirm this weighty conclusion. And in Rev. 16:3 we have an exact NT parallel where "every living soul [Greek *psuche*] in the sea died"; that is, every creature living in the ocean perished.) However, so deliberately has the word "soul" as applied to animals been kept from our English translations that we must wonder why. Why, for instance, did the translators of our King James Bible use the word "soul" almost exclusively for man and almost never for the animals? The answer surely is that these translators all believed in the inherent immortality of man, that man has an immortal soul. They ran into an unpleasant choice in Numbers 31:28 though: "And levy a tribute for the LORD from the men of war which went out to battle: one **soul** [Heb. *nephesh*] in 500, both of persons, and of the cattle, and of the donkeys and of the sheep."

Clearly the translators here were stuck on the horns of a dilemma. They could either call man a "creature," or the cattle and donkeys and sheep "souls"; they opted for the latter. All of which is to say that the Hebrew Bible makes no such arbitrary distinction, for in every case a "soul" is simply a "breathing being," the unique combination of the physical body and the breath of life, whether fish, bird, animal or man.

> The translators of our English versions have rendered us a disservice by concealing this fact. They were apparently so tied to the notion that the word "soul" must mean "immortal soul," the possession of man alone, that they were unwilling to reveal that "soul" is the common attribute of man and animal alike.[5]

---

[5] Anthony Buzzard, *What Happens When We Die?* Restoration Fellowship, 2002, p. 16.

So why make such a fuss about these details? To establish the critical point that neither man nor animals, according to our Hebrew Bibles, are bipartite creatures whose soul at death leaves the body (and continues to independently exist). That dualism which views man as having a physical body that is mortal, and an immortal soul, a spirit, housed in that "shell" is not a Hebrew concept at all. We will explore this point in more detail shortly. But for the moment let us establish the point that at death, an individual (whether animal or human) simply ceases to exist. The Bible's definition of death is this: "You are dust, and to dust you shall return" (Gen. 3:19).

Not: "The 'real you' is immortal, and to the eternal skies you will ascend"! The consistent testimony of all Scripture is: "Do not trust in princes, in mortal man [Heb. *'adam*]...his spirit [Heb. breath] departs, he returns to the earth; in that very day his thoughts perish" (Ps. 146:3-4). Notice, it is "he," the person himself, who "returns to the earth," and not just the body! To die in the Bible is to "sleep in the dust of the earth" (Dan. 12:2). In fact, in death man loses the ability to relate to God, for "The dead do not praise the LORD" (Ps. 115:17); rather they "go down into silence." And, "There is no mention of You [God] in death; in Sheol who will give You thanks?" (Ps. 6:5). At death, the human yields, or God withdraws, the breath or the spirit of life and the entire person dissolves: "You take away their spirit [Heb. *ruach,* breath]; they expire, and return to their dust" (Ps. 104:29). Notice again that it is "they" themselves, the whole persons who "return to their dust." In fact, in Hebrew understanding, when a person dies it is the soul that is dead: "The soul that sins, it shall die" (Ezek. 18:4, 20). To the Hebrew then the "soul" is the individual, either living or dead. Paul carries this kind of thinking into the NT where he writes "there will be tribulation and distress for **every soul of man** who does evil, of the Jew first and also of the Greek, but glory and honour and peace **to every man** who does good, to the Jew first and also to the Greek" (Rom. 2:9-10). Again, "soul" is nothing more and nothing less than the whole person. Rather than returning to heaven at death, the "soul," the person himself/herself, returns to the dust of the earth from which he/she was created.

Let me simply reinforce this point here by quoting three distinguished modern Bible scholars. Emil Brunner: "Not my body dies; *I* die." Karl Barth: "Death means the radical negation of life and therefore of human existence." Helmut Thielicke: "The total person is extinguished in death."

As for immortality, the Old Testament has no distinct word for it. In the New Testament, three Greek words which correspond to the concept occur a total of 17 times: *athanasia,* "immortality"; *aphtharsia,* "incorruptibility"; *aphthartos,* "incorruptible." In his recent monograph on the subject, Murray Harris observes:

> these words never occur [in the Bible] in connection with "soul" or "spirit"...[In every case where they are applied directly to humans (Rom. 2:7; 1 Cor. 15:42, 50, 52-54), the reference is to a future state.]...The concept of the "immortality of the soul" ill accords with the tenor of the New Testament teaching and therefore the expression deserves no place in Christian terminology...Whereas Plato saw immortality as the natural property of all human souls, the New Testament regards it as a conditional as well as a future possession. According to Paul...it is "those who belong to Christ," not all who are in Adam, who at Christ's coming will be made alive by a resurrection transformation that issues in immortality (1 Cor. 15:22-23, 42, 52-54).[6]

In utter contrast to our popular notions the Bible unequivocally states that God alone "has immortality" (1 Tim. 6:16). In Romans 1 we have a contrast between "the glory of the incorruptible God" and "corruptible man and birds and four-footed animals and crawling creatures" (v. 23). Man, therefore, is not in God's immortal class. Rather, man is put in the same class as the birds, animals and crawling creatures that perish! "For the fate of the sons of men and the fate of beasts is the same. As one dies so dies the other; indeed, they all have the same breath and there is no advantage of man over beast" (Eccl. 3:19-20). The Tempter wanted man to believe otherwise from the very beginning, of course. He said, "You will not surely die! For God knows that in the day you eat from it your eyes will be opened, and you will be like God" (Gen. 3:4-5). Funny thing is, that in spite of all the clear evidence to the contrary, man still chooses to believe this Satanic lie by clinging to the notion that he is immortal. The clear choice then is whether to believe God's word: "For you are dust, and to dust you shall return" or to believe

---

[6] Murray Harris, *Raised Immortal*, quoted in Warren Prestidge, *Life, Death and Destiny*, Auckland, New Zealand: Resurrection Publishing, p. 13.

the Devil's lie: "You shall not surely die" for you are immortal like God. Only one option is true. The New Testament message is that immortality is not an inheritance we get naturally from Adam, but a gift bequeathed — at the Second Coming — to the Christian through the second Adam who is Christ Jesus.

The crucial importance of this difference should not escape any thinking Bible believer. There has been a subtle but damaging shift away from the Bible's emphasis on the resurrection of the dead at Christ's Second Coming, to what happens to the individual at death: "When I die what happens to me? What will I find on the 'other side'?" J.A.T. Robinson notes that this paradigmatic shift in popular Christianity has landed us poles away from the New Testament message:

> For in the New Testament, the point around which hope and interest revolve is not the moment of death at all, but the day of the *Parousia,* or the appearance of Christ in the glory of his Kingdom...The centre of interest and expectation continued, right through the New Testament, to be focused upon the day of the Son of man and the triumph of his Kingdom in a renovated earth. It was the reign of the Lord Jesus with all his saints that engaged the thoughts and prayers of Christians, not their own prospect beyond the grave. The hope was social, and it was historical. But as early as the second century AD there began a shift in the centre of gravity which was to lead by the Middle Ages to a very different doctrine. Whereas in primitive Christian thinking the moment of the individual's decease was entirely subordinated to the great day of the Lord and the final judgment, in later thought it is the hour of death which becomes decisive.[7]

From beginning to end, the apostolic hope centred around the corporate resurrection of the dead at Christ's Second Coming (his *Parousia*). There was no belief that an individual upon death would go immediately into the presence of God. The message of the Old Testament is that the dead know nothing at all (Ecc. 9:5), and "many of those who sleep in the dust of the ground will awake, some to everlasting life [life in the new age], but others to disgrace and everlasting contempt" (Dan. 12:2). Jesus repeated this message

---

[7] J.A.T. Robinson, *In the End God*, London: SCM Press, 1950.

in the New Testament: "Do not marvel at this; for an hour is coming, in which all who are in the tombs shall hear his voice, and shall come forth; those who did the good deeds to a resurrection of life, those who committed the evil deeds to a resurrection of judgment" (John 5:28-29).

Where are all the faithful dead now? According to the Bible, the great heroes of God such as Abraham, Moses, David, *et al* are still in the ground awaiting the voice of the returning Lord Jesus to call them back to consciousness: "All these died in faith...[and] did not receive what was promised...so that apart from us [New Testament believers] they should not be made perfect" (Heb. 11:13, 39-40). "Brethren, I may confidently say to you regarding the patriarch David that he both died and was buried, and his tomb is with us to this day...for it was not David who ascended into heaven" (Acts 2:29, 34). David's "soul" did not ascend into heaven, says Peter on the day of Pentecost, after Jesus himself had gone into heaven! "David," the person himself, is still dead!

Job understood this basic truth: "And as for me, I know that my Redeemer lives, and at the last He will take His stand on the earth. And though worms destroy this body of skin; yet in my flesh I shall see God: Whom I myself shall behold, and whom my eyes shall see and not another. Oh, how my heart yearns for this!" (Job 19:25-27).

Believing the promise of God, Job knows that at the end of this age he will be raised up bodily to behold the glory of God. In the meantime, in death, he will not see the glory of God. Job does not yearn for death so he can immediately go to heaven and see his Redeemer. No, he yearns for the day at the end of the age when he will be resurrected to this glorious new consciousness. Only then will he "see God." Job is not now seeing God in the glory because he himself is without consciousness in the ground.

The heroes of the faith are not in heaven. We all together, both Old and New Testament believers, will be raised "at Christ's coming [Greek *parousia*]" (1 Cor. 15:23). With this apostolic perspective, we are in a position to see how seriously the popular notion of "souls in heaven" undermines the hope of the corporate resurrection at Christ's Second Coming. It has robbed the Church of its powerful eschatological hope. (Eschatology is the study of the last things, the end time.)

The all-important moment of the coming of Christ to establish his Kingdom has been replaced by the moment of the individual's death. The common understanding of this matter is therefore not recognizably Christian by New Testament standards, and on a question so central to the faith! History shows, however, that rather than admit this, we persist with the illusion that a satisfactory compromise can be achieved between original Christianity and its later transformation. There is an unwillingness to disturb tradition.[8]

The Dying "Thief" on the Cross

There are a number of Scriptures that seem to teach the popular view of "immortal souls" already being in heaven. Let's take a look at those verses that are often appealed to. What about the dying "thief" on the cross? He prayed, "'Jesus, remember me when you come in your kingdom!' And he said to him, 'Truly, I say to you, today you shall be with me in Paradise'" (Luke 23:42-43). At first glance this may give the impression that at death this penitent thief would be "today" enjoying conscious fellowship with Christ in Paradise, that is, in heaven. But on closer inspection there is another interpretation which harmonizes this verse with the rest of the Bible.

First, notice that the criminal is not even asking about life after death, as we understand it. He is asking for assurance that he will be saved when Jesus comes back as King to introduce his promised Kingdom on earth. "Jesus, remember me when you come in your kingdom!" he asks. This dying man is expressing in the strongest possible faith terms that contrary to all appearances in the hour of his rejection, Jesus really is the Messiah of God. In Jewish minds, including those of Jesus and his apostles, the Kingdom of Messiah was always a future day of glory, when God's people would be resurrected and enter the life of the Age to Come.

In the previous chapter Luke records Jesus' own words about this. He promised his disciples, "I will not drink of the fruit of the vine from now on until the kingdom of God comes" (Luke 22:18). And just a few verses later he again says to the disciples, "You are those who have stood by me in my trials; and just as my Father has covenanted to give me a kingdom, I covenant with you that you may eat and drink at my table in my kingdom, and you will sit on thrones administering the twelve tribes of Israel" (Luke 22:28-30). The Kingdom was always a future event, never the present possession of dead saints already in heaven. The word "Paradise" is a classic

[8] Buzzard, *What Happens When We Die?* p. 40.

Jewish expression of this coming Kingdom. It refers to the hope that all that man lost in the Garden of Eden through Adam's sin will be restored when Messiah comes. What a magnificent faith this dying thief expresses to Jesus! The criminal on the other side of Jesus is still hurling insults at Jesus; the crowd around the cross is jeering, "He saved others, let him save himself"; the soldiers under the cross are callously gambling for Jesus' last possessions; the religious leaders of Israel when they hear Jesus cry to God say, "Let us see if God will have him now!" and above his head Pilate had written a mocking inscription: "This is the King of the Jews." Jesus is dying abandoned by all. But in this dreadful hour, the penitent thief is Jesus' only encouragement. He looks forward and sees Jesus as the Messiah vindicated as God's King, the ruler of the promised New Age!

But what about the difficult word "today"? Jesus promised this man, "Today you shall be with me in Paradise." There is a disputed point in the original Greek text here. Because the Greek texts have very little punctuation it is a matter of personal choice where the English translators put their commas, full stops, paragraph breaks, etc. In other words, does the text read: "Truly I say to you, today you shall be with me in Paradise?" Or does it read: "Truly I say to you today, you shall be with me in Paradise?" Whilst the Greek is ambiguous, fortunately we are not left to conjecture when we take the rest of the Scriptural testimony into account. According to Jesus, he would not be in Paradise when he died, "for just as Jonah was three days and three nights in the belly of the sea monster, so shall the Son of Man be three days and three nights in the heart of the earth" (Matt. 12:40)! Between his death and resurrection, Jesus locates himself "in the heart of the earth." Paul tells us that Christ when he died was in "the abyss" (Rom. 10:7), which is not Paradise in Bible thinking. And on the day of Pentecost, Peter states that Jesus had been in "hades" and would have completely decayed there, were it not for the fact that God the Father raised him again on the third day (Acts 2:27, 31). Hades is the place of the dead — "gravedom." Again, this is not Paradise! Furthermore, even on the day of his resurrection, Jesus' firm testimony is that he had *not yet* ascended to the Father (John 20:17).

How then can it be thought that Jesus could offer the thief a place in Paradise that very day before his own resurrection? We can be sure that Jesus did not mean he went to Paradise with the thief the very day they both died. In fact, there are a number of times in the Bible when, for added emphasis, the speaker says, "I say to you today..." For instance, in solemn declaration, Moses says "I declare to you today that you shall surely perish" (Deut. 30:18). And Paul, also to stress the gravity of his words, says, "Therefore, I testify to you this day, that I am innocent of the blood of all men" (Acts 20:26). It would appear then, that to give this agonized thief the most solemn of promises, Jesus said, "Truly I say to you today, you shall be with me in Paradise."

In spite of all the Scriptural evidence to the contrary, some have proposed that Paradise here was actually in the world of the departed spirits. Anthony Buzzard makes the point about paradise:

> But the paradise of Scripture is found not in the heart of the earth, but in the restored garden of Eden, which contains the tree of life: "To him who overcomes, I will give to eat of the tree of life which is in the midst of the paradise garden of God" (Rev. 2:7; 22:2). No one would propose that the tree of life is growing in the realm of the dead![9]

Where Are Elijah and Enoch Now?

On the surface of things it might appear to the casual reader that there are two historical exceptions to the rule that all men have died and descended straight to the grave. It will be asked, where are Elijah and Enoch, if as the Bible seems to suggest they went straight up to God in heaven, not seeing death? Was not Elijah transported alive by the fiery horse-drawn chariot straight up into heaven? And was not Enoch taken up so that he should not see death; and he was not found because God took him up; for he obtained the witness that before his being taken up he was pleasing to God (Heb. 11:5)?

The commonly held idea that Enoch is alive in heaven now, seems to fit the first and apparently natural reading of this text. However, upon deeper reflection and further reading of the biblical record it will be seen that this notion represents an importation of Platonic philosophy.[10]

---

[9] *Ibid.*, p. 56.

[10] Readers wishing to take an in-depth look at this interesting topic may refer to *Focus on the Kingdom,* Volume 9, No. 2 & 3, Nov & Dec 2006, at focusonthekingdom.org. The following represents a precis of that excellent article.

Before looking at the actual text itself we firstly observe that Enoch is included in a "hall of fame" that is a list of many outstanding heroes of faith. Then the writer states, "All these died in faith, without receiving the promises" (Heb. 11:13). Every single one of these folks — including Enoch — *died.* When it comes to the question of death the writer to the Hebrews allows no exceptions: "**ALL** these **DIED**."

The author goes on to list other men and women of faith. Again, he sums up his consistent message: "And what more shall I say? For time will fail me if I tell of Gideon, Barak, Samson, Jephthah, of David and Samuel and the prophets...All these, though well attested through their faith, did not receive what was promised, because God had provided something better for us, so that apart from us they should not be made perfect" (11:32, 39-40).

There is no hint here that either Enoch or Elijah the prophets are now immortal in heaven and are enjoying their reward "apart from us." Both these men were supernaturally "removed," but it is an unwarranted leap to suggest they were taken up to the throne of God, as we shall now see.

Elijah

The year Elijah was supernaturally lifted up and carried off in a whirlwind with the fiery chariot of God can be fixed at 852 BC. This was the year when Jehoram, son of Ahab began to reign over the northern kingdom of Israel (2 Kings 1:17; 3:1). When these verses are read it will be noted that there was another king Jehoram who reigned jointly in the southern kingdom of Judah with his father king Jehoshaphat. We know that this Jehoram became sole king of Judah in 848 BC after Jehoshaphat died (2 Kings 8:16). So from the time of Elijah's disappearance in 852 until 841 BC there was a Jehoram in Judah and a Jehoram in Israel. They were in fact brothers-in-law.

Jehoram of Judah turned to idolatry (2 Chron. 21:11). Now read this carefully: In 842 BC, a year before he died, and *ten years after Elijah had gone,* Jehoram of Judah *received a letter from Elijah* (2 Chron. 21:12-15)! *Elijah was still alive on the earth, still active for God ten years after he had been taken up in the miraculous whirlwind!*

In 852 BC Elijah "went up by a whirlwind to heaven" (2 Kings 2:11). The prophets thought he must have been dropped on some mountain or in some valley and fifty men searched for him for three days without success (2 Kings 2:17). They clearly did not think Elijah was next to God's throne in heaven. They expected he had been relocated some place elsewhere on earth. And as it turns out, Elijah had been transported through the sky to some other earthly location.

There may be a NT parallel in the miraculous snatching away of Philip from the eunuch (Acts 8:39). On this occasion Philip "found himself at Azotus" (v. 40). Similarly, Elijah was deposited in a secret place, known only to God, where he continued to exercise a prayerful and watchful concern over the affairs of Israel and Judah, as his letter to Jehoram confirms. (God had done this kind of thing, you may recall, with the body of Moses.) Elijah broke his silence after ten years of secrecy. We are told no more. The manner of his death, the place of his death, we are not told. The next time he "appears" in the biblical record is Matthew 17 where the three disciples see him in *vision* form with Moses talking with Jesus (Matt. 17:9). But according to the author to the Hebrews Elijah "died" in faith as did all the prophets like Moses, and now awaits the resurrection at Christ's return. Anyway, we have the unequivocal teaching of Jesus before his own resurrection that "no one has ascended into heaven" (John 3:13).

What Then of Enoch?

Doesn't the record state that Enoch was transfigured (or transferred) to be with God in heaven? Is he an exception? Genesis says, "And Enoch walked with God; and he [was] not, for God took him" (Gen. 5:24). The Hebrew text has no main verb and simply says, "and he not, for God took him." The other verb "took" is a common Hebrew verb (*laqah*) and means to "take, take away, remove, carry off." Its usage covers the "taking away" of purchases from a market, of a woman from her father's house through marriage, or life by violence. This last meaning bears further investigation, for whenever a person's life (*nephesh*) is the object in every OT instance the meaning is "to take away life, to kill."[11] Let's see.

Elijah uses *laqah* to refer to his opponents' plans to seek his life (*nephesh*)" "to **take it away**" (1 Kings 19:10, 14). The psalmist

---

[11] Robert Bratcher, *Bible Translator* 34, no. 3, July 1983, p. 337.

says, "They schemed to **take away my life**" (Ps. 31:13). Ezekiel says that if a sword comes and *takes a person's life* from them, "he is **taken away** in his iniquity" (Ezek. 33:6). Jonah prays to God, "O Lord, **take away** my **life**" (Jon. 4:3) and Elijah also prayed, "O Lord, **take away** my **life**; I am no better than my fathers before me" (1 Kings 19:4). In these last two examples God may be the one who "takes away" being or life.

However, the verb *laqah* does not carry the sense of killing or destruction in every instance of its usage. God Himself says that in His anger he gave a king and in His wrath He has *taken* him *away* (Hos. 13:11; see also Ps. 73:24; 49:15). So we see that *laqah* does not always mean destroyed or killed.

Putting this evidence together, we note that the phrase "God took him" from Genesis 5:24 is not unique. It is a common Hebrew idiom, and would not of itself suggest a unique experience for Enoch. A Hebrew reader of the OT would understand the phrase "God took him" to imply an intervention by God, probably by death, but not necessarily so. More than the phrase itself would be needed to indicate that Enoch bypassed death and was removed by God up into His heaven. The OT itself gives us no further information about Enoch's whereabouts, except to say that "All the days of Enoch were three hundred and sixty-five years" (Gen. 5:23).

It is the Greek translation of the Hebrew made around 250 BC called the Septuagint (LXX) that expands the Genesis reading. The LXX reads Genesis 5:24 this way: "He was not found because God transferred him." The "he not" of the Hebrew text has become "he was not *found*" and the "God took him" has been nuanced to "God *transferred* him." This translation goes beyond the original Hebrew but need not necessarily mean more, as we will now see. The Greek word rendered "transferred" (*metatithemi*) means to place or position differently, change positions in respect of opinions, relocate, re-site, transfer. It is often used of relocating boundary markers, that is transferring a neighbour's landmarks (see Deut. 27:17; Prov. 23:10; Hos. 5:10, etc.). It can be used of changing allegiances (1 Kings 21:25; 20:25, LXX). It can be used of relocating mountains (Ps. 45:3; Is. 29:14, LXX), or of displacing people and relocating them. In the NT it appears as: "Jacob died, he and our fathers, and they were **transferred** to Shechem" (Acts 7:16). Or, "I am astonished that you are **transferring** so quickly to another gospel" (Gal. 1:6). Or, "The priestly office being

transferred, a **transfer** of law of necessity also occurs" (Heb. 7:12) And of course, "By faith Enoch was **transferred**...God **transferred** him" (Heb. 11:5).

Thus, usage of the verb in the LXX and in the NT strongly suggests that we understand it in Genesis 5:24 (LXX) as God's transferral of Enoch from one place to another site or location. It is NOT the word for transfiguration or transformation and does not speak of being taken up to immortality. We have seen that Elijah was transferred from one earthly location to another in Palestine. Was Enoch similarly transferred?

We note that Hebrews prefaces its quotation with "Enoch was by faith transferred, not to see death." The whole chapter tells us what mighty deeds were accomplished by its heroes of faith, and here we are told that Enoch accomplished something mighty by means of his faith: he was transferred, not to see death. NOTE, it does NOT say he was transferred up to God in heaven. It clearly says the purpose he was transferred was that he might "not see death." What does this mean?

There are a few clues. The same phrase occurs in Luke 2:26 where the prophet Simeon saw the infant Messiah as God had promised him. Simeon holds the child up in his arms and now declares that he is ready to "see death." Simeon prays to God that he is now ready to die in peace. Thus, to "see death" is the opposite of to "see life."

Jesus says that the one who does not obey him will "not see life" but will experience "the wrath of God abiding on him" (John 3:36). He also promises that if anyone keeps his word, "he will in no way see death eternally" and in the next verse speaks of "tasting of death" (John 8:51-52).

We may ask then, in what sense did Enoch not see, experience, or taste death? Was it a deferment of natural death like Simeon's? This would not seem the natural sense because Enoch only lived 365 years in a generation where this was considered very young. Was it an avoidance of experiencing the wrath of God which visited death on the generation that Enoch prophesied against? (i.e., eternal death, the second death of John 8:51-52 and Rev. 20:14?). Possibly.

One suggestion has been that Enoch faced a violent death from his wicked generation and that God rescued him from such a dreadful fate. Enoch seems to have been a fearless prophet who told his generation of the coming judgement (Jude 14-15). Perhaps he was translated or transferred from one place to another (just as Elijah evidently had been) so that he should not see a violent martyr's death from that violent people? Possibly.

One thing, however, is certain. Whatever in reality happened to Enoch, whatever Genesis 5:24 and Hebrews 11:5 mean, ascent into heaven is not claimed for Enoch in either Old or New Testaments. How can we be so sure? Simply because the writer to the Hebrews tells us that Enoch died with all the other heroes of faith. Enoch has not yet received his reward. He is now asleep awaiting the resurrection when Christ returns.

If Enoch is the exception to the rule, then a number of axiomatic scriptural affirmations are proven to be false. First, Paul's statement that through Adam's transgression "death spread to all men" and that "death reigned from Adam to Moses" is false (Rom. 5:12, 14). Paul makes no exceptions, Enoch not withstanding — all men died between Adam and Moses! We also know that by the end of the apostolic first century, no other human being apart from Jesus the Messiah had been resurrected from death to immortality. Before his own death Jesus' own belief was that "no man has ascended up to heaven" (John 3:13). Christ was "the first fruits of those who have fallen asleep" (1 Cor. 15:23). Jesus was "the firstborn from the dead" (Col. 1:18). It is only "after" he returns "at his coming" that "those who belong to Christ" will be raised to immortality and receive the promised reward (1 Cor. 15:23). Between Christ's resurrection and second coming, all saints are "asleep in Jesus" (1 Thess. 4:14). This includes all the OT saints, as Hebrews teaches. David himself "has not ascended into heaven" and is still dead and buried, "and his tomb is with us to this day" (Acts 2:29). The first and so far, only human being ever to ascend bodily into heaven is Jesus himself. This is clear. Axiomatic even.

Second, those who have died have forever perished, unless there is a resurrection (1 Cor. 15:18). Immortality is a gift given to the faithful only when Christ returns and raises them from death (1 Cor. 15:51-54; 1 Thess. 4:13-17; John 5:29, etc.) The NT Church held that resurrection at Christ's return was our only hope of entering God's promised kingdom. The idea that Enoch and Elijah could have preceded Jesus Christ into ascension glory is an unbliblical and Christ-denying notion that must be dropped. The idea that human souls even now enter God's glory in heaven apart from the resurrection that inaugurates Messiah's Kingdom is a Platonic invention with no biblical basis. Elijah and Enoch, according to the Scriptural record, both died, even though they experienced a miraculous transference by God during their lifetimes.

Moses and Elijah on the Mount of Transfiguration

In order to maintain belief that souls are conscious after death some appeal to the experience that Peter, James and John had with Jesus on the Mount of Transfiguration. Up on the mountain, Jesus "was transfigured before them; and his face shone like the sun, and his garments became as white as light. And behold, Moses and Elijah appeared to them, talking with him" (Matt. 17:2-3).

Luke even tells us the topic of conversation: they "were speaking of his departure which he was about to accomplish at Jerusalem" (Luke 9:31).

Does this not prove that Moses and Elijah are now alive with God in heaven? The key is found as the three disciples are descending the mountain. Jesus charges them, "Tell **the vision** to no one until the Son of Man has risen from the dead" (Matt. 17:9).

On the word of Jesus then, what the disciples saw was *a vision*. A vision is not actuality. And like other visions in Scripture, neither is this one meant to be taken as historical fact occurring in the first century literally. Visions in the Bible normally depict prophetic outlines of future events in God's program for the ages.

This is exactly how Peter later remembers this vision on the mountain. Peter says that when they were on the mount of transfiguration they saw "the power and coming [Greek *parousia*] of our Lord Jesus Christ" (2 Pet. 1:16-18). That word *parousia* is the great New Testament word for the Second Coming of Jesus Christ, when he returns to earth to set up God's promised New Age. The whole context of 2 Peter 1 is commentary on the amazing vision at the transfiguration and promises with certainty that Jesus Christ is coming again to inaugurate the Kingdom of God (see 2 Pet. 1:11: "the eternal kingdom" and v. 9: "the day dawns"). And in the middle of Peter's discussion where he is bringing assurance and hope to the persecuted Christians concerning the reality of the return of King Jesus, he mentions the mount of transfiguration, the vision of Jesus appearing in his glory. It was, Peter says, a vision where they not only heard about the imminent death Jesus was facing in Jerusalem (Mark 9:31), but where they also experienced the glory of the *parousia*.

In some wonderful way, on this mount of transfiguration, God let these disciples see in vision form the coming glorious Kingdom of Christ on earth. In that Kingdom, the dead saints like Moses and Elijah will be raised up again. Abraham himself will be there, along with Isaac and Jacob (Matt. 8:11). Indeed, all those who have this hope in Christ will actually be there and talking with Jesus just as Moses and Elijah did in this vision on the mount!

It is certain that Moses and Elijah are not already consciously enjoying the glory of God, for as we have seen it is an axiomatic principle that all the Old Testament heroes of faith have died "without receiving the promises," and "apart from us they [will] not be made perfect" (Heb. 11:13, 40). Those who have already died in faith do not receive immortality until the *parousia.* It is not taught here that Moses and Elijah enjoy a post-mortem existence in heaven.

Samuel and the Witch

To support the notion that OT prophets and saints are now in a state of disembodied consciousness, the account of the witch at Endor summoning up the deceased "Samuel" to deliver a message to King Saul in his time of desperation is often cited. The facts are given in 1 Samuel 28 and 1 Chronicles 10. But the commentators disagree as to the interpretation of those facts: Was it really the "spirit" of the dead Samuel, or was it a deceiving demonic spirit impersonating Samuel that appeared?

We note the following. Samuel really was dead (1 Sam. 28:3). Unless it can be shown that Samuel had not dissolved in the dust of the ground as is the destiny of all men, we have to take it that he really was dead and buried (v. 3). In the words of the southern American, "The de-yad are de-yad!" And the dead know nothing (Ecc. 9:5). Some commentators suggest that whoever it is who is conjured up as "Samuel" here, it is significant that the text does not use the normal Hebrew word for "spirit of the dead" (*'obh*). Rather we are told that the witch sees "a god" (*elohim*), or as the NASB translates it, she sees "a divine being coming up out of the earth" (v. 13). The witch describes this being as "an old man" who "is wrapped with a robe" (v. 14). King Saul bows before "Samuel" and a conversation between these two ensues — whether via the witch or without the medium is not clear.

So is this "Samuel" really the spirit of the dead prophet or is he another personage doing an impersonation of Samuel? Warren Prestidge (whose book I have quoted with approval throughout this chapter) believes that this really is the dead Samuel come up. Samuel's appearing "is presented as a 'one-off' work of God." Prestidge quotes W. Beuken, who says that Samuel "does not come as a dead ghost...but as a prophet of the living God." For Prestidge and Beuken, the clinching part is that "Samuel" really does deliver the true message of God to King Saul. Prestidge hastens to add that "the account gives no credence to spiritism, nor does it say anything at all about the death state, except that there, also, God is in control."[12] (Although the text does not say it, the more likely explanation of the remarkable resemblance to Samuel [his appearance of old age and his "wearing" a prophet's mantle] is that the witch sees a vision. After all, the disciples on the mount of transfiguration were enabled to "see" Moses and Elijah and "hear" them talking with Jesus. Certainly, it is not uncommon for spiritists to go into trance-like states and report all manner of sights.)

I have difficulty with Prestidge's conclusion here, even though I recognize the truth that God is sovereign and could, if He so wished, bring up Samuel to speak to King Saul. The problem I have with this comes from a number of angles. Firstly, it is clear that King Saul cannot actually see "Samuel." Only the witch sees this "divine being," through her witchcraft. Clearly, "Samuel" is not standing there physically, i.e. in a body. The Bible makes it clear that to pass as a human being, one must be in the body. A human being does not *have* a soul. A human being *is* a living soul. In God's economy there is no such thing as a disembodied human spirit. It does not and cannot exist independently of the body. This much is axiomatic as already discussed. To have "Samuel" alive without bodily resurrection is to break the Biblical model of both Old and New Testaments, as we will shortly see.

Secondly, God categorically condemns the practice of necromancy and consulting with "familiar spirits" (see Lev. 19:31; 20:6; Deut. 18:10-11; Isa. 8:19-20, etc.) It is highly unlikely that He would condone a detestable practice just to satisfy Saul's whims. Up until this point the LORD has absolutely refused to communicate with Saul by any genuine means (v. 6). God has utterly rejected

---

[12] Prestidge, *Life, Death and Destiny,* p. 29.

Saul. In the absence of Saul's repentance, there is no reason to believe that God has suddenly changed His mind. Rather God has given Saul over to a spirit of delusion and error.

I conclude, therefore, that the whole episode is a case of demonic impersonation. The Bible indicates that the world of witchcraft is full of danger and deception. But it is not a world of make-believe without substance. The powers there are real. Intelligent demonic personalities there are. "Familiar spirits" are fallen angels who closely monitor and observe our behaviour. They can mimic a dead human with ease. Through spiritist mediums they are able to pass on to grieving relatives amazing personal information causing the vulnerable to believe that this really is their deceased loved one communicating. I conclude then that the witch of Endor really does see "a god," "a divine being," a demon. As Anthony Buzzard notes in his discussion of the story, "the comment in 1 Chronicles 10:13, read in the original [Hebrew], suggests that what Saul consulted was the familiar spirit itself, rather than, as he thought, the ghost of Samuel."[13]

The Souls Under the Altar

Whilst on the subject of visions, let us consider another passage of Scripture thought to teach that upon death, Christians go immediately into heaven in a disembodied state. John sees a vision:

> And when he broke the fifth seal, I saw underneath the altar the souls of those who had been slain because of the word of God, and because of the testimony which they had maintained; and they cried out with a loud voice, saying, "How long, O Lord, holy and true, will You refrain from judging and avenging our blood on those who dwell on the earth?" And there was given to each of them a white robe; and they were told that they should rest for a little while longer, until the number of their fellow servants and their brethren who were to be killed even as they had been, should be completed also (Rev. 6:9-11).

We have already observed that visions are symbolic. John's vision of these souls under the altar occurs in a book which is visionary in character. In this very book of Revelation we see the church called a lampstand (1:20); we see a sword coming out of

[13] Buzzard, *What Happens When We Die?* p. 58.

Jesus' mouth (19:15); we see a woman clothed with the sun with the moon under her feet, and she wears on her head a crown of twelve stars (12:1), but no expositor fails to see their symbolic interpretations. This ought to give us cause to proceed with caution in this vision of the "souls under the altar," for it is a commonly accepted principle of interpretation that a symbolic passage should never be used to overturn what is elsewhere clearly taught. Here, the "altar" and the "robes" are not necessarily to be taken literally. Nor are the loud cryings of the "souls" necessarily literal prayers, either. If the point is pressed literally then we get the ridiculous teaching that conscious "souls" are left under a piece of furniture, the altar, for centuries!

Once again, if we put our Hebrew eyes on, we will discover the key to the interpretation. According to Genesis 4, God says to Cain who has just murdered his brother Abel, "The voice of your brother's blood is crying to Me from the ground" (Gen. 4:10). Figuratively then, Abel's innocent blood is calling to God for justice.

There are in fact a number of Scriptures that depict dead people in the grave as talking and showing emotions. In Isaiah 14 "sheol," the Hebrew word for "grave," is portrayed as excitedly anticipating the death and the descent of the wicked king of Babylon. All the dead leaders of the earth and the "spirits of the dead" arouse themselves in anticipation of the king's demise. They say, "You have become like us. Your pomp and the music of your harps have been brought down to Sheol; maggots are spread out as your bed beneath you, and worms are your covering." Even "the cypress trees" and "the cedars" are seen to rejoice at the news. This is clearly poetic imagery. "Mythological pictures of the death-state are being used for rhetorical effect, not as elements of doctrine."[14]

Actually, if we turn over a few more chapters in the book of the Revelation, we are in fact clearly told that these souls are not conscious; they are not alive, but they do come to life again at the return of Christ to earth: "And I saw the souls of those who had been beheaded because of the testimony of Jesus and because of the word of God...and they came to life and reigned with Christ for a thousand years. The rest of the dead did not come to life until the

---

[14] Prestidge, *Life, Death and Destiny,* p. 30.

thousand years were completed. This is the first resurrection" (Rev. 20:4).

This is consistent with the rest of the Scriptural witness. Dead people only come to life again when Christ returns as King to this earth.

The parable of the rich man and Lazarus (Luke 16:19-31) is in the same Hebrew metaphoric mould: "Now there was a certain rich man..." Parables are symbolic representations of truth. The various details in the story are not to be taken at face value. It is never a good idea to build a doctrine on figurative or symbolic language. This is a parable about a poor man who dies and is carried by the angels into "Abraham's bosom." The rich man (symbolizing the Pharisees) dies and finds himself in "hades" in torment.

We know that the story is not meant to teach anything about the state of the dead, for a number of reasons. Firstly, in the parable Abraham is seen as himself being conscious. We have already seen that the dead are constantly said to be unconscious. The OT heroes of faith are "silent" in the ground. Secondly, the rest of Scripture teaches that punishments and rewards do not occur at death in a disembodied state, but are received at the Second Coming, at the *parousia,* after the dead are brought back to life. (When the Lord Jesus is revealed from heaven he will deal out retribution, 2 Thess. 1:7-9. See also Acts 17:31; Rom. 2:16; 2 Tim. 4:8; Rev. 20:13.) Jesus uses this story that was probably in currency and familiar to his hearers for "rhetorical effect." There is one certainty. Jesus did not teach that the dead already have their rewards. Only a few chapters earlier Jesus says that the righteous will be rewarded at "the resurrection of the just" (Luke 14:14).

John's vision of these souls crying to God is in the same Hebrew tradition. Their blood, violently shed, figuratively calls to God for vindication: "It graphically symbolises the urgent need for the coming of God's final Kingdom in order to vindicate His people slaughtered on His behalf, but tells us nothing literal about the state of the dead, other than that it is, at least for some, a state of 'rest' (Rev. 6:11; cp. 14:13)."[15]

---

[15] *Ibid.,* p. 23.

The God of the Living, Not the Dead

It is truly amazing how our tradition-bound minds can read over the blatantly obvious in order to teach "truths" that are not in the text. Surely, if there is any passage that teaches that the dead are conscious in communion with God right now, it is Matthew 22:23-33 (also Mark 12:18-27 and Luke 20:27-40), where Jesus says that God is "not the God of the dead but of the living; for all live to Him" (Luke 20:38). It will be seen on closer examination that Jesus was teaching the very opposite!

Firstly, it is to be noted that Jesus says these words to the Sadducees (who say that there is no resurrection, Matt. 22:23). The subject under discussion is *the resurrection* of the dead. The Sadducees try to tangle Jesus up by proposing a hypothetical situation where a woman loses her husband before she has a chance to have children by him. The man's brother then marries her, according to Jewish practice, so that the family line can continue. But before they have any children, this second brother dies. The woman then marries the third brother, but the same fate happens to him. In the end the woman marries seven brothers, and finally she herself dies. "**In the resurrection** therefore whose wife of the seven shall she be? For they all had her" (Matt. 22:28). The theme is the resurrection and not whether dead people survive their bodies as disembodied spirits. Now, concerning the resurrection, Jesus gets a bit cranky[16] with the Sadducees, saying:

> You are mistaken, not understanding the Scriptures, or the power of God. For **in the resurrection** they neither marry, nor are given in marriage, but are like angels in heaven. But **regarding the resurrection of the dead**, have you not read that which was spoken to you by God, saying, I am the God of Abraham, and the God of Isaac, and the God of Jacob? God is not the God of the dead but of the living (Matt. 22:29-32).

The whole context clearly is *the resurrection of the dead.* Repeat: The topic of discussion has nothing to do with whether the dead are in living fellowship with God in heaven now. Jesus had only one point to make: There is going to have to be a resurrection; otherwise the currently dead patriarchs will not be in the Kingdom.

---

[16] *Cranky* — angry.

Jesus argues for the fact of the future resurrection of the dead, precisely because the patriarchs Abraham, Isaac and Jacob *are dead*! However, they cannot remain dead because God must keep His word of promise to them that they will live again in the land. God will raise them up from the dead in that *coming age*, because He has forever linked Himself with them in promise to do so. Abraham, Isaac and Jacob, though now dead, can be spoken of as "alive" in view of God's promise to raise them up. Is He not "the God of Abraham, the God of Isaac, the God of Jacob"? Precisely because Abraham, Isaac and Jacob are forever associated with God in covenant-promise they will rise to life again. But if Jesus believed that the patriarchs were already enjoying life with God, his argument for the resurrection would be shot, since in that scenario, immortality would come without resurrection! As Robert Hach correctly observes, Jesus is here using a very Hebrew manner of speech called "prolepsis." Prolepsis is a figure of speech defined as "anticipating; especially, the describing of an event as taking place before it could have done so, the treating of a future event as if it had already happened."[17]

It is evident that Jesus did not believe that Abraham, Isaac and Jacob were living, for the only way for them to live and enjoy God is by God's promise in the Scriptures for a future resurrection of the dead to occur by His power. God's word and power will yet be vindicated through resurrection in the Age to Come. Abraham, Isaac, Jacob and all of God's people will rise again.

Absent from the Body and to Be at Home with the Lord

There is perhaps no more popular "proof-text" quoted by those believing that death ushers us straight into the presence of God than 2 Corinthians 5:8 (as so often recited, but as we will soon see misquoted): "To be absent from the body is to be at home with the Lord."

This is one of those cases where "a text out of context is just a pretext." As E.W. Bullinger says:

> It is little less than a crime for anyone to pick out certain words and frame them into a sentence, not only disregarding the scope and context, but ignoring the other words in the

[17] Hach, *Possession and Persuasion*, p. 131 quoting *Webster's New World Dictionary*, 1962.

> verse, and quote the words "absent from the body, present with the Lord" with the view of dispensing with the hope of the resurrection (which is the subject of the whole passage) as though it were unnecessary; and as though "present with the Lord" is obtainable without it.[18]

Before we zone in on this so-called "proof-text" then, the context must be established. Unfortunately our task is not made easy because of the unnatural break in our English Bibles between chapters four and five. In the original Greek manuscripts there are no chapter divisions. And a glance backwards will show that the context of Paul's remarks in chapter five is specifically *the resurrection hope*: "Knowing that He who raised the Lord Jesus will raise us also with Jesus and will present us with you" (2 Cor. 4:14).

Paul is not hoping at death to become a disembodied soul; he is looking for the resurrection at Christ's return:

> For we know that if the earthly tent which is our house is torn down, we have a building from God, a house not made with hands, eternal in the heavens. For indeed in this house we groan, longing to be clothed with our dwelling from heaven; inasmuch as we, having put it on, shall not be found naked. For indeed while we are in this tent, we groan, being burdened, because we do not want to be unclothed, but to be clothed, in order that what is mortal may be swallowed up by life (2 Cor. 5:1-4).

Now it is right here that our Platonically-mesmerized minds jump back into their tradition-bound tracks. As soon as we read "the earthly tent which is our house" we tend to think in dualistic terms of a body housing a soul. When we read, "while we are in this tent, we groan, being burdened" we immediately slip into Greek-dominated ideas of the body being a shell that is trapping our immortal souls and keeping them from their true heavenly destiny.

Perhaps the best way to show why this dualistic interpretation cannot be is to compare and "context" this passage with what Paul wrote to the same people only about a year earlier in 1 Corinthians 15. It is always a good idea to work from what is clear and unambiguous to what is more abstruse. In 1 Corinthians 15 the whole subject concerns the resurrection:

---

[18] E.W. Bullinger, *Companion Bible.*

> Now if Christ is preached, that he has been raised from the dead, how do some among you say that there is no resurrection of the dead? But if there is no resurrection of the dead, not even Christ has been raised; and if Christ has not been raised, then our preaching is vain, your faith is also vain...and if Christ has not been raised, your faith is worthless; you are still in your sins. Then those also who have fallen asleep in Christ have perished...But now Christ has been raised from the dead, the first fruits of those who are asleep...but each in his own order: Christ the first fruits, after that those who are Christ's at his coming; then comes the end, when he delivers up the kingdom to the God and Father...But some one will say, "How are the dead raised? And with what kind of body do they come?"...If there is a natural body, there is also a spiritual body (1 Cor. 15:12-14, 17-18, 20, 23, 24, 35, 44b).

The whole chapter concerns the certainty of the resurrection from the dead when Christ returns at the end of the age. The significance of quoting this passage is to observe how closely it parallels the 2 Corinthians 5 passage. Let's note the contact points:

Both Have the Same Context:

1 Cor. 15: Context is the resurrection hope at Christ's Second Coming: "But now Christ has been raised from the dead...and those who are Christ's at his coming."

2 Cor. 4, 5: Context is the resurrection hope at Christ's Second Coming: "Knowing that He who raised the Lord Jesus will raise us also with Jesus and will present us with you" (4:14).

Both Have the Same Metaphors:

1. Clothed with immortality.

1 Cor. 15:54: "But when this perishable will have been **clothed** with immortality, then will come about the saying that is written, 'Death is swallowed up in victory.'"

2 Cor. 5:2, 4: "For indeed in this house we groan, longing to be **clothed** with our dwelling from heaven...We do not want to be unclothed, but to be **clothed**."

2. Christ arrives from heaven.

1 Cor. 15:47: "The first man [Adam] is from the earth, made of dust; the second man [Christ] is the Lord [coming] **from heaven**."

2 Cor. 5:2: "We are longing to be clothed with our dwelling **from heaven**."

3. Mortality supplanted by immortality.

1 Cor. 15:54: "But when this mortal will have put on immortality, then will come about the saying that is written, 'Death is **swallowed** up in victory.'"

2 Cor. 5:4: "[We want to be clothed] in order that what is mortal may be **swallowed** up by life."

In light of the fact that in both passages the context is the same (the hope of resurrection glory at Christ's *parousia*), and in light of the fact that the metaphors are the same, we must conclude that the theme in both passages is identical. Therefore the statement "to be absent from the body and to be at home with the Lord" cannot mean that dead Christians go immediately to heaven, because in the 1 Corinthians 15 passage the Christians' hope is realized at the *parousia.* The theme deals with the dead being raised at the end of this age; it is not a question of souls departing to heaven at death.

> These points of contact, involving the use of identical language, surely rule out any possibility that Paul has two entirely different events in mind — not least in view of the fact that he is writing to the same people, and within a short space of time. To take 2 Corinthians 5 as referring to the moment of death, to mean that each individual *receives immortality independently at death* is, as J.A.T. Robinson says, "to read the passage in clear opposition to 1 Corinthians 15."[19] The time has surely come to stop making Paul contradict himself and to acknowledge the remarkable consistency and unity which extend to all his writings on this central issue of life after death.[20]

As Prestidge comments on 2 Corinthians 5:

> Most scholars today would agree that *verses 1-5,* at least, refer to the prospect of a resurrected, re-embodied life, and not to any disembodied state. Actually, the case is overwhelming! The hope in the context is resurrection (2

---

[19] *In The End God,* p. 106.

[20] Buzzard, *What Happens When We Die?* p. 45.

Cor. 4:14). The clothing metaphor (2 Cor. 5:2-4; "further clothed") matches 1 Cor. 15:53-54 ("put on immortality"), where it clearly refers to receiving the resurrection body. Similarly, the "swallowing up" of the "mortal" by "life" in 2 Cor. 5:4 occurs at resurrection, according to 1 Cor. 15:54. The "glory" awaited (2 Cor. 4:17) is resurrection as part of God's new creation, according to Rom. 8:18-23, and it is in anticipation of this hope, through the Holy Spirit (2 Cor. 5:5; Rom. 8:11, 23), that we "groan" (2 Cor. 5:2; Rom. 8:22-23) and "sigh" (2 Cor. 5:4, RSV; Rom. 8:26). The parallels with 1 Cor. 15 and Rom. 8 are decisive, that "our heavenly dwelling" (2 Cor. 5:2) is our future resurrection state.[21]

With this background, let us now look particularly at the idea that "to be absent from the body is to be present with the Lord" means that at death the Christian's soul leaves the body and wings its way to a pre-resurrection bodiless state of bliss. It is worth noting that the word "soul" is used by Paul a total of nine times in his letters, but never once does he say it departs from the body at death. Paul also uses the word "spirit" 134 times, but not once does he say our "spirits" leave our bodies at the point of death. This goes to prove that any talk of a "soul" or "spirit" separating from the body at death uses language quite unlike Paul's. This, of course, by itself, is not conclusive, but it sounds a warning that we must use Paul's words the way he uses them.

We may even go further. And this is the shock: Any thought of such a disembodied soul actually causes Paul to wince in horror. He says he does *not* want to be "found naked" (2 Cor. 5:3)! He says "we do **not** want to be unclothed" (v. 4)! To be "naked" and to be "unclothed" mean to be disembodied. Paul knew that the culture of his day was steeped in Platonic belief that the soul escapes the body at death. But he shrinks from such a thought.

On the positive side, what condition does Paul long for? Answer: "For indeed in this we groan, longing to be clothed with our dwelling from heaven" (v. 2). And, "For indeed while we are in this tent, we groan, being burdened, because we do not want to be unclothed, but to be clothed, in order that what is mortal may be swallowed up in life" (v. 4). If it be insisted that in verse 8 Paul is

[21] Prestidge, *Life, Death and Destiny,* p. 45.

saying he prefers to be absent from the body and immediately in God's presence *before the resurrection*, then why in verses 3 and 4 did he just say this is a condition he does *not* want to be in? Whatever else this verse is saying, it cannot mean that Paul longs for death so he can go into heaven in a disembodied, that is, in a "naked" state! This is to make Paul intolerably contradictory. It is to make Paul forgetful of what he has just written in verses 3 and 4.

No. What he yearns for is his resurrection body. He is not groaning to lose his body. He is longing to gain the resurrection body, for that would mean that Jesus has already come back and is here with us now! *Paul wants two things at once*: "to be absent from the body **and** present with the Lord" (v. 8). *These are the very same things he says he desires in verses 2 and 4: the resurrection!* Paul wants to be absent from the body *and* thus present with the Lord, but this cannot happen until the resurrection day when Christ comes back to planet earth. While we are at home in this body "we are absent from the Lord" because Jesus has not yet returned. In the meantime Paul does not want to be found naked and unclothed; that is, he has one real goal and that is to be clothed at the resurrection. He wants to continue living, knowing that those who do not "sleep" and survive until the glorious return of Christ from heaven will be changed instantly (see 1 Cor. 15:51-52: "Behold, I tell you a mystery, we shall not all sleep, but we shall all be changed, in a moment, in the twinkling of an eye, at the last trumpet; for the trumpet will sound, and the dead will be raised imperishable, and we [Paul still hopes to be among those still living when Jesus comes back] shall be changed"). Yes, Paul wants these two things simultaneously. It is amazing how many *misquote* even this proof text. It does not say, "to be absent from the body *is to be* present with the Lord." Paul says, "to be absent from the body **AND** to be present with the Lord." An entire doctrine is thus being promoted on the basis of something Paul did not write and on the strength of half a verse pulled out of a long context! Paul says he wishes to be absent from the body *and* to be present with the Lord. And the only way believers can expect to be present with the Lord is when he is present here on earth.

If he should in the meantime die before the reappearance of Christ from heaven, Paul simply ignores the intervening time of unconscious "sleep."

> And this he may do precisely because the intervening state is not consciously experienced at all by the dead. After death, the next thing we *know* is that we are summoned by Christ...In the consciousness of the departed believer there is no interval between dissolution [i.e. death] and investiture [i.e. resurrection], however long the interval may be in the calendar of earth-bound human history.[22]

This interpretation fits Paul's teaching everywhere else: "**When** Christ, who is our life, shall be revealed, **then** you also will be revealed with him in glory" (Col. 3:4).

"For our citizenship is in heaven, from which also we eagerly wait for a Saviour, the Lord Jesus Christ; who will [then] transform the body of our humble state into conformity with the body of his glory, by the exertion of the power that he has even to subject all things to himself" (Phil. 3:20-22).

"For the Lord himself will descend from heaven with a shout, with the voice of the archangel, and with the trumpet of God; and the dead in Christ shall rise first. Then we who are alive and remain shall be caught up together with them in the clouds to meet the Lord in the air, and thus [in this way and no other] we shall always be with the Lord. Therefore comfort one another with these words" (1 Thess. 6:16-18)

This interpretation fits the other apostles' teaching: "We know that **when** he appears, [then] we shall be like him, because we shall [then] see him just as he is" (1 John 3:2).

This interpretation corresponds to Jesus' own belief:

"For this is the will of my Father, that everyone who beholds the Son, and believes in him, may have eternal life, and I myself will **raise him up on the last day**" (John 6:40).

"No one can come to me, unless the Father who sent me draws him; and I will raise him up **on the last day"** (John 6:44).

"In my Father's house are many dwelling places; if it were not so, I would have told you; for I go to prepare a place for you. And if I go and prepare a place for you, I will come again, and [then] receive you to myself, that where I am, there you may be also" (John 14:2-3).

If the believers are not received by Christ until he comes again, then how can he be receiving each of them individually when they

---

[22] *Ibid.,* pp. 46-47.

die? For it is certain that Jesus did not say "I go to prepare a place for your bodies, and if I go I'll come again for your bodies, even though the 'real' you will have been with me in heaven for millennia." That is nonsensical. If we do not appear with Christ in our glorified and resurrected state until he returns to earth at the last day of this age, how can we then say we go immediately at death to him in the heavenly glory in the meantime? All the way through, the Lord himself and his apostles teach that the resurrection will be a corporate experience of those who wait for him. We are all changed, raised up together. The New Testament knows no doctrine where the individual receives glory apart from and in isolation from the entire body of believers. In fact, the whole of creation is waiting for this universal event: "For the anxious longing of the creation waits eagerly for the revealing of the sons of God" (Rom. 8:19).

To Die and Be with Christ Is Far Better

A similar "proof-text" often quoted by dualists is Paul's statement: "For to me, to live is Christ, and to die is gain...But I am hard-pressed from both directions, having the desire to depart and be with Christ, for that is very much better; yet to remain in the flesh is more necessary for your sake" (Phil. 1:21-24).

Here Paul says he has "a desire to depart and be with Christ, which is very much better." Better than what? Popular opinion will answer, "Better than living in the flesh, because in death Paul can go immediately to be with Christ, even though he will have to wait for his new body at the resurrection." But this response creates one huge problem. Namely, in 2 Corinthians 5:2-4 Paul states categorically that this is the very state he does *not* desire. There he says he does not want to be "naked," and he does not want to be "unclothed." In fact, given the choice Paul clearly says that it's *better* to have the earthly body than *no body at all.* He does not want to die before the return of Christ. Yet, apparently, here in Philippians 1 on the popular theory, Paul says that such a disembodied condition in heaven is "very much better"!? Obviously, this popular interpretation creates a schizophrenic apostle.

Wherein lies the solution? If I may take the advertising slogan of real estate agents, "position, position, position" (in the States, "location, location, location"), and apply it to Bible study, the solution lies in context, context, context:

> Now I want you to know, brethren, that my circumstances have turned out for the greater progress of the gospel, so that my imprisonment in the cause of Christ has become well-known throughout the whole praetorian guard and to everyone else, and that most of the brethren, trusting in the Lord because of my imprisonment, have far more courage to speak the word of God without fear. Some, to be sure, are preaching Christ even from envy and strife, but some also from good will; the latter do it out of love, knowing that I am appointed for the defense of the gospel; the former proclaim Christ out of selfish ambition, rather than from pure motives, thinking to cause me distress in my imprisonment. What then? Only that in every way, whether in pretense or in truth, Christ is proclaimed; and in this I rejoice, yes, and I will rejoice. For I know that this shall turn out for my deliverance through your prayers and the provision of the Spirit of Jesus Christ, according to my earnest expectation and hope, that I shall not be put to shame in anything, but that with all boldness, Christ shall even now, as always, be exalted in my body, whether by life or by death. For to me, to live is Christ, and to die is gain. But if I am to live on in the flesh, this will mean fruitful labor for me; and I do not know which to choose. But I am hard-pressed from both directions, having the desire to depart and be with Christ, for that is very much better; yet to remain on in the flesh is more necessary for your sake (Phil. 1:12-24).

The context is clear. Whether Paul lives or dies — in this case it means by martyrdom for he is in prison — is not important to him, as long as the cause of Christ is furthered. Whether in prison or free, whether Christ is preached out of sincere motives or selfish, whether in life or in death, Paul's driving ambition is the success of the Gospel of Christ. If his chains have helped spread the Gospel "throughout the whole praetorian guard," and if his time in jail has given others courage to preach the word with greater boldness, then what might his martyr-death do for the cause? Paul's driving motivation is that "whether by life or by death" the name of Christ might be exalted. One thing is for sure: Paul is not seeking to escape his ministry by death just so he can get some personal and selfish benefit. Context makes it impossible to believe that Paul is thinking of dying for reasons of *personal gain.* Where indeed in all of his writings does Paul seek for any *personal gain?* He wants to be alive when Christ comes back, yes, but either way, whether alive or dead, Paul wants Christ to be honoured.

If Paul really is saying (according to the popular notion) that he'd rather be dead so he could fly away from earth to heaven to be with Christ, he is acting out of character. This scenario would make Paul say that preaching the Gospel is no more important than getting what he wants, which is to escape by dying! It is to make Paul very confused. For although he is "hard-pressed between life and death" and knows that if he lives it will be better for the Philippian Christians, nevertheless he ends up saying he really wants to die! What a contradiction. What a denial of the whole context this interpretation is. What a denial of Paul's outstanding and selfless apostleship.

The popular notion that here Paul wants to die so he can go as a disembodied soul into Christ's heavenly presence also is at odds with what he has already written in verse 6, namely that the goal of Christian living is "the day of Messiah Jesus." Everywhere in the NT "the day" refers to the triumphant Second Coming of Christ to set up God's earthly rule. Paul's personal goal would not be different from that of the rest of the church. The popular notion that Paul can't wait to die and go straight "to heaven" is also at odds with what he writes just a few lines later: "For our citizenship is in heaven, from which also we eagerly wait for a Saviour, the Lord Jesus Christ; who will transform the body of our humble state into conformity with the body of his glory, by the exertion of the power that he has even to subject all things to himself" (Phil. 3:20-22).

Clearly, Paul's hope and desire are firmly fixed on the return of Christ from heaven. So, if we keep this consistent theme of death followed by resurrection at Christ's *parousia* in mind, Philippians 1:21-24 cannot teach immediate presence in heaven with Christ at death.

There is another possibility here worth considering for a moment. A closer look at the Greek in verse 23 reveals this thought-provoking possibility: "But I am hard-pressed from both directions, having the desire to depart [Greek *analusai*] and be with Christ, for that is very much better." The word in our English Bibles "depart" (*analusai*) occurs in one of Jesus' parables: "And be like men who are waiting for their master when he **returns** [Greek *analusai*] from the wedding feast, so that they may immediately open the door to him when he comes and knocks" (Luke 12:36).

The context in this parable is Christ's return, his *parousia,* which everywhere in the New Testament occurs at the end of this wicked age. As will be seen, the Greek word *analusai* can be translated as either "depart" or "return." The translator must make a decision which English idea he will use. Is there a compelling reason in Philippians 1:23 why Paul could not have said that his great longing was for the *return* (of Christ)? Furthermore, in the Greek text there is a definite article before *analusai.* Paul wrote about a defined event: either "the departure" or "the return." This definite article does not appear in our English translations. We pose the question for reflection: Is there good evidence that Paul may have been referring to *the return* of Christ and not his own departure at death? In our English Bibles it seems that Paul is holding up only two options for himself: either life or death. But if we understand Paul to mean he is longing for Christ's second coming, Paul is actually giving three options (life, death and resurrection at Christ's return).

It is true that the natural reading seems to make Paul the subject of the sentence. Paul is desiring that he himself will depart and so be with Christ. From his subjective point of view this hope may appear quite reasonable, because he knows that the next moment of consciousness for him will be at the resurrection, when he will be raised to receive his new body and thus be forever with the Lord Jesus. There may be many long years between the death of Paul and his next waking moment at the return of Christ when he will be raised up. He knows it will seem but a moment between closing his eyes in the sleep of death and the glorious moment of new consciousness. Furthermore, at the end of his life Paul wrote that "the time of my departure [*analusis*] is at hand" (2 Tim. 4:6). This is a clear reference to "departure" meaning the individual's death. We will expound this verse more fully shortly, but for our purpose at this point it is sufficient to note that it is not a wrong translation to make Paul say in Philippians 1:23 that he desires his departure, that is, his death. But is it the best translation? Does it fit the context? I am not convinced it does.

To translate *analusai* in Philippians 1:23 as "the return" has a certain appeal to me. This way it will be seen instantly to perfectly harmonize with Paul's hope everywhere else in the NT. Paul's overwhelming passion is always for Christ's return. Let us compare Philippians 1:23 with 2 Corinthians 5 to illustrate this. Both verses tell us what Paul finds least desirable: dying before Christ's return. (In Corinthians he shrinks from being found "naked" and "unclothed" and in Philippians he is "hard-pressed" but wants to live for the Philippians' sake because that is preferable to dying and not being able to help them any more.) Both verses tell us what is at least bearable: living on in this present situation (even though this means currently "being burdened"). And both verses teach what Paul really longs and yearns for. (In Corinthians it is "to be clothed with our dwelling from heaven" which is our resurrected glory and in Philippians it is a desire for *the return* so he can be with Christ which is "far better.") As already noted above, Paul specifically states this hope just a few verses later in Philippians 3:20-21 where he says the return of Christ from heaven will transform us into a position of glory.

What Paul positively longs for is the return of Christ, so he can be with him. Because this hope is not now realized, he is currently "hard-pressed" between living and dying. Whatever the immediate outcome, whether he lives or dies, Christ will be glorified — either in ongoing ministry or at the day of Christ's return. This interpretation fits the wider context everywhere where Paul teaches that we only enter Christ's presence (if dead through resurrection; if living at that moment of the return through being caught up, or raptured, to meet the Lord in the air) when he returns again. This interpretation also fits the immediate context and is permissible in the original Greek text. It eliminates all the difficulties that are unnecessarily placed on Philippians 1 by reading into it a "departing immortal soul" concept where no such notion really belongs. However, if we still prefer the translation that makes Paul long for his death, under no stretch does he mention that this will free his soul to fly up in consciousness to Christ in heaven. As we have already proved, that Platonic notion played no part in Paul's belief. As we asked earlier, where else in all the NT does Paul ever desire and long for death as an escape from present personal trouble? This does not fit the context here where he wants to serve the Philippians more and benefit them.

Christ Preaching to the Spirits in Prison

> For Christ also died for sins once for all, the just for the unjust, in order that he might bring us to God, having been put to death in the flesh, but made alive in the spirit; in which also he went and made proclamation to the spirits in prison, who once were disobedient, when the patience of God kept waiting in the days of Noah, during the construction of the ark, in which a few, that is, eight persons, were brought safely through the water (1 Pet. 3:18-20).

Here surely is one of the most challenging passages of Scripture, not only because it conjures up graphic images of Christ preaching to "spirits in prison," whatever this means, but also because various explanations have been offered. Some have used the passage to teach that Christ really does have two parts to his person: the "flesh" or his human nature and the "spirit" or his divine nature: "For Christ [was] put to death in the flesh, but made alive in the spirit" (v. 18). Therefore, on this notion, although Jesus was killed bodily, his divine nature survived, that is, his "spirit" descended into "hell" where he preached the Gospel to all the dead people who once were alive in Noah's day. Here in the nether world of the (conscious) dead, Christ declared to the righteous dead that he had conquered the Devil and had come to lead these captives to freedom, and that they would be now going to heaven with him. Here in the "spirit" also, Christ had some bad news for the wicked dead, namely that they were now forever doomed, with no hope of escape.

Still others see here no reference whatsoever to Christ preaching to the souls of dead humans, but rather he preached to fallen angels, thus announcing their fate. One thing all these interpretations have in common is that they teach Christ was conscious while dead. Is this really possible?

Obviously, we must proceed carefully if we are to unravel this passage. Firstly, does the phrase "put to death in the flesh, but made alive in the spirit" imply that Christ was composed of two natures, the human and the divine, and that the divine nature survived consciously? In a previous chapter we have seen that this cannot be so. Jesus of Nazareth was a man with the same human nature that Adam had. Adam did not have two natures, a human and a divine; nor did Adam have a soul living in a body. Adam was a living soul "and he died" (Gen. 5:5). He returned to the ground and became dust. So has every dead man since, with the notable exception of Jesus of Nazareth, who was dead for three days and then came back to life by resurrection.

Where was Jesus when he was placed in the tomb? Traditional church dogma says he was conscious "in the spirit" and doing some important work. Such an idea, however, would not have occurred to the Hebrew writers of the New Testament. They did not approach the subject of death with the Greek presuppositions about the nature of man which have become so deeply ingrained in our theology. The Biblical fact is that Jesus died. He, Jesus, was in *hades,* the grave. If it were not for God the Father's intervention, Jesus would have forever rotted in the tomb. But "he was neither abandoned to Hades [the grave], nor did his flesh suffer decay" (Acts 2:31).

In contrast to pagan ideas of a two-natured Jesus, it can be demonstrated that the expression "in the flesh" refers to Christ's earthly life before his crucifixion and the phrase "in the spirit" relates to his post-resurrection condition:

> It was at his resurrection, as Paul says, that he "was vindicated in spirit" (1 Tim. 3:16) and "became a life-giving spirit" (1 Cor. 15:45). C.E.B. Cranfield explains: "it means that, while the body of Christ that was crucified was subject to the frailty and limitations of an ordinary human body, the body that was raised up...is no longer subject to such limitations." Christ, who once lived and died subject to all the limitations of human existence, now lives on the plane of God Himself.[23]

In his resurrection existence, now exalted at the right hand of God on high, the Lord Jesus is no longer subject to the possibility of death. Wicked men can no longer touch him or violate him for he is no longer "in the flesh." This is to say that since his resurrection Christ is in another realm altogether; he is now "in the spirit." As Paul put it elsewhere, "For the death that he died, he died to sin, once for all; but the life that he [now] lives, he lives to God" (Rom. 6:10). Christ, who was once offered to bear the sins of many, will appear a second time, not to bear sin, but to bring salvation to those who eagerly await him (see Heb. 9:28). "In the flesh" and "in the spirit," therefore, are terms that refer to the two different phases of

---

[23] *Ibid.*, p. 19.

Jesus' life; "in the flesh" to his 33 years as a man subject to frailty and death, and "in the spirit" to his present resurrected glory. These expressions have nothing to do with any alleged two natures in Jesus.

Having cleared this phrase up, we proceed to 1 Peter 3:19-20a where we are told that it was "in the spirit" that Christ "went and made proclamation to the spirits in prison, who once were disobedient, when the patience of God kept waiting in the days of Noah, during the construction of the ark." It is clear that if we take the phrase in verse 18 "in the spirit" to refer to Christ's resurrection mode, then it is certain that Christ "made proclamation to the spirits in prison" after he had come out of the tomb, and not while he was dead. After all, while he was in the grave there was no complete Gospel to preach, for the resurrection is indispensable to the Gospel announcement (see 1 Cor. 15:3-4, 17; 1 Pet. 1:3). If, however, on the traditional interpretation, Christ preached the Gospel to the spirits of dead people while he was in the grave for three days, then what gospel did he preach? He had not yet conquered death. He was not yet arisen. The way to the Kingdom was not yet guaranteed. There was no complete good news *yet.*

If we compare a parallel passage in 1 Timothy 3:16, we get the necessary interpretative key. That verse reads: "And by common confession great is the mystery of godliness: he who was revealed in the flesh was vindicated in the spirit, beheld by angels, proclaimed among the nations, believed on in the world, taken up in glory."

Here we are told that Christ appeared to angels after he "was vindicated in the spirit," that is, after his resurrection, though prior to his being seated in glory. Surely 1 Timothy 3:16 and 1 Peter 3:18-20 refer to the same event? Scripture does not let us see too much here, but we get a tantalizing hint that for whatever reason the Lord Jesus announced his triumph to angels after his resurrection. But who or what are these "spirits in prison" that heard Christ's Gospel preaching?

The first part of the answer is that nowhere in the Bible are men ever called "spirits," with the possible exception of Hebrews 12:22-23: "But you have come to Mount Zion and to the city of the living God, the heavenly Jerusalem, and to myriads of angels, to the general assembly and church of the first-born who are enrolled in heaven, and to God, the judge of all, and to the spirits of righteous men made perfect."

There are a number of good reasons why these "spirits of righteous men" cannot be the "souls" of those who have died and gone to heaven. Firstly, because they are said to have been "made perfect" (Greek is *teleioo,* meaning to bring to full completion). Even those who hold that souls go to heaven do not believe that disembodiment is a state of perfection or completion. They still believe that disembodied souls await their resurrection bodies. Such perfection can only come at the *parousia* as we have already observed (see 1 Cor. 15:52-54; Col. 3:4; 1 Thess. 4:16, 17). One thing is certain: The condition of perfected "spirits of righteous men" spoken of in Hebrews 12:23 is not possible until after the resurrection. The author to the Hebrews is stating his absolute conviction that the promised glory is sure. Paul wrote similarly in Ephesians that Christians who are joined to Christ by faith are *already* seated with Christ in the heavenly places in Christ Jesus (Eph. 2:5-6). The promised future is so certain in God's plan that it is spoken of as already having come to pass.

In the Bible, whenever "spirit" is used to denominate an intelligent being, it refers to God (Who is spirit, John 4:24), to angels (who are ministering spirits, Heb. 1:14), to demons (who can possess and enslave, Mark 1:23-27; 5:1-13), or to one man after the resurrection (Jesus the life-giving spirit, 1 Cor. 15:45). "Wherever *pneuma* ('spirit') occurs in the Bible without some phrase to show that the spirit belongs to human beings, the word almost always means a supernatural angelic being or demon (Matt. 8:16; 12:45; Mark 1:23; Luke 10:20; Heb. 1:7, 14; Rev. 1:4, etc.)."[24]

Our provisional conclusion is that the "spirits in prison" that Jesus preached to are not men, but some kind of fallen angel, for they are imprisoned. Peter gives us a bit more information when he says these spirits were associated with the time of Noah's flood: "they were once disobedient, when the patience of God kept waiting in the days of Noah, during the construction of the ark" (1 Pet. 3:20).

More information can be teased out by comparing 2 Peter 2:

> For if God did not spare angels when they sinned, but cast them into hell [Greek *tartaros*] and committed them to pits of darkness, reserved for judgment; and did not spare the ancient world, but preserved Noah...when He brought a

[24] *Ibid.,* p. 108.

> flood upon the world of the ungodly; and if He condemned the cities of Sodom and Gomorrah to destruction by reducing them to ashes, having made them an example to those who would live ungodly thereafter… (v. 4-6).

Jude also refers to these wicked spirits or angels who are now in prison:

> And angels who did not keep their own domain, but abandoned their proper abode, He has kept in eternal bonds under darkness for the judgment of the great day. Just as Sodom and Gomorrah and the cities around them, since they in the same way as these indulged in gross immorality and went after strange flesh, are exhibited as an example, in undergoing the punishment of eternal fire (Jude 6-7).

Putting these passages together, we get the information that at the time of Noah, and at the time before Sodom and Gomorrah were destroyed, wicked angels were involved in some kind of gross sexual activity with humans that so outraged God that He imposed some kind of special punishment on them: He locked them up in a place of "darkness for the judgment of the great day," a place called *tartaros* (2 Pet. 2:4). (In Greek literature *tartaros* is an abyss in the underworld, not for humans, but for fallen angels.) The particular sin appears to be that these wicked angels lusted after "the daughters of men" (see Gen. 6:2). The result of the ungodly union of sinful angels and human women was some kind of mongrel, half-breed creature called "the Nephilim" (Gen. 6:4). These monstrosities were evidently huge in stature and "were the mighty men who were of old, men of renown" (Gen. 6:4).

Some Bible scholars hold the opinion that the old Greek myths of the gods producing offspring with humans are based on these actual historical events. Perhaps this "super-human" race explains the mysterious phenomena such as the pyramids, and the amazing stone structures found in places like South America? The number one best-seller *Fingerprints of the Gods* by Graham Hancock speculates concerning these phenomena in a similar way.

As to why these "sons of God" (a common Hebrew expression for angelic beings as seen in Job 1:6; 2:1; 38:7; Dan. 3:25) should want to pervert the natural order of humans on earth, we can only speculate. It makes good sense to believe it was a deliberate ploy by Satan who had heard God's sentence pronounced on him in the garden, that the woman's "seed" would crush his head (Gen. 3:15).

Satan it seems then set out to frustrate this purpose of God to defeat him, by polluting the channel through which the redeemer of men was to come. If the redeemer was to be a man, of true human stock, the "seed of a woman," then Satan would contaminate the human race, thereby averting his own doom by thwarting God's promise of salvation through a man.

How nearly Satan succeeded in this bold plan is evident from the fact that with the exception of one human family, "all flesh had corrupted their way upon the earth" (Gen. 6:12). Noah and his family were the only purebred humans left! The offspring of this outrageous union between the "sons of God" and the "daughters of men," as we have noted, were the Nephilim. This word means "fallen ones," from the Hebrew *naphal* meaning to fall.

Against this view that the "sons of God" were wicked angels and had sex with human women, it is often objected that angels being "spirits" are sexless. Matthew 22:30 is often quoted in support of this objection. Had Jesus said, "For in the resurrection they neither marry, nor are given in marriage, but are like the angels of God" and stopped there, the objection would have weight. But notice that Jesus added a qualifying clause about the angels. He said, "but are like the angels of God **in heaven**." These last two words make all the difference. In heaven the holy angels do not marry. But the angels referred to as "sons of God" in Genesis 6 were no longer in heaven. Jude 6 informs us that they "did not keep their own domain, but abandoned their proper abode." The angels who rebelled against God, and who were under His impending judgment, evidently came to earth and tried to bastardise God's promise of salvation through Eve. This explains the absolute necessity of the great flood. In order to cleanse the earth of this polluted half-bred race, God must act in judgment. The Nephilim must perish.

The same holds true after the flood, for the Nephilim start appearing again. We read, "So they gave out to the sons of Israel a bad report of the land which they had spied out, saying, 'The land through which we have gone, in spying it out, is a land that devours its inhabitants; and all the people whom we saw in it are men of great size. There also we saw the Nephilim'" (Num. 13:32-33).

Here we begin to understand the LORD's orders to completely kill all the men, women and children who were living in that land. Evidently, more intercourse between the "sons of God" and humans was occurring, for the Nephilim were in the Promised Land. In fact, this hybrid race of beings occurs many times in the Old Testament under various names such as Anakim, Rephaim, and Nephilim. It is rather unfortunate that our English Bibles do not always indicate this distinction, for one of the most mysterious of all truths is hidden from our attention. If we take Isaiah 26 as an example, this becomes glaring: "Your dead [Heb. *muth*] will live; their corpses will rise. You who lie in the dust, awake and shout for joy, for your dew is as the dew of the dawn, and the earth will cast out the departed spirits [Heb. *Rephaim*]" (v. 19).

Notice the two different Hebrew words in this verse. The first word translated "your dead" refers to the sons of Israel. They shall rise again. Their corpses will be resurrected. They will come back from the dust. But in contrast, the second group, "the departed spirits" will be cast out by the earth, or better and more literally, cast away by the earth. The translators have done us a disservice here by rendering the proper name *Rephaim* as "the departed spirits." For the Rephaim are a specific race of giants, like the Nephilim. The point should not be missed here. Isaiah is pointing to a contrast between the way two different races of beings are going to be dealt with in the coming resurrection. Dead Israelites will be raised to new life again. The dead Rephaim will be cast away, cast out.

This is confirmed in the same chapter of Isaiah: "O LORD our God, other masters than You have ruled us; but through You alone we confess Your name. The dead [Heb. *muth*] will not live, the departed spirits [Heb. *Rephaim*] will not rise; therefore You have punished and destroyed them, and You have wiped out all remembrance of them" (Is. 26:13-14).

The "other masters" (*adonim*) who have oppressed the land may be parallel to the Rephaim, the hybrid race of angels and men. Here the picture is completed. Isaiah prophesies that the Rephaim "will not rise" in the resurrection because God has "wiped out all remembrance of them." These beings, the Nephilim, the Rephaim, the Anakim, will never rise again in the resurrection. This race is not the pure genetic descendants of Adam for whom Christ died. Their judgment is complete. God remembers them no more. In contrast, all men, whether good or bad, will be raised from their graves to receive their judgment. But the third class of beings, the demonic angels responsible for siring these half-breeds, are now incarcerated by God. They are reserved "in eternal bonds under darkness for the judgment of the great day" (Jude 6). This place is called *tartarus* (2 Pet. 2:4).

We have arrived at the salient point for our discussion. "The spirits in prison" to whom Jesus announced his resurrection victory are these wicked angels, who under Satan's command had the effrontery to try to thwart God's plan of sending a Redeemer to save mankind. One can only imagine the note of triumph, the sense of elation and joy, when the Son of God announced his victory through God. God's age-long promise had come to pass. The "seed of the woman" had crushed the head of the Serpent! Christ's victory over death through his resurrection confirmed to these demonic spirits that their defeat was sealed. From then on the Lord Jesus would indeed be "at the right hand of God" in heaven, because "angels and authorities and powers had been subjected to him" (1 Pet. 3:22).

All of this is to say that 1 Peter 3:18-20 does not teach that Christ went to hades in a disembodied form while dead to preach to disembodied spirits of dead men. 1 Peter 3:18-20 speaks rather of the vindicated Christ (cp. 1 Tim. 3:16) announcing his resurrection victory over Satan's kingdom, particularly to those rebellious angels associated with the blackest of human history in the time of Noah, and Sodom and Gomorrah. The "spirits in prison" are held fast in doom, awaiting the final judgment. Peter is writing to the still living Christians who are being persecuted by evil government. He wants these persecuted Christians to be courageous, because the final victory is assured. Christ has conquered sin and death and his triumph has already been proclaimed from the lowest depths to the highest heights of all God's universe. In him, we are guaranteed final salvation.

Jesus Comes Again with His Saints

Another passage used to justify belief that at death souls go to heaven is 1 Thessalonians 4:

> But we do not want you to be uninformed, brethren, about those who are asleep, that you may not grieve, as do the rest who have no hope. For if we believe that Jesus died and rose again, even so God will bring with him those who have fallen asleep in Jesus. For this we say to you by the word of the Lord, that we who are alive, and remain until the coming of the Lord, shall not precede those who have fallen asleep. For the Lord himself will descend from heaven with

> a shout, with the voice of the archangel, and with the trumpet of God; and the dead in Christ shall rise first. Then we who are alive and remain shall be caught up together with them in the clouds to meet the Lord in the air, and thus we shall always be with the Lord. Therefore, comfort one another with these words (1 Thess. 4:15-18).

It is amazing that the very passage in which Paul informs us about our future hope when Jesus comes back is used to teach that souls are in heaven with Jesus Christ now. The rationale is that the souls of those who have already died in Christ will be brought back with him when he returns to earth, so they can be reunited with their sleeping bodies, which will rise up from the ground. This is what is supposedly seen in the phrase, "Even so God will bring with him those who have fallen asleep in Jesus."

To get our thinking straight we must see what Paul is aiming at. The question he is answering is this: What hope does the Christian Gospel offer to those whose loved ones are already dead? This first generation of Christians were fully expecting the return of the Lord Jesus from heaven within their own lifetime. We have seen that Paul himself expected to be living when his master came back. However, time was marching on. Jesus was delaying his coming. He was to this point a no-show. And in the meantime, many Christians had died. Would they miss the coming glory of God's Kingdom on earth? Was their grief no different from the pagans who were not looking for Jesus? To answer this concern Paul applies the Gospel hope.

If the dead are with the Lord already in heaven, now would be a good time for Paul to say so. Just tell the church that "those who have fallen asleep" are already enjoying the presence of God! Paul does not say anything of the sort. Rather, the comfort he offers is that "the dead in Christ shall rise first" when Jesus "descends from heaven" and "thus [i.e. in this way] we shall always be with the Lord." As elsewhere Paul describes the dead as those who are "asleep." He says that they will rise first. In the NT death is spoken of as sleep 19 times. This word picture of the dead being asleep is meant to convey hope, for just as we expect to wake up in the morning after going to bed, when we lay our dead in the ground we do so in the full knowledge that true to his word, Jesus will come back and wake them up.

We must not fail to understand that Paul here says that the one hope for those who are dead is the resurrection. And this resurrection happens when Jesus returns "with the voice of the archangel, and with the trumpet of God." The pattern is always the same: "Christ the first fruits, then at his coming those who belong to Christ" (1 Cor. 15:23).

After the voice of the Son of Man calls his own back to life, "then we who are alive and remain until the coming of the Lord shall be caught up together with them in the clouds to meet the Lord in the air." The living meet the Lord the same time the dead meet the Lord; we meet him "together" in one huge celebration. If the dead are already with the Lord in heavenly enjoyment, then they are meeting Christ before the living on earth. God's program is for the whole church to meet Christ together, as a corporate body. If Jesus is now individually receiving the (conscious) dead when they die, then this "togetherness" is a lie. In contrast to the individualistic hope of "soul immortality" the apostolic teaching sees the individual's hope only in the overall context of a corporate resurrection of all who belong to Christ. The dead and the living will meet the returning Lord *together*.

But what does Paul mean when he says "the time of my departure is at hand"? He says:

> For I am already being poured out as a drink offering, and the time of my departure has come. I have fought the good fight, I have finished the course, I have kept the faith; in the future there is laid up for me the crown of righteousness, which the Lord, the righteous Judge, will award to me on that day; and not only to me, but also to all who have loved his appearing (2 Tim. 4:6-8).

This is the last NT letter Paul wrote. He knows he is going to die. He knows he will not be one of the living ones when Jesus returns. We no longer see the indifference he talks of in Philippians 1:23 where he is "hard-pressed" between life and death, not knowing which to choose. But is his hope that his immortal soul will depart to be immediately with Christ in heaven?

There is not one word here about the soul departing in consciousness. Nor is there any word about going to heaven. Paul uses the metaphor of a drink offering being poured out. Simply put, Paul is dying, and he knows he is departing *from this life*. And as is the case every single time he discusses hope beyond the grave, he looks forward to the "**appearing**" of Christ in resurrection power. He looks forward to "**the future**" when he will stand before the Lord, the righteous Judge, "**on that day**." Facing imminent death, Paul says nothing about going straight up to the Lord in heaven. This should settle once and for all time that after death Paul's hope is in the resurrection when Christ returns to earth. This also confirms what we found earlier in Philippians 1:23 where he states that what he desires is to meet Christ in the next second of consciousness after falling asleep in death. Paul looks for *the return of Christ*, so he can be with him, "which is very much better."

Confirmation of Church Fathers

It is a matter of historic interest that for a long time after the apostles, the church by and large held firmly to the biblical position on this issue. In the mid-second century Irenaeus wrote:

> Some who are reckoned among the orthodox go beyond the prearranged plan for the exaltation of the just...and entertain heretical opinions. For the heretics, not admitting the salvation of their flesh, affirm that immediately upon their death they shall pass above the heavens. Those persons, therefore, who reject a resurrection affecting the whole man, and do their best to remove it from the Christian scheme, know nothing as to the plan of resurrection. For they do not choose to understand that, if these things are as they say, the Lord himself, in whom they profess to believe, did not rise again on the third day, but immediately upon his expiring departed on high, leaving his body in the earth. But the facts are that for three days, the Lord dwelt in the place where the dead were, as Jonas remained three days and three nights in the whale's belly (Matt. 12:40)...David says, when prophesying of him: "Thou hast delivered my soul from the nethermost hell (grave)." And on rising the third day, he said to Mary, "Touch me not, for I have not yet ascended to my Father" (John 20:17)...
>
> How then must not these men be put to confusion, who allege...that their inner man [i.e. soul] leaving the body here, ascends into the super-celestial space? For as the Lord...after the resurrection was taken up into heaven, it is obvious that the souls of his disciples also...shall go away into the invisible place...and there remain until the

> resurrection, awaiting that event...Just as the Lord rose, they shall come thus into the presence of God. As our Master did not at once take flight to heaven, but awaited the time of his resurrection...so we ought also to await the time of our resurrection.[25]

Irenaeus thus condemns the modern tradition that Christians go *directly* into heaven as disembodied souls at death. It was not until the next century that such Platonic (to use Irenaeus' own word) "heresy" swamped the Church. Another early writer, Justin Martyr, protested against what later became accepted orthodoxy:

> They who maintain the wrong opinion...say the soul is incorruptible, being a part of God and inspired by Him...Then what thanks are due to Him, and what manifestation of His power and goodness is it, if He purposed to save what is by nature saved...but no thanks are due to one who saves what is his own; for this is to save himself...How then did Christ raise the dead? Their souls or their bodies? Manifestly both. If the resurrection were only spiritual, it was requisite that he, in raising the dead, should show the body living apart by itself, and the soul living apart by itself. But now He did not do so, but raised the body...Why do we any longer endure those unbelieving arguments and fail to see that we are retrograding when we listen to such an argument as this: That the soul is immortal, but the body mortal, and incapable of being revived. For this we used to hear from Plato, even before we learned the truth. If then the Saviour said this and proclaimed salvation to the soul alone, what new thing beyond what we heard from Plato did he bring us?[26]

The Latin church father Tertullian also objected to the belief that the soul departs the body at death and goes to heaven:

> Plato...dispatches at once to heaven such souls as he pleases...To the question…whither the soul is withdrawn [at death] we now give an answer...The Stoics…place only their own souls, that is, the souls of the wise, in the mansions above. Plato, it is true, does not allow this destination to all the souls, indiscriminately, of even all the

[25] *Against Heresies,* Book 5.
[26] *Dialogue with Trypho,* ch. 80.

> philosophers, but only of those who have cultivated their philosophy out of love to boys [i.e. homosexuals]...In his system, then, the souls of the wise are carried up on high into the ether...All other souls they thrust down to Hades.[27]

Martin Luther also believed what we are proposing here: "I think that there is not a place in Scripture of more force for the dead who have fallen asleep, than Ecc. 9:5 ('the dead know nothing at all'), understanding nothing of our state and condition — against the invocation of saints and the fiction of Purgatory."

This same reformer put it rather quaintly when he said, "We shall all sleep until he comes and knocks on our little grave, saying, 'Dr. Martin, get up!' Then I shall rise up in a moment and I shall be eternally merry with him."

Tyndale asked, "If the souls of the righteous be in heaven, tell me why they be not in as good case [condition] as the angels be? And then what cause is there of the resurrection?"

John Wesley observed, "It is, indeed, very generally supposed that the souls of good men, as soon as they are discharged from the body, go directly to heaven; but this opinion has not the least foundation in the oracles of God. On the contrary, our Lord says to Mary, after the resurrection, 'Touch me not; for I have not yet ascended to my Father.'"[28]

Dr. Paul Althaus in *The Theology of Martin Luther* comments on the take-over that has occurred within the church concerning the question of life after death:

> The hope of the early church centered on the resurrection of the Last Day. It is this which first calls the dead into eternal life (1 Cor. 15; Phil. 3:21). This resurrection happens to the man and not only to the body. Paul speaks of the resurrection not "of the body" but "of the dead." This understanding of the resurrection implicitly understands death as also affecting the whole man...Thus [in traditional orthodoxy] the original Biblical concepts have been replaced by ideas from Hellenistic, Gnostic dualism. The New Testament idea of the resurrection which affects the whole man has had to give way to the immortality of the soul. The Last Day also loses its significance, for souls have

[27] *A Treatise on the Soul*, ch. 51, 54.
[28] "The Rich Man and Lazarus," Sermon 112.

> received all that is decisively important long before this. Eschatological tension is no longer strongly directed to the day of Jesus' Coming. The difference between this and the Hope of the New Testament is very great.[29]

Big Implications

If only the Church had stuck to the whole biblical testimony that man *is* a soul, and though he may possess soul, meaning animate life, he does not have an immortal soul. If only the Church had taught that when he breathes his last in death man has no hope of ever being conscious again, except for God's rescue plan as revealed in His Son Jesus Christ, who said, "Because I live, you shall live" (John 14:19). Because the Church has bartered the Gospel hope of life through the resurrection at Christ's return for pagan and Greek ideas that man has a soul encased in his physical body, the implications are huge.

Two further points are in order. Firstly, holding a biblical view of the destiny of man is nothing less than a battle for faith. Will we believe God's word or Satan's? Are the dead dead? Or are they still conscious? Is it as a Buddhist workmate said to me, "Death is a part of the cycle of life"? Or is it that death dissolves us in the dust of the earth, as the Bible says? Does death escort us up or down? At the beginning God said, "In the day you eat of it, you shall surely die" (Gen. 2:17). At the beginning Satan said, "You surely shall not die!" (Gen. 3:4). So who is right? Who will we believe? As Warren Prestidge well expresses it:

> *The idea of the immortality of the soul detracts and distracts from faith in God.* The biblical reality is that our salvation is from God alone. It is not our achievement, nor inherent in our own nature. It is the most dangerous delusion to seek salvation within ourselves or our world. Rather, the Bible directs us to God and faith in God, "who raises the dead" (2 Cor. 1:9; Rom. 4:16-22). He alone has immortality (1 Tim. 6:16) and power over death (John 5:21, 26; Rev. 1:17-18).[30]

---

[29] Paul Althaus, *The Theology of Martin Luther,* Fortress Press, 1966, pp. 413, 414.

[30] Prestidge, *Life,Death and Destiny,* p. 53.

If we want to live again, and possess "eternal life," which is life in the Age to Come, we must cultivate a healthy relationship with God through His Son Jesus Christ. Outside this there is no hope. Our destiny lies in God and His great plan to bestow immortality on us on His own terms. The definition of faith is to believe His word and act on it.

Secondly, the Church has by and large scuttled the central plank of its Gospel platform. Instead of being in possession of the sure and certain hope in the coming of Jesus from heaven to set up the promised Kingdom of God, what has become the all-important moment is the individual's death. The challenge to unbelievers has become, "If you died today are you 100% sure you would go to heaven?" This is language completely foreign to the New Testament. Our centre of interest has shifted drastically from what is taught in the New Testament. Consequently, the Church has lost its power to proclaim to the world that its only hope is the coming again of Jesus Christ to raise the dead and inaugurate the Kingdom of God on earth.

The issue here affects nothing less than the nature of our Saviour. Is he a Saviour who can completely save us and the whole of creation? Is the salvation Christ offers merely an escape from the world and our troubles or is it nothing less than the complete redemption of the whole man and our whole world? Paul was expecting that the return of Christ would bring a renewed earth with all of nature freed from its current state of futility and bondage. This powerful hope based on the prospect that God would intervene once more in human history in regenerating glory at Christ's Second Coming enabled Paul and the early Christian church to overcome their persecutors:

> For I consider that the sufferings of this present time are not worthy to be compared with the glory that is to be revealed to us. For the anxious longing of the creation waits eagerly for the revealing of the sons of God. For the creation was subjected to futility, not of its own will, but because of Him who subjected it, in hope that the creation itself also will be set free from its slavery to corruption into the freedom of the glory of the children of God...And not only this, but also we ourselves...groan within ourselves, waiting eagerly for our adoption as sons, the redemption of our body (Rom. 8:18-23).

Commenting on this pericope, Martyn Lloyd-Jones says (this time I am quoting him with approval!):

> There are many today who regard themselves as Christians who do not believe in the resurrection and glorification of the body. They believe that when the Christian dies he goes to be with Christ; and they seem to think of that as some vague, nebulous, indefinite spiritual state and condition. But that is not the teaching of the Scripture. The Scripture teaches the resurrection of the body as an essential part of our salvation...We shall dwell in these glorified bodies on the glorified earth. This is one of the great Christian doctrines that has been almost entirely forgotten and ignored. Unfortunately, the Christian church — I speak generally — does not believe this, and therefore does not teach it. It has lost its hope.[31]

The contrast between these two world views is huge. Plato (and also Hinduism and Buddhism) says that it is the soul that really matters, so escape up yonder. The Bible says that the whole man, the body, all of nature, all of human history is going to be redeemed. Plato says that the body does not count; it's just a shell, indeed, even evil. The Bible says that all of creation, our bodies included, are "very good" (Gen. 1:31) and God has a master plan for His cosmos. He is going to decisively reclaim His creation when He sends His Son Jesus Christ back to this world (Heb. 1:6). Unfortunately, the early Church's defence against this Hellenistic invasion gave way after a few centuries. The wall burst. The church swilled the poisonous Platonic draft that it is the "soul" alone that really counts. The body may even be mistreated, disparaged. So the church built its monasteries, filled them with hermits who took vows of silence and celibacy and fostered a mistrust of women and the good sex which God had invented. They flagellated their bodies. By drinking the poison of Platonism the Christian church traded the robust apostolic hope of total renewal for all of creation for a pale imitation of departed-from-the-body other-worldly "spirits." No wonder today's Christians are open to spiritism and mysticism, a point I shall substantiate shortly in summary point number four.

---

[31] M. Lloyd-Jones, *Romans: Exposition of Chapters 8:17-39, The Final Perseverance of the Saints,* pp. 71-72.

Thirdly, the church has taught that "immortal souls" will forever suffer consciously in hellfire. This doctrine, which I confess I used to believe and teach with all my might and main, has brought much disgrace to the Church and to the God we have wanted others to accept. The medieval notion of paying indulgences to the Church in order to ease the suffering of those in purgatory is a direct consequence of immortal soulism. Plato said the soul cannot be destroyed and never perishes.[32] The church conveniently adopted this philosophy for its own ends, both to fill her coffers and to keep the faithful from straying. Praying to the saints — another unbiblical notion — also has its origins in the belief that the dead are already alive with God and can therefore intercede and help the living still on earth. This God-dishonouring practice would never have developed if the Church had early spat out the poison of Greek dualism. Paul warned that the view that the dead are already alive would be a fatal cancer in the church (2 Tim. 2:18).

Modern evangelicalism admittedly does not promote purgatory or indulgences, nor praying to the saints, but it still adopts Platonic dualism for its own ends. If we can't succeed in loving people into the Kingdom, then frighten them in with images of souls forever burning. Now of course the Bible does call people to repentance and faith in God, to "flee from the wrath that is to come." The destiny that awaits every human being is to stand before the judgment bar of Christ and answer for the deeds we have done in this life. This alone ought to strike great dread into any thinking person. To know that God "has fixed a day in which He will judge the world in righteousness through a man whom He has appointed, having furnished proof to all men by raising him from the dead" is surely a fearful prospect (Acts 17:31).

So where then do the images of eternal burning come from? Surely from the Bible? Ah, but the problem yet again, as we have seen throughout this book, is that we read these words with our Greek glasses on. The fate of all those whose lives are not found in "the book of life" will be to be "thrown into the lake of fire" (Rev. 20:15). Indeed. And didn't Jesus say as much when he warned, "And if your hand or your foot causes you to stumble, cut it off and throw it from you; it is better for you to enter life, crippled or lame, than having two hands or two feet, to be cast into the eternal fire"

[32] *Phaedo* 14, 24, 36.

(Matt. 18:8)? Yes, he did. And what about when Jesus talked about worms never dying: "And if your eye causes you to stumble, cast it out; it is better for you to enter the kingdom of God with one eye than having two eyes to be cast into hell, where their worm does not die, and the fire is not quenched" (Mark 9:47-48)? And what about where it says, "And the smoke of their torment goes up forever and ever; and they have no rest day and night, those who worship the beast and his image, and whoever receives the mark of his name" (Rev. 14:11). Surely these passages speak of people as souls in conscious torment forever?

Anyone at all familiar with the Hebrew Bible will know that each of these pictures of the fate of the wicked is taken from the Old Testament. So, before we jump to any hasty conclusions, let us briefly look at these images through our Hebrew eyes. In the Hebrew Bible, the destiny of the godless is spoken of as "destruction." And the contexts make it clear that *total annihilation* is in view:

"Destroy them in wrath, destroy [margin reads *Bring to an end*] them, that they may be no more" (Ps. 59:13).

"Let sinners be **consumed** from the earth, and let the wicked be no more" (Ps. 104:35).

"For after seven more days, I will send rain on the earth forty days and forty nights; and I will **blot out** from the face of the land every living thing that I have made" (Gen. 7:4).

"You have **destroyed** the wicked; You have **blotted out their name forever** and ever" (Ps. 9:5).

"And have cast their gods into the fire, for they were not gods but the work of men's hands, wood and stone. So they have destroyed them" (2 Kings 19:18).

The wicked will "become **as though they never existed**" (Obad. 16).

The sinner will be "like smoke [disappearing] out the window" (Hos. 13:3).

"You will make them as a fiery oven in the time of your anger" (Ps. 21:9).

Verses could be multiplied, but the message is the same. The wicked will be "destroyed" by God, that is, "blotted out," and will disappear altogether, and it will be "as though they never existed." The fire will "consume" them utterly (Ps. 21:9; Is. 33:10-14; 66:15-17). Annihilation! The Old Testament knows nothing of eternal conscious torment of the wicked. And the New Testament affirms this description of the fate of the wicked and builds squarely on its imagery. Take the imagery of Malachi 4:1-3 as an instance:

> For behold the day is coming, burning like a furnace; and all the arrogant and every evildoer will be chaff; and the day that is coming will set them ablaze, says the LORD of hosts, so that it will leave them neither root nor branch...and the wicked...shall be ashes under the soles of your feet on the day which I am preparing, says the LORD of hosts.

The Lord Jesus refers to this imagery in Matthew 13 where he states, "Therefore, just as the tares are gathered up and burned with fire, so shall it be at the end of the age. The Son of Man will send forth his angels, and they will gather out of his kingdom all stumbling blocks, and those who commit lawlessness, and will cast them into the furnace of fire; in that place there shall be weeping and gnashing of teeth" (Matt. 13:40-42).

This fire will be "unquenchable" (e.g. Mark 9:43, 48), not to suggest that it goes on endlessly (chaff does not take long to burn!), but to emphasise that the fire cannot be prevented from completing its work — of utter destruction. Again, the phrase is straight from the Old Testament, where its force is abundantly clear (e.g. Is. 1:31; Jer. 4:4; 7:20; 17:27; Ezek. 20:45-48; Amos 5:6).[33]

In case it is objected here that the "weeping and gnashing of teeth" points to eternal suffering, it must be stressed that this is to read into the passage what it does not say. Suffering there will be, but there is no indication at all, here, how long the "weeping and gnashing of teeth" are to continue. Furthermore, this phrase, once again, is based directly upon Old Testament precedent and depicts reaction, not so much to ongoing punishment, but rather to God's adverse intervention as such. The "weeping" expresses fearful, perhaps remorseful, anticipation of divine judgment (Zeph. 1:14; James 5:1) and the "gnashing of teeth" expresses impotent, frustrated, perhaps regretful rage against God and the redeemed, before "melting away" (Ps. 112:10).[34]

If any doubt lingers that "the punishment of eternal fire" means total destruction and annihilation then the Bible gives us an example grounded in history to illustrate its own meaning. Again, we note

---

[33] Prestidge, *Life, Death and Destiny,* p. 78.
[34] *Ibid*., p. 79.

how the New Testament reaches back and draws on the Old Testament for its inspiration: "Just as Sodom and Gomorrah and the cities around them, since they in the same way as these indulged in gross immorality and went after strange flesh, are exhibited as an example, in undergoing the punishment of eternal fire" (Jude 7).

Throughout the Hebrew Bible, Sodom and Gomorrah are cited as historical examples of the judgment of God on sinners. Sodom and Gomorrah are types depicting what God's future judgment will be like (see Luke 17:28-30; 2 Pet. 2:6). Note that it was "eternal fire" that fell on Sodom and Gomorrah. There is no thought here that Sodom and Gomorrah are still suffering the burning. They are ashes today — utterly destroyed. In other words, the fire is not eternal because it goes on and on. Rather it is "eternal" because its effects are permanent, having to do with the age to come. The effect of the fiery judgment is eternal in that it will never be reversed.

The same principle holds true when Jesus mentions that in hell "their worm does not die." Jesus draws from Old Testament imagery in Isaiah 66: "Then they shall go forth and look on the corpses of the men who have transgressed against Me. For their worm shall not die, and their fire shall not be quenched; and they shall be an abhorrence to all mankind" (v. 24).

Here Isaiah is gazing at corpses who have been "slain by the LORD" (v. 16). The "fire" and the "worm" are demolishing dead bodies, not immortal souls in hell. Nothing will stop the fire and the worm from accomplishing total annihilation. "It should be noted that according to this imagery it is the worms that never die and the fire that is perpetual or eternal. Everything and everybody else in Gehenna dies, decomposes and is destroyed. Gehenna is the image of complete destruction, the extreme opposite of life."[35] The same holds true for "the smoke of their torment [that] goes up forever and ever; and they have no rest day and night" (Rev. 14:11). It is not the torment that goes up forever, but rather its smoke. This is a picture of ultimate destruction that lasts forever. Once destroyed, there is no coming back, no reversal of God's edict. If it be objected that verse 10 seems to indicate otherwise (where it is said that those wicked sinners who have worshipped the Beast "will be tormented with fire

---

[35] Albert Nolan, *Jesus Before Christianity: The Gospel of Liberation,* London: Darton, Longman & Todd, 1986, p. 89.

and brimstone in the presence of the holy angels and in the presence of the Lamb"), Prestidge again notes that:

> This phrase emphasises the inescapability of the suffering while it lasts. This phrase also derives from the Hebrew Testament: Is. 34:8-18, another passage in the Sodom and Gomorrah tradition, which also includes reference to smoke rising "forever." Yet it is very clear that, in Is. 34, the envisaged effect of the judgment is annihilation: "From generation to generation it shall lie waste: no one shall pass through it forever and ever...They shall name it No Kingdom There and all its princes shall be nothing." Reference to the smoke rising forever is a graphic way of characterising the judgment as an appalling, completed, one-for-all event which memorialises for all time God's justice against evil.[36]

Other texts speak about the wicked being "thrown into the outer darkness." This is another Old Testament figure of speech relating to the day of judgment (see Zeph. 1:14; Amos 5:16-20; 8:9-10) and the picture is one of exclusion from the bright lights of the Messianic banquet when Jesus comes back. "Together, darkness and fire 'fix' for us the invariable twin implications of God's adverse final sentence: *rejection* and *annihilation.*"[37]

Putting this together then, we find that the popular and repulsive notion of eternal punishing is a world away from the Bible's "eternal destruction." "Eternal destruction" means the destruction which belongs to the future Age. It is irreversible. Man's destiny is forever sealed. The "eternal sin" (Mark 3:29) does not mean a sin that is endlessly committed, but a sin that carries everlasting consequences from which there is no reversal, because it keeps one out of the Messiah's Kingdom forever. To suffer "eternal judgment" (Heb. 6:2) likewise does not mean to be in the process of endlessly standing before God, but is rather to suffer the consequences of a judgment that will never be reversed. "Eternal life" in contrast is the life of the Age to Come, that is, a salvation with everlasting consequences, because it bestows immortality.

Straying from the Hebrew Bible's language for God's judgment has resulted in the Church promoting Greek philosophical notions

---

[36] Prestidge, *Life, Death and Destiny,* p. 84.

[37] *Ibid.*, p. 79.

about immortal souls forever in conscious torment. This teaching is foreign to Jesus and the New Testament apostles as well. They build fair and square on their Hebrew roots. Once judged, sinners will be consumed, destroyed, annihilated from all living existence. There is no place in the Bible for any eternal dualism, where evildoers will suffer in some remote corner of God's new age forever and forever. In God's new heavens and in God's new earth there will be no "unrighteousness" (2 Pet. 3:10-13), no screams of the cursed who live on in endless wretchedness. They will have suffered "eternal destruction" from the presence of the Lord (2 Thess. 1:9). Evil is not eternal. "God's purpose in Christ is to overcome and eliminate suffering and evil, not to perpetuate them."[38] The real issue then is not modern evangelicalism's "Where will you spend eternity?" but "Will you spend eternity alive or dead?"

Fourthly, by teaching that humans have or are "immortal souls" the church has unwittingly opened Pandora's proverbial box into the occult. Does this sound too incredible? Then go back to the beginning of this chapter. Remember those who claim to have had NDE's (near death experiences), and in particular ADC's (after death communications). Such experiences are not confined to the secular world. They are rife within the church. They are promoted in popular "Christian" books that support the idea of the survival of the dead.

I remember as a youth boldly entering a Christian Spiritualist Church and asking a lady why she was there, dabbling in so-called "Christian Spiritualism." She was a widow who said she was in weekly communication with her deceased husband. "And how do you know you are communicating with your dead husband?" I inquired. "He visits me often. He comes at night and sits on the end of my bed," she insisted. I pushed for more information. "And how do you know he sits on the end of the bed?" She answered with conviction, "Because I see the indentation he makes at the end of the bed when he comes and sits next to me."

The noted historian Arnold Toynbee studied civilizations across the whole gamut of history. Toynbee concluded that self-worship was the paramount religion of mankind, although it appeared in various guises. By accepting the Satanic lie that man is immortal, we have let man believe he is like God, i.e. divine in nature. This

---

[38] *Ibid.*, p. 95.

belief is nothing but self-worship. Ernest Holmes founded the Church of Religious Science (also known as Science of the Mind) upon the "Supreme Secret" that the "Masters of Wisdom" allegedly revealed to Napoleon Hill. Science of the Mind teaches that the originating and creative power of the universe, the life-source of all things, is a cosmic reality principle which is present throughout the universe and in every human being. Science of the Mind teaches that man controls the course of his own life. Just hitch up by the power of positive thinking to this universal law, and we can create our own world! Man, by thinking, can bring into his experience whatever he desires. Norman Vincent Peale's "power of positive thinking" and Robert Schuller's "possibility thinking" also teach that we can turn wishes into reality when we believe strongly enough. Paul Yonggi Cho, pastor of the world's largest church in Seoul, Korea, declares: "Through visualization and dreaming you can incubate your future and hatch the results."

What has all this got to do with the church's position that man does not die? Simply that once we accept the Satanic lie that man is divine in nature, the Trojan horse has already come through the church's front door. The common denominator is *self,* the desire to become a "god," to determine our own destinies. It's the lie that hooked not only Eve, but all of her descendants. And to whatever extent we seek to manipulate God, pander to our own selfish ends, deny our own mortality and corruptibility and refuse to accept God's verdict that we are dust and mortal — to that extent we are exalting ourselves to the position of gods.

Having accepted the Platonic tenet that man is a body with an eternal spirit dwelling within, the Church has flung its doors open to all sorts of occultic practices. In their book *The Seduction of Christianity* Dave Hunt and T.A. McMahon alert us to the dangers of the practices of meditation, visualization, or "imaging":

> Some Christians even have very real experiences through visualizing themselves in God's presence, in spite of the fact that the Bible declares that He "dwells in unapproachable light; whom no man has seen or can see" (1 Timothy 6:16). Richard Foster writes: "In your imagination allow your spiritual body, shining with light, to rise out of your physical body. Look back so that you can see yourself...and reassure your body that you will return momentarily...Go deeper and deeper into outer space until

> there is nothing except the warm presence of the eternal Creator. Rest in his presence. Listen quietly...[to] any instruction given."[39]

What a dangerous delusion it is to teach men that they have immortal souls which at death leave the body and go into the presence of God immediately. This is a plainly Gnostic teaching not taught in Scripture. It is equally false to teach that man is already divine by nature. Man wants to be like God. But the reality is "All flesh is grass, and all its loveliness is like the flower of the field. The grass withers, the flower fades, when the breath of the LORD blows upon it; surely the people is grass. The grass withers, the flower fades, but the word of our God stands forever" (Is. 40:6-8). Man is but a fragile mortal. Or to use another Biblical metaphor, man is like a puff of "vapour that appears for a little while and then vanishes away" (James 4:14). As we noted earlier, he is in nature no different from the animals that perish at death!

God has imposed death to teach us our true nature, as creatures before Him, to deny our divinity and self-sufficiency, that we may learn to rest in Him. And yet today, against all common sense, most people still cling to the supposition that we effectively survive death! And the Christian Church, contrary to her own Scriptures, has aided and abetted this belief, providing a foothold for belief in our own divinity, undermining her own Gospel!

For the Christian who is in relationship with God through Christ, it is "I *and* Thou." For the spiritualist, the mystic, the soul-immortalist, the Buddhist, it is "I *am* Thou," that is, the immortal soul within me links me forever to the Eternal and I am divine. The teaching that man is somehow divine and un-dying has put its toe in the Church's door and hey presto, a whole host of other "demons" have barged in to sit in the pews! Yes, the implications of accepting "immortal soulism" are huge indeed.

The Bible says that in Christ man can partake in the divine nature, that he can gain immortality which he presently lacks. Jesus taught that immortality is imparted to us through his spirit and words. The Gospel which Jesus preached everywhere brought "life and immortality to light" (2 Tim. 1:10). Our greatest and most

---

[39] Dave Hunt and T.A. McMahon, *The Seduction of Christianity: Spiritual Discernment in the Last Days,* Oregon: Harvest House Publishers, 1986, p. 164.

urgent need is to find out what the Gospel is and to ensure that we believe it and live it out. We now turn our attention to this vital issue.

Eight
ANOTHER GOSPEL

I am amazed that you are so quickly deserting Him who called you by the grace of Christ, for a different gospel (Gal. 1:6).

In his *Honest to Jesus,* Robert Funk tells a story about a man who plays "fetch the ball" with his dog. Every so often he pretends to throw the ball and then, while the dog is looking away, he actually throws it. Because the dog has not noticed this deception, he sits patiently at his master's feet and waits. His master points in the direction of the ball. The dog, not understanding the meaning of that gesture, barks at the pointing finger. Then Funk applies the story to the Church. He says the later followers of Jesus are like that dog: Jesus points to some horizon in his parables, some fabulous yonder, something he called God's estate (or Kingdom), which he sees but to which the rest of us are blind. Like dogs, we bark at the pointing finger, oblivious to the breathtaking scene behind us. All we need to do is turn around and look where he is pointing. The Jesus movement, the NT Church, very early on exchanged the vision. They were unable to hold on to the vision encapsulated in Jesus' parables and other verbal vehicles, and they lost his story. They did not know how to celebrate Jesus' vision of God's Kingdom.[1]

I was like that dog barking in the wrong direction, too. If anybody knew what preaching the Gospel was, I reckoned I did. Born and bred in solid Churches of Christ evangelical tradition, at 12 I went to the front of a church meeting and confessed Christ as my "personal Lord and Saviour" and was baptized by full immersion. I sat under a number of top-notch Australian and American evangelists throughout my teen years and heard them explain the Gospel to the "unsaved." Then I went to Bible college in Sydney for four years and after graduation spent over a decade preaching the Gospel not just as a pastor in local churches, but also as an evangelist all over Australia (except in the state of Western

---

[1] Robert Funk, *Honest To Jesus: Jesus for a New Millennium,* p. 10.

Australia). I "preached the gospel" in all sorts of meetings and settings, from open-air street preaching to large combined city-wide crusades, to one-on-one home door-knocking, to youth conventions, to businessmen's breakfasts, to ladies' coffee mornings, to radio programmes and even overseas. I helped lead hundreds to a personal faith in Christ at a fairly young age. Yes, I knew the Gospel. I could present the "Four Spiritual Laws," and if you wanted to become a member of the Churches of Christ, I knew the longer "Five Finger" version, too!

The following quote from a Billy Graham Gospel tract was typical of my well-practised approach:

> If you will read the epistles of Paul, you will notice the message centers in three things: the death, the burial, and the resurrection of Christ. As far as Paul was concerned, Christ Jesus came to do three days' work: that work was commenced when he was nailed on the cross and was ended when God raised him from among the dead. Paul never discussed the earthly life of our Lord — his baptism, his temptation, his miracles, his teachings, or even his sufferings in the Garden of Gethsemane. This is quite in keeping with the rest of the New Testament, for we must remember that Christ came not primarily to preach the gospel (though he did herald deliverance to the prisoner), but he came rather that there might be a gospel to preach. This gospel was won and brought into being by his work on the cross. We should remember that Jesus Christ had lived the Sermon on the Mount for 30 years before he ever preached it. His teachings and his sinless life never changed a life nor delivered one person from the life of sin. Only his death on the cross could do that.[2]

Yes, sir. I would have given my hearty "Amen" to that version of the Gospel. Did not the apostle Paul tell us that Jesus essentially "came to do three days' work"? Did not Paul agree that the Gospel message "centers in three things: the death, the burial, and the resurrection of Christ"? For he writes: "I delivered to you as of first importance what I also received, that Christ died for our sins

---

[2] Roy Gustafson, *What Is the Gospel?* Billy Graham Evangelical Association, 1980.

according to the Scriptures, and that he was buried, and that he was raised on the third day according to the Scriptures" (1 Cor. 15:3-4).

One day, however, it hit me that this classic definition of the Gospel does not say what most of us have been taught it says. Literally Paul wrote this: "For I delivered to you as **among the first things** what I also received." Crucial and integral as the death, burial and resurrection of Jesus are to the Gospel, they are not the whole Gospel. These are truths *among* others (*en protois*) that constitute the Gospel. We ask, naturally, what are the other things of first importance in the Gospel? More critically, we must ask whether it is possible that the Gospel Paul preached has been (without our being aware of it) exchanged for "another gospel" (Gal. 1:6-7), a depleted gospel. In this chapter I show that much like the cuckoo that tips the legitimate eggs out of the nest to substitute its own — which grows into a monster far larger than the original owners of the nest — the modern evangelical gospel is an impostor that has replaced the Gospel as originally preached with a caricature. We will see that when "orthodox Christianity" encoded its convictions in its early creeds "affirmations about the Christ were fenced off from information about Jesus of Nazareth. The Apostles' Creed implied nothing worth mentioning lay between the miraculous conception of Jesus and his death on the cross. The creed left a blank where Jesus should have come."[3] We will observe yet again how Hellenism reinterpreted Jesus' Gospel in order to service the Church's ecclesiastic programme.

Surely, if we are to understand the Gospel rightly, a good place to start would be with the Lord Jesus himself. It is for good reason he is called the pioneer, the inaugurator of the Christian faith (Heb. 12:2). Scripture insists that our great salvation "was at the **first spoken through the Lord**, and **confirmed** to us by those who heard" (Heb. 2:3). Jesus was the first Gospel preacher (not Peter, or Paul who subsequently "confirmed" the message!), so surely he will define for us his Gospel! And if we are to rightly understand Jesus of Nazareth and his Gospel, we must locate him within the Jewish world of Palestine in the first century. For whatever he said and whatever he did had to make sense — even if it was/is disturbing — within that cultural context. It is often said that Christianity is founded upon a person: Christianity is "Christ-in-you-ity"; its

---

[3] Robert Funk, *Honest to Jesus*, p. 303.

essence is a "personal relationship" with Christ himself. This is true. But it is only a dangerous half-truth. For if we are to understand Jesus the person and his mission, we must ask, *What was the person founded upon?* What was it that Jesus saw and sensed that was so enchanting, so mesmerizing, so challenging that it held him in its spell?

"The answer is that he was founded upon an idea, a strange idea current among the Jews of his time, an idea alien to Western thought which many non-Jewish theologians still find very inconvenient, the idea of Messianism. It was Messianism which made the life of Jesus what it was and so brought Christianity into being."[4] The ultimate conviction on which the whole edifice of Christianity rests is that in Jesus, the Messiah has come. This teaching was the Gospel underlying all the gospels, the Good News that Israel's king and his Kingdom were being announced. Christianity gives lip service to the fundamental fact that Jesus was this Messiah, whose advent fulfilled all the old prophecies, but singularly fails to concentrate on how to understand this Messiah and his Gospel and thus how to get to know him. The Messiahship of Jesus is asserted, and then quickly side-stepped in order to disclose him in a light more congenial to Hellenic rather than Jewish concepts.[5] In our unwrapping of the Gospel of the Kingdom that Jesus taught we must not make the same mistake. We start at the beginning.

At the commencement of his ministry we are told that: "Jesus came into Galilee, preaching **the gospel of God**, and saying, 'The time is fulfilled, and **the kingdom of God** is at hand; repent and believe in the gospel'" (Mark 1:14-15; also Matt. 4:17-23). To some of us with a "traditional" evangelical background it is strange to think that Jesus preached the Gospel! We think the apostles were the first Gospel preachers after Pentecost. After all, what Gospel was there to preach *before* the crucifixion, burial and resurrection? But Mark tells us that Jesus came preaching "the Gospel of God" at the beginning of his Galilean ministry. This was his opening manifesto: "Repent and believe the Gospel."

From start to finish, Jesus constantly emphasized one theme: The promised Kingdom of God. Understanding what Jesus meant by "the Kingdom of God" is the key to understanding his mission,

---

[4] Hugh Schonfield, *The Passover Plot,* pp. 22-23.
[5] *Ibid.*, p. 39.

his God-given purpose, his *raison d'etre.* To understand what Jesus meant by the Kingdom of God is to understand the real Jesus. To miss what Jesus meant by the Kingdom of God is to miss Jesus altogether. For Jesus defined the Gospel as the Gospel of the Kingdom. All other grids of reference in our understanding of his mission and message flow from this key phrase, "the Kingdom of God." We must not skip lightly over this *locus classicus.* To skip over Jesus' preaching of the Gospel of the Kingdom would be to fatally divorce Jesus from his own message and context.

It is axiomatic that Jesus believed that the God of Israel, Jehovah, was his God and Father. He believed he was God's Anointed and destined for rulership in the coming Kingdom of God. He was the son of David with the blood of kings in his veins. "In that *Messiah* refers to the one whom God anoints, or delegates, to rule God's kingdom (see Psalm 2; Mark 15:32), everything that Jesus does from his baptism onward is immersed in the prophetic anticipation of the coming of the Kingdom of God."[6] In announcing the Kingdom Gospel Jesus is announcing himself as the Messiah-designate. The most dramatic moment in all history was believed to have arrived with him. The time was now ripe for people to urgently prepare for that Kingdom's arrival. To ordinary people in that culture this could only mean one thing: Israel was at last going to be redeemed, rescued from oppression. N.T. Wright correctly observes:

> God's "Kingdom" wasn't a state of mind, or a sense of inward peace. It was concrete, historical, real. Twentieth-century Western Christians need to shed a few ideas at this point. When people downed tools for a while and trudged off up a hillside to hear this Jesus talking, we can be sure they weren't going to hear someone tell them to be nice to each other; or that if they behaved themselves (or got their minds round the right theological scheme) there would be a rosy future waiting for them when they got to "heaven"; or that God had decided at last to do something about forgiving them for their sins. First-century Jews knew that they ought to be nice to each other. In so far as they thought at all about life after death, they believed that their God would look after them, and eventually give them new physical bodies in his renewed world. (The phrase

[6] Robert Hach, *Possession and Persuasion*, p. 127.

"Kingdom of Heaven," which we find in Matthew's Gospel, does *not* mean a Kingdom-place called "heaven." It is a reverent way of saying "the King*ship* of God.")

There is no sign that first-century Jews were walking around gloomily wondering how their sins were ever going to be forgiven. They had the Temple and the sacrificial system, which took care of all that. If Jesus had only said what a lot of Western Christians seem to think he said, he would have been just a big yawn-maker. What he in fact said was so revolutionary that it woke everybody up. It was so dramatic that Jesus seems to have adopted a deliberate policy of keeping to the villages, always moving quickly on, never getting into the big Galilean towns like Sepphoris, just over the hill from Nazareth, or Tiberias, down by the sea of Galilee, just south of Magdala.[7]

The Good News — that is, the Gospel of the Kingdom — that Israel was waiting for was that the Messianic deliverance was imminent. To say that "the Kingdom of God is at hand" was to those people a way of saying that Caesar, and his delegate Pontius Pilate, and Herod should not be controlling God's people. It was announcing that God Himself would be stepping in through His appointed delegates, the Messiah with his saints. "No King but God" was the revolutionary catch-cry of the day. Thus, the word "Gospel" had a crystal clear Messianic and political significance to it. To announce that the Kingdom was "at hand" meant Israel's King was here and the Kingdom was coming. The nation of Israel was on tiptoe with anticipation that had built up over many generations. Every year the Messianic hope was felt more keenly. In fact, on every Sabbath in every synagogue in the Jewish world of Jesus' generation, they offered up the prayer: "Speedily cause the offspring of David, thy servant, to flourish, and let his horn be exalted by thy salvation, because we wait for thy salvation all the day. Blessed art thou, O Lord, who causest the horn of salvation to flourish" (*Benediction* 15).

Like a refugee amongst the nations of the world, Israel would soon be liberated. The prophetic word could not fail of fulfilment. Most in first-century Israel believed it was the eleventh hour. And it was certainly not a kingdom in the clouds they longed for. It was the

---

[7] N.T. Wright, *Who Was Jesus?* pp. 97-98.

reign of God over a perfected earth, at a definite point in history, under the Lord Messiah.

Hugh Schonfield makes the point that in the year AD 35 Caesar made a public proclamation throughout the empire signifying his mastery over his subjects; for every citizen of the empire this was Caesar's acceptable year of "Lordship." But in contradistinction, Jesus proclaims in the synagogue *that very same year* that because he is the Messiah it is indeed "the acceptable year of the Lord." (Even if we do not agree with Schonfield's chronology, the point is still culturally valid.) Jesus' Gospel proclamation was a seditious move:

> Messianism represented the conviction that the existing world order would presently be overthrown. The empire ruled by Caesar and his legions would pass away, and in its place there would be the Kingdom of God governed by the Messiah and his people. Christianity identified the Messiah with Jesus. There was "another king," another emperor, to whom allegiance was transferred.[8]

The fact that Jesus was eventually crucified and buried did not mean that Caesar rested easy. Even in AD 70 when the Roman legions finally breached the walls of Jerusalem, Vespasian commanded all of the family of David to be sought and executed so that no one of the royal Davidic stock might be left. Eusebius also mentions that the emperors Domitian (96 AD) and Trajan (120 AD) mercilessly persecuted Jews of the Davidic line of descent.[9]

So to Jewish ears the expression "the Kingdom of God" carried a huge (national) connotation. Their Hebrew Bible contained the recurrent theme that God was going to send the Messiah to be His agent to bring about the end of the world as it is currently run, and introduce a whole new world order. The government of that age would be upon his shoulder (Is. 9:6). This Messiah was to be the son of David. (The title "son of David" is used of Jesus at least 14 times in the gospels and means that he claimed to be the legitimate king of Israel.) It meant that he would sit on the throne of David in a new Jerusalem. The enemies of God's people would be judged. Truth and justice would cover the earth. All nations of the earth would be blessed through Israel's exalted status. Even the very natural order

---

[8] Schonfield, *The Passover Plot,* p. 226.

[9] *Eccl. Hist.* III, xii, xix-xx, xxxii, 3-4.

would be completely transformed, to the point where dangerous animals would no longer hunt and tear apart, and where little children could play unharmed with them; the desert would blossom (Is. 11:6-9). In short, the glory of God, through the Messiah and his people would cover the earth as the waters cover the sea:

> The Messianic mission of Jesus had as its objective the preparation of men for the future Kingdom of God. Jesus constantly looked forward to the coming of the eschatological Kingdom when the final judgment would effect a separation of men, the righteous entering into the life and blessings of the Kingdom, and the wicked into the doom of punishment.[10]

Jesus of Nazareth saw himself as God's appointed agent, the Messiah. He knew his destiny. He was the Son of God who was to bring all of these promises God had given to the prophets to completion. As noted previously, we tend to cloud things somewhat by calling him Jesus Christ. But it must be remembered that Christ is not a proper name, but a title. It is more correct to speak not of Jesus Christ, but of Jesus *the* Christ. To call Jesus the Christ is to give him the title of Messiah. To a Jew to call someone the Christ, the Messiah, was to assign to that person both a political as well as a theological role. Jesus belonged within a world where theology and politics went hand in hand. The theology was that of Jewish monotheism. But not just any abstract monotheism about there being only one God. The Jews believed *their* God YHWH (Yahweh/Jehovah) was the only God, and that all other "gods" were idols, either concrete creations of human hands or abstract creations of human minds. Jesus shared this belief that Israel's God was the only true God. This God was his Father. Thus, Jewish monotheism went hand in hand with the doctrine of "election." They believed they were the "chosen people" of this one true God, destined under God's Messiah to enter his Kingdom when it came. This is and was the essence of the Christian Gospel.

To proclaim Jesus as the Lord's Messiah was as good as proclaiming him as king. When Andrew finds his brother Simon he announces, "We have found **the Messiah...**Rabbi, you are **the Son of God,** you are **the king of Israel**" (John 1:41, 49). Martha confesses, "I have come to believe that you are **the Messiah, the**

[10] G.E. Ladd, *A Theology of the New Testament,* p. 181.

Son of God" (John 11:27). The high priest interrogates Jesus, "'I adjure you by the living God, that you tell us whether you are **the Christ, the Son of God**.' Jesus said to him, 'You have said it yourself; nevertheless I tell you, hereafter you shall see **the Son of Man** sitting at the right hand of power, and coming in the clouds of heaven'" (Matt. 26:63-64). The soldiers mocked Jesus, "'Hail, **king of the Jews**,' and they struck him repeatedly...The Jews answered...'According to the law he ought to die, because he made himself the **Son of God**'" (John 19:3, 7). When he was hanging on the cross the taunt was "Let the **Messiah, the king of Israel** come down from the cross that we may see and believe" (Mark 15:32). These texts could be multiplied many times over. They all prove that the terms Messiah, Son of God, son of Man, and king are synonymous. This usage is strictly in accord with the OT background, especially places like Psalm 2 which uses the descriptions "**My Son,**" "**My king**," and "**Messiah**" interchangeably for the promised saviour who is to come: "The rulers take counsel together against the LORD and against **His Anointed [Messiah]**...but as for Me I have installed **My King** upon Zion...You are **My Son,** today I have begotten you" (Ps. 2:2, 6-7). It can be seen that the NT titles for Jesus were already in existence in the Hebrew Bible:

Messiah = the Son of God = the Son of Man = the king of Israel

It is an incontrovertible fact that for the three centuries before Augustine, the Kingdom was seen this way. It was an altogether *eschatological* Kingdom. (Remember the word *eschatological* comes from a Greek word meaning the study of the end times.) The Kingdom was seen to be the inbreaking of God through Christ at the end of this present age, when the dead "in Christ" would be raised to life again, and the earth would experience the conditions of the garden of Eden all over again. The Messiah would sit on the throne of David and his headquarters would be in a new Jerusalem. There is a famous exchange between a fellow called Trypho and Justin Martyr that highlights the political aspect of the Gospel. It runs like this:

> Trypho: Do you really admit that this place Jerusalem shall be rebuilt? And do you expect your people to be gathered together, and made joyful with Christ and the patriarchs...?
> Justin: I and many others are of that opinion, and believe that this will take place, as you are assuredly

> aware...Moreover I pointed out to you that some who are called Christians, but are godless, impious heretics, teach doctrines that are in every way blasphemous, atheistical and foolish...I choose to follow not men or men's teachings, but God and the doctrines delivered by Him. For if you have fallen with some who are called Christians, but who do not admit the truth of the resurrection...who say that there is no resurrection of the dead, and that their souls when they die are taken to heaven, do not imagine that they are Christians...But I and others who are right-minded Christians on all points are assured that there will be a resurrection of the dead, and a thousand years in Jerusalem, which will then be built, adorned and enlarged, as the prophets Ezekiel, Isaiah and others declare...We have perceived, moreover, that the expression, "the Day of the Lord" is connected with this subject. And further, there was a certain man with us, whose name was John, one of the Apostles of Christ, who prophesied by a revelation that was made to him that those who believed in our Christ would dwell a thousand years in Jerusalem; and that thereafter the general and the eternal resurrection of all men would take place.[11]

The early Christians believed the "Gospel of the Kingdom" related to this glorious future reign of God on earth, through His appointed Messiah. Christians believed God had destined that they "reign upon the earth" with Messiah (Rev. 5:10). All who joined Jesus in repentance and faith would be the elite of the final world order, entitled to the highest honours because of their loyalty to him in this present world. To the early Christians the Gospel of "salvation" related to the reality of God's promised future of a renewed earth. To "be saved" meant being preserved in the day of Messianic judgment, and being entitled to reign with the Messiah in his terrestrial (earthly) kingdom. Gentile believers were assured of equal privileges with Jewish believers and would inherit with them the same promises originally made to Abraham and to Israel. In a moment we will explore this thought further. It suffices for the minute to say that the apostles and the first generation(s) of Christians firmly expected Christ's Kingdom to be publicly

---

[11] *Dialogue with Trypho.*

established in their lifetime. But as their Lord delayed his coming, and with each succeeding generation not seeing this hope materialize, the hope of the future earthly Kingdom began to fade. The Church exchanged its end-time future hope of the Kingdom of God that Jesus preached for the belief that the Church *itself* was in fact the Kingdom of God on earth already. Jesus' Gospel of the *eschatological* Kingdom of God was replaced by a post-apostolic gospel of the *ecclesiastical* kingdom of God. For mainstream Christianity, the Church *became* the kingdom: From Augustine onwards, it became official church dogma that the kingdom had already come! Salvation was no longer to be received when Christ returned. Salvation could only be found in the Church's priesthood and programmes. The Kingdom was no longer without; it was "within the heart." Salvation was no longer tied to God's redemption in future history; it was now an inner spiritual perception, held in custody and administered only by the "Church."

An obvious difficulty in defending the mainstream interpretation that the Kingdom is the Church, and is limited to what is within (spiritual and personal), is that the apocalyptic and cosmic elements in Jesus' view of the coming Kingdom are eliminated. The apostles' hope of resurrection from the grave at Christ's return when he sets up his Kingdom by a spectacular intervention has been replaced by the Platonic heaven-for-the soul-when-you-die gospel. This non-apocalyptic, non-eschatological interpretation of the Kingdom — the Kingdom is primarily a personal religious experience of the presence of King Jesus ruling in the individual's heart — omits two key elements in Jesus' Gospel. Firstly, as we have seen, it dismisses *the historical Hebrew setting in which Jesus did all his teaching*. Theologians call this the *Sitz im Leben,* the real life setting of Jesus. "It is clear, again from Josephus and elsewhere, that the idea of God's becoming King was not about an inner set of ideals, a 'Kingdom' invisible to the naked eye but quietly transforming people's inner motivations. It was about the expected dramatic reversal in Israel's fortunes."[12]

Secondly, it completely ignores *the apocalyptic element* of Jesus' preaching of the coming Kingdom. It ignores the cataclysmic and cosmic climax that will end this present world order. There have been many commentators who would have us believe that

---

[12] N.T. Wright, *Who Was Jesus?* p. 56.

when Jesus preached the Gospel of the Kingdom he was simply giving us the shell. The "real" message is the "spiritual" kernel hidden inside that Hebrew husk. To get to the real message of Jesus we must crack open that useless, out-of-date Jewish capsule before we can swallow the health-giving gospel vitamin. This approach consigns Jesus' announcement of the Kingdom to "interim ethics," only relevant to that day. Fortunately, some contemporary scholarship has seen through this out of character "spiritualizing" view of the Kingdom. They rightly recognize that if we rip the Jew Jesus from his historical setting, we run the risk of creating "another Jesus" and of presenting "a different gospel" (2 Cor. 11:4). Some recent scholarship thankfully is recognizing that Jesus' Gospel of the Kingdom cannot be uprooted from its original first-century soil. For the Hebrew, the prophetic hope expected the Kingdom of God to arise out of history and in history at the end of this present evil age. Jesus never made his Gospel a purely inward, private matter. He kept it in line with this rich Hebrew heritage. Jesus did not deviate from the earthly hope centred in a ruling descendant of David governing the world from Jerusalem, supervising a society redeemed from the curse of all evil. First-century Jews who knew the Hebrew prophets understood this very well. Early apostolic Christianity founded on Jesus' Gospel of the Kingdom also understood it. Subsequent ecclesiasticism serving its own ends conveniently changed it.

There is a critical need to restore the faith that was once for all delivered to the saints (Jude 3). Failure to reinstate the Gospel message in its own native Hebrew environment will guarantee the ongoing confusion that has existed since the Church lost her belief in the Gospel of the Kingdom as Jesus preached it. The call to "accept Jesus" as one's "personal Lord and Saviour" must not be divorced from believing his preaching of the Gospel of the Kingdom. *Jesus made an intelligent understanding of his Kingdom message the indispensable condition for salvation.* He said that "When anyone hears the word of the kingdom, and does not understand it, the evil one comes and snatches away what has been sown in his heart" (Matt. 13:19). Refusal to believe this Kingdom message and to repent is to miss his Good News, for he announced that failure to hear and see "the mystery of the Kingdom of God" would have the disastrous consequence of not being forgiven (see Mark 4:11-12). Repentance, then, is a complete reorientation of one's world view. Repentance involves an understanding of Jesus' message with a heart commitment to his Kingdom ideal. *Without belief in his message, and commitment to his Kingdom vision, there can be no forgiveness and no salvation.* To "receive Christ" is to believe that through his death, burial and resurrection we are assured entrance into the life of that coming Messianic age. To be "born again" is to "see the Kingdom of God," that is, first to understand the Kingdom plan and finally to enter the Life of the Age to Come (John 3:3).

The foundation of Jesus' Gospel centres on the announcement of the Messianic Kingdom. A Kingdom-less Gospel is a Gospel without the Jesus of the Bible, for the authentic Jesus clearly equates salvation with receiving his Kingdom-word. It is this message of the Kingdom that carries the life-giving energy of God, the seed, according to Jesus himself (Matt. 13:19; Luke 8:11). To believe the word of the Kingdom is to receive his seed into our souls. This is to "be born according to the Spirit" which is to be "born according to the promise" (Gal. 4:22-23, 28-29). To hear "the message of truth, the gospel of your salvation" is to be "sealed with the Holy Spirit of promise" (Eph. 1:13). The apostle Peter equates salvation with being "born again" by receiving "the living and abiding word of God" which is "the word which was preached to you" (1 Pet. 1:23-25). When we put these verses together we get the equation:

The Gospel of the Kingdom = the word of God = the spirit of promise = salvation = (the agent of the) new birth

When Paul wrote to the Corinthians that the death, burial and resurrection of Jesus are "amongst things of primary importance," the point under discussion must be kept in mind; some Corinthian Christians were beginning to question and doubt the resurrection. "How do some among you say there is no resurrection of the dead?" Paul asks (1 Cor. 15:12). It is to answer this particular crisis of belief that Paul reminds his readers that the death and resurrection of Jesus are absolutely fundamental to the Christian Gospel. *Without the death of Jesus giving assurance of forgiveness, and without the resurrection of Jesus from the grave, there will be no salvation in the coming Kingdom of God.* If Jesus has not been raised to life again, then the hope of salvation which is the arrival of the Kingdom of God on earth is a forlorn hope. Before Calvary and Easter Sunday, Jesus and the apostles preached the Gospel for years without any inclusion of these great redemptive facts. After Easter Sunday, the apostles (as we shall soon see) still preached the Gospel of the future Kingdom, but were then able to supply as vital information guaranteeing that Kingdom, the facts of Jesus' death and resurrection. Vital and crucial as the death and resurrection of Christ are, they are not the bedrock. They are "among the first things" that Paul preached (1 Cor. 15:3). For Paul the climax of the Gospel is when God's Messiah "delivers up the kingdom to the God and Father" (1 Cor. 15:24). Thus Paul is in total agreement with Jesus' "Gospel of the Kingdom," for there is an unbreakable link between the resurrection of the dead and the coming of the Kingdom.

We are saying that the big reason why the mainstream "orthodox" interpretation that Jesus came only to do three days' work cannot be defended biblically is because it ignores the historical life-setting of Jesus' ministry. Historically, Jesus first preached to Jews, not the Church; Jesus founded his Church with Jewish apostles and converts, though his message was later offered to the nations and has timeless implications of course. Jesus proclaimed his very Hebrew-oriented Gospel of the Kingdom to first-century Jews and later authorized the same saving Gospel for us all. "It makes all the difference to our understanding of Christianity if we are enabled to apprehend that it did not begin as a new religion but as a movement of monotheistic Jews who held Jesus to be their God-sent king and deliverer. Here in a sentence, is what is imperative to know about the origins of Christianity," says Schonfield.[13] To avoid creating a Gentile (pagan!) Jesus, his announcement that "the Kingdom of God is at hand" must be considered within the framework of Judaism. Jesus was not a "Christian" in our modern sense. He was a first-century Jewish prophet. The Jewish world view at that time "grew directly out of Jewish monotheism: Israel's God was the one God of all the world. Theology and politics, piety and revolution, went hand in hand."[14] When Yahweh becomes king, Israel will be rescued from evil domination, and God Himself will return to Zion; the Kingdom will have arrived. "It was about Israel's story reaching its climax, about

---

[13] Schonfield, *The Passover Plot,* p. 22.

[14] N.T. Wright, *The Meaning of Jesus,* HarperSanFrancisco, 1999, p. 33.

Israel's history moving toward its decisive moment."[15] Jesus' call to repent and believe this Gospel announcement had much more than modern connotations of individual salvation in mind, more than "believe in Jesus and when you die you will live forever in heaven." Jesus was summoning his hearers to seize the moment and take up their proper role in God's unfolding drama. If they accepted Jesus as their promised Messianic Lord, and followed him in his new way, then they would be the true Israel, the true people of God, when God's Kingdom day arrived.

He Was Despised and Rejected by All

We must remember that Palestine at the time of Christ was not a fairy-tale land. It was a real world with real people. When Jesus was born, Palestine was ruled by an insecure, egotistical king called King Herod the Great (37-4 BC). His reign overlapped those of other secular figures such as Julius Caesar, Cleopatra, Mark Antony, and Augustus. The contemporary Jewish historian Josephus describes Herod as a megalomaniac whose whole reign was spent listening to his spies tell of plots from all and sundry. He even murdered the wife he loved dearly out of suspicion of a plot to dethrone him. When he knew he was dying, Herod arranged the murders of many prominent citizens, so that instead of celebrations at his passing there would be genuine mourning throughout Palestine! Herod could not even claim to be a Jew by birth. He was a native of Idumea, the non-Judaic desert region to the south of Palestine. In order to gain legitimacy for his kingship, Herod divorced his first wife and married a recognized Jewess. He tried to ingratiate himself with the Jews by rebuilding the Temple of Jerusalem. Such measures did not succeed in winning Jewish affection. He always remained reviled and distrusted. In fact, the Jewish nation considered Herod to be a sign of God's displeasure for their national sins. To many Jews, Herod was a sign that God had abandoned His people. This heightened their desire for a king who would restore Israel to her favoured position. This spiritual leader when he appeared would be the Davidic Messiah, and he would be their rightful king. Sanctioned by God, anointed by God, this man would drive the cursed Gentiles from the Promised Land and bring about a glorious regime in the tradition of David.

---

[15] *Ibid.*, p. 35.

Herod of course is infamous for his Massacre of the Innocents as recorded in Matthew 2. As soon as he heard the rumour that one who might be the long-hoped for Jewish Messiah was to be born, Herod was deeply perturbed. He enquired of the chief priests and scribes where this Christ was to be born. The fact that Herod felt threatened by the baby Jesus was due to powerful public expectation of the arrival of a rightful Messianic ruler. The Romans had a policy of appointing local men to act as kings on Caesar's behalf. Herod would have reasoned that with a legitimate Jewish claimant to the throne of Israel Rome might recognise the infant Jesus' royal bloodline. It was not the son of poor Jews whom this usurper feared, but one who by virtue of inherent and regal genealogical qualification might — when grown — be able to rally popular backing. Herod also burned the archives of Jewish families, including those descended from Ruth and thus David, so he would not be embarrassed by references to his own base origins. Presumably Herod was most interested in the genealogies that could challenge his own position as king. Our point is simply to stress the very real national milieu in which Jesus arrived. The appellation "Messiah" was loaded with political gunpowder. When Jesus preached that the Kingdom of God was at hand, this was the kind of talk which signified that God's intervention was near. It was equivalent to announcing his heaven-sanctioned kingship.

The Roman legate at the time, Pontius Pilate, was ruthlessly loyal to Rome. He probably arrived in Caesarea during the spring of 26 AD. Josephus, the Jewish historian who was born a few years after Jesus' death, tells us that Pilate, the procurator of Judea:

> removed the army from Caesarea to Jerusalem, to take their winter quarters there, *in order to abolish the Jewish laws.* So he introduced Caesar's effigies, which were upon the ensigns, and brought them into the city...Pilate was the first who brought these images to Jerusalem, and set them up there; which was done without the knowledge of the people, because it was done in the night time.[16]

Eusebius tells us that Pilate's agenda was to carry out the policy of his mentor Sejanus. This was to achieve "the destruction of the whole Jewish race."[17] Setting up Rome's offensive military

---

[16] *Antiquities,* 18, 3, 1, italics mine.

[17] Eusebius, *Proof,* 11, 5.

standards was a deliberate part of Pilate's campaign "to abolish the Jewish laws." These standards displayed portraits of Caesar and Roman eagles, graven images highly provocative to Jews. Perhaps even worse, Pilate's Tenth Legion flaunted their own insignia of a bull and a boar. To Jews the pig was an unclean animal, whose flesh they were forbidden to eat or even touch. Josephus does not tell us where these effigies were set up, but historians conjecture that it must have been in the Antonia Fortress directly overlooking the Temple courts. Come daybreak, the city was in an uproar.

A Jewish delegation protested to the Roman tribune, but Pilate refused to remove the standards "because it would tend to the injury of Caesar." For five days the pressure continued. Pilate would not budge. Josephus continues the story:

> On the sixth day he ordered his soldiers to have their weapons privately, while he came and sat upon his judgment-seat, which was so prepared in the open place of the city, that it concealed the army that lay ready to oppress them; and when the Jews petitioned him again, he gave a signal to the soldiers to encompass them around, and threatened that their punishment should be no less than immediate death, unless they would leave off disturbing him, and go their ways home. But they threw themselves upon the ground, and lay their necks bare, and said they would take their deaths very willingly, rather than the wisdom of their laws should be transgressed.

It was a tense moment, with thousands of Jews ready to have their throats cut for the sake of their faith, and a thousand Roman soldiers at the ready with swords drawn, looking to Pilate for his signal. Josephus says Pilate was deeply affected "by their firm resolution to keep their laws inviolable." Perhaps the repercussions of such a large-scale massacre unnerved Pilate, but in any case, he removed the Roman effigies from Jerusalem. Some commentators suggest that this action had immediate impact on Israel. Daniel the prophet had forewarned of "the abomination of desolation" when a brutal ruler will vent his fury on the Holy Covenant: "His soldiers in his command will desecrate the sanctuary and citadel [fortress]; they will abolish the regular offering, and will set up 'the abomination that causes desolation'" (Dan. 11:31).

Although Jesus later puts this "abomination of desolation" as still future and close to the end of age (see Matt. 24:15-16) it is easy to see how Pilate's action in that day would have made tongues wag. They had just witnessed an abomination. This was a portent of the coming Kingdom. The end time had surely come. If Pilate's desecration of Jerusalem was a fulfilment of the Daniel prophecy, then Messiah would soon set up the Kingdom of God. It was at about this time that John the Baptist stepped out of the desert, calling the nation to "Repent, for the kingdom of heaven is at hand" and "make ready the way of the Lord" (Matt. 3:1-3). At the risk of repetition, let us understand that in that first century such talk was not "pie-in-the-sky" stuff. The Kingdom was not going to be set up in the clouds. It was a Kingdom-rule of God through His Messiah in Judea with ultimate control over the world.

But if Jesus' announcement of the Kingdom of God was the equivalent of placing sticks of political dynamite around Palestine, challenging Herod and Caesar, it was also the equivalent of placing religious gelignite amongst his own countrymen. Wherever he went, Jesus turned accepted religious convention on its head. How could Israel enter God's promised Kingdom when they themselves were a society full of social and economic injustices? How could this people enter the Kingdom with such an oppressive and corrupt Temple priesthood? How could those revolutionaries who believed the Kingdom would only come by violent means enter that new society based on love and service and equality? God's people must themselves first repent. They must become worthy of this high calling. That is, they must give up their own agendas and commit to Jesus' way. "This is not to say that Jesus did not give this challenge what we would call a religious and spiritual dimension. It is to insist that we cannot use that to screen out the practical and political challenge that the words would convey."[18] Failure to accept Jesus' Gospel agenda would also disqualify *them*. Jesus called these blind, self-righteous Jews "children of the Devil" (John 8:44). This went down like a lead balloon. What scandal. What effrontery to call Abraham's children accursed! They thought they were being loyal to Jehovah. But instead of the light of the world, Jesus called them darkness. They were not going to enter the Kingdom unless they repented and took up his cross. Nor were they prepared to accept Jesus' risky agenda of turning the other cheek, going the second mile, losing their lives in loving service, forgiving the debts and sins

---

[18] N.T. Wright, *The Meaning of Jesus,* p. 38.

of their oppressors, and praying for their enemies. Jesus' Kingdom would be filled with the meek, the kind and gentle, the poor in spirit. As N.T. Wright correctly asserts, the Sermon on the Mount:

> is not simply a grand new moral code. It is primarily the challenge of the Kingdom: the summons to Israel to be Israel indeed at the critical junction of her history, the moment when, in the Kingdom announcement of Jesus, the living God is at work to reconstitute his people and so fulfill his long-cherished intentions for them and for the whole world.[19]

But as it turned out, Jesus' agenda was too risky, too radical. His own people "did not receive him" (John 1:11).

The Cleansing of the Temple Announces Jesus' Messiahship

Jesus' clash with the established secular and sacred symbols of the day reached its climax in the week before his crucifixion. Israel's moment of destiny had arrived. "Israel, the historical people of the one creator God, was swimming in the stream of history just above a roaring waterfall. If she didn't watch out, she would be swept right over, and fall to her doom."[20] Would the nation accept his Messianic credentials and agenda or miss their hour? The nation was deeply divided. The Pharisees were harsh and critical of their fellow Jews. The Essenes regarded all other Jews — the Pharisees included — of being worthy only of God's anathemas. The Temple priesthood was corrupt and oppressive. Jesus claimed to be the way to fulfill all Israel's promised Kingdom hopes that God would vindicate him and those who trusted his word. He claimed to fulfill the Law and all that the prophets had spoken. He claimed to be Lord of the Sabbath. He claimed to have the authority to forgive sins, but they accused him of blaspheming, for who can forgive sin but God alone (Mark 2:7)?

But these various skirmishes with his countrymen reached their climax when Jesus entered the Temple precinct at the close of his ministry. The Temple possessed huge royal significance. In fact, Temple and kingship went hand in hand. David had planned the first Temple. Solomon had built it. Two great men of God, Hezekiah and Josiah, had restored it. The Maccabees had cleansed the Temple.

---

[19] *Ibid.*, p. 39.
[20] N.T. Wright, *Who Was Jesus?* p. 101.

Herod, having received his kingship from Rome, was eager to make it good by rebuilding it. The Temple was the symbol of Israel's special place in God's plan for the world. (Even many years after Titus had razed the Temple, the last great messianic pretender, Bar-Kochba, minted coins depicting the facade of the Temple, which no doubt he was planning to rebuild.) So when Jesus marched into the precinct of this national symbol and turned their tables over, announcing, "Take these things away. Do not make my Father's house a den of thieves!" he was acting out a parable of judgment. He stood in the reforming sandals of Jeremiah before him who had railed against Israel:

> Thus says the LORD of hosts, the God of Israel, "Amend your ways and your deeds, and I will let you dwell in this place...for if you truly amend your ways and your deeds, if you truly practice justice between a man and his neighbour, if you do not oppress the foreigner, the orphan, or the widow, and do not shed innocent blood in this place, nor walk after other gods to your own ruin, then I will let you dwell in this place, in the land that I gave to your fathers forever and ever. Will you [continue] to steal, murder, and commit adultery, and swear falsely...and walk after other gods?" (Jer. 7:3-9).[21]

Jesus' judgment on the Temple also was a clear reference to Zechariah's picture of the Messianic age when "It will come about that any who are left of all the nations that went against Jerusalem will go up from year to year to worship the King, the LORD of hosts, and to celebrate the Feast of Booths [tabernacles]...**and there will no longer be a trader in the Temple of the Lord of hosts in that day**" (Zech. 14:16, 21).

Here is perhaps one of the clearest indications of what motivated Jesus' triumphal entrance into Jerusalem and his attack on the corrupt Temple system. Zechariah's prophecy is a prediction concerning the Messianic Kingdom. Jesus is now demonstrating the reality that the old is being done away with. This is not just an outburst of righteous anger. The Kingdom is being announced in acted out parable. It is an announcement of authority: "By what

---

[21] I freely acknowledge my indebtedness to N.T. Wright for much of this material, and encourage the reader to review his chapter titled "The Mission and Message of Jesus" in *The Meaning of Jesus.*

authority are you doing these things, and who gave you this authority?" (see Matt. 21:23; Mark 11:27-28; Luke 20:1-2; John 2:18). In the triumphal entry and the Temple cleansing, it is hard to imagine any other action so calculated for Jesus to announce his Messiahship so openly.

The message was that now, at Israel's supreme hour, and through himself as God's Anointed, Israel's God was showing His wrathful rejection of the whole corrupt system. This was his Father's house, the place where Israel and all the nations should be able to see the light of the one true God. But they had turned it into "a den of thieves." We have already met this word for "thieves" (*lestai*) and seen that it was regularly used to denote brigands and rebels, as well as swindlers. The Temple had become the focal point for the nationalists in their plans for revolt against Rome, as well as for the rich and powerful in their oppression of the rest of the nation. For Jesus, the distorted Temple system was a symbol that was now horribly wrong. His action in this symbolic parable of judgment was as good as saying that the Temple would be once and for all replaced. Jesus challenged, "Destroy this temple and in three days I will raise it up" (John 2:19). That is, the Messianic community would now be focused on Jesus himself. This was too much. Jesus' Kingdom aspirations were far too controversial and confronting for the nation. These were considered by the "establishment" as subversive acts. "It would be like announcing in a Muslim country that one was fulfilling the will of Allah — while apparently vilifying Muhammad and burning a copy of the Koran."[22]

Jesus' healings were also highly symbolic. They are often called "signs" and so pointed to the fact that the Kingdom of God was arriving through his own work. (Healing and restoration are often joined in the Hebrew Bible, for instance in Isa. 35.) Jesus had to go. Not only had his Gospel announcement of the Kingdom of God confronted the corrupt and oppressive systems of Caesar's world, but it was a double-edged sword that cut at the corrupt heart of Judaism. At the end of his earthly ministry, the official verdict of Israel was that Jesus' claim to be their Messiah was rejected. They would not have him to reign over them as their king. "Away with him. Crucify him" was their judgment.

---

[22] N.T. Wright, *Who Was Jesus?* p. 99.

However, being under the jurisprudence of Roman law, the Sanhedrin still needed Pilate's authorization before they could execute Jesus. There is no question but that Jesus was crucified by the Romans because he was recognized to be a political revolutionary. Certainly, for the most part of his ministry Jesus had hushed up this expectation. On one occasion the crowds wanted to forcibly coronate Jesus as their King Messiah, but he "withdrew again to the mountain by himself alone" (John 6:15). He said again and again to those he healed, "See that you tell no one" (Matt. 8:4). He commanded the demoniacs to "Be quiet" when they announced his true identity (Mark 1:25). He even "gave orders" to his own disciples "not to relate to anyone what they had seen, until the Son of Man should rise from the dead" (Mark 9:9). Jesus knew how politically explosive it was to openly call him Messiah. Palestine was a tinder box awaiting God's Anointed King. But at the end when he came riding into Jerusalem in the most open manner with the crowds chanting the Hallel chant of Psalm 118, "Hosanna! [Save us!] Blessed is he who comes in the name of the Lord," the die was blatantly cast. Jesus accepted the honour of being the King of Israel, long-awaited. When the Pharisees were offended and called out for Jesus to silence his admirers Jesus replied, "I tell you, if they are silent the stones will cry out" (Luke 19:40). Jesus boldly accepted the public plaudits that he was indeed their rightful leader. Trouble was, this act made him at the same time treasonous against Caesar. This much is stated by Tacitus, the Roman chronicler, and:

> constitutes the one sure assertion about Jesus to issue from a non-biblical, yet contemporary, source. There is no question but that the Romans perceived Jesus as a military and political figure, and dealt with him strictly according to that perception. Crucifixion was a penalty reserved for transgressions against Roman law, and *Rome would not have bothered to crucify a man preaching a purely spiritual message, or a message of peace.*[23]

Thus, if the real Jesus is to be properly interpreted, as N.T. Wright states, he must be earthed in first-century Judaism with their eschatological longing, the readiness to see in a new movement the possibility that this might be God's great, final, decisive hour with Israel and the world. "Jesus belongs within the first-century world

[23] Baigent et al, *The Messianic Legacy,* p. 73, emphasis added.

of rival eschatologies, not within the 20th-century world of 'patterns of religion.'"[24] No other setting does justice to his context or position within it. As Wright follows this historical sketch, he says:

> I discover a Jesus who was not simply an example, even the supreme example, of a mystic or Spirit person, such as one might meet, in principle, in other cultures. I find, rather...a first-century prophet announcing and inaugurating the kingdom of God, summoning others to join him, warning of the consequences if they did not, doing all this in symbolic actions...and in cryptic sayings, *that he believed he was Israel's Messiah, the one through whom the true God would accomplish his decisive purpose.*[25]

In other words, Jesus did not abandon the true and prophetic hope of Israel. He came to reconstitute Israel under his own Messiahship. He was therefore a thoroughly credible first-century flesh and blood Jew, whose Kingdom message earned the ire of his own country's religious establishment and — under Pilate's verdict — the wrath of Rome.

It is clear that Pilate felt a great deal of sympathy for Jesus and preferred rather to release him. Pilate announced, "I find no guilt in this man" (Luke 23:14). But the Jews, led by Caiaphas, howled for Jesus' death: "If you release him you are not Caesar's friend. Anyone who makes himself a king, speaks against Caesar" (John 19:12). Sherwin-White, a specialist in Roman law, sees here a convincing technicality. The term "Caesar's friend" (*Caesaris amicus*) "recalls the frequent manipulation of the treason law for political ends in Roman public life" and is a notable political term. Caiaphas won.

But note that he has won, not on the spurious grounds of blasphemy supposedly introduced in an eleventh hour change of strategy (John 19:7); Pilate could release a blasphemer and remain Caesar's friend. "Caiaphas has won on the grounds of Messiahship, which has been revealed in this trial...as a political issue — one that is potent enough to threaten even the Prefect of Judea."[26]

Although it has been hotly debated, the evidence seems to suggest that the Jews could stone men and women to death for

---

[24] N.T. Wright, *The Meaning of Jesus,* p. 43.

[25] *Ibid.*, p. 50.

[26] Ian Jones, *Joshua: The Man They Called Jesus,* Melbourne: Griffin Press, p. 238.

offences against *religious* law.[27] Adulterers could be stoned to death (John 8:7-11). The first Christian martyr, Stephen, was in fact later stoned to death (Acts 6:8-8:1). Josephus tells us that James, Jesus' brother, was stoned to death by the Sanhedrin.[28] These actions were obviously allowed by Rome. But where Jesus' execution is concerned, Caiaphas and the priests seek crucifixion for political treason: "We found this man perverting our nation and saying not to pay taxes to Rome and claiming that he is the Messiah, a king" (Luke 23:2). Pilate accordingly asks Jesus, "Are you the king of the Jews?" As Ian Jones contemporizes it, "Pilate's question to Jesus is like a Second World War German military governor asking a citizen of an occupied country: 'Are you the leader of the Resistance?'"[29] "If...Jesus were a rightful king, then one [i.e. Pilate] would indeed assert one's authority by humbling him."[30]

The Gospels are unanimous. Jesus was charged with a crime against Rome. True, the Jewish Sanhedrin wanted Jesus out of the way because of his challenge to their Temple. So they told Pilate that Jesus was a rebel king. They told the people that Jesus was a false teacher, who by claiming to be the Messiah was a blasphemer leading them astray. Thus, Jesus was led to his death in the most brutal and sadistic way possible. His crucifixion "proclaimed, within that symbolic universe, that Caesar was the master of the world and that the gods of the nations, including Israel, were powerless before him."[31] In that day Rome, and Rome alone, was authorized to build the kingdom and rule her mini-realms. There was no separation of church and state then, no way to separate religion and politics in first-century kingdom-building. Indeed, from Caesar's viewpoint, why would anybody want to oppose the *Pax Romana,* the new world order of political reformation and spiritual rearmament, his bandit-free roads and his pirate-free sea lanes, his cities linked by common culture and economic prosperity, and his legions guarding the borders behind which the barbarians prowled?

This historical fact is often lost sight of in discussions concerning Jesus' execution. Jesus did not die because he preached "the kingdom of God is within you" (Luke 17:21), meaning God's

---

[27] Josephus, *Against Apion* 25, 31.
[28] Josephus, *Antiquities* 20, 9, 1.
[29] *Ibid.,* p. 233.
[30] Baigent et al, *The Messianic Legacy,* p. 45.
[31] N.T. Wright, *The Meaning of Jesus,* p. 102.

peace rules in your hearts as a spiritual reality. That message was not offensive then, and is still not offensive today. Lots of folks today talk easily about their "spiritual journey" and their life of "faith in God." Nobody bats an eyelid. But let a true believer in the Jewish Messiah announce that Christ will yet rule the governments and nations of this world from Jerusalem, and that all powers and authorities will bow before him, and see the kind of reaction it inevitably engenders! Proclaim the Gospel's exclusive announcement that only those who love this kind of Lord Jesus Messiah will be co-rulers with him, sharing the executive positions of that government, and conversely that those who do not work for and long for that kind of new world regime are "accursed," and see what kind of response is evoked! Paul says, "If anyone does not love the Lord, let him be accursed [literally *anathema*]. Maranatha [meaning, O our Lord come!]" (1 Cor. 16:22). Those who do not live for the coming Kingdom of this Lord Christ are excluded! To put this in a stark modern-day setting, let a Christian say to a Muslim, "Your prophet Mohammed will bow before King Jesus and confess that he alone is sovereign" and see the hostile response. The message of the Kingdom of God as preached by Jesus has lost none of its stigma. "A Jewish-Christian theocracy is hardly what the world expects or desires."[32] Herein lies a good litmus test as to which gospel is the true Gospel: the one the modern Church is preaching today about "the Kingdom of God within you and when you die you go to heaven" or the one that announces "the Kingdom of the world has become the kingdom of our Lord, and of His Christ; and he will reign forever and ever" (Rev. 10:15).

The apostolic preaching which announced Jesus' vindication by God through resurrection must be understood in this light also. Forgiveness was preached not just in today's terms of personal guilt expunged with relief for a guilty conscience. Rather:

> it was the early Christian deduction, from Jesus' resurrection, that his death had been after all effective, *as the hinge upon which the door to God's new world had swung open. To say that the Messiah had died for sins in fulfilment of the scriptures was to make a claim, not so much about an abstract atonement theology into which*

---

[32] Anthony Buzzard, *Our Fathers Who Aren't in Heaven,* Restoration Fellowship, 1995, p. 122.

> *individuals could tap to salve their guilty consciences, as about where Israel and the world now were within God's eschatological timetable.*[33]

Early Christianity continued Jesus' Messianic ministry after Easter. That is to say, the message of the early Church was to continue Jesus' announcement of the Gospel of the Kingdom. This message still offended the existing lords of the world, most notably Caesar. The early Christians, after Jesus' resurrection, rebuilt their agendas and aims on the understanding that God's promises had not failed, and that when the cord had pulled back the curtain revealing God's future Kingdom they had seen a vision worth dying for. God had raised this very Jesus and vindicated his Messianic claims. Therefore, Jesus' message of the Kingdom was not dead and buried. The king was indeed going to come back from heaven to complete his Father's agenda.

In an earlier chapter we noted that the emperor Constantine, three centuries after Jesus, saw himself as the saviour and unifier of the Roman Empire. He endeavoured to combine in his kingship the messianic ideals of military and spiritual rulership. By aligning itself with Constantine, the Church compromised its independence and sold its soul to secularism, thereby denying the very Christ it believed in. The Jesus of history was effectively buried. The Church no longer proclaimed the coming apocalyptic Kingdom of Christ as Gospel, and corrupted the message about the coming Kingdom that Jesus and the apostles had preached with a new "gospel" message: "The kingdom has arrived. That kingdom is the Church." All traces of Messianic Christianity were transformed, and to all intents and purposes erased:

> In order to diffuse itself through the Romanized world, Christianity transmuted itself — and, in the process, *rewrote the historical circumstances* from which it arose. It would not do to deify a rebel against Rome. It would not do to exalt a figure who had been executed by the Romans for crimes against the Empire. As a result, responsibility for Jesus' death was transferred to the Jews — not only to the Sadducee establishment, who undoubtedly had a hand in it, but to the people of the Holy Land in general, who were among Jesus' most fervent supporters. And *Jesus himself*

[33] N.T. Wright, *The Meaning of Jesus,* p. 103, emphasis added.

> *had to be divorced from his historical context, turned into a non-political figure — an other-worldly, spiritual Messiah who posed no challenge whatever to Caesar. Thus, all trace of Jesus' political activity was de-emphasized, diluted or excised. And, so far as possible, all trace of his Jewishness was deliberately obscured, ignored or rendered irrelevant.*[34]

The Roman Church of the middle ages was fiercely anti-Semitic. They hated the "Christ killers" and sought to destroy anything Jewish. We only have to remember the pressure that was applied to Mel Gibson to edit (delete!) certain scenes that were considered offensive by the Jews in his blockbuster film *The Passion of the Christ* to understand the deeply ingrained residual feelings this issue still raises. The Jews suffered horribly from anti-Semitic views promoted by the Church, post-Constantine. The Church came to be presented as a Gentile organization that was supposedly not foreseen in the OT. The Church era was the "mystery" now come to light. However, the NT does not tell Jews that they must become Gentile Christians to be saved. Rather, Gentiles are told to become believers in the (Jewish) Messiah. It is we Gentiles who were once "separate from Messiah, excluded from the commonwealth of Israel, and strangers to the covenants of promise, having no hope and without God in the world" (Eph. 2:12). It is Gentile believers who are included or "grafted" into the blessings of Israel. It is a Jewish Messiah we love and serve. But the Church has taught that if a Jew wants to become a Christian he has to forsake his prophetic Hebrew heritage. This is wrong.

It will be argued of course that Jesus' political agenda (political in the sense of proclaiming a Gospel that promised the literal reign of God through Messiah on a renewed earth over the nations) was wrongly perceived by his contemporaries. After all, did he not say to Pilate whilst on trial, "My kingdom is not of this world. If my kingdom were of this world, then my servants would be fighting, that I might not be delivered up to the Jews; but as it is, my kingdom is not of this realm"? (John 18:36). The argument which dismisses the political nature of Jesus' message of the Kingdom will be shortly examined. It will suffice for the moment to observe that the only thing Jesus denied here was that his time for coronation had come. Jesus did not deny that he was the King of the Jews. He did

---

[34] *Ibid.*, p. 107, emphasis added.

not deny his God-given right to the throne of David and to inherit all the promises God had decreed involving governmental control of the (future) world. All Jesus said to Pilate was that his kingdom did not belong to this present system, did not arise out of the present wicked order dominated by Satanic values. Anybody who doubts that Jesus was waiting for his government to come need only see how his assertions to this effect so inflamed his jurors. Under oath Jesus said to the high priest, "hereafter you shall see the Son of Man sitting at the right hand of power, and coming in the clouds of heaven" (Matt. 26:64). Incensed, the high priest tore his tunic, saying with indignation, "He has blasphemed!"

The Mystery of the Kingdom

What was it that so offended the Jews and caused them to reject Jesus' claim to be their King and the fulfilment of all God's promises? The blasphemy was *not* that Jesus was claiming to be Almighty God in human flesh. That is an incongruous charge and makes no sense in the historical and biblical context of the time. That idea is an imported, foreign, later invention. As Schonfield rightly states:

> By admitting that he was the Messiah, the rightful and foreordained king of Israel, Jesus had committed a "blasphemy," not of God in Jewish law but of Tiberias Caesar in Roman law. He was guilty, they held, of *laesa maiestas*, violation of the emperor's sovereignty, and it was therefore proper for the scandalised authorities, not as Jews but as Roman subjects, to act as *delatores* and inform against Jesus to Caesar's representative. Because a Jewish court reached this verdict, we are not to imagine, as the Church was later concerned to establish, that Jesus had declared his Deity, and consequently from the viewpoint of the Mosaic Law had blasphemed the name of the Lord. In that case the penalty would have been stoning, not crucifixion. Jesus had not even uttered the sacred Name of God, and referred to himself as the Son of Man. Early Nazorean teaching knew nothing of Trinitarianism. The Council had neither cause nor any interest to condemn Jesus on religious grounds, since their whole purpose was to stand well with Rome and at the same time to divert the odium of

> the Jewish people for what they were doing from themselves to Pontius Pilate.[35]

Yes. The scandal was that Jesus was claiming to be God's anointed, the Messiah, the rightful heir to David's throne of Israel. But Jesus did not fit the divine-hero mould the Jews had come to expect. Nor were evil doers conquered. All things appeared to continue on as they had always done. Theirs was the picture of a Messiah coming — immediately, in their own day — to take "dominion, glory and a kingdom, so that all the peoples, nations, and men of every language might serve him. His dominion is an everlasting dominion which shall not pass away, and his Kingdom is one which will not be destroyed" (Dan. 7:14). Even the disciples were offended that the Messiah should be ignominiously killed (Matt. 16:21-23). A suffering Messiah had no place in the disciples' plans, nor in the estimation of the nation of Israel. The Kingdom Jesus announced did not look like what they expected. George Ladd suggests the answer to the scandal of Jesus is found in the concept of this "mystery." Jesus said to his disciples, "To you has been given **the mystery of the kingdom of God**, but for those outside everything is in parables; so that they may indeed see but not perceive, and may indeed hear but not understand; otherwise they might turn again, and be forgiven" (Mark 4:11-12).

That Jesus believed the Kingdom was to come with apocalyptic power is quite certain. As the Messiah he would come "at the end of the age" with the angels of God and raise the dead. He would come with a blazing light universally witnessed from one end of the sky to the other (Luke 17:24). After a brief and intense period of great tribulation, the sun would be darkened, the moon would turn blood-red, and the stars would fall (Mark 13:24-25; Matt. 24:21, 29-31). There would be a cataclysmic "crunch." He would come with such power that there would be "weeping and gnashing of teeth" from all the wicked who would be cast out of his Kingdom. Yes, he believed the prophets.

But the mystery so unexpected to Jesus' contemporaries was that the Kingdom that is to come in such cosmic upheaval has in fact entered the world in advance in a hidden form, and is already at work secretly within and among men. The mystery of the Kingdom is the coming of the Kingdom into history in advance of its

[35] Schonfield, *The Passover Plot,* p. 170.

apocalyptic manifestation. It is, in short, "fulfilment without [present] consummation." There is a now, yet not now, aspect to the Kingdom. There is a tension between the already present, and expected future. The NT must be read with both this present and future aspect of the Kingdom held in tension.

There is "*both* a present preliminary manifestation of the spirit and power of the Kingdom as well as its future worldwide inauguration and establishment at the Second Coming."[36] This is the single truth illustrated by the several parables of Mark 4 and Matthew 13.[37] An illustration or two of this is in order. Take the parable of the mustard seed: "The kingdom of heaven is like a mustard seed, which a man took and sowed in his field; and this is smaller than all other seeds; but when it is full grown, it is larger than the garden plants, and becomes a tree, so that the birds of the air come and nest in its branches" (Matt. 13:31-32).

The Jews were familiar with the picture of Israel as a great tree (see Ps. 104:12; Ezek. 17:23; 31:6). They fully expected, under Messiah, to be the grandest and biggest tree of all the nations. So how could this insignificant Galilean be the Messiah? And his band of half-literate disciples, how could they represent the Kingdom of Heaven? The Jews could not understand how one could talk about the Kingdom apart from such an all-encompassing manifestation of God's rule. "How could the coming glorious Kingdom have anything to do with the poor little band of Jesus' disciples? Rejected by the religious leaders, welcomed by tax collectors and sinners, Jesus looked more like a deluded dreamer than the bearer of the Kingdom of God."[38] Jesus' answer is first, the tiny seed, later at the end, the huge tree. The smallness of his present ministry does not exclude the future glorious invasion of the Kingdom of God. The parable of the mustard seed illustrates the truth that the Kingdom, which one day will be a great tree, is already present in the world in the person of Jesus and his followers, even if currently, according to the world's standards, an insignificant form.

It is true that many commentators see in this parable a forecast of the growth of the Church into a great institution — the so-called Kingdom-Church. This interpretation, however, has the weakness of

---

[36] Anthony Buzzard, *The Coming Kingdom of the Messiah,* Restoration Fellowship, 2002, p. 28.
[37] G.E. Ladd, *A Theology of the New Testament,* p. 94.
[38] *Ibid.,* p. 98.

not giving proper recognition to the historical setting of the parable. It rips Jesus out of his social setting and the context of Israel's faith. In short, it has no exegetical ground whatsoever. That the Church is not the Kingdom is clear when we remember that it is the Church's task to preach the Kingdom. Through her message of the Gospel of the Kingdom it will be decided who will enter the Kingdom at the end of this age, and who will be excluded. The Church does not preach itself! "*The Church is the people of the Kingdom but cannot be identified with the Kingdom.*"[39] Therefore, "This interpretation is based on the identification of the Kingdom and the Church, a view that we hold to be untenable."[40]

The parable of the leaven presents the same truth as the mustard seed. That is, that the Kingdom of God, which one day will rule over all nations on the earth, has already — in the preaching of Jesus — entered the world in a form that was hardly perceptible to the Jews (and the rest): "He spoke another parable to them: 'The kingdom of heaven is like leaven, which a woman took, and hid in three pecks of meal, until it was all leavened'" (Matt. 13:33).

Many commentators have seen here again the idea that through a slow permeating process the Church will eventually penetrate all society and thus the world will be transformed. Other commentators interpret the leaven as evil doctrine that has permeated an apostate Church. However, these ideas were foreign to Jesus' mind and to the Jewish context in which he taught. The interpretation that best fits the historical setting in which Jesus' ministry worked is that the leaven represents the Kingdom now hidden, which one day will control all.

This parable gains its significance only when interpreted in the life setting of Jesus' ministry. The mighty, irresistible character of the eschatological Kingdom was understood by all Jews. The coming of the Kingdom would mean a complete change in the order of things. The present evil order of the world and of society would be utterly displaced by the Kingdom of God. The problem was that Jesus' ministry initiated no such transformation. He preached the presence of the Kingdom of God, but the world went on as before. How then could this be the Kingdom?

---

[39] *Ibid.,* p. 58, emphasis added.
[40] *Ibid.*, p. 97.

Jesus' reply is that when a bit of leaven is put in a mass of dough, nothing seems to happen. In fact, the leaven seems quite engulfed by the dough. Eventually something does happen, and the result is the complete transformation of the dough. No emphasis is to be placed upon the way the transformation is accomplished. The idea of the Kingdom of God conquering the world by a gradual permeation and inner transformation was utterly foreign to Jewish thought. The idea of gradualness is contradicted by the parables of the tares and the dragnet where the Kingdom comes by apocalyptic judgment and destruction of evil rather than by a gradual transformation of the world.

The emphasis of the parable lies in the contrast between the final, complete victory of the Kingdom when the new order comes, and the present, hidden form of that Kingdom as it has now come into the world. One would never guess that Jesus and his small band of disciples had anything to do with the future, glorious Kingdom of God. This is the mystery, the new truth about the Kingdom. How or when the future Kingdom will come is no part of the parable.[41]

Jesus used many other parables to illustrate this hidden mystery of the Kingdom of God. The parables of the pearl of great price and the treasure hidden in a field (Matt. 13:44-46), the dragnet (Matt. 13:47-50), and the man sowing the seed (Mark 4:26-29) all illustrate the point that in Jesus the Christ the Kingdom had come among men in an unexpected way. Jews everywhere longed for the Kingdom of God to be fully manifested. But it had come in a form that they did not recognize, so they overlooked and even despised it, rejecting Jesus as the Messiah. Jesus just did not fit the expected historical, religious and political moulds of the day. As another has observed:

> Jesus was neither a man of the religious and political establishment (a priest or a theologian like the Sadducees) nor a man of the violent political revolution (a political liberator like the Zealots). He was neither a man who joined the apolitical emigration (he was not a monk like the Qumran people) nor a man of religious legal compromise (he was not a pious observer of the law like the Pharisees). This distinctive profile of Jesus, his otherness in comparison

[41] *Ibid.*, pp. 99-100.

> to other politically relevant groups, was the first reason for the conflict over Jesus. Jesus was different![42]

It was the difference in Jesus and the motley band of followers he attracted and his sayings that was so puzzling to what we would in our society call the "conservative middle class majority." How could he be the King of Israel? How could he announce that the Kingdom is "at hand"? How could one who broke the Sabbath and the rules of purity and who mixed with the wrong company — prostitutes, tax collectors, lepers — be their promised King? Jesus welcomed "sinners," lepers, the unclean, the blind, the lame, the deaf, the mute, prostitutes, and tax collectors. Sure, he claimed to fulfill all the old hopes and ideals of Israel, but he did it in a way that appeared to cut across all conventions with a totally new agenda. In that society, such outcasts were excluded from the Messianic hope. But:

> Contrary to every superficial evaluation, discipleship to Jesus means participation in the Kingdom of God. Present in the person and work of Jesus without outward display or visible glory was the Kingdom of God itself...Historically the parable[s] answer the question of the strange character of Jesus' followers. He attracted tax collectors and sinners. In the popular expectation, the coming of the Kingdom would mean not only that the Messiah would "destroy the godless nations with the words of his mouth...and...reprove sinners for the thoughts of their hearts"; he would also "gather together a holy people whom he shall lead in righteousness"...Jesus did not gather such a holy people. On the contrary he said, "I came not to call the righteous, but sinners" (Mark 2:17)...How could the Kingdom of God have anything to do with such a strange fellowship? Is not the function of the Kingdom by definition to destroy all sinners and to create a sinless community? Jesus' answer is that one day the Kingdom will indeed create such a perfect community. But before this end-time event, an unexpected manifestation of God's Kingdom has occurred.[43]

This is the same line of thinking that still causes Jews to this day to reject Jesus as the Messiah. Jews today reason that since the

---

[42] Kuschel, *Born Before All Time?* p. 461.

[43] G.E. Ladd, *A Theology of the New Testament,* pp. 100-101.

Hebrew prophets predict a Messiah who will conquer evil governments, and since Jesus did not overthrow the Roman Empire in Palestine or bring the Kingdom of God, Jesus was deluded and his disciples were deceived into believing he was the promised Messiah. Therefore (modern-day Jews still argue), the New Testament is a false document.

So Jews past and present have failed to understand that the Kingdom of God involves two great moments: fulfilment in the ministry of Jesus of Nazareth and climax at the end of the age, introducing a new era of history, when the Messiah returns in glory. If the matter stopped there, it would be sad enough. But alas, even Christians have lost faith in the central message of Jesus and the apostles, namely the Gospel of the Kingdom. Ask yourself, When you hear the Gospel proclaimed today do you hear anything concerning the Kingdom of God? Or are you invited simply to "ask Jesus into your heart"?

We have replaced the robust end-of-the-age emphasis with heaven-for-disembodied-souls-when-we-die stuff. (To many the idea of being a disembodied soul in heaven suggests eternal boredom. One of my workmates recently told me he *wants* to go to hell where the real party is going to be.) We have turned God's master plan for the redemption of the world and society into a pathetic subjective caricature. No Hebrew grounded in his Bible would have entertained such a nebulous concept. Where does this form of the Gospel invitation appear in the New Testament? On the contrary, as Anthony Buzzard so powerfully states:

> The Gospel as Jesus preached it invites you also to dedicate the rest of your life to preparation for participation in the supervision of that future Kingdom on a renewed earth. You are invited to be a co-heir of the Kingdom with the Messiah. In short, the Jesus of history, the original "theocrat," continues his work of recruiting members of his royal household, the theocratic party, who are urged to prepare themselves with divine help to take part in the Messiah's government of the future. This will be the first and only administration to rule the world successfully.[44]

Sadly, we do not hear this eschatological emphasis today. There is an antipathy to the Gospel of the Kingdom as Jesus preached it. It

---

[44] Anthony Buzzard, *The Coming Kingdom of the Messiah,* p. 7.

was not always so. "For Christians of the first three centuries, the Kingdom was altogether eschatological. An early second-century prayer says, 'Remember, Lord, Thy church, to...gather it together in its holiness from the four winds to Thy kingdom which Thou hast prepared for it.'"[45]

How has this shift away from the Gospel of the Kingdom happened? The reasoning is this: Since Jesus claimed to be the Messiah, and since he did not destroy Roman rule in Palestine and bring in an age of glory for Israel, setting up the earthly Kingdom of God, Jesus obviously did not intend such a literal meaning of his Gospel teaching. Such political and earthly interpretations are way too literalistic. They are misguided Jewish ideals. What Jesus really came to bring was a "spiritual" kingdom, that is, a kingdom of God's rule and sovereignty within men's *hearts.* Did he not say, "The kingdom is within [or, among] you" (Luke 17:21)? It was Augustine of Hippo (354-430 AD) who popularized this position.

Part of this misunderstanding comes from the very phrase "Kingdom of Heaven." To Western ears "heaven" is away out there in ethereal space, beyond human perception. To modern ears "heaven" is where we go when we die. To our minds "heaven" is mystical. But not to the Hebrew mind. "In contrast, the biblical heaven is a metaphor signifying God's promised future, the age to come, the Kingdom of God (which is also called 'the Kingdom of Heaven'). What better metaphor to picture the promised future of God than the heavens, the sky above, to which it is natural to look when envisioning the future?"[46] That is to say, what exists "in heaven" to the Hebrew exists in God's promised future. Heaven, then, is a Hebrew figure of speech synonymous with the coming life of the age to come which will arrive on earth when Jesus Christ returns in kingly glory to set up God's reign over the world, according to all the promises of God.

> Heaven does, then, represent the everlasting home where God and His people will enjoy unending fellowship, but rather than an invisible home in the sky to which they *go* when they die, it is a visible home which will *come* out of the sky — that is, out of the future, so to speak, at the

---

[45] G.E. Ladd, *A Theology of the New Testament,* p. 105.
[46] R. Hach, *Possession and Persuasion,* p. 138.

> second coming of the Messiah to renew the earth; it is the coming Kingdom of God.[47]

The only way I can internalize this hope and make it a present spiritual possession (saying that "Jesus lives and reigns in my heart now") is to understand that by committing myself to this Gospel of the coming Kingdom, I am identifying myself and all of my future dreams and aspirations with this promised future of world renewal when Jesus Christ comes back to earth. It is not just by praying parrot-fashion, "Your Kingdom come." It is by "repenting and believing the Gospel" about the Kingdom. It is by adopting the Kingdom values of love and non-violence that Jesus espoused. Jesus is the prototype of the New Man that God will bring into that coming age. Jesus rejected all worldly approaches of domination and intimidation over others. He came to serve. He will share his Kingdom with those who live in this day and age with these, his values. Jesus "lives in my heart" only when I am so persuaded by this Gospel of the coming Kingdom that his word is the motivation force in my daily living: "And everyone who has this hope fixed on him purifies himself, just as he is pure" (1 John 3:3).

I remember sitting in a church service once, when the person leading the communion service, the Lord's Supper (in Churches of Christ circles we call this person "the president" because he/she presides over the table), invited anybody from the congregation to share publicly what communion meant to them. One stood up to say it meant his sins were forgiven by the blood of Jesus. Another stood up to say it meant he could renew closeness with God for the week to come. Still another stood up and shared that by eating the bread and drinking the cup he felt he belonged to the body of Christ. Probably eight individuals testified along these personal lines. It was significant that not one person shared that it meant to them what it did to Jesus. For it was in the shadow of the cross, as he instituted the Lord's Supper, that Jesus told his followers:

> "I have earnestly desired to eat this Passover with you before I suffer; for I say to you, I shall never again eat it until it is fulfilled in the kingdom of God." And having taken the cup...he said, "Take this and share it among yourselves; for I say to you, I will not drink of the fruit of

---

[47] *Ibid.*, p. 139.

the vine from now on until the kingdom of God comes" (Luke 22:15-18).

For Jesus, eating the bread and drinking the cup with his followers meant a promise. It meant he would eat and drink with them in the coming Kingdom of God: "Just as my Father has covenanted to give me a kingdom, I grant you that you may eat and drink at my table in my kingdom, and you will sit on thrones judging the twelve tribes of Israel" (Luke 22:29-30). Jesus firmly believed that sitting around that table would be the resurrected patriarchs of Israel, Abraham, Isaac and Jacob, along with "many from the east and west" (Matt. 8:11). The apostle Paul also said to the church that "as often as you eat this bread and drink the cup, you proclaim the Lord's death **until he comes**" (1 Cor. 11:26). It was this hope of the promised future of the Age to Come that was the prime and unifying force in Jesus' own life and faith. Only when it becomes ours can we truly say "the kingdom is within you."

The Gospel Jesus preached concerned firstly this future Kingdom of God. Jesus equated "the Kingdom of God" with "the age to come, eternal life." He said to the disciples, "Truly I say to you, there is no one who has left house or wife or brothers or parents or children, for the sake of **the kingdom of God**, who shall not receive many times as much at this time and in **the age to come**, eternal life" (Luke 18:29-30).

Jesus said that being "born again" — modern evangelicalism's great catch-cry — is the necessary condition for entering the Kingdom when it comes: "Jesus answered and said to him, 'Truly, truly, I say to you, unless one is born again [or, born from above], he cannot **see the kingdom of God**'" (John 3:3).

Then note how he changes the phrase slightly: "Jesus answered, 'Truly, truly, I say to you, unless one is born of water and the Spirit, he cannot **enter into the kingdom of God**'" (John 3:5).

Just a few verses further on, the Lord Jesus explains what it is to "see" or to "enter" the kingdom of God. He says that to believe in him will be to "**have eternal life**" (literally, life in the Age to Come, John 3:15, 16).

The disciples also equated "salvation" with "entering the kingdom of God." When Jesus tells them that it is hard for a rich man to enter **the kingdom of God**, and that it is easier for a camel to go through the eye of a needle than for a rich man to enter **the**

Kingdom of God, they ask in astonishment, "Then who can be **saved**?" (Matt. 19:24-25).

Putting all this together, we get the equation:

The Kingdom of God = the life of the age to come = eternal life = salvation

It is a remarkable fact, then, that Jesus' disciples preached this Gospel of the Kingdom long before they understood that Jesus was to be crucified and raised again. One day Jesus took the twelve aside and said to them:

> Behold, we are going up to Jerusalem, and all things which are written through the prophets about the son of man will be accomplished. For he will be delivered up to the Gentiles, and will be mocked and mistreated and spit upon, and after they have scourged him, they will kill him; and the third day he will rise again. And they understood none of these things, and this saying was hidden from them, and they did not comprehend the things that were said (Luke 18:31-34).

Four times at least after Peter had confessed Jesus as the Christ at Caesarea Philippi, Jesus predicted that he would be killed and rise again, though the disciples on each occasion were unable to make sense of it (Mark 8:31, cp. v. 34-37; 9:9, 31; 10:33-34). I repeat: *The disciples were preaching the Gospel of salvation, the Gospel of the Kingdom, the Gospel of eternal life, before they had any comprehension of the death, burial and resurrection of Jesus!*

> Clearly the Kingdom of God was the *first* item on the agenda in apostolic presentations of the Gospel. This is hardly surprising, since Jesus had always proclaimed the Gospel of the Kingdom — and this was long before anything was said about his death for our sins, which the disciples did not understand! (Luke 18:31-34). It is immensely instructive to note that the subject matter of the Kingdom cannot originally have included the death and resurrection of Jesus.[48]

It is true that only on the basis of the finished work of Christ on the cross and his resurrection that we may enter the coming Kingdom of God. But not for one moment did Jesus abandon the earthly hope he inherited from his Hebrew heritage. It was just that

---

[48] Anthony Buzzard, *The Coming Kingdom of the Messiah,* p. 72.

he knew the Messianic Kingdom would not come the first time round. He must die first and be raised again to open the way for us. There would be no harvest unless the grain of wheat first falls into the ground and dies (John 12:24). His whole energy and focus was in preparing his followers for this great universal event. The foundational fact is that Jesus claimed to be the Messiah destined not only to die for our sins, but also to rule this world in a future commonwealth to be set up at his Second Coming. Any theology that does not live and breathe in this atmosphere has lost touch with the Jesus of the Bible. It is in this background that we now delve a bit deeper.

The Promises to the Fathers

Few readers of the Bible today seem to realize that the Gospel has to do with the fulfilling of certain oath-bound promises that God made to Abraham and later expanded to David. The rubric over the NT is Matthew 1:1: "The book of the genealogy of Jesus Christ, the son of David, the son of Abraham." The conclusion of the NT is the confession of the risen Jesus: "I am the root and the offspring of David" (Rev. 22:16). Everything between these "book-ends" is concerned to show how Jesus meets the criteria of "the son of David." These promises "to the fathers" form the basis of Jesus' whole Kingdom ministry and Gospel message. We may summarize the story of these foundational promises this way: God promised Eve that one of her descendants would reverse the curse that entered the world in Eden. That descendant — later delineated as the Messiah — would arise from the family of Abraham, and he will gain possession of the land of Palestine and the world forever. Abraham himself, even though he dies in the meantime, is told he will also enjoy this promised inheritance forever. An everlasting inheritance, however, can only make sense if Abraham will be brought back to life. Here are the first hints that in God's scheme there is going to be a resurrection from the dead.

In the meantime, generations from Abraham's line of descendants come and go. Even though this people called Israel enter the Promised Land under Joshua, the promise to Abraham is not yet fulfilled. Abraham is still asleep in the dust of the earth. But the promise has not failed. In fact, God further clarifies that this promised descendant of Abraham is going to be a mighty king, also descended from David (2 Sam. 7:12-16). So the promise gains specificity and is magnified. The King and his Kingdom become the hope of every true son of Abraham. "On these mighty themes of permanent security, monarchy and territory, the whole structure of the biblical story rests. The Message, it should be carefully noted, is never merely 'religious.' It is both national and universal — and related to the future of the earth."[49] *It is these OT promises to Abraham of land and throne that form the very basis of Jesus' announcement of the Gospel of the Kingdom!* If I may once again borrow one of Anthony Buzzard's statements, "It would be no exaggeration to say that failure to grasp the terms of God's arrangements with Abraham is the root of the massive confusion now existing in the minds of churchgoers in regard to the whole purpose of the Christian faith."[50]

The apostles announced that they preached "**the good news of the promise made to the fathers**" (Acts 13:32). Time and again the NT declares a connection between the mission of Christ and the promises God made through the prophets of old: "For I say that Christ has become a servant to the circumcision on behalf of the truth of God **to confirm the promises given to the fathers**" (Rom. 15:8).

Somehow God's honour, "the truth of God," is tied in with the need for Christ to fulfill "the promises given to the fathers." Whatever these promises are, they evidently have to do with the Jews, for earlier Paul states: "My kinsmen according to the flesh, who are Israelites, to whom belongs the adoption as sons and the glory and the covenants and the giving of the Law and the temple service and **the promises**" (Rom. 9:3-4). Even more definitely Paul says, "**Now the promises were spoken to Abraham and to his seed**. He does not say, 'And to seeds,' as referring to many, but rather to one, 'And to your seed,' that is, Christ...and if you belong to Christ, then you are Abraham's offspring [literally, 'seed'], heirs according to **promise**" (Gal. 3:16, 29).

Evidently, if we would know what promises Paul has in mind, we must refer to the history of Abraham, for this is where he derived his information. Most of us are familiar with the outline of the story of Abraham. We know God called him to leave his home in Chaldea and become a tent-dweller, a "pilgrim" in the land of

---

[49] Anthony Buzzard, *Our Fathers Who Aren't in Heaven,* p. 26.
[50] *Ibid.,* p. 22.

Canaan. We know that God promised Abraham that one day the Saviour of the world would come from his line and that through the preaching of the Gospel all the nations of the earth would be blessed through him. But that there is any more relevance to the promise made to Abraham quite escapes us. After all, "father Abraham" is significant and applicable to the past history of the Jews, but what relevance do the promises made to him over 3,000 years ago have for the Christian today?

This dismissive attitude is a sad reflection on how far modern Christianity has strayed from the very essence of the NT Gospel. There are a number of old Sunday school songs and hymns which talk about crossing the River Jordan when we die and go up to heaven: "Where is now the prophet Daniel? Safe in the Promised Land." The idea that the Promised Land is heaven, and that all the faithful dead, including Abraham, Daniel and the "fathers," are already in the glory, is widespread. Such modern sentiments give the impression that for most, the promises made to the fathers have already come to pass and therefore have no current relevance. But this is a far cry from the teaching of the NT which views the promises made to the fathers as both the basis of the saving Gospel and *still awaiting* a future fulfilment. After Pentecost Stephen said Abraham had not yet inherited Canaan. To that day God had given Abraham "no inheritance" in "this country in which you [Jews] are now living...not even a foot of ground" (Acts 7:4-5). Stephen believed God's promise to Abraham was *still waiting* to be fulfilled.

We have already had occasion to note Hebrews 11: "All these [fathers] died in faith, **without receiving the promises**, but having seen them and having **welcomed them from a distance**, and having confessed that they were strangers and exiles on the earth. For those who say such things make it clear that they are seeking a country of their own" (v. 13-14).

So Abraham, Isaac and Jacob, and Daniel and the prophets died without receiving what God had promised them: a country of their own! The fathers are not yet safe in the Promised Land. This sentiment is repeated towards the end of Hebrews 11: "And all these, having gained approval through their faith, **did not receive what was promised**, because God had provided something better for us, **so that apart from us** [NT Christians] **they should not be made perfect**" (v. 39-40).

So at the time of the writing of the NT the promises God had made to Abraham and the fathers of Israel were still not fulfilled. Evidently, Christians also have a stake in these promises made to the fathers. We are "heirs of the promise"; we are Abraham's descendants because we have faith in the same God who made the promises (Gal. 3:16, 29). When on trial for his faith, the apostle Paul testified that the salvation offered through Christ was a fulfilment of the promises made to the fathers: "And now I am standing trial for **the hope of the promise made by God to the fathers; the promise to which our twelve tribes hope to attain**" (Acts 26:6-7).

This faith was in the good Hebrew tradition as expressed by many. Mary the mother of Jesus also understood that Jesus was to fulfill the promises made to the fathers of Israel: "He has given help to Israel His servant, in remembrance of His mercy, **as He spoke to our fathers, to Abraham and his offspring forever**" (Luke 1:54-55).

The father of John the Baptist also praised God for remembering His promises to Abraham and to David:

> Blessed be the Lord God of Israel, for He has visited us and accomplished redemption for His people, and has raised up a horn of salvation for us in the house of David His servant — **as He spoke by the mouth of His holy prophets from of old** — salvation from our enemies and from the hand of all who hate us; to show mercy toward our fathers, and **to remember His holy covenant, the oath which He swore to Abraham our father** (Luke 1:68-73).

The fact that Christ Jesus has been raised from the dead and is now in heaven awaiting his Second Coming is, according to Peter, proof that the promises to the fathers are still waiting for a future fulfilment. Peter commands his hearers to repent and believe so that God "may send Jesus, the Christ appointed for you, whom heaven must receive **until the period of restoration of all things about which God spoke by the mouth of His holy prophets from ancient time**" (Acts 3:20-21).

These verses show that the promises made to the fathers were still unfulfilled even as late as the first century AD, still unfulfilled after Christ's ascension into heaven, still unfulfilled thousands of years after God had originally spoken them, still unfulfilled after the NT church had been started, still unfulfilled at the writing of the

NT! We are now in a position to ask what the promises to the fathers involve and why are these promises the key to unlocking the meaning of the whole Gospel that Jesus himself preached?

When God told Abraham to leave his home country and his family ties behind him, He promised to lead him "to **the land** which I will show you, and I will make you **a great nation**...and I will bless those who bless you, and the one who curses you I will curse. And in you all the families of the earth shall be blessed" (Gen. 12:2-3). The two central planks to God's promise to Abraham were to give him the Promised Land and to make of his descendants a mighty nation. This promise was repeated again and again:

> And the LORD said to Abram, after Lot had separated from him, "Now lift up your eyes and look from the place where you are, northward and southward and eastward and westward; for all **the land which you see**, I will give it **to you** and to your descendants forever. And **I will make your descendants as the dust of the earth**; so that if anyone can number the dust of the earth, then your descendants can also be numbered. Arise, **walk about the land** through its length and breadth; for I will give it to you" (Gen. 13:14-17).

The careful reader will note that the land of Canaan is promised to Abraham himself, in person, as well as to his descendants. The text states, "I will give it **to you**." Furthermore, observe that God did *not* say to Abraham, "I will give the land to you *through* your descendants forever." Rather God promised, "I will give the land to you **and** to your descendants." Clearly this promise is yet to come to pass. It must be central to God's plan for this world, for God reiterates the same two essential elements to His promise: the Promised Land to Abraham and loads of descendants to fill that country (see also Gen. 12:7; 15:8-18; 17:8). God ties His honour and His word to this Abrahamic covenant time and again with the divine "I will." Again, after Abraham had not withheld his only son Isaac from sacrifice, God underscores the promise further:

> "By Myself I have sworn," declares the LORD, "because you have done this thing, and have not withheld your son, your only son, indeed I will greatly bless you, and I will greatly multiply your seed [descendants] as the stars of the heavens, and as the sand which is on the seashore; and your seed shall possess the gate of their enemies. And in your

> seed all the nations of the earth shall be blessed, because you have obeyed My voice" (Gen. 22:16-18).

Isaac and Jacob are called "fellow-heirs of the same promise" (Heb. 11:9). To them the promise of the land and many descendants was repeated: "And the LORD appeared to him [Isaac] and said, 'Sojourn in **this land** and I will be with you and bless you, for **to you and to your descendants I will give all these lands**, and I will establish the oath which I swore to your father Abraham'" (Gen. 26:2-4).

> And may God Almighty bless you [Jacob] and...give you the blessing of Abraham...that you may possess the land of your sojournings, which God gave to Abraham…I am the LORD, the God of your father Abraham and the God of Isaac; the land on which you lie, I will give it **to you** and to your descendants. Your descendants shall also be like the dust of the earth, and you shall spread out to the west and to the east and to the north and to the south; and in you and in your descendants shall all the families of the earth be blessed (Gen. 28:3-4, 13-14).

We have already noted that Jesus took these promises quite literally, for he believed that the individuals Abraham, Isaac and Jacob would be personally raised up by God to live in the Promised Land in the Messianic age to come (Matt. 22:23-33). This is why Jesus argued for the resurrection of the dead: Abraham, Isaac and Jacob had died without having received God's promise to them, and it was impossible that God's word should fail of fulfilment.

1. A Great and Mighty Nation

No wonder the Hebrews were passionate about "the promises to the fathers." Two key elements stand out. First, Abraham's descendants would become a mighty nation through whom the earth would be blessed. Unfortunately, the Jews rejected God's prophets all the way through and proved unworthy of this high privilege and destiny. Ultimately, they even killed the Son of God, Jesus the Christ. Natural Israel, "Israel according to the flesh," was "broken off" from the stem and root. And so the Gentiles who accept that Jesus is the Messiah and believe his Gospel of the Kingdom are "grafted" into the olive tree and so become a part of the true Israel of God, that is, those who believe the promises (see Rom. 11). The great nation that numbers more than the stars of heaven that was promised to Abraham, now consists of people from every race, whether Jew or Gentile, who by their faith in God's Christ show that they are of the same faith as Abraham. For:

> It is not as though the word of God [His promise of the Kingdom] has failed. For they are not all Israel who are descended from Israel; neither are they all children because they are Abraham's [physical] descendants, but: "Through Isaac your descendants will be named." That is, it is not the children of the flesh who are children of God, but the children of the promise are regarded as descendants (Rom. 9:6-8).

The Gospel NT Christians are to believe is the *same* Gospel Abraham believed. It is "the Gospel of the Kingdom" that Jesus himself believed in. We are to be true to the faith of Jesus. In Romans 3 Paul says that God will justify the believer "who has faith in Jesus" (v. 26). However, as the NASB translation in the margin correctly says, this phrase literally rendered is that God will justify the one "who is **of** the faith of Jesus." We are to have the faith of Jesus, the faith he lived by. There can be no faith *in* Jesus if we do not have the faith *of* Jesus, the faith he lived by, the faith he modelled, the faith he taught. This phrase is found in the next chapter where Paul speaks of "the faith of Abraham" (Rom. 4:16). It is the same Greek construction. There is no reason (other than theological necessity!) to translate one instance as "the faith **of** Abraham" and the other as "faith **in** Jesus." Jesus had Abraham's faith, that is, faith in the same promises of God.

This phrase, "the faith **of** Jesus," is often obscured in our English Bibles, even though this is how the Greek text states it. Romans 3:22 is translated: "the righteousness of God through faith **in** Jesus Christ [is] for all those who believe." However, there is no preposition before the words "Jesus Christ," and the latter phrase is in the genitive case. It is more accurately translated: "the righteousness of God through faith **of** Jesus Christ" (which is how the KJV translates it). The same holds true in Philippians 3:9. Here Paul is willing to count all things as "rubbish" if only he may have a right relationship with God through Jesus, "not having a righteousness of my own derived from law, but that which is through faith **in** Christ, the righteousness which comes from God on the basis of faith." Again, there is no preposition here, and "Christ" is in the genitive case, which the KJV more naturally translates as "that which is through the faith **of** Christ." The same applies in Galatians 2, where we read, "knowing that a man is not justified by works of law, but through faith **in** Christ Jesus, we have believed in Christ Jesus, that we may be justified by faith **in** Christ, and not by works of law" (v. 16). It really reads, "a man is justified through faith **of** Messiah." Just a couple of verses later Paul says, "I have been crucified with Christ, and it is no longer I who live, but Christ lives in me; and the life which I now live in the flesh I live by faith **in** the Son of God, who loved me and delivered himself up for me" (Gal. 2:20). Again we have a "subjective genitive," so the accurate translation is "the faith **of** the Son of God."

The practical implication is significant. What is the faith that brings righteousness before God the Father? It is the faith *of* Messiah Jesus. What faith did Jesus live by? Faith in his Father's promise given to Abraham (and confirmed in the Davidic oath), that God would raise the righteous dead and bring them into a Kingdom of glory through His Anointed King. That is, faith in the promised announcement of the eschatological Kingdom. This is the "faith **of** Jesus." What is the steadfastness of the true believer, but to "keep the commandments" of God and to keep "**the faith of Jesus**" (Rev. 14:12). There is no way to have faith in Jesus except to believe what Jesus believed. To believe in Jesus is to believe his word or Gospel announcement. All of which is to say, *the only way to express true faith in Jesus the Christ is to live according to the faith he walked by and was motivated by.* Jesus' faith in God's word of promise becomes our faith in the *same* Gospel-promise. Paul's Gospel was his preaching of the faith of Jesus, Jesus' Gospel announcement of the Kingdom of God explained in light of the facts of Jesus' death and resurrection. The only way to be righteous before the Father is to honour the faith of His Son, i.e. to believe the Good News of the coming Kingdom of God he believed in. This is to believe *in* Jesus. This is to be *of* Abraham's faith, to be a true son/daughter of God. It is to have the faith of Abraham which Paul recommended.

The true descendants of Abraham, Isaac and Jacob are the ones who please God by believing His word of the promise. The flesh and blood descendants of Abraham, the Jews, to this day mostly do not show that they are of Abraham's faith, for they reject the Messiah that Abraham looked forward to. It was Jesus' complaint that although "Abraham rejoiced to see my day; and he saw it and was glad," his contemporaries did not (John 8:56). The promised race of Abraham's descendants today comes from the rest of the world. God is "taking from among the Gentiles a people for His name" (Acts 15:14). The NT mystery "which in other generations was not made known...as it has now been revealed to His holy apostles and prophets in the Spirit...[is] that the Gentiles are fellow-heirs, and fellow-members of the body, and **fellow-partakers of the promise in Christ Jesus through the gospel**" (Eph. 3:3-6). Those "who also follow in the steps of the faith of our father Abraham" are the inheritors of the promises made (Rom. 4:12). Today then, the promise comes through faith by grace (and not according to the old Law) "in order that **the promise** may be certain to all the descendants...who are **of** the faith of Abraham, who is the father of us all" (Rom. 4:16). When a new believer is baptized into Christ he/she becomes "Abraham's offspring, [an] heir according to promise" (Gal. 3:29). Christ's mission was to redeem not "the nation [of Israel] only, but that he might also gather together into one the children of God who are scattered abroad" (John 11:52).

Speaking of the future day when this great company will be gathered together, Jesus promised, "And I say to you, that many shall come from east and west, and recline at table with Abraham, and Isaac, and Jacob, in the kingdom of heaven" (Matt. 8:11).

When Christ returns to earth Abraham will in his resurrection body see the literal fulfilment of the promise God made to him long ago. He will see his offspring in number as the stars of heaven or the dust of the earth. The dead of all the generations who are of his faith will be in that Kingdom. "Behold! A great multitude, which no one could count, from every nation and all tribes and people and tongues" (Rev. 7:9). Abraham's royal descendants will at last inherit the promised Kingdom of God.

That Jesus will be the king of this Kingdom is also a key part of this promise. For the promise God made to Abraham received further refinement when God prophesied to David that one of his descendants would sit on his throne forever. David would have a royal heir so that his dynasty would never end. That Jesus is the promised heir to the Davidic throne is clear. The angel Gabriel announced to the virgin Mary: "Behold, you will conceive in your womb, and bear a son, and you shall name him Jesus. He will be great, and will be called the Son of the Most High; and the Lord God will give him **the throne of his father David**; and he will reign over **the house of Jacob** forever; and **his kingdom will have no end**" (Luke 1:31-33).

Gabriel the angel is very precise in his choice of words here. He does not say that Christ is to reign over "Israel" but over "Jacob," that is, over the literal flesh and blood descendants of Abraham — the same race over which David had reigned. Had we been told that Christ will reign over the house of "Israel" many might have felt even more inclined to say it meant a "spiritual" reign in the hearts of a "spiritual" Israel. But the angel announces that the Kingdom of Christ will be a literal Jewish Kingdom over the house of Jacob on the literal throne of David. The force of this is highlighted when we compare it with 1 Kings 2: "Then Solomon sat **on the throne of David his father**, and his kingdom was firmly established" (v. 12).

If the Bible means Solomon sat on the literal throne of his father David, why should it not mean a literal reign for Christ who will also sit "on the throne of his father David" in Luke 1:32? This was based on a covenantal agreement God made with King David:

> When your days are complete and you lie down with your fathers, I will raise up your descendant after you, who will come forth from you, and I will establish **his kingdom**. He shall build a house for My name, and I will establish **the throne of his kingdom forever**...and your house and your kingdom shall endure before Me forever; **your throne** shall be established forever (2 Sam. 7:12-16; see also 1 Chron. 17:11-14).

It is clear that *the throne of Israel was synonymous with the Kingdom of God.* Every king of Israel and Judah knew that his throne was given by divine appointment. He ruled in God's name. To resist the king was to oppose God: "Do you not know that the LORD God of Israel gave the rule over Israel forever to David and his sons by a covenant of salt? So now you intend to resist **the kingdom of the LORD**" (2 Chron. 13:5, 8). When the queen of Sheba saw the glory of Solomon's kingdom she exulted: "Blessed be the LORD your God who delighted in you, setting you on **His throne as king for the LORD your God**; because your God loved Israel establishing them forever; therefore He made you king over them, to do justice and righteousness" (2 Chron. 9:8). "Therefore Solomon sat **on the throne of the LORD as king** in place of his father David" (1 Chron. 29:23).

> The Kingdom of God, then, is an empire ruled by the king of Israel enthroned in Jerusalem. This definition will throw a flood of light on what Jesus meant by the Good News about the Kingdom of God. The Hebrew term "kingdom of the Lord" reappears in Revelation 11:15 where, at the seventh trumpet blast, the power of present political states is to be transferred to the "Kingdom of our Lord and of His Christ."[51]

Thus, when we talk about "the promises to the fathers" we are to understand that the Hebrew Bible is full of the prophets' persistent belief that on a glorious day in the future God will set up His Kingdom on earth to be administered under a just Davidic king, the Lord Messiah. When Jesus came "preaching the kingdom of God, and saying, 'The time is fulfilled, and the kingdom of God is at hand; repent and believe the gospel'" (Mark 1:14-15), these were his terms of reference. And we can understand that every Jew would immediately think that the promises to Abraham and David were about to come to pass. The threshold of Israel's glorious promised future had arrived!

2. The Promised Land

The second key element in the promise made to the Jewish fathers involves the land of Palestine. Abraham was promised "all the land of Canaan" that he walked in (Gen. 17:8). That Abraham never once possessed this Promised Land is clear because he had to buy a plot of ground even to bury his dead (Gen. 23:4). Abraham was only a "stranger" in the land of promise, "as in a foreign land, dwelling in tents with Isaac and Jacob" (Heb. 11:9). Stephen says, God "gave him no inheritance in it, not even a foot of ground; and yet, even when he had no child, He promised that He would give it to him as a possession, and to his offspring after him" (Acts 7:5). It is clear, then, that Abraham never entered into the enjoyment of the Promised Land. For Abraham that promise is still unfulfilled. Certainly Abraham had every opportunity to return to his home country of Ur of the Chaldees. All appearances were against him. He could have gone back saying, "I'm jack of all this wandering. I'm fed up with all the flies and the dust in these tents." When it became clear that the promise of God was still future, the temptation

---

[51] *Ibid.,* p. 54.

to give up in disgust must have been great at times. But these fathers kept "looking for the city which has foundations, whose architect and builder is God" and so they were convinced of God's promises and "embraced them from a distance" (Heb. 11:13). And yes, these all died without receiving the promises.

But according to the Gospel of Jesus, receive them they will, for "the time came for the dead to be judged, and the time to give their reward to Your bond-servants the prophets [Abraham, Isaac, Jacob *et al* were all prophets] and to the saints [believers of all ages] and to those who fear Your name" (Rev. 11:18). This will be the time when, as the context indicates, "The kingdom of the world has become the kingdom of our Lord, and of His Christ; and he will reign forever and ever" (v. 15). It is the time when Messiah Jesus will return "to judge the living and the dead" at "his appearing and his kingdom" (2 Tim. 4:1). Hence Jesus' promise to the unbelieving Pharisees:

> There will be weeping and gnashing of teeth there when you see Abraham and Isaac and Jacob and all the prophets in the kingdom of God, but yourselves being cast out. And they will come from the east and west, and from north and south, and will recline at table in the kingdom of God (Luke 13:28-29).

If there is any doubt that this will be in the Promised Land on this very earth, then read again: "And the LORD will possess Judah as His portion **in the holy land**, and will again choose **Jerusalem**" (Zech. 2:12).

"In that day," declares the LORD, "I will assemble the lame, and gather the outcasts...[and make them] a strong nation, and the LORD will reign over them in **Mount Zion** from now on and forever" (Mic. 4:6-7).

"Then I will remember My covenant with Jacob, and I will remember also My covenant with Isaac, and My covenant with Abraham as well, and I will remember **the land**" (Lev. 26:42).

"Indeed, the LORD will comfort **Zion**; He will comfort all her waste places. And her wilderness He will make like Eden, and her desert like the garden of the LORD; joy and gladness will be found in her, thanksgiving and sound of a melody" (Is. 51:3).

A quick glance at a handful of the many verses that could be cited shows that the NT says that these promises will only be fulfilled when Christ comes back from heaven and raises the faithful dead so they will forever live in the land of God's promise, under their anointed Messiah. The NT states that these promises are *still to be fulfilled even though Christ has already come* the first time. He will "appear a second time, not to bear sin, to those who eagerly await him, for salvation" (Heb. 9:28). In this way, all the nations of the earth will be blessed, according to the promises made to "the fathers." By detaching Jesus from "the promises given to the fathers" we rip the very heart out from the Gospel of the Kingdom he preached and for which he died. In the process we rob ourselves of any personal interest in these promises. These promises made to the fathers are the foundation of Jesus' ministry and the salvation he now offers. Christ's mission was to "confirm the promises made to the fathers." God's honour is at stake, His very truth as Romans 15:8 teaches.

I love the way John R. Rice illustrates this truth. He laments that as a child in Sunday School he was taught that at the Second Coming of Christ, this planet earth would be burned up and destroyed and disappear. He was taught that after a general judgment of all humanity, the unsaved would be consigned to everlasting hell and the redeemed would float around and sing and twang their harps in a golden city hanging in space in the "Beautiful Isle of Somewhere"! He also laments that later when he went to theological seminary this notion was only strengthened. If the meek were ever to inherit the earth, they would have to do it in this life. For all the promises to Israel really meant the Church, and the promises to Jerusalem and Mount Zion really meant heaven! He was taught that the golden age when swords will be beaten into ploughshares, and spears into pruning hooks (Is. 2:4; Mic. 4:3) and when the earth will be full of the knowledge of the Lord as the waters cover the sea (Isa. 11:9), would be brought about by the Church preaching the Gospel and setting up a new society through its own efforts. But Rice says that when he started to study the prophetic writings of the Bible he "learned that God had promised to bring the Israelites back to their land to possess it forever, that heaven, then, must be on this earth." He goes on in his *The Coming Kingdom of Christ* with a section subtitled "If God Set Out to Destroy This World." He illustrates the utter impossibility that God should ever forget His promises to Abraham this way:

> Let us imagine that to please all those...who have largely ignored the prophetic portions of the Bible, the Lord should

prepare to burn up and utterly destroy this planet or earth. Let us suppose that, as so many say, the prophecies are highly figurative anyway and that to study and teach or preach them is largely speculation, and so the Lord prepares to strike the match or say the word that will utterly destroy this whole planet. What a multitude is gathered, let us imagine, to behold that great event. But wait! I see an old man who walks like a king who comes forward to interrupt the ceremony. His face has the look of authority and his voice is bold as he cries out, "Wait, Lord; You cannot destroy my property!"

I can imagine the Lord might say, "This man is a friend of mine; let us hear what he has to say. Speak on, friend, tell the people. What is your name: To what possession do you refer: What title do you hold to the property?"

"My name," says the venerable patriarch, "is Abraham! From Ur of the Chaldees I came at Thy command. To Canaan I came and the land Thou didst give to me, teaching me by faith to know that I should afterward inherit it. To Isaac and Jacob Thou didst make the same promises, and all our days, though rich in gold and silver, cattle and servants, we lived as sojourners and pilgrims in tents, patiently waiting until we should inherit and possess forever our own land. This scroll in my hand, O Lord God, is a written deed to the land of Canaan, called by name, and signed by Thyself. It is a warranty deed, guaranteeing to me and my faithful children after me — the children of promise — the possession of the land forever. You may burn up, if You will, the weeds and thorns and thistles. Destroy, if You will, all disease germs and insect pests, which have increased the curse on the land because of man's sin through the centuries. O Lord, You may shake down and burn the cities, for I look for another city which hath foundations whose builder and maker is God. The elements may melt with fervent heat, but the land is mine; to me Thou didst give it with the promise that I should inherit it with my seed. Shall not the Judge of all the earth do right?"

> If God wanted to please the ignorant and the scoffers concerning His prophecies, how would He face Abraham? The deed which Abraham has is the Bible.[52]

John Rice describes the issue at stake here in beautiful and poignant language. He goes on to say that the Scriptures teach that "the heavens shall pass away with a great noise, and the elements shall melt with fervent heat, the earth also and the works that are therein shall be burned up" (2 Pet. 3:10). But the same chapter explains that that will be a judgment like the flood. 2 Peter 3:6-7 says: "The world at that time was destroyed, being flooded with water. But the present heavens and earth by His word are being reserved for fire, kept for the day of judgment and destruction of ungodly men" (2 Pet. 3:6-7).

The world once "perished" in the flood. The earth shall yet be "laid bare" in a coming day of judgment. But as the earth reappeared from the waters of the flood, to be restocked and repopulated and replanted, so in a much greater way this planet, purified of pests, disease, and the marks of sin by the literal fire of God's wrath, will be planted again as the Garden of Eden. This planet will never be entirely removed; it can never cease to be. The fires of judgment will purge this earth, but it will not pass out of existence. It will remain to be the home of God's people through eternity. Canaan shall in truth be the possession of Abraham and his seed, and at that time they shall possess it forever![53] Or, if I may again borrow the words of another, "If the throne of David were not to reappear in Israel, with the Messiah as King, the whole Old Testament revelation would dissolve into pious legend, if not fraud."[54]

We may positively take it, then, that there is a well-defined doctrine in the Old and New Testaments that there must appear a great descendant of David who will reign on David's throne in Jerusalem, and the monarchy of David in Palestine will be restored again in an everlasting Kingdom on earth. George Ladd says:

> The truly Hebraic, prophetic hope expects the Kingdom to arise out of history and to be ruled by a descendant of David in an earthly setting...It always involves an inbreaking of

---

[52] John R. Rice, *The Coming Kingdom of Christ*, Murfreesboro, TN: Sword of the Lord, 1945, pp. 28-30.
[53] *Ibid.,* p. 30.
[54] Anthony Buzzard, *The Coming Kingdom of the Messiah,* p. 21.

> God into history...The Kingdom is always an earthly hope, although an earth redeemed from the curse of evil..."The Kingdom of God" stands as a comprehensive term for all that the messianic salvation included.[55]

Or, as John Rice puts it:

> All the unfulfilled promises and prophecies of the Bible centre around one land, one race and one throne. These three, the throne of David, over the people Israel, in the land of Canaan, form the triple centre of all prophecy. One who understands God's covenant with Abraham about the land Canaan, His covenant with Israel about their restoration and conversion, and the covenant with David about his throne, has the heart and centre of the prophecies. Almost as prominent in the prophecies as these three is the city of Jerusalem.[56]

We commenced this sub-section by saying that the rubric over the NT is that Jesus is "the son of David, the son of Abraham" (Matt. 1:1). We also noted that Jesus' last confession concerning his identity in the NT is that he is "the root and the offspring of David, the bright morning star" (Rev. 22:16). In the meantime we have shown that Jesus' whole ministry and message was to confirm the promises made to "the fathers." It is appropriate before moving on to the next section to take a moment for reflection and adoration of our Lord. It is all summed up in this last confession from Revelation 22. These are the words of our exalted Lord Jesus. He says two things about himself. First, he is the descendant of David and second, he is symbolized by the morning star.

As the descendant of David, Jesus is the heir to all God's promises made to David. He is of the Davidic royal line, the Messiah. At God's right hand, he is *still* David's son, "the offspring of David." He is *a human being.* Yes, a resurrection/glorification — a coronation — has taken place. But not a transmutation. He has not been changed from one nature into another, from humanity to the Deity. As David's son, he is destined to sit on the throne of his father David (Luke 1:32; Rev. 3:21). Peter reminded his hearers that God has determined "with an oath to seat one of his [David's] descendants upon his throne" (Acts 2:30). In the meantime, David's

---

[55] G.E. Ladd, *A Theology of the New Testament,* p. 61.

[56] J.R. Rice, *The Coming Kingdom of Christ,* p. 60.

Lord Messiah sits at the "Lord's [Yahweh's] right hand waiting until his enemies are made his footstool" (Ps. 110:1; Acts 2:34-35).

The second description of Jesus here at the very end of the NT is "the bright and morning star." He is the one who heralds the dawn of the new day, the new age. As the "star" he fulfils the prophecy: "There shall come a star out of Jacob" (Num. 24:17). As the "bright" star, he will come in great and shining glory, bringing a new era of glorification for all who look for his light, for "we shall be like him, for we shall see him as he is" (1 John 3:2; Dan. 12:3). Lastly, as the "morning" star he is the introducer of the dawn, the dawn of the Kingdom of God. As God's anointed one, he and he alone is qualified to bring this world into that New Age. What a fitting summary to the Gospel message of the NT: Jesus, the son of David, the son of Abraham, our "bright morning star." Blessed be his Name forever.

Imminence

One of the difficulties confronting our Western minds is the language that Jesus used when speaking about the coming of the Kingdom. Jesus opened his ministry with the announcement that the Kingdom was "at hand." The impression given is that the Kingdom was going to appear any minute. Once Jesus even said to his disciples, "Whenever they persecute you in this city, flee to the next; for truly I say to you, you shall not finish going through the cities of Israel, until the Son of Man comes" (Matt. 10:23). To our ears this sounds as if Jesus really did expect that he would return to bring in the Kingdom of God before the first generation of Christians had passed.

This has caused many commentators to believe that Jesus was either mistaken in this hope of a literal Kingdom of God on earth, or that his message must be taken in a spiritual sense, namely, that after the day of Pentecost he would bring the Kingdom to men's hearts by sending the Holy Spirit. Perhaps after all, Augustine was correct to believe that the Kingdom is the Church, ruled by the Spirit of God? Otherwise, the Kingdom cannot have been "at hand," because over 2,000 years have since intervened and Jesus has not yet appeared. We have the apparent absurdity that Jesus believed that the disciples must be still themselves going through the land of Israel to this very day and preaching the Gospel. If, on the other hand, we maintain that the Kingdom of God that Jesus proclaimed is the eschatological inbreaking of God at the end of this world, in what sense was it "at hand" when Jesus spoke? In the face of these apparent difficulties, the Church radically altered the message of the Gospel of the Kingdom taught by Jesus and his apostles. According to this revised theory the Kingdom cannot be a future restoration of Israel in a renewed earth ruled by Messiah and his fellow servants.

The solution lies in understanding the Jewish concept of "imminence." We have already noted that very Hebrew style of speaking called the "prophetic past." That is, when God decrees a thing to be, the Jews could speak of it as already having happened. God calls those things which are not yet in history, as though they already are (Rom. 4:17). The concept of immediacy is allied to this way of thinking. Immediacy is an expedient of OT prophecy by which a predicted event certain to occur is spoken of as being imminent. It is quite clear that Jesus himself did not know when the Kingdom was actually going to arrive. He plainly said he did not know the day or the hour. Only his Father in heaven knew this detail (see Mark 13:32). Although Jesus did not know the day or the hour, and although the apostles did not know it either, what they do know is that the Kingdom of God *will come; it is an absolute certainty.* This is why they can speak of it as being on the horizon.

But this still does not solve our difficulty concerning Jesus' instructions to the disciples to keep moving throughout the towns and cities of Palestine "until the Son of Man comes" in his power. Once again, the problem is solved when we understand that:

> in typical Hebrew fashion he addresses the Apostles as the representatives of an end-time preaching of the Gospel of the Kingdom in the cities of Israel. Speaking to the eleven Apostles, after his own resurrection, Jesus promised, "I will be with you till the end of the age" (Matt. 28:20). The promise incorporates all those "descendants" of the Apostles, i.e. disciples of Jesus who undertake the work of preaching the Kingdom until the end of the age, the return of Jesus.[57]

It simply will not do, then, to eradicate Jesus' preaching of the Kingdom of God as a still future reign of Messiah on earth at the end of this present era. We must understand the Hebrew way he spoke and taught. It is a simple fact that "references to the Kingdom

---

[57] Anthony Buzzard, *Focus on the Kingdom,* vol. 7, no. 5, p. 4.

as future outnumber about 20 to 1 the small number of statements in which the Kingdom is said to be, in a different sense, present."[58]

A Misguided Question?

A certain Bible college professor had just preached a whole sermon on Acts 1. Everyone in the congregation seemed very impressed and satisfied with the modern and contemporary approach this erudite scholar had taken. But I sat there feeling that I had enjoyed the veggies but wanted a steak to go with them. Where was the meat, the substance, the protein? I decided to approach the Bible college speaker and politely ask him the question that was on my mind. After complimenting him (always a courteous way to start) I said, "You omitted verse 6 from your sermon. The disciples asked Jesus, 'Lord, is it at this time you are restoring the kingdom to Israel?' What do you make of their question?" The answer I was given did not surprise. It is what I was taught in Bible college myself. It is what most expositors and commentators say. His reply was: "The disciples still did not get it, did they? Their minds were still stuck in that old Jewish idea that Jesus came to beat back the enemies of Israel and to set up a political empire where Israel through their Messiah would rule the world. The disciples' question shows how thick and slow they were. It was a misguided question. It must have frustrated Jesus big time."

There is perhaps no other verse in the NT that has been more misunderstood than Acts 1:6. Let's set the scene. The Lord Jesus has been raised from the dead. "By many convincing proofs" he has demonstrated to the disciples that he really is alive. But soon he is to leave them for good. He will be taken up into heaven. No doubt these forty days between the resurrection and Jesus' ascension were very precious to the disciples. Luke summarizes the final topic of conversation between the disciples and the Lord Jesus. If I read it rightly, there really was only one main topic on Jesus' agenda for that whole post-resurrection period. Jesus was "**speaking of the things concerning the kingdom of God**" (v. 3). This is precisely the same burden and topic that had occupied his whole pre-crucifixion ministry!

One has to wonder: since Jesus was always "speaking of the things concerning the kingdom of God" — even after his

---

[58] *Ibid.*, p. 6.

resurrection — why has the belief that the disciples were thick and slow to ask their question in verse 6 persisted? The reformer John Calvin is typical of an inept exposition of the Gospel. Amazingly Calvin said that this question from the disciples has more errors in it than there are words! Calvin maintained that their blindness was remarkable, that after careful instruction over three years they betrayed no less ignorance than if they had never heard a word! William Barclay concurs with this sentiment:

> Throughout his ministry Jesus laboured under one great disadvantage. The centre of his message was the Kingdom of God (Mark 1:14). But the trouble was that he meant one thing by the Kingdom and those who listened to him meant quite another...They took that to mean that they were inevitably destined for special honour and privilege and for worldwide dominion...They looked for a day when by divine intervention the world sovereignty they dreamed of would be theirs. They conceived of the Kingdom in political terms. How did Jesus conceive of it? [Barclay will now give his own understanding based on the petition in the Lord's prayer: "Thy kingdom come; Thy will be done on earth as it is in heaven."] We see that, by the Kingdom, Jesus meant a society upon earth where God's will would be as perfectly done as it is in heaven.[59]

Here Barclay has spoken a part-truth. The Kingdom will indeed be a society on earth, but equally it will be a society ushered in by the return of Jesus to rule the world with his people from all ages. Barclay commits the classic error of equating the Kingdom with the Church. In another place Barclay states unequivocally, "The only throne he [Jesus] could ever occupy was a throne in men's hearts."[60] This is typical traditional thinking. The idea that the Kingdom of God is merely "spiritual" and that wherever God's people are found "labouring in the cause of human brotherhood, love and compassion, there the King of the Jews is enthroned" is ubiquitous and destructive of the Gospel of the Kingdom Jesus preached.[61] Mathew Henry's commentary also follows this traditional pattern. According to Henry the disciples "thought Christ would *restore the*

---

[59] William Barclay, *The Acts of the Apostles,* Edinburgh: Saint Andrew Press, 1953, pp. 3-4.

[60] William Barclay, *Jesus as They Saw Him,* p. 243.

[61] Schonfield, *The Passover Plot,* p. 206.

kingdom to Israel, whereas Christ (actually) came to set up his own kingdom, and that a kingdom of heaven, not to *restore the kingdom* to Israel, an earthly kingdom."[62]

Many commentators and Christians have been misled for centuries about the nature of God's Kingdom by the well-known mistranslation of Luke 17:21, "The kingdom of God is **within** you." Today all serious scholars and translators agree that the text should read: "The kingdom of God is *among* you or *in your midst.*" The Greek word *entos* can mean "within" or "among" but in the present context to translate it "within" would mean that in answer to the Pharisees' question about when the Kingdom of God would come (Luke 17:20), Jesus told them that the Kingdom of God was within *them*! This would contradict everything else Jesus ever said about the Kingdom or about the Pharisees. Moreover, since every other reference to the Kingdom presupposes that it is yet to come and since the verb in every other clause in the passage (Luke 17:20-37) is in the future tense, this verse must be understood to mean that one day they will find that the Kingdom of God is suddenly and unexpectedly in their midst.[63]

This false concept that the Kingdom of God was the reign of God "within the believer's heart" historically grew out of the fact that the Church had early on to face the acute problem of the postponement of its earthly expectations. Clearly, God's Kingdom through His Messiah had not arrived on earth in its final form. Perhaps then Jesus had got his Messianic hope wrong? Perhaps all Jesus meant to do was to set up his throne in men's hearts? Rather lamely and unconvincingly, the Church "spiritualized" its Jesus and his message was divested of its Messianic content. However, the assumption that the personally-instructed disciples of Jesus did not know what the Kingdom of God meant rests on a failure to understand the Messianism of Jesus' Gospel and poor exegesis of Acts 1. It points to the Church's rejection of and failure to comprehend the message of all the prophets of Israel. It also misrepresents the message constantly preached by the apostles throughout the book of Acts, as I will now show.

---

[62] Matthew Henry, *Commentary on the Whole Bible, Genesis to Revelation,* London: Marshall, Morgan & Scott, 1960, p. 435, emphasis original.
[63] Albert Nolan, *Jesus Before Christianity,* pp. 46-47.

Let us first firmly fix in our minds that Acts 1:6 records the disciples' final question to Jesus before he is taken away from them. No time any more for leisurely chats by the seaside. When somebody we love dearly is about to leave us for good, there is no idle chit-chat. The whole of Jesus' program hangs in the balance here, with this handful of selected men who have been with him from the beginning. The subject under discussion (just to underline the context again) is "the things concerning the kingdom of God" (v. 3). In the same breath (note the conjunction "and" in v. 4) Jesus commands the disciples to wait for the promised Holy Spirit. To the Hebrew mind, mention of the coming of the Spirit was associated with the coming of the Messianic glory prophesied in the Old Testament. Many passages in the Hebrew Bible predicted that when Messiah sets up his earthly Kingdom, that Age will be an age of the Spirit of Lord. That glorious Age will be marked by an unprecedented outpouring of the Spirit and knowledge and power of the LORD. That Kingdom age of the Spirit will be marked by the renewal of all nature and the blessing of Israel (e.g. Is. 11:1-9). In the Jewish mind, the Kingdom of God was synonymous with the renewing power of the Spirit. So when the disciples hear that the Spirit is about to come, their antennas go up immediately! They ask their *logical* question: "Lord, will you at this time restore the kingdom to Israel?" (v. 6).

Let's not miss the point now. Jesus does give a caution, but it is a caution only about *the time* of that expected restoration, not *the fact* of the restoration: "It is not for you to know times or epochs which the Father has fixed by His own authority; but you shall receive power when the Holy Spirit has come upon you; and you shall be my witnesses both in Jerusalem, and in all Judea and Samaria, and even to the remotest part of the earth" (Acts 1:7-8). Two distinct events are in mind here: The coming of the Spirit "not many days from now" (v. 5) *and* the coming of the Kingdom at a time unknown in the future (v. 6-7). Empowerment for ministry by the coming of the Spirit — only days away — *and* the coming of the Kingdom for the renewal of all things on earth — down the track at a time only known to the Father. Thus, *two distinct times and events* are in mind here, proving beyond any shadow of doubt that the Kingdom did not come on the day of Pentecost! The coming of the Spirit on the day of Pentecost was the deposit, the downpayment, "the pledge of our inheritance" (Eph. 1:14) for that future Kingdom. The coming of the Spirit gives the enablement to live as Christ's witnesses *until* the hope of the restored Kingdom to Israel becomes reality. In the interim period the Church is to announce "the testimony of Jesus," the Gospel of the Kingdom, and thus speak prophetically in "the spirit of prophecy" (Rev. 19:10).

The disciples' question about Jesus now restoring the Kingdom to Israel represents the *climax* of Jesus' life and ministry. Far from being block-headed dolts, they prove only how "thick" subsequent theology is when it interprets the Kingdom as being this current Church age! Equating the coming of the Spirit on the day of Pentecost with the (as yet future) Kingdom of God has ripped the heart out of Jesus' Gospel of the Kingdom. It has deprived the people of a brilliant future hope.

In the medical field, there is anecdotal information that occasionally after undergoing a complete heart transplant a person's personality can change. I have from time to time heard this in my work as a paramedic. With someone else's heart now beating in the patient's chest, sometimes relatives are amazed at the personality changes. In parallel allegorical fashion, the Church has unknowingly lain on the operating table and agreed to a heart transplant that altered its whole personality, so to speak. Instead of a Hebrew heart beating with the pulsating hope of the coming Kingdom of God under God's appointed Lord Messiah, we now find ourselves in a weakened, insipid state, drugged by a substitute donor (Gentile) heart transplant which shows every sign of being rejected by its body. Or, to use the illustration I used at the beginning of this chapter, a cuckoo gospel — "another gospel" — has installed itself in the nest!

If further proof is necessary that the disciples got it right with their question, we only have to read the rest of the book of Acts to see how prominent a place the coming Kingdom of God played in the apostles' preaching and witness. In Acts 3 the apostles Peter and John miraculously heal a lame man. The man who was born lame is now walking and leaping and yelling praises to God. This creates no small stir. A crowd of curious people gathers and Peter starts preaching to them. He tells the crowd that the man has been healed in the name of Jesus, the Jesus they were responsible for crucifying. Peter explains to the crowd that Jesus has been raised from the dead by God and taken to heaven, and is waiting for the appointed time to return to earth, exactly as "announced beforehand by the mouth of all the prophets" (Acts 3:18). Peter adds that because Messiah Jesus is now in heaven, God's promises for the Kingdom are guaranteed. In fact, *Peter uses language almost identical to the question the disciples had asked before Jesus' ascension in Acts 1:6:*

> Repent therefore and return, that your sins may be wiped away, in order that **times of refreshing** may come from the presence of the Lord; and that He may send Jesus, the Messiah appointed for you, whom heaven must receive until **the times of restoration of all things** about which God spoke by the mouth of His holy prophets from ancient time (Acts 3:19-21).

The careful reader will observe the close connection between these verses and the question the disciples put to Jesus concerning the restoration of the Davidic throne. Luke who wrote the Gospel of Luke and the book of Acts is very consistent on this point. The angel Gabriel announced to Mary before she bore Jesus that "he will be great, and will be called the Son of the Most High; and the Lord God will give him the throne of his father David; and he will reign over the house of Jacob forever; and his kingdom will have no end" (Luke 1:32-33).

It is clear that for Dr. Luke, the restoration of Israel under the Messiah who appears from heaven is synonymous with the restoration of the throne of David and the coming of the Kingdom of God. Anthony Buzzard draws our attention to Luke's "interchangeable phrases" with this summary:

The arrival of the apocalyptic Kingdom (Luke 21:31) = the redemption of the disciples (Luke 21:28) = redemption in Jerusalem (Luke 2:38) = the redemption of Israel (Luke 24:21).

The expected future Kingdom (Luke 23:51) = the expected consolation of Israel (Luke 2:25).

The restoration of the Kingdom to Israel (Acts 1:6) = the times of the restoration of all that was promised through the mouth of the prophets (Acts 3:21) = the restoration of the house of David as promised through the mouth of the prophets (Luke 1:70) = the enthronement of Jesus on the throne of David to which he is heir (Luke 1:32, 33).[64]

If the reader will take the time to compare these references, he/she will clearly see that the great events Luke talks about

---

[64] Anthony Buzzard, *Our Fathers Who Aren't in Heaven,* p. 189.

concerning the throne of David and the expected consolation of Israel were not fulfilled when the Spirit was poured out at Pentecost, and therefore do not apply to the Church this side of Christ's return. Jesus' absence in heaven is a temporary interlude pending the end of this present age. "Gabriel's opening announcement about the restoration of the throne of David (Luke 1:32) and the disciples' closing question about the restoration of Israel (Acts 1:6) bracket the whole of Luke's account of the Christian faith."[65]

An examination of the content of the Gospel preached in the book of Acts also proves that the disciples understood that Jesus was going to return to fulfill all that the Hebrew Scriptures had predicted concerning the Kingdom, Israel and the Davidic dynasty of the Lord Messiah. In Acts 8 Philip was conducting a very successful evangelistic campaign in Samaria. We read that he was "**preaching the good news about the kingdom of God and the name of Jesus Messiah**" (v. 12). The apostles "in Jerusalem heard that Samaria had received **the word of God**" (v. 14). Here again we observe Luke's synonymous terms. "The Kingdom of God" is equivalent to "the word of God." Wherever we read that the apostles preached "the word" or proclaimed "the gospel" or preached "the name of Jesus Messiah" (as further on in verses 25 and 35) we are to understand that Luke means they preached "the Kingdom of God" with all of its Hebrew content. This interchange of terms is recorded also in Acts 14: "And after they had preached **the gospel** to that city...they returned to Lystra and to Iconium and to Antioch...saying, 'Through many tribulations we must enter **the kingdom of God**'...And when they had spoken **the word** in Perga, they went down to Attalia" (v. 21, 22, 25).

Again, "And he entered the synagogue and continued speaking out boldly for three months, reasoning and persuading them about **the kingdom of God**...And this took place for two years, so that all who lived in Asia heard **the word of the Lord**, both Jews and Greeks" (Acts 19:8, 10).

When the apostle Paul describes the preaching ministry which he received from the Lord Jesus "to testify solemnly of **the gospel of the grace of God**" he immediately defines this gospel of grace as "preaching **the kingdom**" (Acts 20:24-25)! And right up to the end of his life, as recorded in the last chapters of Acts, Paul reminds his

---

[65] *Ibid.*, p. 190.

audience that he always testified about the Gospel of "**the kingdom of God**" and attempted to persuade them about Jesus as the centre of God's plan and how the Messiah fit all that "the Law of Moses" and "the Prophets" had predicted (Acts 28:23). Indeed this Kingdom of God emphasis is underlined in Luke's very last verse: Paul welcomed all who came to him, "preaching **the kingdom of God**, and teaching concerning **the Lord Jesus Messiah**" (Acts 28:31). As George Ladd comments, "It is of great interest that Luke summarizes the content of Paul's preaching to the Gentiles by the utterly non-Hellenistic phrase 'the kingdom of God.'"[66]

Many have tried to promote the idea that Paul preached the Gospel of the Kingdom to the Jews, and that he did not speak of the Kingdom to Gentiles. This fallacy is easily disposed of. We have already observed how he applied the Abrahamic promises to all Christians, whether Jew or Gentile (e.g. Gal. 3:14, 29). Paul warns that all who do not live in the faith, purity and power of that coming Kingdom "shall not inherit the kingdom of God" (Gal. 5:21). One of Paul's great rallying calls to the Corinthian church, who were taking each other before the civil courts, was to ask rhetorically, "Do you not know that the saints [true believers] are to manage the world? If the world is to come under your jurisdiction, are you incompetent to adjudicate upon trifles?" (1 Cor. 6:2-3, Moffat). Paul echoed Jesus' teaching that we are in training for positions of authority and management (cp. "fellow-heirs with Christ," Rom. 8:17) in the coming Kingdom. How out of character then, says Paul, for these Christians not to be showing they were fit for this future royal office in the Kingdom of God, by currently treating each other poorly. Nor should we overlook the connection the writer to the Hebrews (many believe the writer was Paul) makes between the promised "great salvation" and the hope of supervising the coming "future inhabited earth" (Heb. 2:3, 5). No matter what trials and sacrifices the believer may undergo in this present evil world, the apostolic hope was always that "If we suffer with him [now], we shall reign with him [then]" (2 Tim. 2:12). And "the momentary, light affliction [now] is producing for us an eternal weight of glory far beyond all comparison [then]" (2 Cor. 4:17).

The united testimony of all NT Gospel preaching is the good news announced to all, Jew and Gentile, male and female, about the

---

[66] G.E. Ladd, *A Theology of the New Testament,* p. 333.

coming Kingdom of God. It is about how Jesus is the promised Lord Messiah who will bring all of God's promises to "the fathers" to pass. It is about how God's appointed Man will come to destroy Satan's hold on this world (Acts 17:31), and how the Messianic Age to Come will be the time when the Spirit of the Lord will bring the promised refreshing and restoration of all things on earth that the prophets had spoken. For Luke then, the disciples' question in Acts 1:6 was the right question. The coming of the Spirit at Pentecost would empower them to proclaim the coming Kingdom, when Jesus the Messiah will sit on the Davidic throne of Israel, and all the nations of the earth will be under his reign of righteousness and everlasting peace.

> When the cloud of confusion over the Kingdom of God is lifted and when commentators believe what the New Testament says about the future, it will become clear that Acts 1:6 is a text which sits in judgment on our failure to believe the prophets and Jesus and our reluctance to accept that the Apostles knew better than we do what Jesus meant by the Kingdom of God.[67]

Following Jesus involves believing what he believed, that he will judge the nations and establish his royal palace in Jerusalem. To believe in the Jesus of the New Testament is to be persuaded of and committed to the Kingdom he will preside over. May God give us all grace to share the same apostolic hope that "we through the Spirit, by faith, [may be] waiting for the hope of righteousness" (Gal. 5:5) and that we may *not* be amongst those who "shall not inherit the kingdom of God" (Gal. 5:21). Faithfulness to his Gospel of the Kingdom in this life prepares us for positions of joint rule with King Jesus (Luke 19:17). The apostles believed his Gospel-word: "Just as my Father has granted me a kingdom by covenant, I covenant with you that you may eat and drink at my table in my kingdom, and you will sit on thrones judging the twelve tribes of Israel" (Luke 22:29-30). We must believe the Gospel-word of Jesus delivered by him and later by his commissioned apostles, so that when Jesus the Messiah returns we too, if found loyal to him, will help manage his affairs on a renewed earth. We will by his resurrection power enter the enjoyment of our citizenship as sons of

---

[67] Anthony Buzzard, *Our Fathers Who Aren't in Heaven,* p. 196.

the Kingdom in new and never-dying, never-diseased bodies (Phil. 3:20-21; Rom. 8:23), with all tears wiped away (Rev. 21:4).

The Christian Gospel tells us that what mankind lost through Adam is going to be regained in the Kingdom of the Messiah. The Gospel calls us to co-rulership with Christ over the new Paradise on earth. This alone answers that deep sense within man's soul that something he was initially made for is missing. The glory lost will be glory restored. Originally made for dignity under God, originally made to "subdue" the earth and to rule over this world with a management of love and care, man tragically lost his right to kingship. The Gospel of God's Kingdom announces that it will be fully restored. God's great plan promised to Eve, Abraham and David is moving towards this great goal. It will finally be made good through our Lord Jesus Messiah. History is going somewhere. When the fullness of time has come, God the Father, the one true God of Jesus is going to sum up all things in Christ, whether they be things in heaven or things upon the earth (Eph. 1:10). God's honour and ultimate glory depend on this Gospel of the Kingdom. At Christ's coming all hostile rule and power will be abolished under the headship of Jesus the Messiah. After a thousand years our blessed Lord and Saviour will hand over the Kingdom to his Father, "that God may be all in all" (1 Cor. 15:24-28). If this hope of a renewed earth under God's universal King Jesus is not realized, then God's great covenant with Abraham and David will have failed utterly. The Gospel of the Kingdom will have turned out to be one big hoax. The "fathers" and the prophets and the apostles will have been deluded fools. They will have died in vain. They have led us astray. God is a liar. Christ is darkness. The Devil and evil win. There is no justice. There is no Good News.

But we are not of those who have no hope. We are not among those who shrink back in unbelief. Christ is alive! Christ is alive! "Behold, he comes in the clouds, and every eye shall see him, even those who crucified him will see the King and mourn" (Rev. 1:7). Even now we can taste of the powers of that age to come (Heb. 6:5). We, with all the faithful of all generations, look for that Kingdom "which cannot be shaken" (Heb. 12:28). We anticipate the day when "the salvation, and the power, and the kingdom of our God and the authority of His Christ have come" and when "the accuser of our brethren" (Rev. 12:10), the one now deceiving the whole world, will be bound "so he cannot deceive the nations any longer" (Rev. 20:3).

What a privilege to be among those to whom "it has been granted to know the mysteries of the kingdom of heaven" (Matt. 13:11). God grant us all to intelligently receive and commit to this "word of the Kingdom" so that the Devil may not rob us of the hope God has given us all through His Son Jesus Christ our Lord (Matt. 13:19).

May I repeat Anthony Buzzard's ringing challenge quoted earlier in this chapter? It captures the Gospel invitation beautifully:

> The Gospel as Jesus preached it invites you also to dedicate the rest of your life to preparation for participation in the supervision of that future Kingdom on a renewed earth. You are invited to be a co-heir of the Kingdom with the Messiah. In short, the Jesus of history, the original "theocrat," continues his work of recruiting members of his royal household, the theocratic party, who are urged to prepare themselves with divine help to take part in the Messiah's government of the future. This will be the first and only administration to rule the world successfully.[68]

The challenge is clear. As Christians we must go back to the beginning and search out anew in the context of the Jewish vision, which the Church forsook, the mysteries of the Kingdom of God. As Schonfield challenges:

> Reading through reams of modern Christian theology it is hard to find any awareness that the Messianism which gave Christianity its name, Messianism in its native Jewish expression, may hold the secret which could give the Church life from the dead. We must say that either Messianism was the essence of the Gospel, or that Christianity from its very inception was a fraud. Everything else can go, but here is the rock on which the Kingdom of God was to be founded.[69]

---

[68] Anthony Buzzard, *The Coming Kingdom of the Messiah*, p. 7.
[69] Hugh Schonfield, *Those Incredible Christians,* p. 239.

Epilogue

According to the three synoptic gospels, Matthew, Mark and Luke, at Caesarea Philippi Jesus asked his men, "Who do people say that I am?" and "Who do you say I am?" (Matt. 16:13; Mark 8:27; Luke 9:18). Two things stand out.

First, we see both the brilliant insight of Peter and his confusion. He confesses that Jesus is indeed "the Messiah of God." Jesus commends him: "Blessed are you, Simon Barjona, because flesh and blood did not reveal this to you, but my Father who is in heaven" (Matt. 16:17). We are told, "From that time Jesus began to show his disciples that he must go to Jerusalem and suffer many things from the elders and chief priests and scribes, and be killed, and on the third day be raised" (Matt. 16:21; Mark 8:31; Luke 9:22). No sooner had Jesus told them of his impending violent death and subsequent coming back to life, than Peter himself stridently rebukes Jesus for this plan: "God forbid, Lord! This shall never happen to you" (Matt. 16:22; Mark 8:32). (Luke omits Peter's rebuke.)

Peter's shock was caused by the notion that "the Son of Man" could possibly suffer an ignominious death. In popular Jewish expectation, "the Son of Man" was the promised Messiah who was to lead the nation of Israel to triumph in the glorious New Age. What had the majestic, divine glory of the Son of Man to do with humiliation and rejection? What had the irresistible might and triumph of the Son of Man to do with a criminal's death on a cross? To Peter, Jesus' statement was not only personally heart-breaking; it was completely incredible and utterly impossible. In that moment, Peter was confronted with teaching which his whole Jewish conditioning made him quite unable to grasp. This explains his vehement incredulity.

The second part of this episode that stands out is the unexpectedly fierce reaction of Jesus to Peter's rebuke: "Get behind me, Satan! You are a stumbling block to me; for you are not setting your mind on God's interests, but man's" (Matt. 16:23; Mark 8:33). In Peter's words the Devil was again speaking to Jesus. Jesus knew the popular idea that the Son of Man would ride triumphantly over the earth. The whole point of the wilderness temptation which he underwent at the beginning of his ministry just after his baptism, was that he was tempted to be that popular Messiah without suffering. The Devil had tempted him to go the way of power and might and force to get the Kingdom. Was this not the dream all Israel cherished? Wasn't this the traditional and orthodox "faith"? But in that wilderness temptation Jesus turned his back on the Devil's suggestions and showed that God's plan involved sacrificial love. In this pivotal moment in Caesarea Philippi Peter was mouthing all over again the very temptation that Satan had presented to Jesus in the desert. In the stunned devotion of Peter, in the shock-horror of Peter, all unknown to Peter, the Devil himself was speaking to Jesus. In that moment Jesus was again being tempted to take the role of the popular Messiah and not of the suffering servant which his Father had planned for him.

It is clear that from this moment on Jesus *began* again and again to instruct his disciples that he must go up to Jerusalem to suffer a dreadful death: "From that time Jesus the Messiah began to show his disciples that he must go to Jerusalem, and suffer many things from the elders and chief priests and scribes, and be killed, and be raised up on the third day" (Matt. 16:21; Mark 8:31; Luke 9:22). The big question, then, is, why were the disciples so utterly unprepared for Jesus' death when it finally came? Why did Jesus' death disintegrate their whole world? It is important to note that Jesus never told of his death without also telling them of his resurrection. So again, we ask, why did his resurrection come as such a huge surprise? All three synoptic writers indicate that Jesus clearly foretold these events, and yet the disciples were caught completely off-guard. Why?

Perhaps the answer is found in the way our human minds work (or don't work). At the end of the day the disciples did not succeed in making any connection between the popular notions they had been brought up on of a gloriously triumphant Messiah and the idea of a suffering, rejected, humiliated, dead Messiah that Jesus predicted. The human mind is notorious for being unable to accept data that is objectionable and alien to it. The human mind has the amazing capacity to shut out data that it cannot emotionally or rationally compute. Any idea so new, so revolutionary, so unexpected, so contradictory to all that is believed and loved stands very little chance of reception.

This is what happened to Peter and the disciples. They connected Jesus only with a conventional idea, and despite Jesus' clear teaching to the contrary, they did not see beyond that idea. They did not cope well with it. They were shocked by the cross. It also explains why they initially failed to grasp the reality of Jesus' resurrection.

Throughout this book, I have presented unconventional, non-traditional ideas that for many people no doubt are shocking. Perhaps our minds have reacted like Peter's. I remember the night when I received that "hospital pass" that left me on the ground so winded. To use another Australian image, I was left for about two years like a "stunned mullet." A mullet is a fish. When a fisherman pulls his catch in, he will often knock it on the head with a lump of wood. The fish lies there stunned. An apt description when the mind is hit with the unexpected.

The thought that perhaps after reading the Bible for so long we have failed to understand its core message, that we have been blinded by centuries of tradition, is certainly shocking. But that is the thesis of *They Never Told Me* This *in Church*! It is also the position of sound Bible scholars:

> throughout the centuries the Bible has been interpreted in a Greek context, and even the New Testament has been interpreted on the basis of Plato and Aristotle. This may be justifiable, but we hold that those who adopt this method of interpretation should realize what it is that they are doing, and should cease to maintain that they are basing their theology on the Bible.[1]

Strong words indeed. We have read the Bible as though it is a Greco-Western book instead of a Hebrew book. We have not taken into account one of the most basic and fundamental of all Jewish notions, namely the principle of Jewish agency, that an agent is as the principal himself. Jesus as the Lord Messiah is God the Father's Son, His fully authorized and divinely empowered king. We have not understood the key tenet of Jewish monotheism, that God is one and not three. We have not understood the important Old Testament verse most often quoted by Jesus and his apostles in the New Testament, Psalm 110:1 that speaks of two Lords — only one of whom is God. We have not understood the Hebrew doctrine of the

---

[1] N.H. Snaith, *The Distinctive Ideas of the Old Testament,* p. 185.

soul and so have opened the floodgates to spiritualism and spiritism. We have failed to grasp that in Hebrew thinking the Spirit is the presence and mind and energy of God Himself, not a third hypostasis. We have "spiritualized" Jesus' Gospel of the still future Kingdom of God on earth, and replaced it with a foreign and pale chimera. And the hallucinatory power of Greek thinking mesmerizes to this day.

The Jewish scholar Hugh Schonfield advises that:

> the Christian must become a Jew in comprehension, sympathy and spirit before he is qualified to address himself to matters Christian. Scholarship is not enough, because it does not necessarily involve commitment and identification with the Jewish soul. While there lingers any sense of what is Jewish being alien, and still worse hostile or opposed, there is not the slightest possibility of getting Christianity in correct perspective.[2]

The history of the Christian Church is a sad commentary on our failure to follow this most basic and commonsense approach. If we continue to ignore such advice it will be to our everlasting shame. One thing is certain though. As early as the first half of the second century AD Christianity moved decisively away from Judaism, from the hope of the Kingdom of God on earth, from any real identification with the Jesus of history, and became as a result very much the religion with which we are familiar.[3] In other words, Christianity took a radical deviation from what Jesus and his apostles taught and the Church became increasingly Gentile in outlook. The result was that "in little more than a century after the death of Jesus Christianity for all its relics of a Jewish origin...patently presented itself in the guise of a religion of the Gentile world."[4] In blunt terms Christianity accommodated itself to paganism.

The Gentile scholar Snaith concurs. He writes that the reinterpretation of apostolic Christianity "in terms of the ideas of the Greek philosophers has been both widespread throughout the centuries and everywhere destructive to the essence of the Christian faith."[5] Dieticians tell us that we are what we eat. For centuries we

---

[2] Hugh Schonfield, *Those Incredible Christians*, p. 51.
[3] *Ibid.*, p. 211.
[4] *Ibid.*, p. 222.
[5] Snaith, *The Distinctive Ideas of the Old Testament,* p. 187.

have been fed the wrong diet of Greek philosophy mixed with supplementary pills from the extract of Biblical remnants. The result is that the Church, the body of Christ, has become emaciated, divided, malnourished.

Just like Daniel and his mates, Shadrach, Meshach and Abednego, we now find ourselves deported to a foreign Babylon, as it were. The time has come for us to issue the challenge Daniel did to the court. Feed us no more the delicacies of the king. Defile us no more! Put it to the test. Give us the plain diet from Israel our homeland. After a short period you will see how strong and healthy we are. I am convinced that after even a brief period of time we would see the same kind of results the Babylonians saw, when they observed that the plain but pure diet made the Hebrew boys "better" looking and "fatter than all the youths who had been eating the king's choice food" (Dan. 1:15). If the judgment of this book is sound (and we will let the reader weigh it up):

> then neither Catholic nor Protestant theology is based on Biblical theology. In each case we have a domination of Christian theology by Greek thought...We hold that there can be no right answer until we have come to a clear view of the distinctive ideas of both Old and New Testaments and their difference from the pagan ideas which so largely have dominated "Christian" thought.[6]

It has been rightly said that when a man who is honestly mistaken hears the truth, he either ceases to be mistaken or he ceases to be honest. This is now the choice that confronts us all.

---

[6] *Ibid.*, p. 188.

Appendix 1
Adonai and *Adoni*: The Two Hebrew Lords

For readers wishing to follow further this little-recognized distinction between the two Lords in the Hebrew Scriptures, the following will supply a good springboard for thoughtful reflection. There are many examples scattered throughout the OT. One or two examples of quite heavy concentration should be sufficient.

The first interesting example concerns the time Abigail begs David for mercy on account of the stupidity of her husband Nabal. I quote from the NASB which makes the correct distinction between God and man. The Hebrew text actually has the Tetragrammaton — YHWH — which is God's personal name Yahweh (or Jehovah) but is usually translated into English as though it were *Adonai* as "the LORD." The human lord (in this case the man David) appears in lower case as "my lord":

> When Abigail saw David, she hurried and dismounted from her donkey, and fell on her face before David, and bowed herself to the ground. And she fell at his feet and said, "On me alone, **my lord**, be the blame. And please let your maidservant speak to you, and listen to the words of your maidservant. Please do not let **my lord** pay attention to this worthless man, Nabal...but I your maidservant did not see the young men of **my lord** whom you sent. Now therefore, **my lord**, as **the LORD** lives, and as your soul lives, since **the LORD** has restrained you from shedding blood, and from avenging yourself by your own hand, now let your enemies, and those who seek evil against **my lord,** be as Nabal. And now let this gift which your maidservant has brought to **my lord** be given to the young men who accompany **my lord**. Please forgive the transgression of your maidservant; for **the LORD** will certainly make for **my lord** an enduring house, because **my lord** is fighting the battles of **the LORD**, and evil shall not be found in you all your days. And should anyone rise up to pursue you and to seek your life, then the life of **my lord** shall be bound in the bundle of the living with **the LORD** your God and it shall

> come about when **the LORD** shall do for **my lord** according to all the good that He has spoken concerning you, and shall appoint you ruler over Israel, that this will not cause grief or a troubled heart to **my lord,** both by having shed blood without cause and by **my lord** having avenged himself. When **the LORD** shall deal well with **my lord**, then remember your maidservant" (1 Sam. 25:23-31).

The reader is encouraged to take a highlighter and continue on through the rest of chapter 25 and on into chapter 26. Some surprises are no doubt in store. Note particularly verses 15 to 19 of 1 Samuel 26 where King Saul is called "your lord the king" and "my lord the king" and even (as per Psalm 110:1) "your lord, the LORD's anointed" (that is, Jehovah's Messiah/Christ), which is significant when we come to the New Testament with its designation of Jesus as "our Lord the Messiah/Christ/king." The astute reader should also note the correlation between this very Hebrew way of designating a human superior and Thomas' affirmation that the risen Jesus is "my Lord and my God." It may well be that the second title "my God" shows Thomas finally grasping that to see Jesus means to see God in him (see John 14:5-11).

Should the reader still require more evidence of the two Hebrew Lords, s/he could try 2 Samuel 14 or even 2 Samuel 19. The highlighter will get a good workout!

Appendix 2
Jesus and Michael

Since the first edition of *They Never Told Me This in Church!* not a few readers have expressed the desire for me to expand on the question as to why Jesus could not possibly have personally preexisted his human birth as an angel, and in particular, as the Jehovah's Witnesses teach, Michael the archangel. The following is an excerpt of a reply to one such JW reader:

In so far as our discussion on the identity of Michael the archangel vis-a-vis Jesus is concerned, I guess this is a rather large topic. Firstly, though, I appreciate your concurrence that the JW position is purely inference (though you state reasonable inference), which is to say, it is not a clearly stated teaching in Scripture. (The doctrine of the Trinity is also inference, there being no definitive statement in the Bible that God is three in one, or that Jesus has two natures — a divine and a human — in his person, or that the Holy Spirit is the third member of the Godhead, etc.) You will understand, therefore, my hesitancy at embracing your enthusiastic endorsement of the doctrine that Michael the archangel is Jesus based on inference, considering that I once believed another doctrine of inference and found I was completely deluded. I am prepared to respectfully disagree with your bold claim for infallibility (Inference is correct, you write) on this one.

Before I enter into that area, may I ask a question? You quote "Insight on Scripture" p. 393 to the effect that the name Michael is applied to the Son of God before he left heaven to become Jesus Christ. I cannot recall any Scripture that states these as facts: Nowhere is Michael delineated as "the Son of God." He would certainly be included in the term "sons of God" which of course includes all God's angels, but nowhere is Michael called "the Son of God." And nowhere in Scripture is it stated that Michael left heaven in order to become the Son of God. Nor is there any statement as you suggest that when he went back to heaven as a spirit-being the Son of God again took on the alter-ego of Michael. This does not mean that all this is not so, just that I cannot find it clearly announced this way (inference on JW part only it seems?).

You quote 1 Thessalonians 4:16 to infer that when the Lord Jesus himself descends from heaven "with the voice of the archangel" this must *ipso facto* prove Jesus is Michael. I know that you hold this teaching most sincerely. Probably no less sincerely than I once believed that Jesus is God Almighty. But I cannot accede to this identification for many reasons. For starters, the assumption you mention that Michael is the only archangel is just that — assumption. In the OT Michael is called "one of the chief princes" (Dan. 10:13). This clearly means there are other "chief princes" besides Michael. (I am well aware that the description "archangel" does not appear in the OT, and is purely a NT description. In the OT there are "cherubs" which are covering angels, which may or may not be a reference to arch authority. This category may indeed be the OT equivalent of archangel, but I cannot definitely assert this, nor can anybody definitely rule it out, either. So as to whether or not a "chief prince" is the OT equivalent of the NT archangel again is not certain. But at the very least *Michael is only one of a particular hierarchy*...i.e. he is only one of the chief princes. His particular sphere seems to be in relation to the nation of Israel.)

Even 1 Thessalonians 4:16 says that Jesus descends from heaven with "a voice of **an** archangel," there being no definite article in the Greek which finds its way into our English translations, unfortunately. Furthermore, when the NT speaks of "principalities" the word is *arche* which you will recognize as the prefix to the word "archangel" (see Eph. 1:21; Col. 1:16; Rom. 8:38). This (by inference!) does also suggest that there are a number of archangels. This is reasonable when we know that there are many ranks or orders and hierarchies within God's angelic hosts. I *infer* that there are possibly many archangels from these Scriptures, but I will not be dogmatic on this point, since it is only reasoned inference.

An archangel, however, whilst exercising a high (or covering?) rank, is for all that still an angel only, which leads to my next difficulty with your proposition. Scripture clearly places Jesus in a rank *outside* of the angels altogether. I am sure you are aware of the writer to the Hebrews' position here. The Son is in a different class altogether to the angels. When the Son had sat down at the right hand of the Majesty on high it was because he had "become superior to the angels" and had inherited "a more excellent name than they" (Heb. 1:4). If Michael was the only archangel prior to his assumed earthly existence as Jesus then he already had this high authority before his resurrection and exaltation back to heaven. But the text states that Jesus was rewarded with what he previously did not possess, namely, he "inherited a more excellent name" and he became superior to the angels. Jesus is here clearly distinguished from the angels. He is not one of them. Unless we ignore all the rules of grammar and plain sense, when all is said and done, an archangel is still an angel. (I am aware that you might reason that an archangel is not an angel, but a different creature, but this idea is not found anywhere in the Bible, only in some extra-biblical writings. If I may put it this way, the queen bee is still a bee, and an archangel is still an angel.)

The following verses in Hebrews 1 clearly distinguish Jesus from all the angels: "For **to which of the angels did He ever say,** 'You are My Son, today I have begotten you?'" (v. 5). God has never said to any angel, "You are My Son; this day have I begotten you!" Yet He said this to Jesus. If Jesus is Michael the archangel, this verse makes no sense. And following on we read, "And **of the angels** He says...**But of the Son** He says..." A clear distinction between the two, between the angels and the Son. And verse 13 clearly states that no angel has ever been invited to sit at the right hand of Jehovah on high. God has never said to an angel, "Sit at My right hand till I make your enemies your footstool." If this was spoken to Messiah, then Messiah cannot be an angel.

And in Hebrews 2:5 we are clearly told that God "did not subject to angels the world [age] to come, concerning which we are speaking." Michael an archangel is clearly excluded from lordship in the new age or the coming Kingdom of God. The new age coming is to be subjected to "the Son of Man," for God has put all things under his feet. Here is a clear reference to Messiah, the Son of Man, and to all his redeemed people. Jesus, the Son of God, the Son of Man, to whom the Father has subjected the coming new age, is not therefore an angel. Michael will not be the Lord or head of the new age according to this clear and definitive statement, for God has not subjected that world/age to angels!

Yes, my original concern still stands: if Jesus the Messiah, the Son of God is not a man in exactly the same sense as the first man Adam was, then he cannot be our redeemer. If he preexisted his own conception and was an angel before becoming a flesh and blood man like the rest of us humans then he is disqualified from humanity. It is axiomatic: you cannot be pre-human and human. A human being cannot preexist his/her own begetting and conception. Otherwise, we have entered the Gnostic heresy of the Redeemer-myth. There were many belief systems in the ancient world that spoke of preexisting spirit beings who came to earth among men. God would not become a man to save us (Trinitarian). An angel (a son of God) would not become a man to redeem us (Arianism). The gods would not become men (Greek myths). However, the Jewish belief stood out alone. Jehovah would raise up "from among you, from your brothers" a prophet "like me" (Moses, Deut. 18:15). He will be a man. Otherwise, where is the Scripture that tells us the Saviour will be an angel who becomes a man? There is total silence here. Inference must bow to clear statements.

You state that you are theoretically open to the metaphysical possibility that Jesus was a divine/heavenly/spiritual being who could have become a real human being by divesting himself of his divine condition. To my mind, such a possibility raises a number of awkward questions: Would this divested human condition still retain all the memory of his pre-incarnate glory? (If so, then he had an unfair advantage over the rest of us sons of Adam, for such memory would have been an extremely powerful motivation to victory over temptation. Indeed, such memory would, it could be argued, mean that there was very little need to live by faith because he could now live by sight, so to speak.)

It is extremely hard, if not impossible, for me to classify such a person as being anything like a real human being. It most definitely also fudges the scriptural meaning of "beget" which in both Hebrew and Greek clearly connotes creation (beginning, generation, coming into being). As we have seen, Gabriel's precise definition of the Son of God is that he is the one who is miraculously begotten in the womb of Mary by God's creative energy. It is the Son of God whose existence began in history in Mary. Jesus was not the Son of God before his begettal in Mary, according to Luke 1:35. He was not transmuted from another existence into a human one.

Furthermore, now as you suggest that he is exalted back to where he once was, does he forever remain "a real human being" or does he revert to what he once was — an angel — which of course he can never really be, if he is going to qualify as a real human being, albeit an exalted, glorified man? If he still retains the human condition, he obviously must have a dual nature, which possibility is strongly suggestive of docetic dualism, surely? Even worse, such a possibility would disqualify Jesus now from being our great high priest, who by definition must be taken from among men to be appointed on behalf of men in things pertaining to God (see Heb. 5:1).

These are a few of my initial concerns with your openness to a preexistent Son of God. I like your insistence that your line of thinking may not necessarily be the correct interpretation of the scriptural data. However, your admission that a pre-existent Son is logically or metaphysically possible is the same thin-edge-of-the-wedge type of inquiry that brought the whole Trinity disaster into being in the first place. The Hebrews of course did not think in such metaphysical categories. The Greeks did. This would suggest to me that this whole line of investigation is foreign to the biblical revelation and fraught with alarm bells.

As you say, this is a big subject. There is a lot, lot more. But I will close by referring again to 1 Thessalonians 4:16. The inference that because Jesus comes with the voice of an archangel he must therefore be Michael is tenuous. The text says that Jesus' return will be accompanied by a command, by the voice of an attendant archangel, and by God's trumpet. To be accompanied by an archangel does not mean one is an archangel, any more than a trumpet sounding when Jesus returns means that he is a trumpet!

Appendix 3
Divine Agency

The principle of divine agency in the Bible is all-pervasive. For the keen reader the following are just a smattering of other Scriptures to further illustrate the Hebrew understanding that "a person's agent is regarded as the person himself."

In Deuteronomy 25:19 God solemnly charges the Israelites that they themselves must "blot out the memory" of the Amalekites from under heaven, because they had attacked the stragglers and the weak of the Israelites who were marching in to take possession of the land: "**you shall blot out** Amalek." The Amalekites had showed no reverence for God, so the LORD ordered their annihilation by the armies of Israel. However, in the parallel verse in Exodus 17:14 God says, "**I will utterly blot out** the memory of Amalek from under heaven." Thus, it is clear that Israel acted as God's agent in the destruction of Amalek. The Israelites did the actual fighting but to the Hebrew mind it was God Himself who blotted out Amalek. The teaching is: It is you, but it is Me!

Another striking example of this principle is found in Judges 2. The angel of the LORD comes up from Gilgal and speaks in the first person: "**I** brought you up out of Egypt and led you into the land which **I** have sworn to your fathers; and **I said,** I will never break **My covenant** with you...but you have not obeyed **Me**" (Jud. 2:1-2). In disobeying the words of the angel, the people were guilty of disobedience to God Himself. "And it came about when **the angel** of the LORD spoke these words to all the sons of Israel, that the people lifted up their voices and wept" (2:4). The principle is: The angel sent or commissioned is regarded as God Himself.

On another occasion King Saul and his armies are engaged in hot battle with the Philistines. Saul's son "**Jonathan smote** the garrison of the Philistines that was in Geba" (1 Sam. 13:3). However, Scripture records the result this way: "And all Israel heard the news that **Saul had smitten** the garrison of the Philistines" (v. 4)! Again we ask, what is happening here? The solution is that in Hebrew thought a king's personality extended through his entire household so that the messenger-representative was conceived of as being personally — and in his very words and actions — the presence of the sender.

Another classic example of the principle of divine agency is found in 2 Chronicles 4. The furnishings in Solomon's temple are attributed to the work of Huram: "**Huram** also **made** the pails, the shovels, and the bowls. So **Huram finished doing the work which he performed for King Solomon** in the house of God" (2 Chron. 4:11). However, just a few verses on we read, "**Thus Solomon made** all the utensils in great quantities, for the weight of the bronze could not be found out. **Solomon also made** all the things that were in the house of God; even the golden altar, the tables with the bread of the Presence on them, the lampstands with their lamps of pure gold" (4:18-20). Who made? To the Hebrew mind there is no confusion here. Solomon himself acted in person through his commissioned agent Huram.

Other passages worth checking include Joshua 5:13-6:2; Judges 2:1-4; 1 Samuel 12:5-8 in conjunction with Psalm 77:20; 2 Kings 14:27; 1 Chronicles 10:13-14.

Bibliography

Agostini, Mike. *The Dying Experience and Learning How to Live*. Vaucluse Press, 2004.

Althaus, Paul. *The Theology of Martin Luther*. Fortress Press, 1966.

Armstrong, Karen. *The Battle for God: Fundamentalism in Judaism, Christianity and Islam*. London: Harper Collins, 2000.

Armstrong, Karen. *A History of God*. London: Mandarin, 1993.

Baigent, Michael, Leigh, Richard and Lincoln, Henry. *The Messianic Legacy*. N.S.W., Australia: Transworld Publishers, 1987.

Bainton, Roland H. *The Reformation of the Sixteenth Century*. Boston: Beacon Press, 1952.

Bainton, Roland H. *The Travail of Religious Liberty: Nine Biographical Studies*. Philadelphia: Westminster Press, 1951.

Barclay, William. *The Acts of the Apostles*. Edinburgh: Saint Andrew Press, 1953.

Barclay, William. *Jesus as They Saw Him*. Amsterdam: SCM Press, 1962.

Brown, Dan. *The Da Vinci Code*. Australia: Random House.

Brown, Raymond. *The Birth of the Messiah: A Commentary on the Infancy Narratives in the Gospels of Matthew and Luke*. New York: Doubleday, 1993.

Brown, Raymond. *An Introduction to New Testament Christology*. New York: Paulist Press, 1994.

Brunner, Emil. *The Christian Doctrine of God, Dogmatics*. Philadelphia: Westminster Press, 1949.

Buswell, J.O. *A Systematic Theology of the Christian Religion*. Zondervan, 1962.

Buzzard, Anthony. *The Coming Kingdom of the Messiah: A Solution to the Riddle of the New Testament*. Restoration Fellowship, 2002.

Buzzard, Anthony. *Jesus Was Not a Trinitarian,* Restoration Fellowship, 2007.

Buzzard, Anthony. *Our Fathers Who Aren't in Heaven: The Forgotten Christianity of Jesus the Jew*. Restoration Fellowship, 1999.

Buzzard, Anthony. *Who Is Jesus? A Plea for a Return to Belief in Jesus, the Messiah.* Restoration Fellowship.

Buzzard, Anthony and Hunting, Charles. *The Doctrine of the Trinity: Christianity's Self-Inflicted Wound*. Lanham, MD: International Scholars Publications, 1998.

Chang, Eric H.H. *The Only True God: A Study of Biblical Monotheism.* Xlibris, 2009.

Criswell, W.A. *The Holy Spirit in Today's World.* Grand Rapids, MI: Zondervan, 1966.

Dunn, James D.G. *Christology in the Making*. London: SCM Press, 1989.

Duran, Will. *The Story of Civilization from Wycliff to Calvin: 1300-1564*. New York: Simon & Schuster, 1957.

Edwards, Douglas. *The Virgin Birth in History and Faith*. London: Faber & Faber, 1941.

Ehrman, Bart D. *The Orthodox Corruption of Scripture: The Effect of Early Christological Controversies on the Text of the New Testament*. Oxford University Press, 1993.

Erickson, Millard J. *God in Three Persons: A Contemporary Interpretation of the Trinity*. Grand Rapids: Baker Books, 1995.

Freke, Timothy and Gandy, Peter. *The Jesus Mysteries: Was the Original Jesus a Pagan God?* London: Harper Collins, 1999.

Funk, Robert W. *Honest to Jesus: Jesus for a New Millennium*. Sydney, Australia: Hodder & Stroughton, 1996.

Gade, Richard E. *A Historical Survey of Anti-Semitism*. Grand Rapids: Baker Book House, 1981.

Gibbon, E. *The Decline and Fall of the Roman Empire*. Penguin Classics, 1976.

Goldstone, Lawrence and Nancy. *Out of the Flames: The Remarkable Story of a Fearless Scholar, A Fatal Heresy, and One of the Rarest Books in the World*. New York: Broadway Books, 2002.

Graeser, Mark H., Lynn, John A., and Schoenheit, John W. *One God and One Lord: Reconsidering the Cornerstone of the Christian Faith*. Indianapolis: Christian Educational Services, 2003.

Hach, Robert. *Possession and Persuasion: The Rhetoric of Christian Faith*, Xlibris, 2001.

Haight, Roger. *Jesus: Symbol of God*. Maryknoll, NY: Orbis Books.

Harrison, Everett F. *Romans, Expositor's Bible Commentary*. Zondervan, 1976.

Henry, Matthew. *Commentary on the Whole Bible, Genesis to Revelation*. London: Marshall, Morgan & Scott, 1960.

Herrin, Judith. *The Formation of Christianity*. London: Fontana Press, 1987.

Hopkins, Richard R. *How Greek Philosophy Corrupted the Christian Concept of God*. Horizon Publishers, 2005.

Hunt, Dave and McMahon, T.A. *The Seduction of Christianity: Spiritual Discernment in the Last Days*. Oregon: Harvest House Publishers, 1986.

Jones, Ian. *Joshua, The Man They Called Jesus*. Melbourne, Australia: Griffin Press.

Kahl, Joachim. *The Misery of Christianity: A Plea for Humanity Without God*. Pelican Books, 1971.

Kimel Jr., Alvin, ed. *This Is My Name Forever: The Trinity and Gender Language for God*. Downers Grove, IL: InterVarsity Press, 2001.

Kuschel, Karl-Josef. *Born Before All Time? The Dispute over Christ's Origin*. New York: Crossroad, 1992.

Ladd, G.E. *A Theology of the New Testament*. Grand Rapids: Eerdmans, 1974.

Lewis, C.S. *Mere Christianity*, New York: Macmillan, 1943.

Lloyd-Jones, Martyn. *God the Father, God the Son: Great Doctrines Series.* London: Hodder & Stoughton, 1996.

Lloyd-Jones, Martyn. *Romans: Exposition of Chapter 10, Saving Faith.* Edinburgh: Banner of Truth, 1997.

Lockhart, Douglas. *Jesus the Heretic: Freedom and Bondage in a Religious World.* Melbourne, Australia: Element, 1997.

Manson, T.W. *On Paul and John.* SCM Press, 1967.

Mathes, James. *Address to the Christian Churches: Works of Elder B.W. Stone.* 2nd edition.

McCready, Douglas. *He Came Down From Heaven: The Preexistence of Christ and the Christian Faith,* Intervarsity Press, 2005.

McDowell, Josh and Larson, Bart. *Jesus: A Biblical Defense of His Deity.* San Bernadino, CA: Here's Life Publishers, 1983.

McGrath, Alister E. *A Life of John Calvin: A Study in the Shaping of Western Culture*, Oxford: Blackwell, 1993.

Morgridge, Charles. *The True Believer's Defence Against Charges Preferred by Trinitarians for Not Believing in the Deity of Christ.* Boston: B. Green, 1837.

Morris, Leon. *Spirit of the Living God: The Bible's Teaching on the Holy Spirit.* London: InterVarsity Press, 1974.

Moulton, J.H. ed. *Grammar of New Testament Greek.* T & T Clark, 1963.

Nolan, Albert. *Jesus Before Christianity: The Gospel of Liberation.* London: Darton, Longman & Todd, 1986.

Packer, J.I. *Keep in Step with the Spirit.* InterVarsity Press, 1984.

Packer, J.I. *Knowing God.* London: Hodder & Stoughton, 1973.

Pagels, Elaine. *Beyond Belief: The Secret Gospel of Thomas.* New York: Random House, 2003.

Prestidge, Warren. *Life, Death and Destiny.* Auckland, New Zealand: Resurrection Publishing, 1998.

Rice, John R., *The Coming Kingdom of Christ.* Murfreesboro, TN: Sword of the Lord Publishers, 1945.

Robertson, Nicoll. *The Expositor's Greek Commentary.* Grand Rapids: Eerdmans, 1967.

Robinson, J.A.T. *In the End God.* London: SCM Press, 1950.

Rubenstein, Richard E. *When Jesus Became God: The Epic Fight over Christ's Divinity in the Last Days of the Rome.* New York: Harcourt Brace & Co., 1999.

Schonfield, Hugh. *Those Incredible Christians.* New York: Bantam Books, 1968.

Selwyn, E.G. *First Epistle of St. Peter.* Baker Book House, 1983.

Snaith, N.H. *The Distinctive Ideas of the Old Testament.* Epworth Press, 1944.

Spong, John Shelby. *Born of a Woman: A Bishop Rethinks the Birth of Jesus.* San Francisco: Harper, 1992.

Torrey, R.A. *The God of the Bible.* New York: George Doran Co., 1923.

Vermes, Geza. *Jesus the Jew.* London: SCM Press, 1994.
Walker, Benjamin. *Gnosticism: Its History and Influence.* Crucible, 1989.
Werblowsky, R.J.Z. and Wigoder, Geoffrey, New York: Adama Books, 1986.
Wright, N.T. "The Mission and Message of Jesus" in *The Meaning of Jesus: Two Visions*. HarperSanFrancisco, 1999.
Wright, N.T. *Who Was Jesus?* London: SPCK, 1992.

Scripture Index

Nehemiah

Job

Psalms

Mark

Luke

John

Acts

Romans

Subject Index